THE RISE AND FALL OF THE BRITISH WELFARE STATE

THE RISE AND FALL OF THE BRITISH WELFARE STATE

FROM POVERTY IN 1900 TO POVERTY IN 2023

Pat Thane

BLOOMSBURY ACADEMIC
LONDON • NEW YORK • OXFORD • NEW DELHI • SYDNEY

BLOOMSBURY ACADEMIC
Bloomsbury Publishing Plc
50 Bedford Square, London, WC1B 3DP, UK
1385 Broadway, New York, NY 10018, USA
29 Earlsfort Terrace, Dublin 2, Ireland

BLOOMSBURY, BLOOMSBURY ACADEMIC and the Diana logo are trademarks of Bloomsbury
Publishing Plc

First published in Great Britain 2024

Cover design by Chris Bromley
Cover image © Stephen via Adobe Stock

A catalogue record for this book is available from the British Library.

A catalog record for this book is available from the Library of Congress.

ISBN: HB: 978-1-3504-1441-9
PB: 978-1-3504-1442-6
ePDF: 978-1-3504-1969-8
eBook: 978-1-3504-1968-1

Typeset by Deanta Global Publishing Services, Chennai, India
Printed and bound in Great Britain

To find out more about our authors and books visit www.bloomsbury.com and
sign up for our newsletters.

CONTENTS

ILLUSTRATIONS

ABBREVIATIONS

AIDS	Acquired Immunodeficiency Syndrome
ALRA	Abortion Law Reform Association
BMA	British Medical Association
CABx	Citizens Advice Bureaux
CARD	Campaign Against Racial Discrimination
CBI	Confederation of British Industries
CEO	Chief Executive Officer
COS	Charity Organization Society
CPAG	Child Poverty Action Group
CRC	Community Relations Commission
CSA	Child Support Agency
CSE	Certificate of Secondary Education
CTC	Child Tax Credit
DEA	Department of Economic Affairs
DHSS	Department of Health and Social Security
DIG	Disablement Income Group
DOE	Department of the Environment
DWP	Department for Work and Pensions
EC	European Community
ECHR	European Commission on Human Rights
EEC	European Economic Community
EFTA	European Free Trade Area
EHRC	Equality and Human Rights Commission
EMA	Educational Maintenance Allowance
EPA	Educational Priority Area
ERM	Exchange Rate Mechanism
EU	European Union
FIS	Family Income Supplement
FPA	Family Planning Association
GCSE	General Certificate of Secondary Education
GLC	Greater London Council
GLF	Gay Liberation Front
GNP	Gross National Product
GP	General Practitioner
HE	Higher Education
HIV	Human Immunodeficiency Virus

HRA	Human Rights Act
ILP	Independent Labour Party
IFS	Institute for Fiscal Studies
IMF	International Monetary Fund
IS	Income Supplement
JRF	Joseph Rowntree Foundation
LCC	London County Council
LGB	Local Government Board
LSE	London School of Economics
MO	Mass Observation
MOH	Medical Officer of Health
MP	Member of Parliament
MOD	Ministry of Overseas Development
NAB	National Assistance Board
NCSS	National Council of Social Services
NCUMC	National Council for the Unmarried Mother and her Child.
NCVO	National Council of Voluntary Organizations
NCW	National Council of Women
NEDC	National Economic Development Council
NGO	Non-Governmental Organization
NHI	National Health Insurance
NHS	National Health Service
NIC	National Insurance Commission
NICE	National Institute for Clinical Excellence
NOP	National Opinion Polls
NSPCC	National Council for the Prevention of Cruelty to Children
NUM	National Union of Mineworkers
NUWSS	National Union of Women's Suffrage Societies
ONS	Office for National Statistics
OPCS	Office of Population, Censuses and Surveys
OPF	One Parent Families
OECD	Organization for Economic Co-operation and Development
PAC	Public Assistance Committee
PC	Pension Credit
PEP	Political and Economic Planning
PFI	Private Finance Initiative
PR	Proportional Representation
RRB	Race Relations Board
SBC	Supplementary Benefits Commission
SDP	Social Democratic Party
SERPS	State Earnings Related Pension
SNP	Scottish National Party
TB	Tuberculosis

TUC	Trades Union Congress
UAB	Unemployment Assistance Board
UN	United Nations
UBI	Universal Basic Income
UC	Universal Credit
VAT	Value Added Tax
WAF	Women's Aid Fund
WCG	Women's Co-operative Guild
WFTC	Working Families Tax Credit
WHO	World Health Organization
WLM	Women's Liberation Movement
WTC	Working Tax Credit
WVS	Women's Voluntary Service

CHAPTER 1
INTRODUCTION

This book was driven by my concern at the levels of poverty in the UK at present, in 2023, at least 25 per cent and rising. Also, by the government's apparent lack of concern for the victims, including thousands of children, or feeling of responsibility for their condition, preferring to blame the supposed idleness or fraud of the adults and designing 'welfare' measures to force them into work, despite the clear evidence that most are in work but too low-paid to cover their own and their families' needs.

I was struck by the similarity between conditions revealed in recent surveys and those discovered by the poverty surveys of Charles Booth and Seebohm Rowntree at the beginning of the twentieth century. The numbers in poverty are similar, as are the causes: primarily inadequate pay for precarious work and sub-standard living conditions, with people in poor quality, damp, often overcrowded housing; and children starving, with parents skipping meals to feed them, unable to afford heat or clothing. The only publicly funded 'welfare' then available was the Poor Law, which blamed poverty on the feckless idleness of the poor and its only response was to seek to drive them into work, providing only the most basic 'relief' on punitive terms. Of course, there are major differences between the situation then and in the much richer contemporary world. Researchers allow for this. Since the 1960s there has been an internationally accepted measure of 'relative' poverty: incomes below 60 per cent of the national median. It derives from the realistic assumption that, as national living standards rise, those who fall seriously behind accepted standards, especially of health, education and housing as well as income, are impoverished, with poor chances in most areas of life.

The research of Booth and Rowntree was widely disseminated and created widespread shock that such conditions were possible in the richest country in the world. This was largely due to their conclusions – unexpected by both – that poverty prevailed among hard-working people and was not their fault. This led to growing pressures for state action to help these 'deserving poor'. These were driven also by growing fears that poverty, poor health and poor education not only harmed the poor but the whole of society by diminishing the pool of fit, skilled workers at a time of growing fear of international economic competition especially from Germany and the United States, also fears that Britain's mighty imperial army was failing in the contemporary Anglo-Boer war. Concern about social welfare has never been solely motivated by sympathy for the poor. A striking difference between then and now is how limited is the concern expressed by politicians and the wider public about revelations of poverty and the absence of widely supported proposals for reform, when Britain is undergoing relative economic decline.

The response in the early twentieth century led to the first measures of what was later known as the 'Welfare State'. In 1906 a Liberal government came to power, assisted by a secret tactical voting agreement with the newly formed Labour Party that they would not oppose one another in constituencies where one or other could defeat a Conservative. Supported by Labour they introduced the first state-funded old age pensions, free school meals for needy children, National Health and Unemployment Insurance. This began a long process of expansion of state welfare and state action to grow the economy, especially after 1945, reaching a peak in the 1970s. The book traces and seeks to explain this growth then decline of the Welfare State from the 1980s, with some respite under New Labour 1997 to the financial crisis of 2007–10, followed by further decline to the present.

In the early twentieth century, revelations about poverty gave rise to the beginnings of the Welfare State; now extensive poverty owes much to its decline and the state's withdrawal from effectively promoting economic renewal and growth and high living standards. The book concludes by asking whether this review of history suggests any realistic paths out of the present, sad situation.

CHAPTER 2
'OBVIOUS WANT AND SQUALOR'
POVERTY IN BRITAIN c. 1900

Britain in 1900

In 1900 Britain was the most industrialized and the richest country in the world. The discovery of extensive poverty in its capital, London, the largest city in the world, was a shock which created demands for the state to support destitute people, to introduce what was later called a 'Welfare State'.

This followed major changes to the economy, politics and culture in the late nineteenth century. The economy underwent technical advance and growth as global trade grew. Transport and communications, finance and retail expanded. Demand increased for skilled workers and for unskilled casual work, including in the docks and on the railways, and middle-class employment grew with business, government and the professions. Economic change brought personal gains and social problems, including from the rapid, unplanned growth of towns.

Government responses influenced and were influenced by political change, including an electorate expanded in 1867 and 1884 to enfranchise more skilled working men, who could not be ignored. Then the Labour Party was founded in 1900, led by the growing trade union movement determined to ensure that workers benefitted from the expanding economy made possible by their work, influenced by the emergence of socialism in Europe. They were supported by intellectual reformers, including the Fabian Society (founded 1884), also dedicated to improving working-class living standards and reducing inequalities. Mass demonstrations against exceptional unemployment in the mid-1880s aroused attacks from Conservatives on a 'degenerate residuum'. Reformers, influenced by growing understanding of the economy, argued that unemployment owed more to the fluctuating state of the labour market than to individual failing and unemployed workers deserved understanding and support. As the electorate grew and workers increasingly organized, established politicians had to pay attention if they were to win voters and avoid social conflict.

Voluntary, philanthropic, organizations also demanded government action on social problems that were not necessarily new but were becoming more visible and widely publicized by labour activists and other reformers, including poor housing and starving children. Volunteers used donations to take what action they could, including providing free meals for malnourished children and 'soup kitchens' for hungry adults, funding construction of affordable flats, but only the state had the resources to ameliorate effectively widespread, persistent problems. And not all voluntary organizations were progressive. The Charity Organization Society (COS) was established in 1869 by Conservative philanthropists who shared the conventional belief that poverty was due to personal inadequacy or deceit and that many voluntary organizations encouraged this, giving 'hand-outs' to the poor rather than training them in self-help. Many, perhaps most, charity workers learned from their contact with poor people a less punitive sense of their condition and resisted 'organization' by COS,[1] but it was highly influential especially with Conservative politicians.

Pressure for reform came also from the growing women's movement. Organized women demanded the vote for its own sake, as an essential step towards gender equality, also to end social deprivation neglected by a parliament of elite men. They particularly campaigned for much-needed healthcare for working-class women and children, especially to reduce the high maternal and infant death rates.[2] In 1869 J. S. Mill persuaded parliament to give some women the local government vote, important because local government carried major responsibility for administering social policies. The vote was granted only to property holders – exclusively widowed or unmarried women, since on marriage women were required to surrender all their property to their husbands. Propertied women could vote for and, after further campaigning, stand as Poor Law Guardians, for local Public Health Boards and School Boards, responsible for key social services which were judged in contemporary culture to lie within women's competence and interest, as affairs of state did not. By 1900 over one million women had the local vote and used it to make limited improvements to the Poor Law, and in education and public health.[3] The Labour Party began to establish itself as a reforming influence in local government.

Growing awareness of international competition as other countries, particularly Germany and the United States, industrialized, aroused concerns about social conditions, including fears that such problems as child malnutrition would create adults unfit for hard work, reducing Britain's competitiveness. State action on welfare was thought necessary to facilitate economic growth as well as amelioration of poverty. In Germany Bismarck introduced the world's first national insurance schemes for healthcare and pensions in the 1880s, designed to foster economic growth and to challenge the growing appeal of socialism to workers.[4] The effects of poor diet on health and the causes of disease were only beginning to be understood, but the physical appearance of thin, starving children in ragged clothes, and the high death rates of young children, made the connection inescapable. In Britain it intensified fears that there were already too few productive workers due to long-term deprivation. As Sir Assheton Cross put it in parliament when introducing a Housing of the Working Classes Bill in 1875, 'Health is actually wealth.'[5] The aim of the bill, a sign of growing social concern though it failed to pass, was to create healthier living environments than the mass of damp, overcrowded, insanitary urban dwellings. Fears were intensified by decline in the birth rate from the 1870s. This was widely assumed to be mainly due to the careful middle classes seeking to improve their living standards by reducing their costs, while the feckless poor bred ever more 'degenerates', contributing further to 'racial decline.'

Fears deepened in the Anglo-Boer war of 1899–1902 when the British imperial army had difficulty defeating inexperienced Boer farmers in South Africa. Military leaders ascribed their failures to the poor physical condition of volunteers for the army. The Conservative government appointed an Interdepartmental Committee on Physical Deterioration to examine the issue. Its report in 1904 rejected the idea of deterioration, arguing that the health of poorer people had long been poor, that the fact that one-third of schoolchildren 'went hungry' was not new but due to long-established inequalities. It recommended free school meals and medical care for poor children.[6]

There was a growing sense, especially among intellectuals and reformers, of 'society' as a collective entity, not just a disconnected collection of individuals, that illiteracy, disease and other deprivations among poorer people harmed everyone, and everyone should feel responsible for reducing poverty, that, challenging Margaret Thatcher's claim a century later, there *was* 'such a thing as society'. Concerns previously regarded as private became public; experiences once perceived as normal among the poor, like ill-health, became problems to be solved. There was growing awareness of the relationships of individuals with society and the 'race', an increasingly influential new concept.

Hence there were growing demands from a growing range of sources for government to provide and fund services to improve social conditions. Despite continuing opposition from Conservatives, central and local government services and spending gradually expanded. New government departments were established: the Local Government Board in 1870 to administer the Poor Law and other local institutions, the Board of Education in 1899 as state education expanded. For decades central government had delegated administration and funding of social services, including the Poor Law, public health and education, to local government, but by 1900 this faced resistance to the increased costs especially from poorer authorities where need was greatest but funds from local taxes ('rates') limited. Consequently, there were considerable variations in the level and effectiveness of local services and central government gradually took more control.[7]

Poverty surveys

Pressure for state welfare was intensified by the unprecedented findings of the poverty surveys of Charles Booth and Seebohm Rowntree. Booth was a successful shipowner who grew up in a wealthy business family in Liverpool. Canvassing as an (unsuccessful) Liberal parliamentary candidate in 1865 in an intensely poor area of Liverpool shocked him into a profound sense of obligation to improve the conditions he encountered for the first time. He lost hope that conventional party politics would deliver solutions and was disturbed by sensational reports in the expanding press of conditions and behaviour in the growing cities, reinforcing the widespread belief that the irresponsible poor were to blame for their conditions. He became convinced of the need for accurate accounts of the extent and reality of poverty and the lives of poor people as the necessary basis for reforms, which should be based, he believed, on providing a 'minimum accepted standard' for everyone, similar to twenty-first-century proposals for a Universal Basic Income to resolve contemporary poverty.

In 1885 Henry Hyndman, leader of the recently formed socialist Social Democratic Federation, inspired by Marx, published the results of an inquiry concluding that up to 25 per cent of the population of London lived in extreme poverty. Booth, who now lived in London, believed this overstated the problem and decided to discover the truth. He began in 1886 with a study of East London, believed to be the poorest area of Britain, which was published in two volumes in 1889 and 1891. He later studied the whole London County Council (LCC) area, with a population by the time of the 1901 census of 4,670,177. The largest city in the world was still growing. The full findings were published in seventeen volumes in 1902/3, establishing that Hyndman had understated London poverty.

The study of *The Life and Labour of the People of London*, as the final publication was named, was more than a survey of poverty but a wide-ranging account of the living conditions, work and beliefs of the whole London population, designed to put poverty into perspective relative to general standards and expectations and assess the causes. Booth insisted that he aimed 'to provide facts to help social reformers find remedies, not to bring forward my own suggestions', because unchallengeable facts about the reality of poverty were lacking.[8] Yet, as the work progressed, he was tempted to suggest his preferred way forward: a 'limited socialism' which would restrain capitalism and the damage it could do to workers and society, without seeking a revolutionary assault on capitalists, 'a socialism which shall leave untouched the forces of individualism and the sources of wealth' but end poverty, which he appealed to the labour movement to promote.[9] He proposed gradual expansion of 'state socialism' (reform implemented and funded by the state) to ensure that everyone was 'well housed, well-fed and well-warmed, taught, trained and permanently employed'.[10] He believed trade unionists could pressure parliament to implement this, not through 'taking from the rich', who made economic growth possible, but by ensuring that working people received their fair share of the proceeds of the economy their work helped to construct through higher wages, regular work, shorter hours, safety at work, and training to improve their skills and efficiency, as his research showed they currently did not.[11] Exploitative employers who underpaid workers in intolerable conditions should be regulated by central or local government and fined for transgression.[12]

When the survey began, Booth believed East London 'lay hidden from view behind a curtain on which were painted terrible pictures: starving children, suffering women, overworked men, horrors of drunkenness and vice; monsters and demons of inhumanity; giants of disease and despair'.[13] The research focused upon the precarious trades prominent in East London, especially dock labour and tailoring, employing methods later extended to the whole of London. It was not a house-to-house or representative sample survey. The social sciences and statistical methods were in their infancy and such approaches were untried. It was closer to what would now be called a participant observation survey and itself contributed to the development of research methods. Thirty-four researchers were employed on the whole survey of London, costing the equivalent of £4m.[14] An important source was information from School Board Visitors, officials appointed when state education became compulsory from 1880. They called regularly at the homes of poorer children to ensure their school attendance, giving help to families when needed, becoming familiar with conditions in their districts. Insights were also provided by clergymen about their parishes and by charity volunteers.

Researchers studied trades and living conditions in specific communities. The future Fabian Beatrice Webb (still Miss Potter), cousin of Booth's wife Mary, advised on the project, then lived among and observed dockworkers and tenants of flats in East London, later among the growing Jewish community of East London (mostly recent refugees from persecution in Eastern Europe) working as a jobbing tailoress.[15] Mary Booth played a major, underestimated, role in guiding and managing the project, while running the household and raising the Booths' six children. She wrote substantial parts of the books, rewriting passages by Booth which she judged too 'dreary', successfully maximizing their impact.[16]

Studying East London convinced Booth of the need to gather facts from the whole of London. Investigators studied other London trades to establish wage levels and conditions of work, also 'unoccupied' (unemployed) people and inmates of institutions including workhouses. They constructed maps of every London street, each coloured according to its social composition: black for the 'lowest class, vicious, semi-criminal'; dark and light blue, 'very poor . . . in insecure work . . . at all times more or less in want', and 'poor . . . the great body of the labouring class . . . neither ill-nourished nor ill-clad'; purple (mixed); pink ('fairly comfortable'); red (middle class, well-to-do); yellow (wealthy upper-middle and upper class).[17] The maps were published in the successive volumes.

The descriptions of each class indicate how Booth perceived the poor. He concluded that the poorest class included 'some occasional labourers, street-sellers, loafers, criminals and semi-criminals . . . their life is the life of savages, with vicissitudes of extreme hardship and occasional excess'. But he did not share the widespread belief that this was the condition of most people in poverty and its cause, to be overcome only by incentivizing them to work and live respectably. He concluded that the 'facts' revealed that 'loafers' and others were at most around 4 per cent of the London poor, 0.9 per cent of the population. Most poor people could get only casual, irregular or low-paid work, despite their best efforts: 'The hordes of barbarians of whom we have heard, who, issuing from their slums, will one day overwhelm modern civilization, do not exist,' and these poorest people needed help not condemnation.[18] The study ultimately described the lives of hundreds of thousands of Londoners living on the margins of destitution for whom 'it is only by evading the payment of rent, or going short of food, that clothes and household things can be bought'.[19] Descriptions all too familiar in 2023.

One revelation from the East London study which struck Charles and Mary Booth especially hard was destitution among older people. They discovered that about 39 per cent of residents over 65 were paupers, dependent upon minimal, stigmatizing Poor Law relief. Many people who managed, often with difficulty, to earn adequate incomes during their working lives experienced poverty in old age, not to due to personal failings or family neglect but because they were no longer fit enough to earn a living, had not earned enough to save for old age and had no relatives who could afford to support them. In response, the Booths joined the campaign for state old age pensions which started in the 1870s.[20] Booth became a leading advocate of state-funded pensions for all at sixty-five, universal because he believed this was the only way to ensure they benefitted all in need and did not stigmatize by singling out the poorest.

To convince opponents wary of the cost of universal pensions and/ or believing that aged paupers and their families were to blame for their poverty, he established another survey of the conditions of the aged poor throughout England and Wales. Published in 1894 as *The Aged Poor in England and Wales*, it described the variable treatment of older people by the Poor Law in different districts, nowhere generous but harsher in some than others. The percentage of over-65s receiving poor relief varied from 5 to 85 across unions; 22 per cent received support from relatives, but families were often themselves too poor to help. The findings further convinced Booth and others of the need to give all older people the security of a state pension.[21]

The survey of London continued, providing a detailed account of the overcrowded, damp, unhealthy homes of most low-income people, not only the poorest, in the rapidly growing city, often poorly constructed by profit-seeking builders and owners. Whole families were crammed into one room, with toilets (often filthy 'middens') and water taps shared with many others. It described poor health due to home and work conditions, inadequate diet and the difficulty of accessing healthcare when free care was only patchily available through the Poor Law or charities, including voluntary hospitals, and poor people could not afford other services. Better-off, mainly male, skilled workers accessed GPs through contributions to Friendly Societies or trade unions. Research for the Royal Commission on the Poor Laws, 1905–9, concluded that 49 per cent of working-class women were in permanently poor health, often because they could not afford skilled medical care in childbirth.

Booth demonstrated that families were poorest when they had (often many) children to support, better off when the children started to earn, poor again when the children left home and poorer when the parents aged. He believed that good education could train children in work skills, ambition and thrift, preparing them for better work and lives than their parents. Free education was now available for all, but too often poor children were taken out of school as soon as possible to supplement the family income, mainly by casual work, and the opportunities were lost.

He concluded that poverty throughout London was much greater than generally supposed, afflicting about 30 per cent of the population; 8 per cent were 'very poor'. He did not define poverty by income alone and recognized that his final statistics were estimates derived from observation of the living conditions of the whole London population. People were judged to be in poverty if they could not match the standards judged normal by the general population, when their means were insufficient for 'decent independent life'.[22] Booth's definition of poverty went beyond absolute destitution. It was an approach defined by social scientist Peter Townsend, in the 1950s, as 'relative poverty' then adopted internationally to the present, a condition above total destitution but below conventional standards of comfort, health, education and housing, standards which changed over time as general prosperity rose.[23]

Seebohm Rowntree

Booth's first publications on London poverty inspired another businessman, Benjamin Seebohm Rowntree, to study poverty in the northern city of York where he lived, and his family firm was based. Rowntree was Labour Director of the firm from 1897, much concerned with workers' conditions. He raised wages, established an eight-hour day, later a pension scheme, then a five-day week – the benign employer behaviour he supported. Like Booth, he blamed employer greed for much poverty.

Rowntree wanted to understand the living conditions of workers and the reasons for their poverty to help determine how best to assist them. He was inspired by Booth's survey of London to investigate whether conditions were similar elsewhere in Britain and focused on York, deciding that an intensive study of one city would be more informative than a more superficial view of several. He believed that York 'might be taken as fairly representative of the conditions existing in many, if not most, of our provincial towns'.[24] From 1899 he led an intensive house-to-house survey of all 'wage-earning families' in York. Investigators visited 11,560 families including 46,754 individuals in an estimated city population of 75,812, at a time when the local economy was believed to be prospering.[25] He gained more detailed information than was possible for much larger London. A thorough analysis was first published in 1901, with two further editions in 1901/2. In contrast with Booth's seventeen volumes, it was a single tiny (11cm × 15cm) volume of 495 pages, but no less illuminating and influential. Booth and his researchers supported and commented upon Rowntree's work throughout. Booth admitted to Rowntree in 1901 that his methods were 'more complete than those I found available for the large area of London', while the results were 'very close'.[26]

Rowntree divided poor people into two classes: those whose 'total earnings are insufficient to obtain the minimum necessities for the maintenance of merely physical efficiency', which he described as 'primary poverty'; and those whose 'total earnings are sufficient for the maintenance of merely physical efficiency were it not that some portion of them is absorbed by other expenditure, either useful or wasteful' which he termed 'secondary poverty'.[27] To establish the numbers in each group he first estimated the minimum cost of suitable food, rent and other essentials and a measure of 'physical efficiency', that is, fitness, for men and women of all ages, which he linked with observations of their living conditions and lifestyles.[28]

The house-to-house surveys focused upon housing, occupation, income and spending. The findings were put to clergymen, charity workers and others with local knowledge for confirmation. Details of each household were printed street by street, for example, 'Labourer, age 25, one child, respectable, wife and house dirty and untidy. Very little furniture'. 'Bricklayer, 40, Respectable, looks well-to-do compared with many. House clean and tidy'.[29] Quite typical were the Smith family, 'whose house is scrupulously clean and tidy. Mr Smith is in regular work and earns 20s a week. He keeps 2s a week for himself and hands over 18s to his wife'. When Mrs Smith was asked how she met 'any extraordinary expenditure, such as new dress or a pair of boots', she replied, 'Well, as a rule, we have to get it out of the food money and go short; but I never let Smith suffer – 'e 'as to go to work, and must be kept up, yer know!'[30]

The survey concluded that the diets of people in 'primary poverty' were 'totally inadequate . . . consisting largely of a dreary succession of bread, dripping and tea; bread and butter and tea; bacon, bread and coffee, with only a little butcher's meat and none of the extras'.[31] Households had few cooking utensils or facilities and fuel was expensive. The families were ill-clothed and 'chronically ill-housed' in dwellings hastily constructed in towns which had grown faster than the capacity to provide adequate sanitation and water supplies, overcrowded because they could afford little rent.[32] In York as in London, possibly more than in London Rowntree believed, there was much 'overcrowded, insanitary housing, without modern sanitary conveniences' and many homes sharing water taps and privies.[33] He judged that 51.9 per cent of primary poverty was due to regular work at low wages, 22.16 per cent to 'large family' (4+ children), 15.63 per cent to the death of the chief wage earner, 5.11 per cent to illness or old age, 2.3 per cent to unemployment. 45.6 per cent of households in primary poverty were headed by widows, the largest group of single mothers nationally.[34] Rowntree was impressed that even very poor people helped others in even greater need including by caring for the sick or cleaning. He noted, like Booth, that 'few people spend all their days' in such poverty but rose above it when the man found a better job or children earned, falling back when the children left home, still further as the breadwinner aged or became sick and could no longer work – the 'lifecycle of poverty', as it became known.[35] This reinforced the growing view that 'the poor' were not a class apart, but many, perhaps most, working people experienced poverty at some point in their lives, due to involuntary circumstances rather than personal failings, while living in relative 'comfort' at other times

Those in 'secondary poverty' experienced only marginally better conditions: 'They live constantly from hand to mouth'.[36] While the wage earner was in work, they could manage, but they were always on the brink: illness or unemployment 'means short rations or running into debt or more often both'. Even the most careful households could not buy furniture or boots for a child or pay for medical care, including in childbirth, without falling into debt or some members going without food, normally the wife, sometimes the children, never the worker 'except in extreme circumstances'.[37] They could never spend on transport fares, buy newspapers, pay postage, give children pocket money, smoke, drink or enjoy other extras without sacrifice.[38] Only a minority of children stayed at school past age fourteen due to their families' needs. Rowntree estimated that universal old age pensions would reduce poverty in York from 27.59 per cent to 26.59 per cent, due to the small numbers of older people (4.67 per cent of the York population), but those in poverty would benefit. This indicated 'how large is the problem of poverty' to be solved by other means.[39]

Rowntree concluded that 27.84 per cent of the York population were 'living in poverty', 17.93 per cent in 'secondary poverty'.[40] However recent analysis of his data concludes that he probably overestimated numbers in primary poverty, underestimated those in secondary poverty.[41] Like Booth's, Rowntree's statistics were estimates and he also did not believe that poverty could be measured by income alone. Rather, he described it as a condition visible in individual appearance and living conditions and marked by absence of opportunities to live as most people judged normal.[42]

Rowntree was 'much surprised' that his findings for York were so similar to Booth's for London and believed they were probably true of the rest of urban Britain.[43] He shared the view that the poor physical condition of so many workers and future workers affected 'the industrial future of the community', especially when competing nations, especially Germany, were believed to be increasing their physical efficiency.[44] He wrote that even the 'steady, respectable section of the labouring classes who spend practically nothing upon drink . . . receive only about three-fourths of the food required for physical efficiency', while spending on average half their incomes on food.[45] He concluded that 'No civilization can be sound or stable which has at its base this mass of stunted human life . . . social questions of profound importance await solutions'.[46] Like Booth, he asserted that 'The object of the writer, however, has been to state facts rather than to suggest remedies. He desires, nevertheless, to express his belief that however difficult the path of social progress may be, a way of advance will open out … if inspired by a true human sympathy',[47] which he aimed to arouse, with some success.

Town and country

Further surveys by Rowntree and others before 1914 showed that poverty was not confined to towns, though this received most attention. It had always been endemic in the countryside, exacerbated by late nineteenth-century agricultural decline. Rowntree and his co-researcher May Kendall studied just forty-two budgets from rural areas in eight English counties and found wide regional variation in wages. They did not try to measure rural poverty, but this and other surveys found similar conditions to the towns, without the debilitating pollution: low pay, miserable housing, widespread malnutrition especially among women and children, among girls more than boys (assumed to be future workers, so better fed), though some families ate well because they could grow healthy food as poor urban dwellers could not. Prices were higher than in towns, and there were concentrations of older people and widows as men fled to work for higher pay in the towns or the colonies.[48]

In 1912–14, A.L. Bowley surveyed four towns across England that he judged representative: Northampton, Warrington, Stanley and Reading. Bowley was a mathematician, pioneer of statistical method and influential survey techniques, professor at the newly founded London School of Economics (LSE), established by the Webbs to develop the social sciences to provide understanding and solution of social problems. Bowley rejected qualitative impressions and introduced the sample survey, examining systematically the earnings and outgoings of representative households. He confirmed that low pay was the main cause of poverty, in Warrington, Northampton and Reading more than in York. Much less in coalmining Stanley, Co. Durham, with relatively high earnings. Illness or old age was the next significant cause in all four towns.[49]

The Fabian Women's Group was formed in 1908 to demand the vote and improved social and working conditions, especially for women. Led by Maud Pember Reeves, wife of the New Zealand high commissioner, a successful campaigner for votes for women in her home country (achieved in 1893) and aware that New Zealand led Britain on social reform, including state pensions (introduced in 1898), they recorded the budgets and daily lives of families in Lambeth, South London, asking, 'How does a working man's wife bring up a family on 20s a week?'[50] The report *Round about a Pound a Week* included details of incomes and budgets and described housing, diet, health and family life. It stressed how carefully most poor women managed inadequate, insecure incomes, contrary to the 'improvidence' perceived by critics ignorant of their lives.[51] The Fabians advocated a state-guaranteed national minimum income, sufficient to keep a family, which New Zealand had been the first to introduce in 1894, followed by Australia in 1896.

Most Lambeth wives were not in employment. They had work enough at home, sometimes supplemented with work as part-time cleaners or by letting rooms to lodgers. The Fabian women also campaigned for and with employed women, especially in the low-paid, largely non-unionized, appropriately labelled, 'sweated' trades, including tailoring, cardboard-box-making, lace making, chain-making, carried out in small workshops or by female outworkers in their homes. In 1905 they organized a London exhibition displaying these women's working conditions. The resulting publicity, plus pressure from labour organizations, persuaded the Liberal government to introduce procedures to set minimum wages in these occupations through the Trade Boards Act, 1909, one of the government reforms which resulted from the growing campaigns.

Inequality

The poverty revealed by the surveys was a feature of Britain's vastly unequal distribution of income and wealth at the time. The Liberal economist and politician Sir Leo Chiozza Money calculated this in Table 1.

Table 1 Income and Wealth Inequality

UK Income and Wealth *c.* 1900
Total UK population 1901, 41,438,700
87% private property owned by 882,690 persons, 4,400,000 including families.
13% shared among 38,600,000.
17,000 property holders owned *c.* two-thirds of private wealth.
90% of population left no recorded property at death.
20% employees earned above the income tax threshold of £150 p.a.
0.5% earned above £5,000.

Source: Leo Chiozza, *Money Riches and Poverty* (London: 1905, 1912).

Inequalities of wealth and income had always been vast and they mounted further with industrialization. By 1900–10 they were comparable in all high-income countries, but greatest in Britain: the great majority of people owned almost nothing.[52] Most wealth was inherited and held in land.

Foundation of a 'Welfare State'

Governments, Liberal and Conservative, responded to evidence of poverty and the pressures for state welfare initially by further increasing the social responsibilities of local government, centrally directed but still locally financed. This included expanding education, clearance of poor housing and re-housing, and providing work for the unemployed. The Conservative Unemployed Workmen Act, 1905, permitted urban areas experiencing unemployment to appoint 'distress committees' to provide employment on local works, including road building and repairs, funded by local rates and voluntary donations. It had limited effect not least because local authorities could not always provide enough work to meet the need or afford cash support to the unemployed outside the Poor Law. Unemployed skilled men received no help to find work appropriate for their skills. The Trades Union Congress (TUC) attacked its inadequacy and unemployed demonstrations continued.

Some larger, well-funded authorities in prospering areas – notably Birmingham under Joseph Chamberlain as mayor – moved ahead of central government using their powers to borrow on the market and invest in local business expansion, using the profits to develop local services including improved housing and water supplies, 'municipal socialism' as it became known. These authorities and others, including Bradford and the LCC following its establishment in 1888, worked with voluntary donors to develop technical colleges, free public libraries and, with charities, provided free school meals to needy children and health and welfare centres for mothers and children on models initiated by women's voluntary groups.[53] But poorer authorities, where needs were greatest but income from local taxes small, had trouble funding even obligatory services such as education and increasingly protested at the costs imposed upon them.

To alleviate social deprivation effectively central government had to take full responsibility, but it also had limited funds since successive governments strove to minimize taxation. The Treasury sought new sources of revenue to meet growing defence as well as socio-economic costs. The Conservative budget of 1894 introduced the first death duties on large estates. The costs of the Anglo-Boer war were partially met by a tariff on imported corn, in effect a tax on bread, part of a wider attempt to draw more of the population into taxation. It encouraged Joseph Chamberlain, now Conservative minister for the colonies, to initiate a tariff reform campaign designed to strengthen the unity of the empire by placing tariffs on imports from countries outside the empire, which would also provide funds for social reforms he supported, including old age pensions. This was strongly opposed, especially by Liberals, who were devoted free traders.

Meanwhile Conservative governments introduced further reforms with limited costs for central or local government: in 1897 employers were required to compensate workers for accidents at work; greater controls were introduced over food adulteration, contaminated water supplies and public health generally. These all prescribed standards and punishments for flouting them, without costly supervision. The Midwifery Act, 1902, required midwives to be trained and registered, responding to women's campaigns to reduce high maternal and infant mortality at minimal public cost. But poor families could not afford trained midwives, and there were no controls on untrained women who continued to practice in poor communities. Also in 1902, an Education Act expanded and improved state secondary education in England and Wales. Education was judged so vital to the economy and society that the state funded free places for able children from poor backgrounds and secondary school attendance grew, though poor families still needed their children in paid work as early as possible. Many local authorities appointed school medical officers to diagnose and treat ill-health among schoolchildren whose parents could not afford medical care. In 1905 Poor Law Guardians were permitted, but not funded, to provide free meals for children identified by their school as 'necessitous', supplementing widespread charitable provision, but many parents rejected stigmatizing Poor Law provision.

In the same year a Royal Commission was appointed to investigate the increasingly criticized Poor Law, with members representing the range of known viewpoints, including Charles Booth, Beatrice Webb, George Lansbury representing the Labour Party, representatives of the COS and a trade unionist. It reported in 1909, when the Conservatives had been replaced by a Liberal government. Voters' demands for social reform contributed to the Liberals' success in the election of 1906, defeating the Conservatives after twenty years in government. Labour, which also advocated reform, won its largest number of seats so far, thirty.

Liberal leaders were initially non-committal about reforms, aware of the financial difficulties and that many traditional Liberals still favoured a minimal state, but many reformers were elected to the back benches. What became an unprecedented run of state welfare legislation began immediately with an extension of the Workman's Compensation Act, 1897, improving enforcement. Then a Labour backbencher successfully introduced a Bill allowing, but not obliging, local authorities to provide free meals for needy schoolchildren, funded by the rates and/or charities, without Poor Law involvement. By 1911/1912, 131 of the 322 education authorities in England and Wales provided meals, in 95 funded from rates, the rest from charity. About 100,000 children were fed in London, 258,000 elsewhere. State finances improved, and from 1914 the scheme became compulsory, subsidized by the Exchequer, feeding was authorized during school holidays and need was determined by school medical officers assessing the health of the child. Concern for the 'physical efficiency' of future workers was evident from further legislation in 1907 requiring local authorities to 'provide for the medical inspection of schoolchildren' in state elementary schools to maintain their 'health and physical condition', initially at local authorities' own pressurized expense, from 1912 funded by the Treasury, and treatments available to children were extended. With free meals this improved the health of many poor children.

These extensions of state welfare were possible because the Liberals gradually transformed the tax system. H. H. Asquith, as chancellor, sought reform of the flat-rate income tax of 1s in the £ on incomes of £150 pa and above, but he believed that simply raising it would penalize those on lower taxable incomes. A Select Committee on Income Tax in 1906 recommended an innovative graduated income tax, making higher earners pay more.[54] It was supported by Labour and Liberal reformers, opposed by traditional Liberals and in the Conservative-dominated House of Lords. Asquith proceeded cautiously. In the 1907 budget he took a first step by reducing the tax to 9d on earned income only. To compensate the revenue, inheritance tax was raised on estates worth over £150,000. In 1908 Asquith succeeded Henry Campbell Bannerman as Liberal leader and David Lloyd George became chancellor. He took tax reform further in his notorious budget of 1909.

Meanwhile he introduced the first state old age pensions in 1908. The bill had been largely drafted under Asquith at the Treasury following the long campaign. Asquith and his civil servants rejected the model of contributory insurance pensions introduced in Germany in 1889 and supported in Britain by Joseph Chamberlain among others. The Liberals', and Booth's, chief concern was alleviating old age poverty and Asquith and his colleagues recognized that those at greatest risk, mostly women, could not afford contributions during their working lives. They were too low-paid or, in the case of many women, were employed irregularly or not at all. German pensions mainly benefitted better-off male skilled workers. The alternative was non-contributory, tax-funded pensions, as Booth proposed, already introduced in New Zealand, Australia and Denmark. Booth's campaign for universal pensions for everyone at age sixty-five was resisted by the Treasury due to cost, and the scheme which came before parliament was stringently means-tested, restricted to the very poor and not payable until age seventy, at a maximum 5s pw. Lloyd George admitted in parliament that this was insufficient to live on – indeed British state pensions have never, to the present, provided enough to live on without a supplement of some kind. Claimants had also to prove that they had not been imprisoned for crime or convicted of drunkenness in the ten years preceding the claim and were not guilty of 'habitual failure to work according to his ability, opportunity or need for his own maintenance or that of his legal relatives'.

The pension was scarcely less stringent than the Poor Law, though it faced opposition from traditional Liberals in the Commons and from Liberals and Conservatives in the Lords for excessive generosity with state revenue. But it was not the Poor Law, it was the first tax-funded cash payment to the poor outside the Poor Law, and for all its limitations it was better than anything before, less stigmatized and welcomed by the 490,000 people, two-thirds female, who qualified for the first pensions in January 1909. Pension claims were assessed by committees of volunteers, including charity workers and clergy, appointed and supervised by state officials, and pensions were paid through the Post Office. Like other Liberal reforms it exemplified commitment to encouraging voluntary action and co-operation between charity and the state to encourage 'public spirit'. Workhouses remained the only form of institutional care for older people needing care whose families could not provide it, could not afford private care or access charitable care.[55]

Also in 1908, the Children Act continued the process of building up future generations. Local authorities became responsible for child victims of physical and sexual abuse, to be placed where possible in charitable institutions or with foster parents. The National Society for the Prevention of Cruelty to Children (NSPCC), founded in 1889, had been working with victims for more than two decades and pressing for the state to take over with its greater resources.[56] Child abuse was not new, but it was not publicly discussed or made a public responsibility until the Prevention of Cruelty and Protection of Children Act, 1889, following intense campaigning by NSPCC.[57] The Children Act introduced further penalties for child abuse or neglect. It also established separate juvenile courts, reformatories for under-sixteens and remand homes to keep them out of adult prisons, providing support and work training.

In February 1909, the Royal Commission on the Poor Laws reported. Free school meals, the Children Act and old age pensions had removed some people from poor relief, but many remained. The majority, dominated by the COS, and a radical minority, including Webb and Lansbury, issued separate reports. Both were critical of the failure to prevent or ameliorate severe poverty and recommended abolishing the Poor Law and replacing it with specialized services for specific needs, including allowances to enable mothers of young children to stay home to rear healthy children, non-punitive cash support for the involuntarily unemployed and help to find work, with rigorous investigation of individual circumstances to identify 'shirkers' who should receive compulsory work training. Both also proposed raising the school-leaving age to fifteen; the minority added part-time education to age eighteen. The main differences were majority support for national insurance for sick or unemployed workers, the minority preferring non-contributory benefits providing 'a national minimum of civilized life' for low earners unable to afford contributions. Also, the majority proposed substantial involvement of charities in providing new services, co-operating with the state. The minority supported co-operation but believed that, to ensure efficiency, national uniformity and accountability, policy should be directed and funded by the state, with delivery of services delegated to local authorities. Reform was strongly opposed by the Local Government Board (LGB) which administered the Poor Law, and it survived fundamentally unchanged. But demands for change did not go away. Beatrice Webb and her husband Sidney campaigned vigorously for the minority proposals, especially the 'national minimum'.

Lloyd George's first budget, in April 1909, the 'People's Budget' as he called it, moved closer to a graduated income tax. Earned incomes up to £2,000 pa continued to be taxed at 9d in £, from £2,000 to £3,000 at 1s, later at 1s 2d. An additional super-tax of 6d in £ was charged on all income above £3,000. Death duties rose on estates worth over £5,000 and a new tax took 20 per cent of the profit from land sales. Taxpayers earning up to £500 p.a. received an innovative £10 tax allowance for each child under sixteen, perhaps to encourage respectable people to have more children. A £200,000 development fund was introduced to create rural employment, including through afforestation and developing smallholdings.[58]

The land tax incensed the mostly landowning Lords even more than higher income taxes, and they took the unprecedented step of rejecting the budget. The government held firm, made it an issue of public confidence and called an election in January 1910. They lost seats (from 400 to 275) and their overall majority, but Labour won 40 seats and, with the Irish Nationalists, held the balance in parliament, increasing their influence. The peers refused to back down. At Asquith's request the new king, George V – Edward V11 died during the crisis in May 1910 – agreed to appoint enough new peers to outvote the Tories if the Liberals won another election and the Lords remained intransigent. Another election in December brought similar results. The Liberals introduced the Parliament Act,1911, which significantly curbed the Lords' powers. Finance bills now required approval by the Commons alone, and it could overrule the Lords on any government measure after a maximum delay of two years. To avoid a flood of Liberal peers, the Lords passed it with many abstentions. They were then forced to pass the delayed budget. Lloyd George later made further increases in taxes on higher incomes. By 1914 direct taxes contributed 52 per cent of government revenue compared with 40 per cent in the 1890s.[59]

Lloyd George could now return his attention to social reform. He visited Germany to investigate their unique scheme of National Health Insurance. Unlike with pensions, he was less concerned with poverty than with the health especially of skilled workers, whom he believed could afford insurance contributions, as in Germany. National Health Insurance passed calmly through parliament in 1911. It granted insured workers sickness benefits for twenty-six weeks (10s per week for men, 7s 6d for women – unequal compensation for unequal lost pay) and free access to a GP, to assist recovery and a speedy return to work. They and their dependents received free hospital treatment only for TB, intended to protect society from this highly infectious scourge. Most working-class women and poorer, irregularly employed men were excluded because they could not afford contributions. Severely disabled insured people received a long-term pension of 5s pw and the wives of insured men a maternity benefit of 30s (£1.50) to provide skilled care in childbirth to reduce infant and maternal deaths. This was not, as initially planned, paid to the man, following a campaign by women who feared it would go to the pub, not the wife. Contributions from workers aged 16–65 were 4d pw for men, 3d for women; employers paid 3d and the state a little under 2d per week per worker, 'nine pence for four pence', as Lloyd George put it. Contributions were collected and benefits paid and administered by organizations with relevant experience, mainly Friendly Societies and trade unions, defined in the law as 'approved societies', supervised by a central National Insurance Commission. This further example of co-operation between the state and voluntary institutions soothed the latter's fears of state competition, while the state avoided a costly new bureaucracy.

The same structure was adopted for Part II of the National Insurance Act, the world's first experiment with unemployment insurance. In 1908 Winston Churchill, a Liberal at this time, became president of the Board of Trade, the department responsible for work conditions, amid high unemployment. He recruited William Beveridge, then working among the poor of East London at Toynbee Hall settlement while completing an influential study of unemployment.[60] Beveridge began a long career of advising on state social policy. On his recommendation in 1909, labour exchanges, nationwide offices providing the unemployed with information and advice on available work, were founded, designed to reduce unemployment by improving opportunities to find work. In the same year, the Board of Trade initiated the first attempt to improve low pay. Following the campaign by Fabian women, Trade Boards were established in four non-unionized trades covering 200,000 female workers, on which employer and worker representatives negotiated pay, but they were under-resourced and poorly regulated. Female pay remained low.

Meanwhile Beveridge, with civil servants, devised unemployment insurance. Insurance could not solve the greatest labour market problem: workers in irregular, low-paid jobs could not afford contributions sufficient to cover their high risk of unemployment. Instead, the scheme covered workers in just three, exclusively male, skilled trades important to the economy, shipbuilding, engineering, building and construction, which regularly experienced fluctuations and, generally short-term, unemployment. Workers and employers contributed 2½d pw which provided 7s pw for 15 weeks after the first week of involuntary unemployment, intended to keep them fit to return to productive work as soon as possible. Payments were administered and paid by labour exchanges, where registration was compulsory to assist the search for work. Claimants were expected to seek work but could refuse work in conditions inferior to their regular occupation. It passed easily through parliament and by July 1914 covered 2.3m workers, costing the state about £1 million p.a. It did not solve the major problems of unemployment, but it was a significant start. Also in 1911, after a long campaign by female trade unionists, a Shops Act established half-day closing each week, reducing shop workers' very long hours.

The Liberals also started to tackle another major problem, urban squalor and overcrowding. The Housing and Town Planning Act, 1909, encouraged, but did not fund or require, local authorities to demolish unfit dwellings and plan further development at low density, with gardens and open spaces. It was influenced by the pioneering planners, Ebenezer Howard and Patrick Geddes who inspired the building of Letchworth from 1903, the first 'Garden City', providing homes and work away from London, but only for those who could afford the rents, as the poorest could not. The garden city concept influenced the building of the LCC's (and Britain's) first council housing estates from the turn of the century, and private ventures, including Hampstead Garden Suburb, started 1905, designed for workers by its philanthropic initiator, Henrietta Barnett, wife of the founder of Toynbee Hall. Port Sunlight on Merseyside (opened 1890) and Bournville in Birmingham (with 300 houses by 1900) were built on similar models for workers by Lever Bros soap manufacturers and Cadbury's chocolate business respectively. Few local authorities could afford to follow their example, but the ideas and models were influential, especially after the war, though none were affordable by the poorest.[61]

Conclusion

The Liberals significantly expanded the state's social responsibilities, unintentionally sowing the seeds of what was not then described as a 'Welfare State'. This expanded through future decades, though profound socio-economic inequalities persisted. The conditions that brought this about – approximately 25 per cent of the population in poverty, most due to low wages in work, leading to malnutrition and poor health especially among wives and children and higher death rates than among the better off; increasing dependence upon charitable support including for food; poor, often damp, overcrowded housing due to lack of decent housing at rents affordable by the lower-paid – are remarkably similar to those of Britain in the 2020s, when it is still one of the richest countries in the world, though less prominent internationally than in 1900. These conditions did not persist for over a century but were much ameliorated by the expansion of state welfare that followed, then eroded by its decline. The following chapters will trace this rise and fall of the British Welfare State and the fall and then rise of the conditions that made it necessary.

CHAPTER 3
THE FIRST WORLD WAR

The First World War, 1914–18, caused more international death and destruction than any previous war, but it also triggered the emergence of welfare states and the gradual narrowing of inequalities in Britain and elsewhere. As Thomas Picketty describes, in all high-income countries, 'The wars of the twentieth century to a large extent transformed the structure of inequality'.[1] 'Without the wars at the very least progress would have been slower'.[2]

Financial crisis

This was not obvious as the war began. It opened amid an unprecedented, severe, largely forgotten international financial crisis. The fear, then reality, of war caused panic selling on the European exchanges in late July 1914, and the world's leading stock exchanges closed. The centre of world finance, the London Stock Exchange, closed for the first time since its foundation in 1773, followed by that in New York. In London there was a run on the banks and huge queues outside the Bank of England as people tried to exchange bank notes for the security of gold sovereigns. The Bank's gold reserves fell perilously low. Like the Treasury, where Lloyd George remained chancellor, it was taken by surprise. Both bought time by declaring an unprecedented extended Bank Holiday from 3rd to 7th August; Britain declared war on Germany on 5th August.

After days of intense discussion with officials and advisers, Lloyd George took another unprecedented step by issuing bank notes from the Treasury rather than, as normal, from the Bank. These were new, hurriedly printed, notes for £1, later also 10 shillings (50p). Previously the lowest denomination note was £5, worth over £400 at early twenty-first-century rates, and too large for most everyday transactions. The value of notes and currency in circulation more than doubled. The gold standard, the internationally agreed valuation of the currency in relation to gold, was effectively, though not officially (until 1919), abandoned. When the banks reopened, they were awash with small, shoddily printed notes, produced by the official printer of postage stamps and of similar size. They proved highly popular and became permanent features of the currency in enlarged format. Gold flowed back into the Bank. International debts were repaid, other than to Germany and Austria which were delayed until after the war. The financial system was restored; only one small British bank and a few stock exchange firms (of hundreds) failed. In January 1915 the London Stock Exchange reopened.[3] Decisive action prevented catastrophe and established unprecedented Treasury control over the financial system, valuably in wartime. The banks bought quantities of bonds issued by the Treasury at generous interest rates to fund the war. Lloyd George preferred to pay for the war, as far as possible, through loans rather than by raising taxes. He had prevented the failure of businesses essential to the war effort and interruption to essential supplies from abroad.

Supporting service families

Poorer people faced other crises. Unemployment rose as the economy shifted from peace to wartime production. Many men responded by volunteering for war service, leaving their families in poverty. In previous wars charities supported service families, but they could not cope with the unprecedented numbers serving in this war. Sylvia Pankhurst, daughter of the leading suffragette Emmeline Pankhurst, now a socialist far to her mother's left, helped impoverished families in East London, whom she later described:

> Poor, wan, white-faced mothers, clasping their wasted babies, whose pain-filled eyes seem older than their own. Their breasts gone dry, they had no milk to give their infants, no food for the older children, no money for the landlord.[4]

From October 1914, for the first time, the government paid allowances to service families: for the ranks, 12s.6d per week for the wife, 2s for each child; higher for officers' families.[5] Later they even paid allowances to cohabiting 'unmarried wives' when these emerged in unexpected numbers, but only if the relationship preceded the serviceman's enlistment by at least six months, there was at least one child and 'evidence that a real home had been maintained'. The woman had to prove that the serviceman was her sole support and she 'would otherwise be destitute'. It was paid even if he had a legal wife if the conditions were met. There is no official record of the numbers eligible, but they must have been substantial to bring about such an unprecedented move.[6] It also emerged that many servicemen supported ageing parents who were also left destitute. Up to 10s per week was paid to parents who were judged 'incapable of self-support and in pecuniary need'.[7] From November 1915, as deaths at war rose, widows and children of the dead received weekly pensions, at levels related to rank and pay, 21s maximum for widows of non-commissioned servicemen. 'Unmarried wives' received a maximum 10s pw, plus allowances for children 'if, and as long as, she has children of the soldier in her charge'. Dependent parents received pensions unless they were judged capable of work, when they were paid just a gratuity equal to one year's service pay. Prices rose through the war, causing hardship, and in 1917 the pension limit was raised to 15s and the gratuity paid regardless of assumed capacity for self-support.

Through the war, to 1919, 221,692 pensions were paid to parents of non-commissioned servicemen, 192,698 to widows and 2,645 to 'unmarried wives', suggesting how many sons supported their parents. It was a substantial extension of state welfare, but allowances and pensions were low compared even with average unskilled wages, though they could be more regular and even higher than a precariously employed, unskilled man's take-home pay.[8] But they were often paid only after long delays for assessment and could expose wives (married and unmarried) to moral policing by administrators, since payments were withdrawn for 'immoral behaviour', of which women were widely suspected when free from their husbands in wartime.[9] Nevertheless, they improved the well-being of some families so visibly that feminist Eleanor Rathbone demanded their continuation as peacetime family allowances, sparking another long campaign which reached fruition in the next world war.[10]

Civilian social conditions

Families of civilian workers fared better. After the first months of war, the needs of war production plus service recruitment brought unprecedented full employment. Thereafter through the war unemployment rarely rose above 1 per cent.[11] By mid-1918 wages in agriculture, mining, docks and railways, all vital for management of the war, were 90 per cent above 1914 levels. Food prices and the overall cost of living doubled, but incomes rose faster due to regular work and longer hours. And many households had more earners as women could work often for higher pay in previously male-only jobs, such as bus-driving, vacated by servicemen, especially after the introduction of conscription in 1915. But women rarely received male pay rates. Enlistment of teachers to the services created a shortage, leading some local authorities tacitly to suspend compulsory attendance for older children, who were also employed. Older people remained in or returned to work if they were fit, eagerly forsaking meagre old age pensions. Pensions rose following price rises and campaigns but remained inadequate. A.L. Bowley undertook a survey of wartime conditions and concluded that wage-earners generally gained, the unskilled and semi-skilled most, but many white-collar workers experienced fixed hours and pay and suffered from rising prices.[12]

Another cause of hardship was rising rents in centres of war production, including Glasgow and London, where workers flocked to work, and landlords took advantage. There was a serious shortage of adequate housing even before the war and new building almost ceased in wartime. Some manufacturers of munitions, shipbuilders, and other employers in essential industries, built homes to attract labour, including Vickers Armaments in Barrow-in-Furness, where the population grew by 10,000 in two years. Glasgow was believed to have the worst housing in Europe before the war and rebellion against high rents started there.[13] In May 1915 in Govan, a district of Glasgow of mainly lower-middle-class and skilled workers, women led the first rent strikes, supported by shopkeepers and tradesmen who suffered because high rents reduced demand. As Scottish socialist Willie Gallagher described:

> Mrs Barbour, a typical working-class housewife, became the leader of a movement such as had never been seen before . . . street meetings, backcourt meetings, drums, bells, trumpets – every method was used to bring women out and organize them for the struggle. Notices were printed by the thousand and put up in the

windows. . . . In street after street scarcely a window without one: WE ARE NOT PAYING INCREASED RENT.[14]

Rent strikes and demonstrations followed in London, Coventry and elsewhere. Lloyd George, still chancellor, moved fast to avoid interruption to the war effort, introducing the Rent and Mortgage Interest (Rent Restriction) Act,1915, restricting both to pre-war levels. But there was initially no penalty if landlords broke the law and no means of enforcement, other than victims appealing to the magistrates' courts. Magistrates, often landlords themselves, were not always sympathetic and some rent rises continued alongside housing shortages and overcrowding especially in key centres. Restricted rents gave landlords less incentive to invest in improvements and conditions deteriorated further.[15] Rent control in various forms remained in force, increasingly effectively from 1945, until abolished by Margaret Thatcher's government in 1988.

As Bowley concluded, many families experienced real improvements. The clearest sign that average living standards rose, despite rising costs, was improved civilian health and longevity after the first year of war. In the first year, increasing numbers of malnourished children were identified in large towns.[16] Thereafter, poverty diminished, fewer infants died and mortality fell among adult civilians. Digestive disorders, diarrhoea and degenerative diseases declined, probably due to improved nutrition.[17] Malnutrition in largely working-class Doncaster fell from 31 per cent in 1913 to 5 per cent in 1915.[18] These improvements occurred despite the absence at war of 13,000 of the 24,000 pre-war doctors in UK, but many working-class people, especially women, were not covered by National Health Insurance and had never been able to afford a doctor. Higher incomes and improved diets mattered more than medical care. Workers were also helped by factory welfare facilities installed to help overcome labour shortages and increase productivity, encouraged by the government from 1916 through the Special Welfare Department of the Ministry of Munitions. Canteens provided cheap, hot meals, health centres were installed and improved sanitation and washrooms.

Like doctors, many nurses were recruited for war service. More were trained than before but too few for civilian needs, despite increased pay. Shortage of medical and nursing care in TB sanatoria, combined with greater risk of infection from overcrowding due to high rents and housing shortage, contributed to increased deaths from TB. Perhaps also to deaths in the exceptionally virulent 'Spanish flu' epidemic of 1918–19, in which 151,446 people died in Britain, though the impact was similar, indeed generally greater, internationally including in countries not involved in the war and among both rich and poor. Civilian hospital services deteriorated as war casualties were prioritized, increasing inequalities between improved health for the majority and the deprived minorities. Older people with low incomes were particularly vulnerable. Death rates among men aged 65–74 rose from 64.7 per 1,000 in 1914 to 70.7 in 1915, dropping to 67.5 in 1917; among women, deaths averaged 51.4, 56.2 and 52.2 per 1000.

Women, many of them former suffrage campaigners, volunteered as nurses in voluntary hospitals for service casualties organized in Britain and at the fighting front by some of the very few qualified women doctors. Their numbers, however, grew during the war. Medical training opened up for women as the absence of male doctors at war created a shortage at home. In London, eleven medical schools admitted no women in 1914; they were confined to the London (Royal Free) School of Medicine for Women. Most other UK university medical schools admitted just a few women. By 1915, women were urged to respond to the national need and train as doctors. By 1918 seven London medical schools admitted women and other universities increased their intake, generally specifying this was for the wartime emergency only. After the war, some schools excluded women again and everywhere places were severely cut.[19] Women's medical training remained restricted until the Sex Discrimination Act,1975, enforced equal rights.

Families with small children, especially those headed by a single mother, could fare badly. Numbers in severe poverty probably fell, but the gap between the poorest and the rest grew with the cost of living. Applications for poor relief declined from 1915, but applicants' incomes almost certainly slipped further behind those of employed workers. The income gap between workers who gained from war conditions and the mass of the middle class may have narrowed slightly, though they all fell far behind the employers who profited from war production, especially before business profits were restricted and direct taxation increased in 1916. A minority of landed families were hard hit by death duties following the deaths at war of one or more heirs and some landed estates were broken up in consequence.

Shortage of supplies, including food, caused prices to rise by 40 per cent in 1914–15. Further inflation was fuelled by increased demand as incomes rose and by the weaker pound as Britain became increasingly dependent on supplies from the United States. Before the war, home food production declined due to cheaper imports, but these were disrupted by the war.[20] The government encouraged home production, but this took time. Throughout the war Britain was heavily dependent for food on troublesome Ireland; Irish farmers had too much to gain to resist, and the severe food shortages feared were avoided. Compulsory rationing was introduced only in the last year of war. Britain suffered less from food scarcity than most combatant countries.

Paying for the war

Through the war the basic rate of income tax rose from 1s 2d to 6s in the pound, becoming more graduated and redistributive, ranging by 1918 from 13 per cent on earned incomes above £500 per year to 43 per cent at £10,000 and above. Lloyd George initially increased taxes cautiously, partly due to political opposition from Conservatives and some Liberals and because the likely costs of war were uncertain. He wanted to avoid burdening the population and causing resentment. But as time went on and costs rose it became unavoidable, and in war there was less resistance to tax rises than in peace.

When Reginald McKenna succeeded Lloyd George at the Treasury in 1916 the financial situation was urgent. In his first budget he raised income tax and lowered the threshold from £160 to £130, while raising child tax allowances so that increases fell mainly on single men and childless couples. Income taxpayers increased by 350 per cent, including more working-class people, creating some resistance. McKenna introduced taxes on imported motor cars and films and raised the excess profits duty.[21] Tax revenue rose from £227m in 1914, when it exceeded spending, to £889m in 1918 covering only about 30 per cent of war expenditure. In 1918 income and super-tax accounted for 36 per cent of revenue compared with 29 per cent in 1913/14.[22] War costs were met by sale of government bonds and loans, mainly from the United States on easy terms.[23] The war brought some narrowing of inequalities of income and wealth, as Picketty suggests.

State welfare

One reason for increased spending was wartime demand for more public services, supported by Labour and women's organizations, including for increased state pensions. They rose to a still inadequate 7s 6d pw in 1917.[24] At the other end of the age scale, pre-war campaigns to reduce infant and maternal deaths continued, mainly by women but with greater male support as adults died in the war. The Bishop of Fulham announced: 'While nine soldiers die every hour in 1915, twelve babies die every hour, so that it is more dangerous to be a baby than a soldier.' A *Daily Telegraph* leader proclaimed: 'If we had been more careful for the last fifty years to prevent the unheeded wastage of infant life, we should now have had at least half a million more men available for the defence of the country.' Concern deepened when it was reported that of every nine men conscripted in 1917/18, three were 'perfectly fit and healthy; two were upon a definitely infirm plane of health and strength . . . three could almost (in view of their age) be described with justice as physical wrecks; and the remaining man was a chronic invalid with a precarious hold on life'.[25]

Births declined even faster, not too surprising given the absence of men at war, but deepening concerns for the future of the nation, especially because 'illegitimate' births rose from *c.* 4 per cent to 9 per cent of all births during the war. This unleashed a moral panic about the deterioration of morals among young people in wartime. More probably, as was proven in the next world war, it was due to the absence of men at war delaying marriage following pregnancy, as it delayed births in established marriages. Almost certainly in peacetime premarital pregnancy was more common than moralists believed. But a serious cause for concern was that 'illegitimate' babies had higher death rates than others, often because their mothers were poorer and more isolated, suffering from shame and stigma.[26] Concern about the mothers and babies led a group of women, with some male support, to establish in 1918 the voluntary National Council for the Unmarried Mother and her Child (NCUMC) to support them, as it still does, now named Gingerbread.

Improvements in infant care began before the war. A government circular in 1914 encouraged local authorities to provide comprehensive ante- and post-natal care, as women's groups demanded. The LGB met 50 per cent of the cost of clinics, health visitors, hospital beds and skilled midwives, and, from 1915, local authority depots selling milk at cost price. The Board of Education funded childcare classes for mothers.

From 1916 the LGB funded the full costs of nurses, health visitors, doctors and midwives for poorer mothers, and clinics and hospital treatment of infants in regions where provision remained poor. Health visitors in England and Wales increased from 600 in 1914 to 1,355 in 1918. The improvements owed much to women who saw campaigning and implementing reform as their war service. A volume of heart-rending *Letters from Working Women*, recounting women's experiences of repeated childbearing and child death in poverty, published in 1915 by the Women's Co-operative Guild, expressed the need, typically:

> How I managed to get through my second confinement I cannot tell anyone. I had to work at laundry work from morning to night, nurse a sick husband and take care of my child three and a half years old. In addition, I had to provide for my coming confinement, which meant I had to do without common necessaries to provide doctor's fees, which so undermined my health that when my baby was born, I nearly lost my life, the doctor said through want of nourishment . . .

> I had to depend on my neighbours for what help they could give during labour and the lying-in period. They did their best, but from the second day I had to have my other child with me, undress him and see to all his wants, and was often left six hours without a bite of food, the fire out and no light . . .

> When I got up after ten days my life was a perfect burden to me. I lost my milk and ultimately lost my baby. My interest in life seemed lost.[27]

Voluntary health centres for mothers and children multiplied and donations poured in, assisted by the charitable Infant Welfare Propaganda Fund which launched a week of publicity, National Baby Week, in July 1917. Infant deaths declined: in deprived Wigan, from 139/1,000 to 119/1,000, 1914–18.[28] How much this owed to local services or to rising family living standards is uncertain. The improvements were not shared by other belligerent countries. This was one example of the voluntary welfare work which contributed substantially to the war effort, mostly carried out by women, supported by generous donations and royal patronage. Initially volunteers helped mainly servicemen's dependants and Belgian refugees. Later they provided bandages, dressings and medical care and 'comforts' for men at war, including tobacco, socks, blankets, warm clothes, supplementing state efforts. The press criticized the government for leaving such support to charity.[29]

Reconstruction

The government remained Liberal, led by Asquith, until 1916, when disagreement over the conduct of the war led to a split in the party, his resignation and replacement by Lloyd George at the head of a Conservative-dominated coalition, with Labour representation. Rising wartime living standards raised popular norms and expectations, and government fears of unrest if, as expected, the war was followed by unemployment and recession. The fears were increased by growing support for Labour and the unions whose membership rose from 4 to 6.5 million as war needs strengthened their bargaining power and wages rose, and by the even more alarming Bolshevik revolution in Russia in 1917. The Liberals, then the coalition, decided they should act to maintain and improve living standards after the war, to reward people for their wartime support and sacrifices and avoid conflict.

They recognized it was impossible to continue excluding 40 per cent of adult men from the vote when so many had suffered and died in the war. In February 1918 all men gained the vote at age twenty-one and at any age if they had fought in the war. Conscientious objectors, who refused to fight, were excluded. Promise of male franchise reform aroused the suffragists, the National Union of Women's Suffrage Societies (NUWSS), led by Millicent Garrett Fawcett to resume campaigning.[30] Emmeline Pankhurst, once a supporter of the Independent Labour Party, had become increasingly Conservative (she was later a Conservative parliamentary candidate, unsuccessfully) and did not lead a suffragette revival. Some men argued that because they did not fight for their country, women should not vote, although women's branches of all the armed services had formed for the first time during the war, forbidden to fight but performing essential tasks behind the lines, liberating men to fight. Others argued that women deserved the vote for their essential wartime work. But another problem for the politicians was that most adults were female. This was not only due to male deaths at war, though this increased the disparity it was long-established; in England and Wales there were 107 females per 100 males in 1911, 110 in 1921. A female majority electorate was too alarming and, to keep them in the minority, women were granted the vote in 1918 only at age thirty and if they or their husbands possessed the property qualification that had been abolished for men. Many politicians also believed that propertied older women would be more conservative than younger and poorer women and would counterbalance the danger of socialism among newly enfranchised men who were mainly working class.

The prospect of an unprecedented near-democratic electorate reinforced the belief of Lloyd George and his colleagues that it was essential to promise and deliver improved social and economic conditions after the war. As Lloyd George put it shortly after the Armistice in 1918, he aspired to make Britain 'a fit country for heroes to live in'.[31] In 1917 a Ministry of Reconstruction was established, and committees appointed to examine reform of the Poor Law, pensions, housing, education and health. The coalition retained power in the election of December 1918 and embarked on 'reconstruction'. It helped that the economy remained unexpectedly buoyant until 1920, largely due to reduced competition from defeated Germany and demand for British produce from countries that had suffered more severely from the war (as most combatant nations had) and needed to rebuild. British people had become accustomed to higher taxation than before the war and it could be sustained to some degree, though there was pressure for cuts from Conservatives and businesspeople and for the easing of wartime state controls.

The minister of reconstruction, Liberal Christopher Addison, a medical doctor, supported by civil servants, wanted a coordinated National Health Service, under a Ministry of Health, taking over and extending the health responsibilities of the Poor Law, the school medical authorities and the National Insurance Commission (NIC), to reduce health inequalities. A Ministry of Health was established in 1919 following the lethal influenza epidemic. It absorbed the responsibilities of the NIC and the Poor Law but did not receive powers or funds to deliver a full national health system. The Maternity and Child Welfare Act, 1918, followed the long women's campaign. Wartime deaths, the return of many damaged men and continuing concern about 'national efficiency' made it urgent to nurture fit future generations. It permitted, but did not oblige, local authorities to provide state-subsidized health and social care before, during and after childbirth for mothers and children. Women's groups worked hard to persuade local authorities to implement these powers.[32] The Poor Law otherwise remained unreformed, despite a report by a Ministry of Reconstruction sub-committee in January 1918 recommending comprehensive dismantling, proposed by Beatrice Webb, a member of the committee, pursuing the reforms she advocated in 1909, particularly for transferring the administration and institutions to local authorities. Poor Law administrators successfully resisted change, arguing, dubiously, that they had provided a safety net against starvation in wartime and protected Britain from the near-revolution now threatening much of Europe.[33] Another committee investigated old age pensions. It heard strong arguments that pensioner poverty necessitated a substantial increase, but the Treasury insisted this was unaffordable. In 1919 the maximum pension rose to a still inadequate 10s weekly and the income limit rose.[34]

Addison was also responsible for supplying affordable housing. The major pre-war housing problems were worsened by wartime conditions. In 1917 the Committee of Enquiry into Industrial Unrest, following increased trade union action, argued that poor, overcrowded housing encouraged militancy, which could only be prevented by building more decent, affordable homes. The Ministry of Reconstruction investigated housing design. They found that too much working-class housing had no separate space for food preparation and storage or for washing, and lacked running water and an indoor WC, all causing ill-health. In 1917 it appointed a Women's Housing Sub-Committee, representing the three main political parties, to recommend improved housing design. Their proposals for healthier, easier to manage housing included indoor toilets and washrooms, hot and cold running water, windows which admitted ventilation, looked attractive, excluded draughts and were easy to clean, adequate work surfaces and cupboards at convenient heights. They influenced the Tudor-Walters Committee on housing design which reported in 1918 and set the standard for improved building and design of post-war housing.[35] Intelligence reports in 1919 stressed that housing still caused severe discontent. Addison's Housing and Town Planning Act, 1919, obliged local authorities to survey housing need and create homes at rents workers could afford. The government agreed the first substantial subsidy to local authority house building. As a result, by 1922 170,000 council homes were built. Further legislation in 1919 subsidized private house building and 30,000 more homes resulted. Rents, private and public, remained controlled. But council house subsidies were never sufficient to fund rents affordable by those in greatest housing need, whose problems of overcrowded, insanitary housing remained acute. They were rented mainly by skilled workers, clerks, teachers and other lower-paid white-collar workers, who wanted better housing but were not the neediest.

The government rejected proposals by Beveridge, who advised on employment matters during the war, for planned, staggered demobilization of service people to minimize problems; it feared resistance among servicemen.[36] The government's lack of an alternative strategy when the war ended unexpectedly led to confusion, mutinies and demonstrations by servicemen anxious to return home. Long-serving men were then released first. As Beveridge had recommended, a non-contributory 'Out-of-Work Donation' was hastily introduced for ex-servicemen and civilians whose war-related work terminated. It was more generous than other benefits, with allowances for wives and children, to prevent servicemen returning home to destitution.

Education reform proceeded more smoothly, guided by HAL Fisher, Vice-Chancellor of the University of Sheffield, and Liberal President of the Board of Education. The Education Act, 1918, raised the school-leaving age to fourteen, introduced compulsory part-time continuation schools for young people in employment aged 14–18, abolished elementary school fees and encouraged local authorities to establish day nurseries and schools for disabled children. Elementary schools were obliged to provide more advanced courses for older, more able children, beyond the basic current curricula. The earnings of elementary schoolteachers doubled, and their pensions trebled. Later, a limited number of state scholarships to university were introduced for able, poorer, students. Fisher aimed to improve opportunities for working-class children, who indeed benefitted from more and better education, though fewer than he hoped.[37] The government wanted more education and training to increase economic growth.

New groups needing support after the war were disabled servicemen, their families and those of the war dead. After providing allowances and pensions during the war, administered by a new Ministry of Pensions from 1917, the state could not abandon them in peacetime, especially when discharged, disabled servicemen protested about inadequate allowances and work training. They formed associations, including the National Federation of Discharged and Demobilized Sailors and Soldiers, one of the organizations that in 1921 formed the British Legion, which became their main campaigning and support institution. About 1.2m men – one-quarter of all who had served in UK forces – qualified for disability pensions. The amount was determined by the degree of disability, and the serviceman's rank and was subject to regular medical inspection and review. Two-thirds of disabilities were rated as minor, including loss of fingers or toes. About 40,000 were pensioned due to total or near-total disability, including total paralysis, loss of two limbs or severe psychological disorder. Psychological conditions risked being taken less seriously because they were less understood than visible physical trauma, though the emerging specialisms of psychology and psychiatry developed from serving servicemen's needs. Similarly, the need to treat physical injuries created new skills. Cosmetic surgery developed for the severe facial disfigurement that was all too common; orthopaedic surgery was transformed by the multitude of bone injuries, and prosthetic limbs massively improved, becoming lighter, more flexible and cheaper. But servicemen who contracted TB or malaria on active service suffered lasting ill-effects which were not always recognized as war disabilities or compensated. The British Legion from its foundation worked to help them and aroused public and government awareness of neglected victims of the war.[38]

Conclusion

The Board of Trade concluded in 1918 that there had been 'an almost unbelievable expenditure of effort on the war without this entailing any large amount of suffering to the civilian population'.[39] Privileged people commented on the improved behaviour of the masses. Apart from a distressing tendency to strike, they appeared more regular in their habits, less prone to drunkenness and fighting. The destitute 'residuum' seemed almost to have disappeared. This was widely attributed to restrictions on the sale of alcohol during the war. More plausibly it was due to full employment, long hours of hard work and higher living standards for many, though not all, working people. The 'Great' War certainly led to a significant expansion of state welfare funded by redistributive taxation and some reduction in poverty and socio-economic inequality.

CHAPTER 4
THE 1920s

Introduction

At the end of the war some believed Britain would best recover and repay its substantial war debt by continuing the successful wartime state controls over key sectors of the economy to secure investment and employment, and the improved health, welfare and education services to maximize the security, skills and efficiency of the workforce. Others were committed to a private enterprise economy unconstrained by state controls, with low taxation. These deep divisions persisted through the twentieth century, with shifts in the relative influence of each dimension. State welfare continued, unevenly, to expand.

So did voluntary action. In 1919 the National Council of Social Services (NCSS) was established 'to co-operate with Government Departments and Local Authorities making use of voluntary effort' and coordinate and encourage voluntary action. It is now the National Council of Voluntary Organizations (NCVO), with the same objectives. Between the wars and later it channelled statutory funding to voluntary bodies, cutting costs for the state, published policy documents and held conferences to inform discussion and legislation on welfare issues, always urging greater state action.[1] Established voluntary organizations continued to be highly, indeed increasingly, active, including the NCUMC, as unmarried mothers were still harshly treated.[2] Volunteers were especially active in the growing number of regions of high unemployment where they were much needed. Toynbee Hall and the many other settlement houses which had developed around the country since the late nineteenth century provided a growing range of support for deprived people, including women's healthcare, free legal advice and help for young people to gain education, training and work.[3]

1918–20

The economy remained buoyant from 1918 to 1920. Unemployment rose but by much less than expected. This sustained the unions' bargaining power and, with the wartime constraints gone, there were many strikes.[4] Even police went on strike though they were forbidden to unionize; their pay had not kept up with wartime inflation and they resented controls on their working conditions. They had popular support and achieved most of their demands. Other workers sought to maintain their wartime gains as prices rose a further 20 per cent by 1920, also to preserve the wartime reduction in the average working week from 56 to 48 hours. The eight-hour day became a standard demand, generally successful, though resisted by some employers because it raised costs.[5] Worker militancy reinforced fears of 'Bolshevism', though it had little substance. The Communist Party of Great Britain was founded in 1920, but it remained small, of little influence.

Trade unionists believed they and their industries had benefitted from state controls, including of profits, and supported their retention. Lloyd George and fellow coalition Liberals wished to preserve the controls at least long enough to stabilize and hopefully expand the post-war economy, maintain full employment and keep industrial peace, bolstered by social reform. Rationing survived to late 1920 when world food prices were falling. Some Conservatives, in the party's paternalist tradition, sympathized. Others pressed for tax cuts and tariffs to protect industry from international competition.

Depression

In mid-1920 the post-war bubble burst and an international crisis erupted. Britain's manufacturing output fell by 10 per cent in just over a year, especially in its major exporting industries which faced increased international competition as other economies revived. In 1921 1.8m insured workers were unemployed, causing demonstrations in London and elsewhere; the number would not fall below one million until the next world war, in 1940. Out-of-Work Donation was wound up in 1921, having cost £62m, far beyond the initial £38m estimate. It was replaced by a near-universal unemployment insurance scheme which was expected to be cheaper in the long run. It was more generous than the pre-war system because the government could not risk unrest by reverting to something substantially less generous than the Out-of-Work Donation, though it was lower and less expensive. It covered almost twelve million workers earning below £150 pa, paying unemployed men 15s pw, women 12s, for up to fifteen weeks each year, plus allowances for wives and children. After fifteen weeks' unemployment, workers could claim a lower, locally administered, means-tested 'extended benefit'. The scheme excluded agricultural and domestic workers and many lower-paid, irregularly employed workers, whose only resort in unemployment remained the Poor Law. All too often they were forced into workhouses.

Districts where pay was lowest and poverty greatest had the smallest rate incomes and could least meet local needs. A Labour-controlled borough council in Poplar, East London, held a much-publicized revolt, led by George Lansbury, local Labour councillor, Poor Law Guardian, future leader of the Labour Party and editor of the left-wing *Daily Herald* newspaper. The paper ran a 'Go to the Guardians' campaign, encouraging unemployed workers to march to workhouses and demand relief, knowing there would not be space to accommodate them, exposing inadequate support for the involuntarily unemployed. In 1921 Poplar councillors refused to pay their annual contribution to the LCC budget, arguing that richer should subsidize poorer districts. They were imprisoned, causing further demonstrations and a national crisis as unemployment continued to rise. The Ministry of Health then introduced a slightly more generous poor relief scale and a 'rate equalization' system for London only, whereby richer subsidized poorer boroughs. Protest continued, including in Poplar, against the stringent allowances, and in poor districts elsewhere in Britain the funding problem persisted.[6] To boost employment, in December 1920 an Unemployment Grants Committee was established, with a £3m annual budget to subsidize local authority public works projects; by 1922 this produced £26m worth of schemes. In October 1921, £10m was announced for export credits and cheap loans for job-creation schemes, but such measures only helped a minority of the unemployed.[7]

The crisis fuelled demands for cuts to public spending, promoted by a furious 'anti-waste' campaign mounted by the *Times* and the popular *Daily Mirror* and *Daily Mail*. They pilloried 'squandermania', sponsoring an 'Anti-Waste League'. Their influence demonstrated the growing significance of the popular press in politics and society as the habit of daily newspaper reading grew. It became increasingly influential through the century.[8] Two 'anti-waste' candidates won by-elections in June 1921, taking coalition Conservative seats. The chancellor, Conservative Austen Chamberlain, son of Joseph, cut the basic rate of income tax from 6s to 4s in £. The Treasury called for 20 per cent cuts in all spending departments. The housing budget was slashed and Addison resigned. Lloyd George reluctantly submitted to 'anti-waste' pressures and appointed a committee of businessmen to propose economies. It was chaired by Sir Eric Geddes, Conservative minister for transport, and worked closely with the Treasury before reporting in 1922. It was labelled the 'Geddes axe' for the savagery of the cuts that resulted. They hit hardest the recent reforms of housing and education, but not unemployment benefit for fear of the consequences. The housing subsidy was withdrawn, saving £2m pa, but sacrificing jobs in the building industry. Education was targeted for cuts of £16.5m, potentially sacking 43,000 teachers. Fisher's resistance, supported by teachers, reduced cuts to £5.7m, but grants for free places in secondary schools and the new university scholarships were abolished, disadvantaging poorer young people.

Lloyd George was weakened, and the Conservatives dominated economic and social policy. He was weakened further by revelations that he had raised political funds by selling peerages and other honours. This was not unusual among politicians, but it encouraged the Conservatives to withdraw from the coalition and call an election in 1922, which they won. The Labour vote substantially increased, helped by the cuts, fuelling fears of advancing socialism. It also greatly increased its votes and power in local authorities including for improving local services. Women now had the same voting rights at local as at national level. Women councillors in England increased from 263 to 650, 1918–23, women Poor Law Guardians from 1,546 to 2,039.[9] Women continued to campaign effectively for improved local social services.

They also organized nationally to campaign for equal voting rights with men, which they achieved in 1928 at local and national levels, for other gender equalities including equal pay (less successfully), and for social and economic reforms. In 1918 NUWSS was renamed the National Union of Societies for Equal Citizenship (NUSEC). Still led by Millicent Fawcett, it was dedicated to helping women to use the vote, having campaigned so hard to gain it. It aimed to inform them about political issues and procedures while campaigning with other organizations for reforms. Eleanor Rathbone formed the Women's Citizens Association (WCA) in 1913 with similar aims, and the organizations worked closely together. These and other organizations campaigned to improve women's work conditions, including for equal pay and against the 'marriage bar', which excluded married women from a growing number of jobs including teaching. Also, more successfully, to improve the poorest housing, education, women's healthcare and childcare, for access for women to previously closed professions including the law, and for gender equality in divorce and child custody rights among other equality issues.[10]

Conservative government, 1922–4

The Conservative government of 1922–4 had no clear strategy and achieved little in a divided party. The only significant exception was the Housing Act, 1923, initiated by the minister of health, Neville Chamberlain, another son of Joseph, who inherited his father's commitment to social reform. He reversed some of the cuts many of his colleagues had supported. Following protest at the continuing housing crisis he introduced a subsidy of £6 per year for twenty years for each house built by local authorities or private enterprise, if they met certain standards, though these were below those established in 1919. According to Conservative principles, private enterprise was favoured, and council housing subsidized only when the minister judged that private enterprise could not meet local needs. The act also, for the first time, allowed local authorities to advance loans to potential owner-occupiers unable to afford a deposit. Owner-occupation was rare before 1918, perhaps no more than 10 per cent of all homes in UK.[11] It grew to 32 per cent in 1938, encouraged by the Conservatives.[12] The leader of Conservatives on Leeds city council told his Labour opponents in 1926, 'It's a good thing for people to buy their houses. They turn Tory directly. We shall go on making Tories and you will be wiped out,'[13] a widespread, long-lived belief in his party. Home ownership became a normal aspiration for the growing middle class and increasingly for skilled manual workers. It was assisted by low interest rates, the growth of profit-making building societies and financial institutions supplying mortgages, subsidized by tax reliefs introduced by Conservative-led governments.

Such measures did not resolve the economic crisis. Its persistence and their divisions over strategy forced the Conservatives to call another election in December 1923. The Liberals were still divided. Labour, led by Ramsay MacDonald, promised to pay off the war debt through a wealth tax on those who had profited from the war. The Conservatives again won most seats, but not enough to outnumber the Liberals plus Labour, which won the second largest number of seats. Labour now attracted more white-collar public sector workers (threatened by Conservative cuts) and middle-class radicals, as the only party expected to introduce progressive reforms, expand the public sector and raise living standards. The Conservatives reluctantly gave way to the first, minority, Labour government.

The first Labour government, 1924

Labour faced a weak economy, rising unemployment, no majority in parliament and no guarantee of support from most Liberals. MacDonald became prime minister. For the first, and probably the last, time the PM's family groceries were delivered to Downing Street in a Co-op van. He was determined to create a 'responsible' image which he believed would benefit Labour in future elections, so dropped the proposed wealth tax, upsetting left-wingers. The tax was opposed by Philip Snowden, the very orthodox chancellor, who believed that economic recovery required tax cuts, and it would probably have been rejected by parliament. MacDonald also discouraged strikes, fearing Labour would be blamed.

But, despite likely parliamentary opposition, Labour promoted progressive social reform. John Wheatley, minister of health, a member of the lively Clydeside left, rescinded the 'Poplar Order' restricting poor relief payments which had accompanied imprisonment of the councillors.[14] He then introduced the most radical Housing Act yet, increasing subsidies for building for rent, mostly by local authorities, while extending Chamberlain's subsidy to private construction. House building greatly increased, creating jobs and more council housing, though the poorest could still rarely afford it.

At the Ministry of Labour, Tom Shaw raised unemployment benefit to 27s for a family of four, and (opposed by the Treasury) abolished the unpopular means test for 'extended benefit'. Unemployed people who exhausted their insurance entitlement were thus mostly removed from poor relief, though not to a notably generous system. Shaw retained and toughened the test introduced in 1921 requiring claimants to prove to a Local Employment Committee that they were 'genuinely seeking whole-time employment but unable to obtain such employment', providing evidence of searching for work. Some left-wingers opposed this, but parliament supported it, along with voters with little sympathy for supposed 'scroungers'. Unemployment remained above one million but was falling.

Labour had long been committed to free education to university level, with maintenance grants for poorer students, strongly supported by R. H. Tawney, Professor of Economic History at LSE and a leading Labour advocate of education as the road to social equality.[15] He believed that the state education system undervalued the intellects of working-class children and joined a Labour-appointed committee chaired by Sir Henry Hadow, vice-chancellor of Sheffield University, to explore reform of secondary education. In 1926 it recommended raising the school-leaving age to fifteen (already Labour policy) and reorganization of secondary schooling. Children would be selected by examination at age eleven to attend one of three types of school, judged appropriate to their abilities: academic, technical or a new type of 'modern' school in which 'the courses of instruction though not merely vocational or utilitarian should be used to connect the school work with interests arising from the social and industrial environment of the pupils'.[16] The committee, influenced by ideas prevailing in the growing discipline of psychology, believed these distinctions were realistic, that the lifetime abilities of children could be identified by examination at age eleven and that the three types of school would be equally esteemed and improve educational opportunities for most children, while Britain gained a more educated workforce and reduced juvenile crime. In 1926 the Conservative government was unwilling to promote this system, but the Board of Education encouraged local authorities to adopt it, using their independent powers in such matters (parliament could recommend but not enforce local education policy), as they did especially while

Labour was back in government, 1929–31. By 1931 the new 'tripartite' system was available to one-third of children, and it became firmly established, as the '11+ system', by the Labour government after 1945. In 1924 Labour was also committed to a free National Health Service for all and appointed a Royal Commission to investigate National Health Insurance, following criticism of its uneven provision of services. This also reported to a less receptive government in 1926, and major reform of healthcare was deferred.

Snowden's April 1924 budget removed £14m in direct and £29m in indirect taxes, mainly on imports, a return to free trade intended to promote industrial efficiency and growth. MacDonald promised disarmament and the naval budget was severely cut. Snowden raised pensions as promised in Labour's election manifesto. Following demands for improved support for retired people and civilian widows and orphans, the Conservatives had appointed a committee which in 1924 recommended raising the means limit for old age pensions, which Snowden adopted. About 70 per cent of over-70s now qualified for the pension, suggesting the extent of poverty among older people since the means limit remained stringent. Snowden hoped improved pensions would stop older workers competing for the shrinking pool of jobs, though the committee found that unemployed people over age sixty had much less chance of re-employment than younger workers, an example of deeply embedded discrimination against older people.[17] It also recommended contributory pensions for insured workers aged 65–70 and the wives of insured men, and widows' and orphans' pensions for their families, creating parity with war widows and removing another group from poor relief. Snowden approved the recommendations, but the government fell before he could act.[18]

Labour introduced a minimum wage for miners and backed a private members' bill to nationalize the coal industry, but it also fell with the government, along with other proposals. Labour faced mounting Conservative and Liberal attacks for its supposed Bolshevism, supported by the right-wing press, in particular the *Daily Mail*. This culminated in the Commons passing a censure motion which led to MacDonald's resignation and an election campaign dominated by assertions – promoted by the *Mail* – about Labour's (invented) secret collusion with Moscow to foment revolution in Britain. The Conservatives won. Labour increased its vote, on a higher turnout, but won fewer seats, piling up votes in mainly working-class constituencies as it was prone to do. But, given the disadvantages it faced, Labour's first government achieved significant social and economic reforms and established its capacity to govern.

Conservatism, 1924–9

Again, the Conservative government, led by Stanley Baldwin, lacked a clear strategy, leaving individual ministers much leeway. The chancellor was Winston Churchill, who returned to the party after twenty years as a Liberal and immediately started to prepare his first budget, delivered in April 1925. He reluctantly returned to the gold standard, which Britin had left in 1919, under pressure from the Treasury, the Bank of England and the City of London financiers anxious to restore confidence in sterling and London's pre-war position as the world's leading financial centre, now overtaken by the United States. The influential Liberal economist and wartime Treasury adviser John Maynard Keynes strongly opposed it, believing it would raise the prices of Britain's already weak exports and increase unemployment, as it did. Churchill also reduced income tax by 6d in £. But he felt the need to appeal to the newly democratic electorate 'by doing something for the working class', as he put it to Neville Chamberlain (minister of health again) when seeking permission to appropriate his plan to adopt Snowden's proposed pensions reform. Churchill proposed in the budget a scheme which Chamberlain later in 1925 introduced as legislation, providing pensions at age sixty-five (still at 10s pw too small to live on) for NHI contributors and their wives, who also qualified for 10s widows' pensions, while orphans received 5s pw. Other older people still qualified for a strictly means-tested pension at age seventy. The numbers receiving poor relief to supplement the pension to enable them to survive rose from 8,600 in 1920 to 69,900 in 1928.[19]

Many employers responded to the rise in export prices and falling overseas demand by reducing wages or imposing longer hours. In response miners threatened to strike. To prevent this, Baldwin announced a Royal Commission on the coal industry, chaired by the Liberal Sir Herbert Samuel, and a nine-month subsidy to the industry until it reported. It proposed amalgamation of pits into larger combines, nationalization of mining royalties and abolition of the recently introduced minimum wage for miners, alienating both sides. When the subsidy ended in April 1926, the employers proposed wage cuts. Baldwin attempted mediation, but the miners called a strike, expecting widespread sympathy action. The TUC tried unsuccessfully to mediate and, reluctantly, called an unprecedented general strike in support of the miners from 3 May 1926. They did not aim to overthrow the state as their more apocalyptic opponents believed, but to improve pay. The response was impressive though incomplete. The TUC ruled out disrupting domestic electricity supplies but ordered building workers to strike, except those building essential homes and hospitals, and forbade interference with health and sanitary services or food distribution. It was as anxious as the government to avoid conflict and alienating voters.

The government was prepared for a confrontation long anticipated against workers who, as is often the case, were more reluctant strikers than right-wing stereotypes portrayed, not least because they lost pay despite help from their unions.[20] The government organized volunteers for essential tasks including driving trains and stoking power stations; some desperate unemployed workers replaced strikers. Success in maintaining services was patchy, but it became clear that the government could withstand a long strike, whereas strike pay crippled the unions despite help from street collections.[21] The miners rejected attempted government mediation and, on 12 May, with no settlement in sight, the TUC terminated the strike. The miners struggled on for a further six months to ultimate defeat.

The government introduced the Trade Disputes Act, 1927, which outlawed general strikes. This did not arouse massive opposition in the labour movement since the tactic was unpopular and had failed. Baldwin avoided too punitive a response for fear of further conflict and to preserve his 'one nation' image. He resisted the more extreme curbs on unions proposed on the back benches, including compulsory strike ballots. However, the act obliged individual union members to opt into paying subscriptions to the Labour Party, rather than the established practice of contracting out if they chose, as about one quarter of members did. Baldwin was happy to antagonize Labour, though it had sought to remain neutral in the strike. Labour's income fell by 18 per cent, less than expected or hoped by some, because the act strengthened Labour support and stimulated members to ensure that that maximum numbers of unionists opted into membership.

The General Strike delivered a warning to employers, who had also lost income as a result. There were some reprisals, but no big counterattack and fewer wage cuts. A revival of the world economy helped: commodity, including food, prices fell internationally, reducing the cost of living and discontent among workers, but exports remained lower than before the war and unemployment remained above one million. The government made further spending cuts. It was still reluctant to risk cutting unemployment benefit, despite the cost, but in 1925, harried by a press campaign against 'dole scroungers', appointed an investigation, chaired by a former judge, Lord Blanesborough, which reported in 1927. The Ministry of Health had reminded Guardians in 1921, during the Poplar crisis, that, even amid mass unemployment, poor relief 'should of necessity be calculated on a lower scale than the earnings of the independent labourer who is maintaining himself by his labour' to incentivize the search for work; nor should they pay cash relief long-term.[22] But, as involuntary unemployment grew, more Guardians, especially those in districts controlled by Labour, were reluctant to deposit the unemployed in workhouses. They became mainly depositories for the sick, mentally and physically disabled and aged poor.[23] But areas with the greatest poverty could least afford cash relief, and some Guardians relieved unemployed claimants only in kind – mainly food – in return for unpaid work.

Strikes presented further problems. A Court of Appeal judgement of 1900 (the *Merthyr Tydfil* judgement) established that poor relief could not be paid to anyone refusing available work, as strikers did, until destitution reduced them to a condition no longer definable as 'able-bodied'. Their families could be supported. Local Poor Law practice, as ever, varied. The Ministry of Health greeted the General Strike by lowering relief scales and reminding Guardians to obey the strict letter of the law. The miners' unions had minimal strike funds. Paupers in England and Wales doubled from 1.2 million to 2.4 million during the strike. In most mining districts more than 50 per cent of families were on relief. Strikers and unemployed people were encouraged by strike committees and political organizations to press Guardians to raise payments to those qualifying for relief. Guardians in areas of high unemployment treated strikers more generously than elsewhere, if they could afford it, but in prosperous parts of the Midlands, miners were almost literally starved back to work. Some Guardians went too far even for the ministry. When Lichfield union (Staffordshire) threatened to withdraw all relief to miners' dependents because 'the miners had work to go to and it was the guardians' duty to see that they went back', they were reminded of their legal duty to relieve destitution, whatever the cause. The ministry also tried to restrain the more generous boards. Under the Board of Guardians (Default) Act of July 1926 it could suspend and replace with an appointed board any Guardians persistently raising loans to make higher payments. The Boards of West Ham in East London and Chester-le-Street, a mining area in Derbyshire, were suspended and others followed. Challenges to official policy grew with the number of Labour-controlled boards through the 1920s.

Chamberlain responded by at last reforming the Poor Law. The Local Government Act, 1929, abolished Boards of Guardians and their Scottish equivalents, parochial boards, transferring their powers to county and borough councils in England and Wales, burghs in Scotland, integrating the administration and funding of what was now called 'Public Assistance' with other local responsibilities under Public Assistance Committees (PACs), often using the same officials and buildings as under the Poor Law. Local authorities in areas of greatest need were assisted by carefully regulated government grants. Labour guardians, especially, opposed the reform, believing, rightly, that it was designed to tighten central control over poor relief, reducing scope for democratic action, to the disadvantage of many unemployed people and, especially, strikers and their families.[24]

When the Blanesborough committee reported in 1927, unemployment and the costs of relief had risen further, despite tighter administration of the 'genuinely seeking work' test which trebled the claims rejected, mainly by taking less account of whether there was, realistically, work available to seek. Unemployed married women found it harder to obtain benefits if their husbands were, or in theory could be, working. The committee found no significant evidence of 'scrounging' and optimistically assumed unemployment would soon decline. It recommended, following recovery, return to a fixed ratio between contributions and benefits and retention of the means and 'genuinely seeking work' tests, which were embodied in the Unemployment Insurance Act, 1927. Since unemployment did not decline, indeed worsened from 1929, extended benefit, now renamed 'transitional benefit', continued for a further seven years, while stringent administration of the work test threw many people onto Public Assistance.[25]

Another group often dependent on what became Public Assistance were unmarried mothers. They remained marginalized and stigmatized and found it difficult to bring up their children alone. Landladies/lords refused to rent them homes, and it was hard to find work and childcare. An unknown number lived with their parents who provided childcare; some were supported by the child's father. Mothers could seek affiliation orders through the courts, gaining a weekly payment from the father. From 1918 this was only 10s pw, though it was raised to £1 by the Bastardy Act, 1923, for which NCUMC and other women campaigned. Others felt forced to have the child adopted or resorted to poor relief/public assistance, which was generally minimal. Often, they were forced into the workhouse and separated from their child, though after 1929 the progressive LCC paid for expectant and new mothers 'of previous good character' to stay in approved voluntary homes. Some other authorities followed, urged by the NCUMC. It worked hard to help mothers and children stay together, helping them find hostels with childcare, a rented home, and work, often live in domestic service accompanied by their child, though this might expose them to exploitation. NCUMC handled 600–800 new cases a year through the 1920s.[26]

Chamberlain did little to improve health or housing services, despite concern that poverty due to unemployment increased ill-health at a time when medical knowledge and the capacity of medicine to cure underwent unprecedented improvement. The Royal Commission on National Health Insurance established by Labour produced two conflicting reports in 1926. Both recommended it should provide sickness benefits for dependents of insured workers, medical care in childbirth and dental and optical treatment. Both criticized the lack of coordination among health services and unequal provision of services by different approved societies. The minority report recommended abolition of approved societies, and transfer of their functions to local authorities. The majority opted for pooling and redistributing the societies' funds to equalize services between those with mainly older and/or lower-paid members and limited funds, and societies with younger, healthier, fully employed members and higher incomes, which provided more services including dental and optical care. The government was more concerned with cutting public spending than reform; its only response was substantially reduced state national insurance contributions, which deepened the inequalities.[27] Wheatley's generous housing subsidies were also cut. Conservatives who opposed state action criticized Chamberlain's Poor Law reforms, attacking Baldwin as a 'semi-socialist' for tolerating them and demanding fiercer cuts.

The next general election was due in 1929. The big issue was the economy. The Liberals, led by Lloyd George, had the clearest policies. Briefed by Keynes, their manifesto, *We Can Conquer Unemployment*, proposed, without hope of implementation, a loan-financed £250m (6 per cent of GDP) public works programme employing 600,000 people per year. Labour had no clear alternative. Nor did Baldwin, whose government's record was not an asset. The 1924–9 government exposed very clearly the severe divisions in British society: between militant workers and employers; campaigners for gender equality and opponents; employed and unemployed; rich and poor; supporters and opponents of state welfare. Strikers, suffragists and unemployed workers periodically erupted onto the streets, but they did not cause violent confrontation or a serious threat to social or political stability, especially compared with events elsewhere in Europe. Baldwin's government, like its immediate predecessors, avoided serious conflict by providing unemployment benefits adequate – just – for survival and somewhat expanding other areas of social welfare despite the depression. Despite the cuts, total UK public spending on social services rose from £365m in 1924 (35.5 per cent of total spending) to £438m (39.6 per cent) in 1929.[28] Baldwin also defused growing militancy by women suffragists and hoped to win their votes by granting the equal franchise in 1928, which parliament accepted. Successive British governments since the nineteenth century had avoided severe conflict by timely compromise. The tradition was upheld by all political parties through the interwar years.

Inequalities

In the 1920s regional divisions in the UK grew. The troubled export industries, central to Britain's nineteenth-century industrial expansion, were geographically concentrated, mainly on Clydeside (shipbuilding and engineering), Tyneside and North-East England (shipbuilding, mining), Lancashire (cotton textiles and engineering) and the coalfields of South Wales. In these areas there was little alternative employment and they suffered disproportionately from poverty, ill-health and high infant mortality. Meanwhile, the economy diversified, developing new industries supplying electricity, motor vehicles, cycles, chemicals, aircraft, consumer, including electrical, goods, and cigarettes, products generally depending on home rather than export demand. These industries were concentrated in the Midlands and South – motor manufacture in Coventry and Oxford, electrical goods in West London, Bristol and the South-West – where prosperity grew. Unemployed workers in the depressed regions could not easily move to the new industries, though their children might. Employers could find labour closer at hand, were reluctant to employ potential militants from highly unionized industries and preferred younger to older men, and, especially in new light industries, lower-paid women.

Through the 1920s the share of total income of the top 1 per cent fell from 20 to *c.* 18 per cent and the share of total wealth of the top 1 per cent of wealth-holders from 40 per cent to *c.* 38 per cent, both due to higher taxes.[29] Landed wealth was depleted by death duties following the wartime deaths of heirs, but the wealth of the richest 5 per cent declined only slightly. Its composition shifted as wealth from land declined and commerce, manufacturing, brewing prospered, assisted by an expanding advertising industry. Signifying shifts in popular consumption, two of the largest fortunes were left at death by the first Earl of Iveagh, of the Guinness brewing family, who left £13.5m in 1927 and Bernhard Barron, inventor of the cigarette slot machine and founder of Carreras cigarettes (from a humble background and a major benefactor to the Labour Party) who left £4m in 1930.[30]

Incomes from work, of course, differed between occupational groups and between men and women: See Table 2.

Schools still perpetuated and reinforced class and gender divisions. The most elite, male public schools – Eton, Harrow, Westminster, Winchester – trained and built networks among upper-class men, further reinforced by Oxford and Cambridge Universities, while many of their sisters were still educated at home, though more women demanded education equal with men and attended single-sex independent schools.

The middle class grew in size and diversity with the expansion of central and local government, banking and insurance, publishing, the professions, including architecture and surveying, accountancy, engineering, science and technology, and new areas of business. Professional, managerial and clerical workers increased from 2.4 to 3.4m, 1911–31.[31] Upward mobility from working-class backgrounds became a more realistic aspiration as educational opportunities grew and 'white collar' work expanded. It differed from skilled manual work not only in pay but also in security of employment, often with pensions, less physically demanding work, wearing a suit and tie or the female equivalent, though the 'marriage bar' generally required women to leave on marriage, with a 'marriage gratuity' replacing a pension. Gender inequality in pay and promotion was still taken for granted, with a few exceptions in

Table 2 Average Net Earnings by Occupational Class (£ pa)

Average Net Earnings, by Occupational Class (£ pa)	1922–4	1935–6
• Professional		
A. Higher	582	634
B. Lower	320	308
2. Managers etc.	480	440
3. Clerks	182	192
4. Foremen	268	273
5. Skilled manual	180	195
6. Semi-skilled	126	134
7. Unskilled	128	129
Women		
Professional		
Higher	–	–
Lower	**214**	211
Managers, etc.	160	168
Clerks	106	99
Forewoman	154	156
Skilled manual	87	86
Semi-skilled	98	100
Unskilled	73	73

Source: Guy Routh. Occupation and Pay in Great Britain, 1906–79. (Macmillan 1980) pp 120–1

new organizations striving to be 'modern', including the BBC (founded in 1922), John Lewis stores and the London School of Economics under Beveridge's Directorship from 1919 to 1937.[32]

The spatial and cultural class divide was highly visible between the overcrowded inner cities and the growing suburbs of owner-occupied semi-detached houses, with three or more bedrooms and gardens. The size – smaller than older middle-class housing – was determined by falling family size, as the birth rate continued to decline, and fewer live-in servants, often replaced by 'dailies'. The suburbs grew alongside, and were regarded as socially superior to, council estates, though, due to relatively high rents, council tenants continued to be mostly lower middle class or better-paid skilled workers. Council houses were generally smaller, more often terraced, but with gardens, bathrooms, indoor toilets, a huge improvement on previous lower-income housing. The new suburbs and estates divided their residents from the inner cities and contact with the poorer working-class, often from their own families, though many workers commuted to work in city centres on improving public transport, another expense which confined the lower-paid to city centres.

Poverty

Severe poverty continued. Poverty surveys increased as the social sciences expanded in universities. They revealed less desperate destitution than before the war, but still serious problems. In 1924, Bowley and Hogg repeated their five towns' study of 1913, asking, *Has Poverty Diminished?* They adopted the same stringent poverty measure, with adjustments for changing expectations and standards (the diet now included 2lbs of meat per week). They calculated that the minimum weekly wage required by a family of five was 37s 6d and found 6.5 per cent of working-class people on lower incomes in the five towns. They found especially alarming levels of child poverty, mainly caused by low pay or the absence, death or disability of a male earner. They concluded that the lowest wages had risen, leaving only large families and those without a regular male income vulnerable to severe poverty.

The Social Survey of Merseyside, conducted in 1929–30 by researchers at Liverpool University, used a similar, but more stringent, poverty measure. It found 16 per cent in poverty, only 2 per cent of whom received Public Assistance. Inadequate earnings at work were the main cause, though unemployment was increasingly significant. 10.9 per cent of the people of Merseyside lived below the Registrar General's overcrowding standard of more than two persons per room. In inner Liverpool only 7.6 per cent of families had access to a garden, 9.8 per cent to a fixed bath, one-third only shared access.[33]

In 1929–31, H. Llewellyn Smith, retired Ministry of Labour civil servant and former researcher on Booth's London survey, headed a team at the LSE, advised by Bowley and using a similar poverty measure, to repeat Booth's survey in selected areas. They concluded that 14 per cent of the population of East London were 'subject to conditions of privation which, if long continued, would deny them all but the barest necessities and cut them off from access to many of the incidental and cultural benefits of modern progress'. In the whole LCC area, 9.6 per cent were in poverty (in contentious Poplar 24 per cent) compared with 30 per cent in the 1890s; 16 per cent of children in East London. Inadequate wages caused 38.5 per cent of London poverty, lack of a male earner 37 per cent, old age 16.5 per cent.[34]

Much changed in the 1920s with the gradual expansion of state welfare and reduction in poverty, but major inequalities continued.

CHAPTER 5
THE 1930s

The Great Crash, 1929–31

The next decade opened amid a major financial crisis. It was the Labour Party's misfortune to enter government just before it erupted. Labour's re-election in 1929, when a general election was unavoidable, was a sign of gradual change in this class-divided society. It won most seats but again not an overall majority. Opponents of Labour and of the recent equalization of the franchise, most vehemently the *Daily Mail*, blamed the new, younger women voters for Labour's success, how accurately is unknown. Many middle-class voters had suffered the effects of the return to gold and tight monetary policies. MacDonald returned as premier, still unwilling to alienate the Liberals on whom Labour depended in parliament, or voters, with extreme policies. Lloyd George agreed to support a moderate Labour government but warned that 'the very hour the Ministry becomes a Socialist administration its career ends'.[1] But the Liberal MPs were still divided, many reluctant to co-operate and vote with Labour.

In October 1929 the New York Stock Exchange crashed and world trade collapsed, mainly due to speculative mania on Wall Street following long-term depression in the United States. In 1930 UK unemployment rose to 2.5 million.[2] To make things worse, the Conservatives bequeathed a deficit of government spending over revenue which grew to £14.5m by spring 1930 as tax revenues fell and the costs of unemployment benefit rose. Labour could not resolve a world crisis originating elsewhere, which did not stop Conservatives from blaming them for it. Labour aimed to manage it by creating work, protecting the living standards of the unemployed and raising taxes on higher incomes. During 1929–31, it funded public works costing £100m, creating about 300,000 jobs contributing, as Keynes advocated, to modernization of infrastructure, including roads and bridges. Benefits for dependents of the unemployed increased, and the 'genuinely seeking work' clause was abolished; unemployment benefit could now be refused only if a claimant rejected suitable work. Income tax, surtax and estate duty rose.

Labour attempted other social improvements. By 1929 the more manageable end of the housing problem, affecting many skilled and white-collar workers, had largely been solved. The glaring remaining problem was overcrowded, often insanitary, bug-ridden, privately rented 'slums' as they were known. Labour shifted from house building to 'slum clearance', demolishing the worst housing and releasing land for building low-cost homes near city centre workplaces. The Housing Act, 1930, subsidized local authorities according to the number of families re-housed from clearances. They were instructed to survey their housing stock and produce five-year plans for clearance and replacement. The greatest housing need began to be tackled, slowly in the economic circumstances.

In 1929 widows' pensions were extended to include all widows of insured men from age fifty-five and women whose husbands had died or were over seventy when the pensions were introduced in 1925. Previously they were restricted to widows with children under fourteen when their husband died; women and men protested that the system discriminated against older women and left them in poverty. Employed unmarried women then protested that the lower pension age for widows discriminated against them. In 1935 they formed the National Spinsters Pensions' Association demanding pensions for unmarried working women at fifty-five because they were often forced to retire at earlier ages than men, sometimes as early as their thirties, due to employers' discrimination against 'ageing' women. And many single women gave up work to care for ageing parents, then were left destitute when they died. The Association was founded by a woman shopkeeper and had strong support, though not in the professions where women feared it would encourage their dismissal at earlier ages than men.[3] A parliamentary committee established to investigate the issue reported in 1938 recommending pensions at sixty for all women on the grounds that, on average, married women were five years younger than their husbands, and this would enable them to retire together.[4] This was introduced in 1940 but only for insured women and wives of insured men, others had to wait until seventy.

In 1931 Labour responded to demands by Labour women, and many others, to make birth control more easily available. Births still declined in all classes, but concern persisted about the effects on the health especially of poorer women, and on family living standards, of repeated pregnancy and childbirth for women without access to birth control or good healthcare and facing the risk of illegal abortion. Labour cautiously allowed local authority health and welfare clinics in England Wales to give free birth control advice to married women (only) whose health was endangered by pregnancy. It did not risk a parliamentary vote on this contentious issue but issued a Ministry of Health memorandum recommending it to local authorities. Four years later, 224 councils (of 474) provided birth control clinics, sometimes interpreting their role more flexibly than the strict terms of the memorandum.[5]

There was strong resistance in parliament to other reforms. A move in 1931 to raise the school-leaving age to fifteen was crushed in the Lords. Under parliamentary pressure a Royal Commission on Unemployment Insurance was appointed to investigate potential savings, also a committee to investigate further spending cuts, chaired by Sir George May, former chairman of the Prudential Assurance Company. The government became bitterly divided over unemployment benefits, the largest item of public spending. MacDonald, Snowden, again a cautious chancellor, and Margaret Bondfield, minister of labour, the first woman Cabinet minister, proposed 15 per cent cuts. A Cabinet majority opposed this unless it was matched by equivalent sacrifice by the better-off. Opponents included senior party figures, Arthur Henderson and George Lansbury, and a junior minister outside the Cabinet, the wealthy former Conservative MP-turned-Independent-then Labour, Oswald Mosley. Mosley proposed a large scheme of loan-financed public works, fewer planning controls, raising the school-leaving age and lowering the pension age to reduce competition for work, and tariffs with special arrangements for imperial trade. This was rejected by the leadership, and Mosley resigned to campaign for his programme within the party. He won support from Keynes, among others, and at the party conference in October 1930 came close to winning the vote, but his package was unlikely to get through parliament. And Mosley's domineering personality aroused suspicion. So, even more, did the New Party he then launched, initially to promote his economic ideas, then adopting racist, fascist-style nationalism like that growing in continental Europe.

The Agricultural Marketing Act, 1931 – the work of Christopher Addison, now a Labour MP and minister for agriculture – controlled agricultural and food prices.[6] In June 1931 the first report of the Commission on Unemployment Insurance concluded that there were more jobseekers than jobs but recommended an 11.5 per cent cut in benefits. This was again rejected by the Cabinet. The international crisis deepened. Banks collapsed in Austria and Germany, withdrew their funds from London and the Bank of England's gold reserves shrank. In July the May Committee increased panic with a dramatic report, blaming the financial crisis on the profligacy it claimed was inherent in democracy because it encouraged public spending. It recommended cuts of £96.5m pa, £66m from unemployment benefits alone, through cuts to payments, higher contributions and more means-testing, but no sacrifices by higher earners. Keynes described the report as 'a most gross perversion of social justice'.[7] The Cabinet would only accept higher contributions from workers if taxes also rose. It was one more episode in the ongoing battle between proponents and opponents of state social and economic intervention, always acute at times of economic crisis. As Keynes suggested, it was not obvious that severe cuts to public spending would assist, rather than retard, recovery.

Government finances could now escape bankruptcy only with a large loan, for which bankers required all-party approval since the financial markets lacked confidence in a Labour government. The Conservative and Liberal leaderships refused. On 21 August 1931 the governor of the Bank of England informed MacDonald that gold was draining away, and national bankruptcy was imminent. Nine of twenty Cabinet members still refused cuts, threatening resignation. A meeting of party leaders proposed a cross-party National Government, suggested by King George V, a passionate anti-socialist with no desire to keep Labour in office. MacDonald believed his remaining as premier was essential to maintain confidence at home and abroad. An all-party Cabinet was formed. MacDonald took only a handful of followers into the National Government. The belief that he and Snowden had betrayed the party and the neediest in society in surrender to financial interests was deep, bitter and long-lasting. Arthur Henderson became Labour leader. The National Executive Committee expelled all supporters of the National Government from the party.

A national government

The coalition was an exceptional response to an exceptional situation and exceptional measures followed. Snowden, who remained chancellor, delivered an emergency budget, enacting the 10 per cent cuts to unemployment benefit the Labour Cabinet had rejected, while contributions were raised, the benefit period reduced and a means test introduced for 'transitional' payments to unemployed people who had exhausted their insurance allowance. He balanced these reduced incomes of unemployed people by cutting public sector salaries, including ministers', raising income tax from 4s.6d to 5s in £, raising surtax and reducing exemptions and children's allowances. An Anomalies Act, 1931, withdrew recognition as 'unemployed' from married women who were not personally insured or whose entitlement to insurance payments had expired. It was argued that their husbands should support them and there were always vacancies for domestic servants- suitable work for women whatever their skills or former employment. This caused especial hardship and resentment in Lancashire textile districts, hard hit by unemployment among women whose families depended on their incomes. These measures passed easily through parliament but caused a mutiny of seamen at the Invergordon naval base in Scotland when they faced wage cuts of up to 25 per cent compared with only 7 per cent for admirals. The government responded by limiting all salary cuts to 10 per cent. The mutiny triggered another run on sterling. The gold standard was abandoned again on 21 September. Within three months the pound fell by almost 30 per cent against the franc and the dollar and foreign exchange flowed back into London.

Baldwin and his colleagues were unenthusiastic about coalition, and, when the Bank was forced to abandon the gold standard, they argued for an election to produce a government with a clear mandate, strengthen confidence and the currency. It was called for October 1931 and was particularly strident and unpleasant, with all major parties divided. The Conservative leadership argued they would deal with the crisis better than Labour, unjustly blaming the ideology and incompetence of the 'socialists' for its longevity – the greatest financial crisis then experienced in modern history. Labour held support in mining areas and among the growing numbers of public sector workers who were apprehensive of further Conservative cuts. Henderson declared that capitalism had broken down and demanded planning of industry, import controls and nationalization of banking and credit, which Snowden, who did not stand in the election, and the Conservatives denounced as 'Bolshevism gone mad'. Henderson lost his seat and was succeeded as party leader by Lansbury. The pro-National Government parties won a massive, Conservative-dominated, majority though it remained, in principle, a coalition. MacDonald remained premier until the next election in 1935, while Snowden was elevated to the Lords. Neville Chamberlain became chancellor.

The British economy survived the crisis better than its closest competitors, the United States, Germany and France. Output and employment fell by less, though exports were hit by the international slowdown. Britain was the world's largest importer of food and raw materials, which fell in price, increasing purchasing power at home. It benefitted from retaining free trade, while other industrial countries reacted to falling import prices by increasing tariffs. Abandonment of the gold standard enabled the exchange rate to fall to a level at which it was attractive to hold sterling again. The relative mildness of the depression in Britain helps to explain why extreme politics, especially fascism, were less attractive than elsewhere in Europe. But immediately after the election the

Conservative-dominated government abandoned free trade, which Conservatives had always opposed. Tariffs were imposed on all imports except basic food and raw materials, except from the colonies, which probably slowed recovery. They protected companies facing competing imports but raised costs of raw materials.[8]

But the economy stabilized and output recovered to its 1929 level by 1934, owing little to conscious government policy. Conservatives were still not prepared to manage the economy, but foreign currency flowed in and interest rates fell, reducing payments on the national debt among other advantages. Unemployment rose until January 1932, when 2.7 million were registered unemployed in Great Britain and the actual total was probably well over 3 million. Then it steadily fell. The 1933 budget reduced income tax to 4s 6d in £. Cautiously, the government guaranteed loans for key enterprises, including railways, shipping and expansion of London transport. Low interest rates enabled new industries to invest cheaply and encouraged house building and purchase, creating jobs. Building firms had expanded due to local authority contracts under the Wheatley Act and were well placed to take advantage of increased demand for private housing, though new private homes were not always of high quality. The later 1930s saw a wave of mortgage strikes by home buyers unwilling to pay for houses with leaking roofs and warped window frames.[9]

House sales increased demand for domestic goods, including new, home-produced inventions: vacuum cleaners, electric irons, modern cookers, radios, helped by the new, flourishing hire purchase method of deferred payment. Prices fell, while wages generally did not, increasing purchasing power and feelings of prosperity. Falling family size also helped reduce costs for younger families. The birth rate reached its lowest recorded level in 1933. The two-child family was increasingly the norm in all classes. Until 1938 the economy recovered. The official unemployment total fell to 2.03 million in March 1935, 1.7 million by 1937 as domestic demand grew, including for a growing range of leisure activities which more people could afford: travel by bus and coach, increasing car ownership, purchase of radios and gramophones, attendance at cinemas, theatres and music halls; dance halls especially attracted younger people. Book prices fell with the introduction of paperbacks; Penguin Books was founded in 1935. Spectator sports, especially football, were popular, while alcohol consumption fell. The holiday industry grew especially in Blackpool, a popular working-class centre for holidays and day trips, further encouraged by Butlin's new low-cost, seaside holiday camps, as more workers gained paid holidays, often following strikes. At least one week's paid holiday per year was recommended for all workers by the Labour-backed Holidays with Pay Act, 1938, though implementation was delayed until after the coming war.

Unemployment

But the decline of older industries continued and unemployed people gained little from new consumer opportunities. Profound regional and local inequalities continued.

In London industrial expansion focused on the West, while East London remained depressed; London never had fewer than 100,000 unemployed through the 1930s, alongside some of the most prosperous areas in Britain. The West Midlands and South of England prospered, while the old industrial centres were even more depressed as world trade contracted. Long-term unemployment grew. In 1929 4.6 per cent of unemployed people had been out of work for a year or more; by 1935 26 per cent, in Northern England, in February 1938 35 per cent.[10] Unemployment was concentrated in coal, shipbuilding, textiles and iron and steel: 71 per cent of the workforce in Crook in the Durham coalfield had been unemployed for five years by 1936.[11]

Unemployment payments were costly, and the National Government tightened them further along with other areas of social spending. It restricted eligibility and reduced the length of time insurance benefit was paid. Contributors who exhausted their eligibility, other than married women, remained entitled to 'Transitional Payments'. Central government covered the costs and local authority Public Assistance Committees decided eligibility. This led to further local variations, some authorities doling out government money relatively generously, others very stringent: in depressed, Labour controlled, Rotherham and Merthyr Tydfil 98 per cent of claimants were paid the full rate, against a national average of 50.8 per cent.[12]

Again, Neville Chamberlain, this time as chancellor, faced protests against cuts. In 1934 he introduced a reformed, rather more generous, insurance system administered by an Unemployment Insurance Statutory Committee, headed by Sir (as he now was) William Beveridge, which provided payments for one year in return for sufficient contributions. A safety net, administered by an Unemployment Assistance Board (UAB), provided for people who exhausted or lacked cover, with minimum payments means-tested with a rigour reminiscent of the Poor Law. For the first time a 'household means-test' was employed, assessing the income and possessions of all members of a household if any member claimed benefit. This caused mass protests in January 1935 in areas of high unemployment. The government, with an election looming, hastily decreed that no one should suffer reduction in payments. But new claimants were treated with harshness which gave the 'dole', as it was known, of the 1930s, a lasting, miserable reputation. The test was rigorously enforced: household possessions were intrusively inspected for items required to be sold before payment would be made, including anything beyond basic necessities, even 'excess' chairs. It was hated for its treatment of people who had worked hard and done their best but could not find work. The more generous authorities – generally in areas of high unemployment – were unwilling to apply the test to all household members, which broke up families as working teenagers left home because their incomes reduced their parents' benefits.

Hunger marches

In June 1935 Baldwin replaced MacDonald, whose health was failing. He had become increasingly isolated heading a 'National' government which was essentially Conservative, with minimal Labour support, indeed fierce opposition from most of the party. He died in 1937. In the election of November 1935, the Conservative vote fell slightly, and its share of seats fell from 472 to 432, but it controlled the new government. Labour, fighting as a united party again, led by Lansbury, gained a higher share of votes than in 1929 but only 154 seats. Lansbury resigned the leadership, and his deputy, Clement Attlee, narrowly and surprisingly defeated the more experienced Herbert Morrison to succeed him. Attlee, son of a solicitor, was Labour's first middle-class leader, educated at a public school, Haileybury, and Oxford. After graduating he reluctantly followed his father into the law, then found his real vocation working in his spare time, then full-time, with a boys' club in Stepney, East London, and he became a voluntary social worker at Toynbee Hall. For the first time he encountered working-class life and socialism and joined the Stepney branch of the ILP. In 1912 he became a lecturer in social work at LSE, then fought in the war. After the war he became the first Labour mayor of Stepney, in 1922 MP for Limehouse, East London. In 1920 he published a book, *The Social Worker*, surveying the activities and value of social workers in the voluntary and public sectors and collaboration between them. He was firmly on the left of the party, as he made clear in his volume for the Left Book Club, *The Labour Party in Perspective* (1937), which firmly supported public ownership. His policies and support for the unemployed won him praise in the party.[13] The still-divided Liberals continued to decline, while Labour gained support. It made effective use of the press, BBC and newsreels to challenge continuing Conservative accusations of 'Bolshevism', stressing its moderate, democratic socialism, committed to socio-economic equality, not to revolution.

Protests continued and higher rates of UAB relief were introduced in 1936, but all unemployment payments remained low because administrators, including Beveridge, insisted upon keeping relief levels below wages as an incentive to work, despite the lack of work and inadequate wages in many occupations. In 1937 average insurance allowances were two-fifths of the median wage: 24.s 6d against 55s. 6d.[14] Payments remained unchanged until the war. In 1936, 43 per cent of the registered unemployed drew insurance benefits, 37 per cent UAB payments and about 334,000 were maintained by PACs. In the later 1930s the Ministry of Labour established 'training centres', where unemployed men cleared forests, dug ditches, made roads, levelled land or broke stones, and women were trained in domestic skills. Attendance was voluntary though sometimes 'encouraged' and effectively became compulsory for young long-term unemployed men, but it rarely led to regular, still less desirable, employment.

A minority who previously had very low or irregular incomes could be better off on unemployment benefit, particularly those with large families receiving dependants' allowances. The payments were regular and predictable, and households could plan their outgoings as they could not when it was uncertain how much would come in from week to week.[15] But most unemployed people resented a system they perceived as mean and intrusive, especially skilled workers accustomed to a decent wage and proud of keeping free of poor relief, who knew their plight was beyond their control. 'Hunger marches' of emaciated unemployed men to London and other major cities accompanied demonstrations outside Public Assistance offices, labour exchanges and town halls.

They were generally organized by trade unions and unemployed workers themselves, sometimes by the National Unemployed Workers Movement (NUWM), established by the Communist Party in 1921. The Labour Party officially kept its distance, though local parties were often supportive.

Police confronted marches and demonstrations fiercely. In 1932 they banned a march in Belfast. When the marchers disobeyed, armoured cars were deployed, provoking stone-throwing marchers shouting, 'We must have bread.' The police responded with gunfire, killing one man and seriously wounding others. These were the most violent demonstrations in the UK, fuelled by antagonism between the largely Protestant police and unemployed Catholics and the police were armed as they were not elsewhere in the UK. The events were largely ignored in mainland Britain. It was harder to ignore protests on Merseyside and elsewhere in Britain which were also prolonged by police resistance, wielding batons, not guns, but causing injuries and hostility. They culminated in October 1932 in the Great Hunger March against the means test, from various centres to London to present parliament with a petition with a million signatures. As 2,000 marchers approached central London, about 2,000 police were mobilized. More violence followed, causing severe injuries, and marchers were prevented from presenting the petition. Another march in 1934 was welcomed in London by Labour and Liberal MPs. It was closely watched by police, but police violence was now discouraged by the government for fear of alienating voters and arousing more opposition.

Marches continued. In 1936 came the month-long, 300-mile Jarrow March, which had particular impact. Marchers slept in church halls and community centres and were sympathetically received along the way. Cinema newsreels and sympathetic sections of the press aroused sympathy throughout the country for *The Town That Was Murdered*, as its Labour MP, Ellen Wilkinson, called her book about Jarrow. Seventy-seven per cent of its workforce were unemployed after the closure of its main shipyard in 1932. The book described vividly the reality of unemployment and poverty. Wilkinson helped organize the march and negotiated with the police, stressing its peaceful intentions and political neutrality, but she was reproved by the Labour Party conference for potentially inciting conflict. Baldwin announced that ministers would not receive marchers, who presented their petition to parliament and their leaders took tea with MPs. But the government did nothing for Jarrow and marchers' unemployment pay was stopped because they were judged unavailable for work when marching.

The marches achieved nothing tangible, but they perhaps prevented the government from even more punitive measures. They informed more comfortable people about the plight of the unemployed and aroused sympathy. When they marched through Windsor in 1934 royal servants threw them money. Apart from the newsreels, in 1934 BBC radio ran a series of talks by unemployed men called *Time to Spare*, and the *Times* ran articles on the plight of mining communities. New and older media conveyed the reality of unemployment to the whole country as never before. After 1938, when there was renewed depression in the international economy, Britain was protected by producing armaments which had not been a significant part of the economy since the previous war.

Economic planning

Resentment among unemployed people and growing knowledge of their conditions among sympathetic others stimulated criticism of the government. Lloyd George, echoing Roosevelt's plans of 1933, talked of a British New Deal; Keynes advocated a counter-cyclical investment strategy; Labour increasingly supported newly fashionable economic planning. Political and Economic Planning (PEP) was founded in 1931 as an independent expert think tank (as it would not then have been called) devoted to impartial analysis of social and economic issues, on which they published reports through the 1930s and beyond. In 1933 the young Conservative MP for the depressed constituency of Stockton in North-East England, Harold Macmillan, published *Reconstruction: A Plan for a National Policy*, followed in 1938 by *The Middle Way*, arguing that poverty must be abolished if freedom was to be preserved, and everyone had a responsibility to plan for reconstruction. In 1934 a young, Labour-supporting, female economist, Barbara Wootton, published *Plan or No Plan*, advocating a planned economy, favourably and idealistically contrasting the economy of the USSR, which almost alone escaped the crisis of 1929–31 due to its isolation, with unplanned systems.[16] She was not alone among left-wing intellectuals, most obviously the Webbs, in romanticizing communism compared with the problems of capitalism. Other Labour intellectuals, including RH Tawney, GDH Cole and Harold Laski, and Liberal Beveridge, favoured planning if it allowed for democratic participation. Some employers supported a moderate national economic strategy.

In 1934, with an election looming amid growing protest, the government introduced the Depressed Areas (Development and Improvement) Bill, renamed more positively as it went through parliament, the Special Areas Act. It granted £2m to promote industrial development in four areas suffering long-term depression. Trading estates were developed, unhampered by planning regulations and other 'red tape', but they received too little funding for needs that were not strictly economic, including improved health, sanitary and social services to keep people fit for work, and there were few inducements to business to move to areas regarded as distant (from London), unattractive and full of potentially troublesome trade unionists. They attracted only 34 of 2,000 new factories established in England and Wales, mainly in the English Midlands and South, 1934–7.[17]

Education

Throughout its time in office, the National Government focused more attention on cuts to social spending than on positive reform. Education was severely cut in the early 1930s, second only to unemployment benefit. Teachers' salaries were reduced by 15 per cent and reduced subsidies to Local Education Authorities caused cuts in school building programmes. In 1932 free places were abolished in secondary schools and replaced with means-tested fees. Progressive local authorities responded by fixing the means limit high enough to protect free places for poorer working-class children. Lower-middle-class families suffered when they could not afford fees but had incomes above the means limit. Opportunities for working-class children slumped in areas where they had been improving, including regions of high unemployment in Wales and County Durham, which could not afford to compensate for government cuts. The government claimed to favour expansion of state secondary education and equalizing opportunities, but the cuts undermined this. Local authority education spending from local rates rose 25 per cent, 1921–39, making some compensation for cuts, but improvements were uneven and greatest in Labour and progressive Liberal controlled authorities including Bradford, Manchester and the LCC.

Secondary education expanded from 1926 by admitting more children following a selective examination at age eleven in those, generally better-off, areas where it was adopted, but elsewhere all-age elementary schools suffered. They were almost exclusively working class, with large class sizes and poor equipment. In 1939 more than 2,000 children were in classes of over 50 pupils, 2 million in classes of over 40, many in old, ill-equipped, sometimes insanitary buildings. Nursery education expanded hardly at all. In 1938, 47 per cent of pupils in secondary schools paid no fees, following means-testing, but only 19 per cent of the 14–17 age group were in school. Poorer families still could not afford to keep children at school past the minimum leaving age. In 1936 parliament raised the school-leaving age to fifteen – from 1 September 1939, the day Hitler invaded Poland. It was postponed until after the war.

National insurance

The only improvements to social security payments were insurance-based and largely funded by contributors. In 1936 agricultural labourers were at last included in unemployment insurance. In 1937 the 'Black-Coated Workers Act' enabled lower-middle-class people who earned above the national insurance limit but could rarely afford private pensions and did not receive occupational pensions – including shopkeepers, farmers, clerks, dressmakers – to become voluntary insurers. The income limit was £400 for men, for women £250: justified, as ever, by the assertion that male workers had families to support whereas females had only themselves, regardless of the numbers of widowed and separated single mothers and single women supporting aged relatives. Women protested, fruitlessly. A total of 759,683 people applied to join the scheme by late 1938.[18]

Housing

Council house building dwindled through the 1930s, despite the Labour takeover of more local authorities including Glasgow in 1931, Leeds briefly in 1933, the LCC in 1934. The economy drive of 1931–3 put an end to subsidized council house building under the Wheatley Act. The Rent Act, 1933, decontrolled the rents of 500,000 more expensive private tenancies and other rents were not carefully controlled. Labour Party branches and tenants' associations, notably in Glasgow, formed unofficial rent advice bureaux to aid tenants in challenging landlords. Under strong pressure, the government decided to clear as much as possible of the poorest quality privately rented property, which was the source of most rent disputes since the tenants could least afford high rents. The Church of England issued a national slum clearance appeal; the BBC and leading newspapers made special investigations and published horrifying revelations about slum-living.[19] Slum clearance expanded, and subsidies for local authority housebuilding were retained only for replacing slums. The prince of Wales (the future King Edward VIII) was mobilized to make powerful speeches against slums, with well-publicized visits to a selected few. The Housing Act, 1935, requested, but did not require, local authorities to survey housing and submit clearance plans. It defined 'slums' by an inadequate measure of overcrowding, two persons per room, including all rooms, allowing for segregation of the sexes in bedrooms. By this measure, 3.3 per cent of all housing in England and Wales was overcrowded. A more stringent, and realistic, definition applied in Leeds, including only rooms used for sleeping, found 21.1 per cent of households overcrowded. The official measure took no account of poor sanitation, poor construction and maintenance, which were widespread. By March 1939 472,000 homes officially defined as slums were scheduled for closure and 272,000 had been cleared.

The 1935 Act also specified that council rents should not fall below local market rents for similar property, aiming to support the private sector by ensuring that council housing did not attract those capable of renting or buying in the private market, but it disadvantaged the poorest who could not afford market rents. This was left to local authorities to resolve, while coping with cuts to their education, health and unemployment assistance budgets. One solution, introduced in Leeds in 1933 when it was briefly Labour-controlled, was differential rents: tenants rather than houses were subsidized, according to income. Below a certain income, they paid no rent, causing resentment among tenants who paid rent for the same housing. Leeds Conservatives accused Labour of establishing a 'socialist city state', which helped return them to power in 1934. They then modified the scheme, so that all tenants paid some rent, but did not abolish it. They recognized that some subsidy was essential to provide the poorest with decent housing and to enable themselves to fulfil their legal obligations. Many Labour supporters were dubious about differential rents because they were means-tested and redistributed from better-off working and lower-middle-class tenants whose higher rents subsidized their poorer neighbours, rather than from rich to poor through taxation.[20] But it was the best option available, and by 1939, 110 local authorities of all political colours had adopted it in some form.

In the 1930s more poorer people gained council housing but not all who needed it and not all who did so benefitted. The effect of high council rents on poor families was shown tragically by a survey in 1927–8 by the MOH in Stockton-upon-Tees of the diets of fifty-five working-class families, some of whom had been re-housed on a modern housing estate following slum clearance. Death rates rose despite improved housing, fastest among the unemployed. The MOH attributed this to poor diet because the families could afford less food when they paid the higher council rents.[21] This persuaded the British Medical Association (BMA), in 1933, to set standards for 'the minimum weekly expenditure on foodstuffs which must be incurred by families of varying size if health and working capacity [were] to be maintained'. They estimated that at 1933 prices between 5s and 6s was needed to provide an adequate diet for a man for a week, but this was of little immediate help to low-income families.[22]

Housing at the lower end of the private rental market remained appalling, despite further slum clearance, causing protests and rent strikes. Between 1931 and 1939 2.5 million new homes were built in Great Britain, fewer than 600,000 by local authorities, not helped by a further cut in subsidies in 1938. Three-quarters of new private housing was in the South and Midlands, most council houses in London, Scotland and Northern England. The housing stock embodied the differences between the 'two nations' of depressed and prospering areas. Much rural housing remained poor, though Women's Institutes campaigned with some successes for better housing and improved water and electricity supplies.

City centre rebuilding increasingly took the form of high-density flats. Most private and council houses continued to be built in low-rise, low-density garden estates on the outskirts of towns. Such homes had long been the ideal of town planners, but the reality disturbed many of them as towns and cities spread into the countryside, unrestrained by central control when, from 1932, local authorities were no longer obliged to prepare town-planning schemes, as the government sought to cut 'red tape' and assist private building. Some planners looked to the continental European model of well-planned flats. These were unpopular in England, though not in Scotland where flat dwelling was an established tradition, though larger English cities felt they had little option given the cost and limited availability of land. A model example was the Quarry Hill development in Leeds city centre, begun in 1934, occupied from 1938, replacing some of the worst slums, designed by the City Architect on European modernist lines, including 938 well-equipped flats with communal laundries, gardens and playgrounds. In most towns and cities the out-of-town sprawl of public and private development continued, increasing demand for public transport, railways and roads while car ownership grew.

Health

National Health Insurance still provided uneven services. GPs providing free healthcare under the scheme were scarcer in poorer areas: in Manchester each might have over a thousand patients, in Gloucestershire fewer than 700. The National Government cut its contribution to NHI in 1932. In 1939 it covered fewer than half the population. The families of insured workers still had no access to free healthcare outside the Public Assistance system, apart from unevenly distributed local clinics for mothers and babies and the school medical service providing diagnosis and limited treatment for schoolchildren. In many areas GPs, encouraged by the BMA and Friendly Societies, provided care in return for small weekly payments, which had at least 650,000 contributors by 1939, but the poorest could not afford this.

NHI, outside the most prosperous approved societies, still did not provide hospital treatment, except for TB for insured workers and their families. Traditionally, voluntary hospitals provided free care for poor patients with acute conditions (only), but they were poorly distributed around the country, most in big cities especially London, and they experienced growing financial pressure. Medicine was increasing its capacity to cure, increasing demand for hospital services from those who could afford to pay. For the first time, reputable hospitals were attractive to better-off people as they provided cure rather than, as too often in the past, infection. But the costs of new technology, drugs and staff grew with new discoveries and increased demand. Voluntary hospitals became more dependent on fee-paying patients and less able to afford caring for those unable to pay. Some local authorities subsidized beds for low-income patients, and hospitals established low-cost contributory schemes, like GPs, while vigorously seeking voluntary donations.

Local authorities slowly took over the old Poor Law hospitals, concerned about the costs alongside other demands on their resources. They remained generally poorly equipped, providing poor standards of care while carrying the burden of much chronic illness including victims of stroke and heart disease. In one such hospital in West Middlesex, Dr Marjorie Warren was so shocked by the neglect of 700 bedbound older patients that she started redecorating and brightening the wards, providing activities, rehabilitation, diagnosis, treatment and improved care, enabling some patients to leave hospital. This introduced Britain to geriatric medicine, already established in the US and other countries.[23] Provision for healthcare remained worst in the depressed areas despite some investment by the Special Areas Commission. It was clear by the later 1930s that neither the private nor the public sectors could provide adequately for the national need or demand for healthcare.

Unemployment did not always worsen health since the heavy industries, where it was concentrated, had themselves long been a cause of sickness and disability. But it did not improve health, especially from 1932 when the National Government reduced sickness benefits for the unemployed to 17s pw for insured men, for married women from 12s to 10s. Cuts would have been greater but for opposition from a parliamentary alliance of Labour members and female MPs of all parties. Throughout the interwar years central governments gave low priority to health compared with other social issues. Progressive local authorities were the main sources of initiative and expenditure including on maternity and child welfare and school medical services which improved gradually and unevenly. By the later 1930s, 5,340 health visitors were employed by voluntary bodies and local authorities and about 97 per cent of babies received at least one visit from a health visitor. In England and Wales all 409 local authorities supplied milk to expectant and nursing mothers, free or at cost price. About half of all mothers received antenatal care; more than half of all babies attended local health and welfare centres staffed by, at least, a doctor and a health visitor. They treated only minor ailments and were often overcrowded and under pressure but dispensed free or subsidized food and milk. They were the only source of professional advice available to many mothers. Those who benefitted welcomed it while women's organizations campaigned for more.

A survey of the health of 1,250 working-class women by the feminist Women's Health Enquiry Committee in 1933 found that 404 had received no professional advice on healthcare; 591 learned all they knew from district nurses and antenatal clinics, 245 from a health visitor, only 67 from a GP. The report *Working Class Wives* described how women put the needs of their husbands and families first and were more anxious to learn how to care for their children than for themselves.[24] It gave a devastating account of their ill-health and the inadequacy of healthcare, though it was positive about the role of welfare centres and health visitors in all but their numbers. Women's ill-health was very often the outcome of repeated pregnancy, miscarriage, sometimes illegal abortions, without qualified medical care, all made worse by poverty and bad housing. One example, not untypical, was the wife of an employed miner in Durham:

She is only 32, has been married fifteen years and has seven children the eldest of whom is 14. She lives in a colliery house; it has an open ash-privy at the back; the back bedroom is damp and the rain comes in ; the kitchen ceiling is unsafe; there is no sink under the tap; the coal-house and ash-pit are at the end of a long garden and coal and ashes have to be carried through the sitting room which is used as a bedroom. *The ground-floor windows do not open* (original italics). In her spare time (!) she makes mats for which she gets given clothes in return. She gets up at 4am and goes to bed at any time between 10pm and midnight . . . She does her own baking and the diet given is miraculous. She drinks a lot of water and gets a lot of green vegetables from their own garden including lettuce daily in summer. Her husband helps her with the heavy work when he is at home . . . None of the children has ever been to hospital or needed outside treatment. She consults the health visitor, the district nurse and the colliery doctor and all sickness has been nursed in the home. Now these are her own ailments, (1) Neuritis: from which she has suffered for two years owing, in her opinion, to getting wet, the heavy work of mangling etc. She rubs her shoulder with oils and puts on hot flannels with the advice of the colliery doctor. (2) Pyorrhoea: on the advice of the colliery doctor she has had all her teeth extracted; (3) Kidney trouble due to Bright's disease at 5 years; she takes medicine for this; (5) Cystitis during her last pregnancy due to getting wet and heavy work; for this she rested in bed and kept warm; (6) Pain in right side during menstrual periods, due to ovarian trouble; the colliery doctor gives medicine for this by which 'he hopes to avoid an operation'.[25]

She was fortunate to have access to a colliery doctor.

To limit the effects of repeated pregnancies, women's organizations campaigned for, and, when possible, provided, birth control assistance.[26] For poorer women this came overwhelmingly from the voluntary sector, while better-off women paid doctors. Marie Stopes, a leading birth control campaigner from the early 1920s, converted two horse-drawn caravans into mobile clinics which travelled the country. In 1938 several voluntary organizations merged to form the Family Planning Association (FPA), developing a national network of clinics.[27] The steadily falling birth rate suggests that couples were increasingly controlling births. The most common techniques appear to have been withdrawal and abstention from sex rather than condoms or the more modern cap, which poor people could rarely afford.[28]

Due to better care and, in some areas, improved living standards, infant mortality continued to decline in England and Wales from 80 per 1,000 live births in 1920–2, to 64 in 1930–2, 55 in 1940–2. It remained somewhat higher in Scotland and above average in the depressed areas. Higher survival rates were another reason for fewer births. Unusually among causes of death at this time, maternal mortality rose slowly but persistently from 3.09 per 1,000 births in 1921–5 to a peak of 5.94 in 1934.[29] It affected all classes, especially first births, due mainly to sepsis. The statistical rise may have been partly due to falling births and the corresponding high proportion of first births, while poor diet in pregnancy left poorer women more vulnerable to infection. Most births, in all classes, still occurred at home, though more were in hospital. The numbers, qualifications and regulation of midwives improved, though still in 1939 many poorer women gave birth at home with unqualified assistance, unable to afford a doctor or medication. Maternal deaths declined permanently from the later 1930s following the discovery of penicillin to cure infections.

It was suspected that a significant cause of maternal death was illegal abortion. In 1934 the Ministry of Health attributed 20 per cent of the deaths to abortion, estimating that 68,000 illegal abortions took place that year.[30] It was believed to be most common among older, married, working-class women. The Women's Co-operative Guild (WCG) and the National Council of Women (NCW) campaigned with others for legal abortion. In 1936 the Abortion Law Reform Association (ALRA) was formed by feminists, starting a long campaign for safe, legal abortions for all women. They succeeded in 1967.[31] In 1937 the Birkett Committee was appointed to investigate abortions in response to these pressures and the ministry's concerns. In 1939 it recommended against legalization but suggested that abortion should be allowed if pregnancy threatened a woman's life. This followed a judgement in the *Bourne* case in 1938 involving a doctor who performed an abortion on a teenage girl following her gang rape by members of the King's Guard in London. The judgement set a precedent by ruling the abortion lawful because it was intended to save the girl's life by preserving her psychological health.[32] The law remained unchanged.

Again, the poor physical condition of military recruits was invoked as evidence of low general standards. Of volunteers for the services in 1935, 6,210 were reported as 'below the comparatively low standard of physique required by the army'.[33] This suggested there had been little improvement since 1918. Again, eugenic arguments surfaced as 'explanations' of physical and mental weakness though they were less influential than pressures for positive measures to improve even inherited disabilities. This was especially important amid mounting panic about the declining birth rate while average life expectancy was rising, creating the spectre of a shrinking workforce and an ageing population 'burdening' a reduced younger generation with the costs of their pensions and healthcare. This caused anguished debate involving such figures as Beveridge and Keynes, but no solutions because there was no known way to increase births. The attempts of Hitler and Mussolini to reward mothers of numerous children did not raise their national birth rates, and the British government declined to follow them.[34]

A popular response to concerns about national unfitness was a vogue for physical exercise, encouraged by a government National Fitness Campaign in the later 1930s, sponsored by King George V and his two successors, especially George VI. It was supported by the flourishing Women's League for Health and Beauty, a largely middle-class organization which helped improve health and raise expectations of 'normal' health.[35] *Working Class Wives* suggested that the ideas reached some working-class women, who exercised when they could. The royal family encouraged sport and other outdoor pursuits, such as walking in the countryside, 'rambling' as it was known. The Ramblers' Association was formed in 1935 to encourage this and preserve access to footpaths threatened by landowners fearful of intrusion on their land. These activities became popular among middle-class people with rising incomes and time to spare. Many unemployed people did their best to use their time constructively and keep healthy and active, staving off sickness and depression.

There were growing demands for good healthcare for all, funded and managed by the state. The Commissioner for Special Areas, Malcolm Campbell, repeatedly stressed that the poor quality of 'human capital' was hindering economic development in these areas. The increasingly influential PEP agreed. It was an early advocate of a tax-funded, integrated National Health Service.[36]

Poverty and inequality

Extensive poor health suggests the extent of continuing deprivation. More poverty surveys were conducted by university researchers and independent reformers using ever more refined methods, generally aiming to influence popular perceptions and government policy to improve social conditions. In 1936 (published 1941) Rowntree repeated his study of York, aiming to assess change since 1899. He used a more generous measure of poverty, allowing for higher food expenditure and a small margin above bare necessities for such items as newspapers and a wireless, which had become parts of normal life, but he emphasized, as before, that 'the standards adopted . . . err on the side of stringency rather than of extravagance'. He set 43s.6d per week for a family of two parents and three children as 'a measuring rod by which to gauge the standards of social well-being actually possible for working class families in York'.[37] Average male manual earnings were 56s 9d pw.[38] He concluded that 40 per cent of the working-class population of York lived below this standard, in secondary poverty, 31 per cent (20 per cent of the whole York population) due to lack of means, 9 per cent because of spending on 'non-essentials', including 'drink, cigarettes, gambling or any other purely personal expenditure', though he admitted he had no clear evidence for this judgement.[39]

Using the same methods as before, he judged that those in 'primary poverty', with insufficient income even to buy the bare necessities, were 6.8 per cent of the working-class population (3.9 per cent of the whole) compared with 15.9 per cent in 1899. People in poverty according to his 1936 definition included half of all working-class children above the age of one. Low pay was a lesser cause of poverty than in 1899 though it remained substantial, unemployment was greater, accounting for 44.3 per cent, while old age contributed 14.7 per cent. Rowntree concluded:

This striking reduction in the amount of primary poverty is a tribute to those who have been a driving force during the present century to raise the standard of life of the people, but the fact that nearly seven per cent of the workers were living in abject poverty in 1936 in a typical provincial town in England shows how great a task still lies before social reformers.[40]

A study in Southampton in 1931, a relatively prosperous southern town, using Bowley's measure, found 21 per cent of working-class families in poverty, two-thirds due to unemployment, 11.74 per cent to 'wages insufficient for number of children'.[41] A sample survey of depressed Sheffield in 1931–2, also using Bowley's standard modified for price changes, found 15.4 per cent of working-class families below the poverty line, 3.5 per cent 'on the margins'. Again, two-thirds of poverty was due to unemployment, with widowhood accounting for 10 per cent, old age 6.8 per cent, illness or temporary incapacity for work 6.6 per cent, insufficient earnings 5.2 per cent, permanent incapacity for work 4.8 per cent. A sample survey of *c.* 4,526 working-class households in Bristol, a centre of new industries and one of the most prosperous manufacturing centres, in 1937 using similar measures found 6.9 per cent in poverty. Seventeen per cent of all families were estimated to have no margin for saving, so any crisis could plunge them into poverty.

All the surveys showed substantial numbers in real deprivation even in relatively prosperous areas. They all paid close attention to diet. A study by nutritionist Sir John Boyd Orr in 1936, based on 1,152 family budgets, found 10 per cent of the sample and 20 per cent of children seriously undernourished, up to 50 per cent 'poorly' nourished. He applied not the 'bare subsistence' standard of the poverty surveys but 'a diet that will keep people in health; and the standard of health adopted is a state of well-being such that no improvement could be effected by a change in diet. The standard may be regarded therefore as the minimum for maximum health'.[42] But the sample was small, and there was still uncertainty about appropriate nutritional standards.

Other investigations suggested that cleanliness and general health improved with better housing and water supplies. In London in 1912 school medical inspectors found 39.5 per cent of state school children were verminous; in 1937, there were 7.9 per cent. Nationally standards were rising. In Northampton the average height of twelve-year-old boys rose from 55.4 inches in 1910–13 to 57.3 inches in 1933, their weight from 74.3 lb to 79.9 lb. However, Boyd Orr found the average heights of boys of fourteen at a public school, at Christ's Hospital (a charitable boarding school) and an elementary school to be 63.7, 61.1 and 58 inches respectively: class differences had changed little since 1883.[43]

From 1920 to 1938, average real incomes grew modestly by around 15 per cent, due more to falling prices (by one-third) than rising earnings.[44] The falling birth rate enabled more families to avoid poverty by having fewer people to support. The narrowness of the margin is suggested by the numbers in poverty with more than two dependent children. This was as true in the new industrial as in depressed areas, possibly more so since unemployment benefits included children's allowances but wages did not. The nutritional adequacy of diets improved, though least among the unemployed. In 1938 the German émigré economist Jurgen Kuczynski demonstrated that low wages were still a problem by comparing Ministry of Labour wage statistics for 1935 with Rowntree's 'Human needs' standard of 53s pw for a man, wife and three children. He found that four million adult male workers and two million women earned less than the standard which, including dependents, affected ten million people.[45] Unmarried motherhood continued to cause stigma and poverty, while NCUMC and other charities continued to give support.

There was a slight narrowing of income and wealth distribution. In 1913 working-class people paid more in tax than they received in social services and benefits. In 1925 they still paid 85 per cent of the cost of social services, including through national insurance contributions, but received £55m more than they contributed. By 1937 they received between £200 and £250m more, raising total working-class incomes by between 8 per cent and 14 per cent. Total central and local government spending on social services in the UK was £411.8m in 1920 (6.8 per cent GNP), £596.3m (11.3 per cent) in 1938.[46] In 1938 the top 0.15 per cent of wealth-holders in Great Britain owned 27 per cent of national wealth, the top 5 per cent, 78 per cent.[47] Death duties and super-tax reduced the largest holdings only slightly.[48]

Conclusion

The 1930s are remembered as a time of depression and unemployment, though the economy expanded with new industries. This increased regional, social and economic inequalities and slightly narrowed national income and wealth inequality. It also created exceptional protest against unemployment and deprivation. In response, even reluctant Conservative governments felt driven to respond with improvements to welfare services. These were small and gradual but real enough to provide poorer people with some security and ensure that Britain avoided the right-and left-wing extremism that pervaded other European countries, leading to another world war in 1939. They also stimulated pressures for further reforms which increased during this war.

CHAPTER 6
THE PEOPLE'S WAR

In 1937 Baldwin, exhausted and in poor health, retired from the premiership as another war loomed. He was succeeded by Neville Chamberlain, who became notorious for seeking to avoid war by 'appeasing' – negotiating with – Hitler. This failed and political and public pressure to declare war intensified as Hitler's persecution of Jews became unmistakable, and he invaded Czechoslovakia then Poland. On 3 September 1939 Britain, with France, declared war on Germany. Opposition to Chamberlain grew within his own party, and he resigned in May 1940, dying of cancer shortly after. He was succeeded by Winston Churchill, who had been a strong proponent of war. He led a wartime coalition government including leading Labour figures.

Churchill quickly established a Ministry of Information with a brief to sustain morale and strove to foster the perception that the shared stresses of war drew British people together, softening social divisions and conflicts and strengthening collective patriotic resistance.

Adjusting to war

Lessons were learned from the previous war and conscription was introduced immediately. It was a partial social leveller, though upper-class men, as ever, were perceived as the natural officer class. Shared fear of bombing and invasion early in the war, then the experience of bombing, rationing and queuing for scarce goods, brought together people who might not otherwise meet. So did the rushed evacuation of children from districts that were expected targets of German bombing. This was expected soon though the destructive 'blitz' did not begin until September 1940. The potential psychological damage from suddenly taking children from their families into wholly strange environments was not understood, though the experience of evacuation eventually made it clear. The transition sometimes from very poor homes to those of better-off families could exacerbate social divisions. Some hosts blamed mothers for the impoverished appearance, lice-ridden heads and poor table manners of underweight children from desperate homes, who wet their beds due to what was not recognized as trauma. Others felt compassion for depths of poverty they had never encountered and demanded reforms to end such conditions. Some evacuees were generously received and benefitted lifelong from better education, food and environments than they had known. Others suffered undetected abuse. Much was learned from the experience of evacuation, including about the psychological impact on children, though at some cost to many children.[1]

Evacuation could be stressful for women who were expected to look after sometimes more than one, unknown, bewildered child, and for mothers separated from their children. Hosts were paid 10s.6d pw for the first child, 8s.6d for others, more than the maximum service allowances of 5s for the first child, but insufficient to cover costs, especially when growing children needed shoes and clothing their families could not afford. Reluctantly, against Treasury opposition, the Ministry of Health sanctioned small clothing grants. Following protests there were small increases for children over fourteen in 1940.[2]

Rich people retreated to country homes from the dangers of the cities, including encountering other classes. They suffered some deprivations. The London social season was suspended, but they could enjoy luxury foods in smart restaurants since all restaurants were 'off-ration', when food rationing was quickly introduced. As in the last war, one of the greatest deprivations suffered by better-off families was the flight of servants to more appealing work, this time permanently.

Women in all classes again supported the war effort through voluntary action. As part of war planning, which began pre-war despite Chamberlain's efforts at appeasement, in 1938 the Home Secretary established the Women's Voluntary Service (WVS), initially to help with evacuation and the effects of the anticipated bombing. It fulfilled these and other functions throughout the war, invaluably supplementing stretched official services. It was a cross-class organization, with elite leadership, directed by Lady Stella Reading, widow of a former viceroy of India, experienced in public and voluntary service.[3]

Social conditions and social welfare

The government intervened to improve social conditions more vigorously than in the last war, following the growth of state welfare between the wars. Again, social conditions for most manual workers and their families improved and there was some narrowing of socio-economic inequalities due to full employment from 1940 and government policies. Allowances for service families, including again 'unmarried wives', were provided from the start, more efficiently than in the First World War, though still not generous. A soldier's wife with two children received 32s weekly in 1939, 33s in 1940, 38s in 1941, 43s in 1942. Average weekly male manual earnings in 1939 were 56s.9d. These payments were hard to live on. Public concern led to an increase to 60s by 1945. Officers' wives also received low payments by the standards of their class and service personnel themselves were relatively low-paid.[4]

From early 1941, rationing prioritized healthy foods at controlled prices, improving the diets of many low-income families, and most local authorities established British Restaurants, as Churchill insisted they were called, providing low-cost, nutritious, off-ration meals. By September 1943, 2,160 British Restaurants served about 630,000 meals daily.[5] The Food Policy Committee was chaired by Attlee who was prominent in the mainly Conservative/Labour coalition and directed domestic affairs while Churchill conducted the war. From 1940 Attlee approved grants of subsidized milk to mothers with children under five and daily milk and meals for schoolchildren. By February 1945 1,650,000 children received meals, 14 per cent free, the remainder paying 4d–6d per meal; 73 per cent of schoolchildren received free milk. Free vaccination of children against diphtheria eliminated a major pre-war killer. Pre-war efforts to reduce child deaths and improve health progressed, benefitting the poorest most. Rationing was extended to clothing and other essentials including furniture. A basic range of sound, plainly designed goods was provided under the 'Utility' label, with purchases limited by ration tokens.

Keynes served as unpaid economic adviser to the government, advocating progressive taxation and controls on prices, wages and supplies to avoid inflation while financing the war. The tax changes further eroded inequalities. Purchase tax, to restrain consumption especially of luxury goods, and 100 per cent excess profits tax were introduced at the beginning of the war, continuing throughout. In 1939 the standard rate of income tax was 29 per cent, the additional surtax 41 per cent on incomes over £2,000. Ten million people were liable for tax, and the sum raised was £400m. The standard rate rose to 50 per cent in 1942, surtax to 48 per cent. Tax allowances were reduced. By 1944–5 there were 14 million taxpayers paying almost £1,400m p.a. Tax collection became easier and cheaper in 1943 with the introduction of Pay As You Earn (PAYE) which placed the onus of collection on employers through deduction from pay in place of the long-established system of individual assessment by government officials and payment once or twice each year.[6] From 1938 to 1948 the purchasing power of the top one-sixth of income earners fell by about 30 per cent while that of the remainder increased by about 25 per cent, though tax avoidance appears to have grown on an unprecedented scale; among the lasting gainers from the war were accountants.

Price controls helped stabilize the cost of living at 30 per cent above its pre-war level, avoiding the inflation of the last war. Wages rose, but higher earnings made more manual workers liable for income tax. In 1938 the average adult male wage was £175 pa; a married man did not pay tax until he earned £225 or, if he had one child, £300. From 1941 a married man with one child paid tax on earnings of £161 pa, with two children £265. Average male pay was then £288 p.a. National insurance contributions rose. The tax structure became more regressive at lower levels and more progressive from middle incomes upwards. This aroused resentment but not serious conflict since most workers enjoyed higher real incomes. Despite criticism in parliament and the press, the government, urged by Ernest Bevin, the former trade unionist minister of labour, avoided wage controls to prevent industrial conflict, without total success: days lost through strikes were fewer than in the last war but similar to the later 1930s, peaking at 3.7m in 1944.[7]

The belief that plans for 'reconstruction', designed to create a more equal and united society, had largely failed after the previous war made some determined to do better this time. The idea that the experience of this war promoted social solidarity and support for redistributive state welfare, was developed influentially by Richard Titmuss, Professor of Social Policy at LSE, in his official history of wartime social policy, *Problems of Social*

Policy (1950). He argued that bombing and evacuation in particular revealed poverty, malnutrition and ill-health to people previously unaware of their reality. He concluded that war conditions increased government awareness of the value of creating, in peace and war, a fully employed, well-fed, fit, contented and socially cohesive population and increased popular support for extended state welfare. His analysis of the causes has been challenged, but the government, far more than in the previous war, worked to improve wartime social conditions and a flow of influential reports proposed post-war reforms.[8] On 18 June 1940, the day after the fall of France, the director-general of the Ministry of Information urged the government to promise social reform to boost civilian morale.[9] The War Aims Committee was established in August 1940 to plan post-war reconstruction, though it did little until 1942 when the war looked realistically winnable. Meanwhile, reform proposals emerged from Whitehall, parliament and elsewhere.

Education

Education was affected by teacher shortages due to enlistment, by bombing of school buildings and evacuation of children and schools. Revelations of illiteracy among conscripts, while no surprise, increased demands to improve schooling. In 1941, R. A. Butler became president of the Board of Education. He was a Conservative reformer, chair of the party committee on 'post-war problems', a title which avoided committing the party to radical change. Churchill was reluctant to devote government time to social issues amid wartime crises, and he was too preoccupied with the war to pay attention to discussions in the home departments. The board supported the tripartite system of secondary education already developing and the concepts of 'parity of esteem' and 'equality of opportunity' between children of different backgrounds and aptitudes. The TUC, Labour Party, LCC and some Welsh county councils advocated non-selective, multilateral (later known as 'comprehensive') secondary schools for all children. The concern to raise standards was widely shared. In 1943 a report by a Board of Education committee chaired by Sir Cyril Norwood, head of independent Harrow School, rephrased the Hadow report's assertions in 1926, that children were divided into three 'rough groupings' with 'different types of mind', requiring different forms of education from age eleven. The Norwood report referred to those 'interested in learning for its own sake, who can grasp an argument or follow a piece of connected reasoning'; those 'whose interests and abilities lie markedly in the field of applied science and applied art'; and those 'who deal more easily with concrete things than with ideas . . . abstractions mean little to him (*sic*) . . . his horizon is near and within a limited area his movement is generally slow'. The report was criticized by educationists and psychologists for unscientific assertions and, more widely, for its pejorative description of the third 'type', contrary to the language of 'parity of esteem'.

It impressed Butler, who was anxious to reform secondary education before party politics revived after the war. He believed this would improve the Conservatives' electoral chances, pre-empt Labour moves to reform or abolish private schools and right-wing

Conservative pressure to minimize spending on poorer children. Butler introduced the only major wartime item of social legislation, the Education Act, 1944, though it was not to be implemented until after the war. This raised the school-leaving age to fifteen, to rise to sixteen as soon as practicable. It abolished all-age elementary schools, dividing state education at age eleven into 'primary' and 'secondary' sectors. The board was renamed the Ministry of Education. It put its influence behind the tripartite secondary system, though this was not specified in the act, nor any method of selection. It still could not insist that all local authorities adopt it, given the established principle of local autonomy, but specified that within one year all local authorities must submit plans for reorganization of secondary education. The LCC, still Labour-controlled throughout the war, immediately planned reorganization of London schools, many of them destroyed by bombing, on a 'multilateral' basis. Most authorities proposed tri- or bi-partite structures suited to their school stock.

The act abolished secondary school fees and increased grants to universities and students. Grants to faith schools increased, and, for the first time, all state-funded schools were required to provide daily religious (it was assumed Christian) instruction, following pressure from Anglicans and Nonconformists to compensate for the declining number of Protestant schools. It passed smoothly through parliament until women MPs introduced an amendment granting equal pay to teachers. Moved by Conservative Thelma Cazalet Keir, this passed the Commons by 117 to 116 votes. The following day Churchill diverted his attention from the war to insist in parliament that this was a matter of confidence in the government and the amendment must be withdrawn. In 1936 Baldwin had similarly forced reversal of a vote for equal pay in the civil service, to the fury of the staff associations.[10] Protesting that the amendment hardly threatened the war effort, the House gave in, then Churchill, under pressure, appointed a Royal Commission on Equal Pay which reported in 1946. The women MPs won another amendment abolishing the marriage bar in teaching, which the Board of Education accepted because it anticipated a teacher shortage due to higher student numbers in the reformed post-war system. The Education Act progressed pre-war changes in the education system, owing much to Butler's efforts.

Health

Reorganization of health services to meet war needs featured in the careful pre-war planning. An Emergency Medical Service (EMS) was established immediately war was declared, a centralized state system taking over voluntary and public hospitals and establishing new ones in buildings of variable suitability, initially intended to treat victims of the expected bombing. Doctors and nurses were employed and paid by the government, often at higher rates than before. Access to non-war-related civilian healthcare was curtailed by the recruitment of doctors for war service, and long-stay patients, including many older people, were transferred from city centre to rural and suburban hospitals.

The reorganization alerted the Ministry and the BMA to deficiencies in existing services. Healthcare reform was constantly discussed in the *Lancet* and the *British Medical Journal*. Ministry officials became convinced of the need for a comprehensive health service for everyone. Again, the poor physical condition of many recruits to the services and fear of the loss of young men at war, together with the condition of children evacuated from poor neighbourhoods, aroused demands for a healthier nation. In October 1941, the minister of health, Liberal Ernest Brown, announced that immediate reorganization was impossible, but a comprehensive hospital service would be introduced after the war. He set up a survey of hospitals and proposed that, following reform, patients 'would be called on to make a reasonable payment towards the cost whether through contributory schemes or otherwise'. Local authority MOHs and GPs working with poorer people supported change enthusiastically. MOHs favoured requiring, rather than the present system of allowing, local authorities to provide services, including for maternal and child welfare; these expanded further during the war, partly due to demand from mothers and children evacuated to rural areas and small towns where services were sparse. Additional health and welfare centres, maternity homes and nurseries were staffed by volunteers, often from WVS.[11]

In 1943 a Mass Observation (MO) survey for the Ministry of Information found widespread enthusiasm for a free national service, though some fears of bureaucratized, impersonal care. Many Conservatives opposed a state-managed service. In February 1944 a Ministry of Health White Paper proposed compromise. It stressed the need for adequate healthcare for all and early treatment. On Labour insistence it included free health centres with salaried GPs, of the sort established by a few local authorities between the wars- the first in Peckham, South London – alongside fee-charging GP practices. The voluntary hospitals would keep their independence but would be encouraged to co-operate with public hospitals and paid to perform certain functions for the national service. All medical services would be regularly inspected, and medical education expanded. Churchill initially opposed its publication, but the issue was too popular to ignore. The BMA, representing the elite of well-paid consultants benefitting from private practice, opposed a universal state-run service, but when it polled the whole profession it found that 60 per cent of doctors favoured a universal free service, 62 per cent a wholly or partially salaried service. The war gave ammunition to those already committed to reform of healthcare and made converts, but the shape of reform remained uncertain in 1945.[12]

As in the last war, the health of most people not directly affected by bombing and war service improved. This was partly due to improved access to health services, also to full employment, better diets due to higher incomes, adequate supplies and rationing of unhealthy foods, including sugar. From 1939 to 1945 infant mortality fell by 20 per cent as more mothers received expert antenatal care and delivery, support from local health centres and access to cheap milk, orange juice and other supplements.[13] Deaths of older children also fell, mainly due to prevention of infectious diseases. Deaths from TB, which mainly killed adults, and other respiratory diseases, including bronchitis, influenza, pneumonia, fell significantly following the development and more widespread provision of effective drugs plus improved living standards.[14] For similar reasons, especially the discovery of penicillin, maternal mortality declined from 1938 to 1945 from 4.22 deaths per 1,000 births in England and Wales to 2.33, with similar falls in Scotland and Northern Ireland.

Housing

Housing was another focus of post-war planning, especially of future building following bombing, including of many low-cost homes since bombing targeted inner-city and industrial areas. Planners and architects seized the opportunity to generate plans, building on their growing pre-war expertise, influence and international status. They were encouraged by the Ministry of Works, under John Reith (previously first director-general of the BBC), 1940–2, which ensured efficient repair of damaged housing, though new house building and repairs to property unaffected by bombing virtually ceased. Evacuation, fear of bombing and bombing itself depleted the populations of large cities – that of East London fell by half. The drift of population from pre-war 'depressed areas' continued, while the location of war industries away from big cities increased overcrowding in towns such as Reading, though not to the crisis proportions of the last war.

Reith supported proposals for central planning of the location of housing, jobs, transport, industrial and urban growth, persuaded the Cabinet to establish a national planning authority and initiated planning of post-war redevelopment of London and other towns and cities. Churchill dismissed Reith in 1942, probably for personal reasons, but proposals continued from committees he had established, including for nationalization of the rights to land suitable for development which became Labour, but not Conservative, policy. Also for planning of the countryside to protect good agricultural land from urban development, and enabling public access to unspoiled countryside by establishing National Parks where development was prohibited, which became post-war policy. The Town and Country Planning Act, 1944, provided the machinery for comprehensive redevelopment.[15]

Women's organizations still campaigned for improved housing. In May 1942 a Women's Housing and Planning conference was organized by prominent women's associations, determined that plans for post-war housing should take account of women's views and needs.[16] The Ministry of Health established the Design of Dwellings Committee to improve home-design and the layout of suburban estates. It included seven women representing leading campaign groups. Campaigners formed the Women's Advisory Housing Council and issued a questionnaire. More than 40,000 women of all classes responded, as summarized in a report to the Committee. Most wanted houses with sufficient living space and gardens, upstairs, tiled, bathrooms and hot and cold running water; large, bright, soundproof rooms with rounded corners for easy cleaning; kitchens with conveniently placed cupboards and work surfaces, gas and electric cooking appliances and ventilated larders. In 1944 the Committee endorsed many of their recommendations, proposing national minimum standards which were introduced after the war.[17]

Planning for a better future was extensive, but in wartime emergency measures came first. In 1944 local authority building of prefabricated houses was subsidized to cover urgent needs. They were cheap (*c.* £1,000 per house), quickly constructed and intended to be temporary, but the speed with which they caught the national imagination suggests their advantages and the prevalence of poor housing. Affectionately called 'prefabs', for many tenants they were unimaginably better than their previous homes: unpretentious in appearance, two-bedroom bungalows with gardens, fitted kitchens, even refrigerators, water heaters and indoor bathrooms and toilets. Many survived for thirty years and more, some into the twenty-first century.

Beveridge and social insurance

Planning was also proposed for national economic and social reconstruction, notably by William Beveridge. He was not, this time, immediately recruited to assist the war effort. His limited diplomatic skills made him unpopular with politicians and civil servants, especially when he publicly criticized what he believed, sometimes wrongly, was inadequate planning for the war. He wanted to return to planning civilian labour and in July 1940 Bevin appointed him an adviser. But Beveridge underestimated Bevin and bombarded him with unwanted advice on the direction of labour and criticism when he was ignored. To escape, Bevin had him appointed chair of an interdepartmental committee on the coordination of social insurance, composed otherwise of civil servants. This was intended as a low-key committee, making no important recommendations. Beveridge was deeply disappointed, 'tears stood in his eyes when the new appointment was offered to him'.[18]

The committee arose from trade union pressure to revise the workmen's compensation scheme and wider demands to improve National Health Insurance, and there was a need, which Beveridge had long recognized, to coordinate the various social insurance and income support schemes that had developed since early in the century.[19] The need for reform was clear early in the war. Pensions, especially, remained inadequate. In 1940 responsibility for the welfare of older people was transferred from local PACs to the former UAB, now the Assistance Board, and means-tested supplementary pensions of up to 5s per week were introduced for impoverished pensioners. Applications soared to 1,275,000 in the first months, double the number anticipated. It was, commented *The Times* 'a remarkable discovery of secret need'.[20] A government survey in 1942 revealed the wretchedness of many pensioners, unable to afford medical care, adequate food or heating.[21]

The terms of reference of Beveridge's committee were vague. The civil service members were too busy to give it much attention. It became a one-man enterprise. Little was expected but Beveridge grasped the opportunity to promote some long-cherished ideas. He was determined to propose 'a comprehensive policy of social progress' to abolish 'want' (he rarely referred to 'poverty'). Its components were full employment, good education, adequate housing, a National Health Service and children's allowances to improve the health and life chances of children, plus improved social security benefits. As he wrote in his final report of November 1942:

> Social Insurance fully developed may provide income security; it is an attack upon Want. But Want is one only of five giants on the road of reconstruction and in some ways the easiest to attack. The others are Disease, Ignorance, Squalor and Idleness.[22]

The details of policies to attack the other four 'giants' were outside his brief, but he argued they were vital for the elimination of Want, by preventing it, whereas social insurance only provided for periods of crisis.

Beveridge's proposals embodied some of the enduring themes of his long career: dislike of means tests for their stigmatizing effects on recipients, the costs of assessment and inefficiency in relieving need since in all known systems substantial numbers of eligible people failed to apply due to fear of stigma, failure to recognize their eligibility or to negotiate the complexities of application. This remains true today. He was also anxious to avoid commercial bodies profiting from need, 'police supervision' of claimants and the 'Santa Claus state' encouraging dependency rather than independence. Always politically Liberal, he believed in the psychological value of contributory insurance for encouraging self-sufficiency and thrift and providing cash allowances as rights that had been paid for rather than hand-outs from the taxpayer. The report also expressed his commitment to voluntary action, encouraging the 'haves' to help the 'have-nots', building social cohesion across classes, co-operating with state welfare. He wanted the state to ensure that every need 'from the cradle to the grave' was covered to genuinely adequate subsistence level, but no more. Those desiring a higher standard of living when they could not work should save for it, preferably through non-profit institutions like friendly societies.

Universal old age and widows' pensions, unemployment, sickness, disability, maternity and other benefits would be funded by contributions (paid by employee, employer and the state), both flat rate, not income-related as in Germany and elsewhere in Europe. Beveridge, supported by the Treasury, rejected this because he did not believe the state should subsidize above-subsistence benefits. The whole employed population would be covered, in all classes, hopefully encouraging universal support for the system and social cohesion. He realized that some – just a few he expected – would fall through this 'safety net' because they could not work or contribute, including long-term disabled people and unmarried women who gave up work to care for ageing parents. He concluded, with regret, that they could not be fitted into contributory insurance and could only be helped by a means-tested public assistance scheme, an attenuated, he hoped very limited and less stigmatizing, version of Public Assistance.

Married women not employed outside the home also presented difficulties because they could not contribute yet needed pensions and other benefits. Beveridge believed they should receive these by right, funded by their husbands' contributions, as partners, not dependents, of their husbands, because they 'must be regarded as occupied on work, which is vital though unpaid, without which their husbands could not do their paid work and without which the nation could not continue'.[23] These views echoed those of Eleanor Rathbone, a friend of Beveridge and his feminist partner, soon to be wife, Jessie Mair, and many women's organizations.[24] He did not, as has been suggested, believe that married women *should* stay at home, subordinated to their husbands in a 'male breadwinner welfare state',[25] but, realistically, that many of them did so, given the difficulties of combining work inside and outside the home, the inadequacy of affordable childcare and the marriage bar which excluded married women from work in many occupations. This mostly died out during the war, but this was not yet evident in 1942. Beveridge feared, presciently, that if wives' benefits were funded directly by the state rather than by their husbands' contributions they would be undeservedly denigrated as dependents upon hard-working taxpayers.

Married women in paid work would contribute and receive benefits, both at lower rates than their husbands because, being normally better paid, he should bear the housing costs. Beveridge also proposed insurance benefits for divorced and separated wives, funded by their former husbands' contributions, funeral allowances, and universal, state-funded children's allowances. Old age pensions for the first time should be paid on condition of retirement, from age sixty-five for men, sixty for women, but with higher payments for each year worked beyond the minimum, to encourage older people to keep working, to combat the costs of the ageing society about which Beveridge was still much concerned. Experts and interest groups supported the proposals. Employers complained of the costs and of growing state power, though some recognized the potential gains to the economy of a more secure, healthy workforce. Keynes declared himself 'in a state of wild enthusiasm about the proposals', though concerned that the Treasury would resist the costs. He persuaded Beveridge to propose a gradual transition to full implementation over twenty years, to enable the insurance fund to grow and reduce the burden on the revenue. Allowances for the stigmatized groups of deserted and divorced wives met fierce resistance for 'subsidizing sin'.

Beveridge drafted the report with help from Jessie. He wrote in the introduction, 'A revolutionary moment in the world's history is a time for revolutions, not for patching'[26] and worked hard to publicize his attempted revolution in the press, on the BBC and in newsreels. The Conservative minister of information, Brendan Bracken, Churchill's ally, tried to delay publication because it was too socialistic. He then realized its morale-building potential but was restrained from promoting it too enthusiastically by Churchill and party colleagues, fearing it would raise excessive hopes and boost Labour's electoral chances. It sold 600,000 copies, unprecedented for an official document. It would be interesting to know how many people read the dense 299 pages. Within two weeks of publication a Gallup poll found nineteen out of twenty people had heard of it and 90 per cent, including in higher income groups, believed it should be implemented, though many feared it would not.[27] Churchill opposed issuing a summary to the armed forces but had to retreat. He and other leading Conservatives refused to commit to reconstruction plans until after the war, but Attlee welcomed it with backbenchers of all parties. Popular enthusiasm killed Conservative hopes that the report could be quietly shelved. In February 1943 backbenchers won the largest anti-government vote of the war for a commitment to implementation.[28]

Beveridge continued his publicity drive. He revealed and stimulated a widespread desire for state action to create an improved, more equal and just society. He was disappointed not to be involved in government planning to implement his proposals, especially the most ambitious, full employment, at least for men. He did not oppose women's employment but did not think it so essential or full female employment realistically attainable. Full male employment had never been achieved in peacetime, but he was convinced that greater equality and reduced 'Want' was impossible without it, that the free market had irretrievably broken down, while full employment had been achieved in wartime with a sizeable extension of state planning and control and no breakdown of democracy. He believed similar practices could continue after the war. To promote this ambition, in 1943 he formed a committee of young economists, mostly to his left. Their report, published in November 1944 as *Full Employment in a Free Society*, recommended state investment in key industries, especially transport and power; increased state spending on essential services, including roads, hospitals, schools and defence; state subsidies to housing, medical services, food and fuel; state regulation of private investment and consumer demand through control of interest rates, taxes and income distribution; planned location of industry and labour mobility, all managed by a Ministry of National Finance, relegating the Treasury to supervising departmental expenditure. It spurred the government to rush the publication of a *Full Employment* White Paper. This proposed greater management of the economy than before the war, but much less than Keynes or Beveridge envisaged, with little planning or close control.[29]

Women at work

The need for civilian labour was so great that in 1941 unmarried women aged 18–50 were conscripted to work in the armed services, teaching, nursing, or other essential occupations in the absence of men. A higher proportion of British women were mobilized than in the previous war or than in other belligerent countries except Russia, improving the living standards of many families. The female Land Army was relaunched to help maximize food production as in the last war. Married women without children under fourteen or other essential household (mainly caring) duties were required to register for war work and prosecuted if they failed to take work as directed.

More women were recruited to the services than in the Great War. The Auxiliary Territorial Service (ATS) was founded in 1938 and became the largest women's service, with 214,420 members by June 1943, working as cooks, waitresses, clerks, gaining skills including shorthand, switchboard operation, motor mechanics. The Women's Auxiliary Air Force (WAAF) and the Women's Royal Naval Reserve (WRNS) continued as non-combatant support units. Women were forbidden to use weapons in any service, no matter how vulnerable their situation. They went on guard duty bearing sticks, while male colleagues carried firearms.[30] 494,000 women were in the services by 1944.[31] There were 43,000 'Land Girls', plus 4,900 in the Timber Corps, cutting trees and managing forests.[32]

At the peak in 1943, *c.* 7,250,000 women were in civilian work, the services or civil defence, 46 per cent of all women aged 14–56. Female civil servants increased 1,214 per cent 1939–45, from 14 per cent to 54 per cent of all government workers. Insured women in industry increased by 128 per cent, the proportion from 28 per cent to 39 per cent. Women in commerce, banking, insurance and finance increased from 31 per cent to 63 per cent. A minority continued in these occupations after the war. Due to labour shortage, the marriage bar was lifted in most occupations and generally did not return after the war.[33] A total of 8,770,000 women were full-time 'housewives'. Married middle-class women were most likely to serve as volunteers, as the conscription laws allowed.

As labour became increasingly scarce, the Ministry of Labour in September 1941 held a conference of women to discover how to encourage more women into the workforce. They heard that married women, especially, were concerned about work conditions, hours and childcare. Limited improvements followed: reduction of women's daily working hours in industry to ten and encouragement of employers to provide part-time work and childcare.[34] In 1938 only about 10 per cent of under-fives in England, Wales and Scotland, generally the poorest, attended publicly funded day care.[35] From April 1941 the Ministry of Health established and funded nurseries and registered child-minders. Training courses were created for staff, opening further work opportunities to women. Nurseries opened and some employers provided day care.[36] Publicly funded, affordable childcare reached its highest level in UK history. Mothers of young children were not conscripted, but the absence of a male breadwinner and the small service allowances forced many into employment despite the difficulties. By April 1943 the labour shortage was so acute that women previously exempt because of domestic responsibilities were directed into part-time work, often in shops, where staff shortages added to queues and the stress of wartime life.

War work intensified the equal pay campaign. Feminism did not die in wartime but was invigorated by women's indispensable contribution to the war effort and their poor treatment. In September 1939 women's associations established the Women's Group on Public Welfare, chaired by Labour MP Margaret Bondfield, which informed people, especially women at home, of their rights to welfare, health and other services and pressed government and official bodies to extend those rights. They investigated the circumstances of children and mothers whose problems had been exposed by evacuation, and in 1943 published *Our Towns: A Close-Up* advocating, among other things, better housing, nursery schools for all children from age two and domestic training for schoolgirls, as part of women's long campaign to improve social conditions and opportunities.[37]

Early in the war Conservative MP Irene Ward formed the Woman Power Committee of women MPs to urge government to employ more women in skilled work. It criticized the Personal Injuries Act, 1939, which allowed unmarried male civilians 7s pw more in compensation (total 21s) for war-related injuries than unmarried woman, on the usual grounds that it was compensation for unequal pay. Mavis Tate, Conservative MP, and Labour's Edith Summerskill protested in the Commons that the cost of living was equal for men and women, demanding equal compensation. When this failed, they and leading women's associations organized rallies and deputations which in 1942 forced the government to establish a Select Committee which recommended equal compensation. In 1943 the government complied. Women established a very active Equal Pay Campaign Committee (EPCC) in January 1944 which continued after the war.[38]

Population and families

Marriages surged from 1938 to 1940 throughout the UK to the highest rates since official records began, surely driven by impending separation for war service. They fell in 1943–4, then rose again in 1945–8, as the men returned.[39] The early surge of marriages did not lead to an equivalent rise in births. Births declined early in the war, reaching the lowest recorded levels in England, Wales and Scotland in 1941. Then they rose, reaching 17.7 per 1,000 population in England and Wales, 18.5 in Scotland, 22.8 in Northern Ireland in 1944.[40] This was the beginning of a sustained rise – the 'baby-boom' – confounding pre-war projections of indefinite decline. During the war, the rise was attributed to wartime conditions; decline and population ageing were expected to return post-war.[41] In 1944 the government appointed a Royal Commission on Population to clarify what was changing and why and propose policy responses. It reported in 1949.

Again, births to unmarried women increased, from 4.2 per cent to 9.14 per cent of live births in England, 1939–45, in Wales, 3.7 per cent to 7.9 per cent, in Scotland, 6 per cent to 8.6 per cent, in Northern Ireland 4.7 per cent to 5.4 per cent.[42] From 1940 to 1945 almost 300,000 more 'illegitimate' children were born in England, Wales and Scotland than in the six years before the war.[43] As in the last war, this sparked moralizing about young women liberated from parental control, 'running wild', 'going out for a good time', especially with overseas, especially American, including Black, servicemen. Married women with husbands absent at war aroused suspicion too. But in this war statistics challenged the moralizers. From 1938, parents were obliged to record their date of marriage on birth certificates, and in 1939 the Registrar General published a *Statistical Review of England and Wales* which estimated, to great surprise and shock, that almost 30 per cent of first children born in 1938–9 were conceived out of wedlock, based on births within eight and a half months of the parents' marriage. Some births might have been premature, but the Registrar General believed these were balanced by parents who misrepresented their marriage date to hide premarital conception. Later *Statistical Reviews* showed that premarital pregnancies fell, 1939–45, from 60,346 to 38,176, while 'illegitimate' births rose from 26,569 to 64,743. It is unknown how many children were legitimatized by the parents' marriage when the father returned from war.

The wartime statistics showed that younger women were less prone to sexual irregularities leading to childbirth than their seniors. The number of premarital conceptions plus births to unmarried mothers among women under twenty in England

and Wales declined from 12.1 to 10.7 per 1,000 during 1939–43, returning to pre-war levels by 1945. Among those aged 25–30 they rose 26.6–46.5 in 1945, at ages 30–35, 15.8–33.2.[44] The Registrar General concluded that the wartime rise in unmarried motherhood

> is almost unquestionably to be found in the enforced degree of physical separation of the sexes imposed by the progressive recruitment of young males into the Armed Forces . . . rendering immediate marriage with their brides increasingly difficult- and in the case of many quite impossible . . . .
>
> . . . Taking the six war years as a whole the average increase of 6% in the total number of irregularly conceived births will hardly be regarded as inordinate, having regard to the wholesale disturbance to customary habits and living conditions in conjunction with the temporary accession to the population of large numbers of young and virile men in the Armed Forces of our Dominions and Allies'.[45]

It is unlikely there was significant change in sexual behaviour during the war, rather some behaviours, including premarital pregnancy, became more visible.

Clearer evidence emerged about the unmarried mothers and their experiences. The official historians of the wartime social services, Sheila Ferguson and Hilde Fitzgerald, reported:

> it would appear that the women who bore illegitimate children during the war belonged to all classes, types and age groups. Some were adolescent girls who had drifted away from homes which offered neither guidance nor warmth and security. Still others were married women with husbands on war service who were unable to bear the loneliness of separation. There were decent and serious, superficial and flighty, irresponsible and incorrigible girls among them. There were some who had formed serious attachments and had hoped to marry. There were others who had had a single lapse, often under the influence of drink. There were, too, the 'good time girls' who thrived on the presence of well-paid servicemen from overseas and the semi-prostitutes with little moral restraint. . . . Some of the unmarried mothers of the war were of a 'new type' and surprised the moral welfare workers to whom they were referred. Their spirit of independence was considerable and there was little of the sinner or penitent among them.[46]

Pregnant wives of husbands absent at war could be particularly desperate. They could not disguise the fact that their absent husband was not the father. They could not have the child adopted legally because any child born to a married woman was legally the child of her husband and his permission was required. The Forces' Welfare Services gave sympathetic help to husbands and wives and the NCUMC continued to help many women, assisted by government funding.[47] Unmarried mothers of 'coloured' children faced especial hostility and difficulty in finding lodgings and foster-care, while white British women who married Black Americans faced even greater discrimination in the

United States. Officially, the government opposed discrimination or singling out mixed-race children for support lest it encouraged discrimination, but without positive action it was hard to achieve equal treatment.[48]

Wartime conditions made life even harder for unmarried mothers who lacked family support or an adequate income. There were fewer foster-mothers, as women could find better-paid work, and fewer voluntary and local authority welfare workers, who were diverted to urgent war work.[49] The outcome was, as the founder of the NCUMC wrote, a 'fever of adoptions' by desperate women 'often arranged with the minimum of care and the maximum of irresponsibility'.[50] Babies were offered in newspaper advertisements, until legal regulation of adoption was tightened in 1943, though lurid press reports of sales of babies continued. In 1944 George Orwell and his wife adopted a baby straight from hospital, arranged by Orwell's sister-in-law, a doctor, though his wife was sick and died of cancer nine months later. The boy was brought up by Orwell's sister.[51]

Public sympathy for the mothers and children grew, alongside the opprobrium. In 1943 the bishop of Derby asked the government to take responsibility because local services could not cope, supported by letters to *The Times* from public figures.[52] The Ministry of Health urged local authorities to help but provided no funding and little changed. It gave minimal financial help to just thirty-six unmarried pregnant workers in essential industries. Pregnant servicewomen might receive advice from officers about social services and/or adoption before being dismissed without pay. Due to concern for the reputation of the armed services, amid excited press comment, the government appointed a committee to review sexual behaviour in the services chaired by Violet Markham, long active in voluntary and government work and support for women's rights.[53] In the First World War she was secretary to an official investigation into reports of immorality among the Women's Auxiliary Army Corps stationed in France, which concluded they had no foundation.[54] Her report in 1942 on 'Amenities and welfare conditions in the women's services' rejected the latest outcry equally firmly.[55] The Ministry of Health then funded pregnant servicewomen who could not return to their families to live in voluntary homes or government hostels before and after confinement, giving more generous support than to civilians, providing care and advice, including on future work and training. This was kept secret during the war. The birth rate among unmarried servicewomen was never revealed, and all records were destroyed after the war. For the first time, a government department was closely involved with helping unmarried mothers and their children, providing more than the bare necessities of food, shelter and maternity care. The wartime experience, in this as in other fields, contributed to the post-war reform of services whose inadequacy was exposed.

Conclusion

How far war conditions encouraged greater social cohesion, lessening inequalities, is uncertain, but there were some changes and hopes grew of more profound post-war transformation.[56] The war again improved the living standards of many people, raising their expectations for the future and, more than the last war, exposed to the government and many of the public unacceptable conditions, generating proposals for change which shaped politics and cultural change after the war.

CHAPTER 7
FACING THE FUTURE

The making of the 'Welfare State', 1945–51

Germany was defeated in April 1945, Japan surrendered in August following devastation by US atomic bombs. Britain's coalition government ended in May and Churchill formed a largely Conservative caretaker government, with no Labour members. Party politics resumed, preparing for the first general election for ten years. Labour campaigned on a programme of social and economic reconstruction and no return to pre-war depression: *Let Us Face the Future*, its manifesto urged.

Labour gained because many voters who admired Churchill as wartime leader doubted his peacetime capabilities. Also, from its commitment to wartime proposals for social and economic reform, especially from Beveridge, amid the widespread desire not to return to pre-war conditions, while Churchill equivocated. Labour Party individual membership climbed after publication of the Beveridge report to a record 487,047 in 1945.[1] Labour ministers, including Attlee, performed well in highly visible domestic roles. Labour fought a well-organized campaign. There was little sign of the 'consensus' on social and economic policies between the major parties some historians have perceived, though they disagreed less profoundly than in later decades.[2] The Conservatives, consistent with their past and future inclinations, to varying degrees supported free enterprise, decontrol, reduced state action and lower taxation, without which, claimed their manifesto, full employment was unsustainable. The manifesto *Mr Churchill's Declaration of Policy to the Electors* was, as the title implied, Churchill's personal statement, hurriedly drafted, stressing the national victory, and attacking the 'socialism' of his former coalition partners. This, he claimed in a radio broadcast, 'is abhorrent to the British ideas of freedom. . . . There is to be one State to which all are to be obedient in every act of their lives. . . . I declare to you from the bottom of my heart, that no Socialist system can be established without a political police. . . . They will have to fall back on some form of Gestapo'.[3]

This equation of Labour with Nazism shocked many voters. Labour gained further support by responding calmly. Their manifesto stated, 'The Labour Party is a Socialist Party and proud of it,' in moderate terms, seeking to appeal to the middle ground and middle-class voters. It was drafted mainly by Michael Young, head of the party's research department 1945–51, later a prominent civil society innovator.[4] He was another former Toynbee Hall resident and wartime director of PEP. The manifesto stressed that, after 1918, 'the people lost that peace' to the 'hard-faced men who did well out of the war', as Stanley Baldwin is believed to have claimed at the time, his family business having been among the beneficiaries.[5] This time, Labour ministers had taken 'the profit out of war' with the 100 per cent profits tax, and continued controls would ensure 'Peace for the People'. Central to Labour's programme was economic planning and 'Jobs for All' at fair wages, achieved by increased production, especially in export industries, controlled location of industry, encouragement of science and technology to assist competitiveness as it had helped win the war, regulation of banking, nationalization of the Bank of England, of fuel and power (including mining), transport (including railways) and iron and steel, with 'fair compensation' to owners. Labour did not oppose a liberal market economy but aimed to control and reform it, practising a modified Keynesianism. A National Investment Board would direct its development and modernization using public funds where necessary. There would be controlled development of agriculture and supervision of monopolies and cartels, complemented by reformed social services, including a National Health Service providing excellent healthcare for all, family allowances, universal comprehensive social insurance, a vigorous housing and planning programme, rent and price controls, implementation of the 1944 Education Act and 'taxation which bears less heavily on lower income groups' .

Economic reconstruction would take priority. Labour had argued since its foundation that the best route to 'welfare' for most people was work with decent pay, with social assistance when they could not work for good reasons including age, sickness, unemployment.[6] The term 'Welfare State' appeared nowhere in the manifesto, nor in Beveridge's publications or statements, despite his subsequent popular association with the term. He, with Michael Young, disliked what they believed was its implied dependency of individuals on the state.[7] Young wrote in a later report to the Labour Party:

> 'The very name . . . is against it. It must have been invented by a diabolical copywriter who knew that if the nation was not poisoned by the first cold word [welfare], recalling the smell of carbolic acid and the tough brown paper of ration books, it could be done to death by the second cold word [state] suggesting the Law Court, the Sanitary Inspector and the Recruiting Officer'.[8]

Beveridge preferred the term 'social service state', implying the mutual responsibilities of citizens and the state to promote general social improvement rather than dependence, a popular term between the wars.[9] Associated though it is with the post-1945 Labour government, 'Welfare State' did not come into common use until the 1950s, initially as a term of right-wing Conservative abuse of measures which they claimed, as Beveridge and Young feared, created dependence.[10]

Labour in power

For the first time, Labour won a large majority in the July 1945 election, and an unprecedented number of middle-class votes. It went on to fulfil many of its election promises, but the costs of war and the high costs of continuing defence commitments, among other obligations, prevented full implementation. The British and US governments were committed to rebuilding the German economy to avoid the crises caused by its weakness following the last war and British occupation of part of north-west Germany until 1949 was costly.

About 20 per cent of the UK economy became publicly owned, against less parliamentary opposition than some Conservatives later cared to remember. Churchill said that nationalization of the Bank of England in 1946 did not raise any issue of principle. There was little opposition to nationalization of the coal industry, which was vital but notoriously inefficient, nor of the unprofitable but indispensable railways and canals, all in 1947. The inclusion of profitable road haulage was controversial. The nationalization of cable and wireless companies in 1947, the establishment of public corporations to run British European Airways (BEA) and the British Overseas Airways Corporation (BOAC) in 1946, the formation of the British Electricity Authority in 1948 and the Gas Council in 1949 to manage these essential public utilities, took existing controls further. Nationalization substantially improved performance. It proved harder to regulate and improve the private sector. Harold Wilson, the young president of the Board of Trade from 1947, tried unsuccessfully to persuade colleagues to appoint government directors to the boards of private companies, to increase controls, and nationalize uncooperative, inefficient companies.

Rationing and price controls continued, to restrain consumption, maximize exports and real earnings and improve the balance of trade. Income tax was more steeply graduated, and the threshold raised, exempting most manual workers. Budgets in October 1945 and April 1946 increased surtax on incomes above £10,000 and death duties on larger estates, to 75 per cent on those worth over £21,500, raised to 80 per cent in 1950. Consumption was further restrained by increasing purchase tax, with punitive rates on luxuries like champagne, while wartime utility goods, including clothing and furniture, continued and were exempt. The standard rate of tax fell from 50 per cent to 45 per cent, while personal allowances and earned income relief increased. Average working-class wages after tax rose in real terms by 21 per cent, 1938–49, while salaries fell by 16 per cent causing some middle-class disenchantment with Labour, despite their gains from the health, social security and education reforms their additional taxes helped to fund.[11] By 1947/1948 income tax was payable by 14.5 million people compared with 6 million in 1937/1938, largely due to full employment and increased population. A total of 6.5 million lower earners, mainly manual workers, still paid no direct tax.[12] Interest rates remained low to encourage borrowing for investment.[13] From 1938 to 1951 total personal wealth of the top 0.1 per cent in Great Britain fell from 27 per cent to 18 per cent, that of the top 5 per cent from 78 per cent to 68 per cent, still substantial inequalities but narrowed by change during and since the war.[14]

Labour tried hard to modernize and increase the efficiency of British industry, raise management standards and increase the participation of workers in decision-making, with limited effects. Businesses were reluctant to change while they experienced buoyant overseas demand including for products to aid post-war reconstruction. The unions accepted wage restraint in return for price controls, to achieve full employment. Labour repealed the 1927 Trade Disputes Act, removing the restrictions on general strikes and public sector unions and on party membership which increased by 25 per cent. Union membership grew to almost 10 million by the early 1950s.[15]

Managing the economy became even harder when the US government, led by Harry S. Truman, suddenly cancelled the US/UK wartime 'lend-lease' agreement when the war with Japan ended, instead of the staged termination expected, increasing costs of imports from the United States. To cover the costs, in 1946 Keynes negotiated a large dollar loan from the United States and Canada on stringent terms. Bread was rationed for the first time, to limit US wheat imports. The *Daily Mail* called it 'the most hated measure ever to have been presented to the people of this country',[16] though the restrictions were moderate, had little effect on consumption and ended in 1948.[17] The loan assisted the government, but the pound sank following the worst winter of the century so far, with a prolonged freeze during January–March 1947 followed by severe flooding. Potatoes were rationed for the first time because the weather ruined the crop. Energy supplies could not cope, and manufacturing, transport and trade were severely disrupted when electricity was cut off. Restoring the balance of trade became even more urgent, leading to further increases in taxation, reduced clothes rations, and suspension of foreign currency for pleasure travel. Food imports from dollar economies were cut further, including meat.[18] Nevertheless nutritionists pointed to reduced malnutrition since the 1930s and much improved health especially among poorer children. The rationed diet was certainly monotonous, but that of poorer people always had been. It was more nutritious, and full employment enabled more people to eat better.

Defence costs in 1947 took almost 18 per cent of GNP. This was controversial in the Labour Party, and some (including Keynes before his death in 1946) accused the government of seeking to maintain an unsustainable 'great power' role. Attlee agreed that the costs were excessive (Bevin did not), and they fell gradually until the outbreak of the Korean War in 1950, though maintained at quite a high level following the decision of Attlee and Bevin in 1948 to begin construction of a British atom bomb as a defence measure in the emerging Cold War, though it was kept secret. Also, Britain could not withdraw from commitments in the Middle East and Commonwealth.

The Cold War led the United States in 1948 to seek to strengthen Western Europe against Communism with funds, described as Marshall Aid after their initiator, US general George Marshall. Aid was granted to European countries with credible economic recovery plans. Britain received the largest share, around $2,700,000 to the end of 1950, when it needed no further assistance. This helped the economy stabilize, and in February 1948 Harold Wilson announced a 'bonfire of controls', removing some restrictions on industrial production, supply of items including perambulators, toys, cutlery, linoleum, cosmetics and relaxing others. But derationing could increase demand uncontrollably, that of sweets and chocolate in April 1949 by so much that they vanished into a flourishing black market and rationing was reintroduced. Clothes were derationed in May 1949. Women could now experiment with fashion, including the 'New Look', with long, swirling skirts, rejecting wartime constraints and uniformity, launched in Paris in 1947. Paris fashion was expensive, but women made copies, despite humourless disapproval: 'the ridiculous whim of idle people', sniffed Liverpool Labour MP Bessie Braddock.[19] Petrol rationing ended in 1950, having been progressively relaxed amid protests by motorists.

Creating a 'Welfare State'

Labour was committed to expanding and improving social services, but its prioritization of economic reconstruction, plus relentless Treasury pressure to cut costs, constrained reforms. Far from recklessly diverting funds from economic development, as some have suggested,[20] 'the "welfare state" of the 1940s was an austerity product of an age of austerity', organized to assist economic expansion.[21] An early indicator came in 1946 when Labour implemented family allowances under an act passed by parliament in 1945, at 5s per week, not 8s as Beveridge believed necessary to dispel family poverty.

Education

The 1944 Education Act was implemented quickly by Ellen Wilkinson, minister of education, the only woman in the Cabinet. Improved education was still judged essential for economic growth. Selection by examination was introduced at age eleven for 'grammar schools' for children judged academically able, technical schools for those with technical or scientific aptitude, or 'secondary modern' schools for the rest. Labour no longer promoted 'multilateral'/comprehensive schools, now believing that '11+' selection would promote equality of opportunity as all state secondary schools became free, though local authorities retained their independence in education policy and some continued to run and establish multilaterals. Independent schools were not abolished as some hoped. More teachers were trained, including many ex-service personnel who received special funding; 10,000 teachers were in training in 1937/1938, 21,000 in 1949/1950.[22] The school-leaving age rose to fifteen in 1947. There were more state scholarships to universities and increased university funding, especially for science and technology to assist economic development. But there was little school building unless enforced by war damage and few of the promised technical schools materialized. They required costly buildings, equipment and teachers with skills needed for the urgent task of modernizing the economy. Not until 1950 did education spending exceed pre-war levels, by only 4 per cent. Most wartime nursery schools closed, and new ones opened only 'where exporting industries need the services of working mothers'. Publicly funded childcare was again limited.

More children received more and better education, continuing pre-war trends, but working-class pupils overwhelmingly left secondary modern schools (which educated almost two-thirds of secondary pupils) at fifteen without qualifications and the selective grammar schools for the 'academically able' were disproportionately male and middle class. There were fewer grammar school places for girls, since most of these schools had been built for boys, most remained single sex and no new schools were built: girls had to achieve higher grades in the 11+ exam in most districts to gain a place. This went largely unnoticed at a time when girls were still expected to aspire to marriage rather than education and careers and most left school at fifteen.

Housing

Housing was a major issue for voters in 1945, and Labour's promised housing drive was more convincing than Churchill's vague statements. The Town and Country Planning Act, 1947, built on wartime proposals, making all new development subject to planning permission and allowing local authorities to plan 'green belts' around towns to check sprawl, as already introduced around London. The New Towns Act, 1946, inaugurated a succession of New Towns, publicly financed to encourage construction of factories and housing away from conurbations and develop declining areas. Stevenage (Essex) was designated first in 1946. Twelve followed by 1950, six in southern counties to take London overspill, two in Scotland, two in North-East England and Cwmbran in South Wales, while Corby (Northants) became a major steel-producing centre. Each was controlled by a government-appointed Development Corporation, which purchased land compulsorily, antagonizing many farmers and landowners. They were briefed to attract businesses and build low-density housing mainly for affordable renting. New Towns were intended to be socially mixed, self-sufficient communities, mainly providing work and good homes at reasonable rents for working-class people.

Nationally, private housebuilding was limited to 20 per cent of the total. Labour's priority was resolving the working-class housing crisis. Rents were frozen at 1939 levels. But only in 1948 did Labour meet its target of 240,000 new homes each year. In the crisis year, 1947, only 189,000 were completed. A total of 1,192,000 had been built by 1951, 189,000 for owner-occupation. The shortage was estimated at up to two million, and housing was again a major issue in the elections of 1950 and 1951. Numbers were held back partly by the insistence of the minister, Aneurin Bevan, that council houses met high standards: well-built, cottage style, with adequate space, indoor toilets, bathrooms and gardens, which raised costs. Also, the Treasury imposed strict spending controls and Labour prioritized building directly related to economic development, including factories and housing for essential workers, especially in export industries. Hence the failure to build schools and hospitals and constraints on the rebuilding of towns devastated by severe bombing. Reconstruction began but plans were scaled back, and rebuilding was more conventional than planners hoped.[23] Still, in 1951 in England and Wales, 1.8 million households shared a dwelling compared with 1.9 million in 1931; 37 per cent lacked access to a fixed bath, 8 per cent shared with another household; 8 per cent lacked a WC, 13 per cent shared.[24]

Health

Bevan's, arguably Labour's, greatest achievement was the National Health Service (NHS). Bevan lacked experience of health administration but, growing up in South Wales, he had experienced ill-health and poor services in working-class communities. The NHS became law in 1946 and was implemented in 1948. It reorganized and improved coordination of existing services, nationalizing the voluntary hospitals and dental, optical and other ancillary services. All services became 'free at the point of delivery' for everyone, following long, often fraught, negotiations with the BMA. Bevan overcame the resistance of many senior consultants by 'stuffing their mouths with gold', as he put it, responding to their hostility to a salaried public service by agreeing to payment by fees based on numbers of patients and allowing continued lucrative private practice within NHS hospitals. Younger doctors were generally more supportive. There was also opposition in the Cabinet, including from Herbert Morrison who as leader of the LCC had headed a successful public health programme, to the centralized structure which reduced the health powers of local government. Bevan wanted a national service ideally providing equal standards of care across the UK, as local services had not.[25]

The NHS transformed the lives of many people, especially working-class women who previously had little access to good medical care, providing universal free access to hospitals and GPs. Free access to optical care and spectacles, dentistry and chiropody was transformative, especially for many older people. One doctor described a woman who was bed-ridden, apparently deaf and thought to be suffering from mild dementia. Once her corns were treated under the NHS, impacted wax removed from her ears and her severe constipation cured, she was active again.[26] It was no longer common for working-class people to have all their teeth extracted as twenty-first birthday presents to prevent future agony. Fewer people needed false teeth. Need for such services was underestimated, and costs rose faster than anticipated. Despite impressive improvements in staffing and treatment, no new hospitals were built until the late 1950s, though repairs and reconstruction were unavoidable. The stigmatized area of mental healthcare lagged behind services for physical health, though 50 per cent of NHS beds in 1948 were occupied by mentally ill people.

National insurance

The National Insurance Act, 1946, transformed the social security system based, broadly, on Beveridge's recommendations. National insurance was universalized to cover the whole employed population and wives of insured men, providing flat-rate old age and widows' pensions, maternity and funeral benefits. Sickness and unemployment allowances were provided for those normally in paid work, plus payments for wives and children. Payments were funded by flat-rate contributions from workers and employers, subsidized by taxation. Labour, like Beveridge, stressed that benefits were a right, purchased through contributions, not 'handouts' from the state, but they were lower than Beveridge proposed. He recommended their introduction gradually over twenty years, to build up a sufficient fund to cover full subsistence-level payments and payment of unemployment and sickness allowances for the whole period of need. Labour was anxious to deliver speedy improvements to voters. Higher pensions were paid immediately to mainly working-class contributors to the existing national insurance scheme and their wives. New, generally better-off, entrants to the insurance system had to build up contributions for ten years.

'Approved Societies' were removed from the administration, for which they had been much criticized between the wars, and it was taken over by the state.

Unemployment benefits rose by 2s per week, sickness benefits by 8s, pensions by 16s, but, on Treasury insistence, to cut costs they did not provide full subsistence.[27]In 1948, 495,000 pensioners needed means-tested supplements to their pensions to survive, by 1951, 767,000, as Beveridge had never intended.[28] For the first time the pension was conditional on retirement. Beveridge's proposal to pay higher pensions for each year of deferred retirement, to encourage longer working lives, was implemented minimally, with additional payments too small to encourage continued work. A proposal by James Griffiths, minister for national insurance, to link payments to an index of prices or wages was rejected by the Treasury. Sickness and unemployment payments were restricted to fixed time periods; then those still in need had to apply for means-tested benefits. To encourage safe births, the maternity grant was raised from £4 to £12.10s and 14 weeks' maternity benefit of 36s per week was payable to all mothers including, for the first time, unmarried mothers.

Means-tested supplementary benefits were paid by the National Assistance Board (NAB), under the National Assistance Act, 1948. This at last formally abolished the Poor Law, replacing Public Assistance with a theoretically less stigmatizing, somewhat more generous, 'safety-net' for those whose insurance payments were inadequate or they could not fit into national insurance because they had not worked. These included single mothers who were now, minimally, supported at home, and not required to seek work while they had children at school. They and others on NAB benefits could receive additional payments, e.g., for clothing or household equipment, when needed. Such support was basic but better than before, though unmarried mothers still faced much shame and stigma.[29]

Post-war social insurance covered more people with higher benefits than before, but these soon slipped behind levels in other West European countries. The system was rigid, regressive, since flat-rate contributions took more from the incomes of the lower than the higher-paid, and only partially redistributive due to taxpayer contributions. Beveridge was deeply disappointed and critical of the outcome and unhappy that he was not involved in the development or administration of the policies.[30]

Social services

Local authority social services expanded. A furore over the death in January 1945, due to neglect and cruelty, of a twelve-year-old boy, Dennis O'Neill, placed in foster-care by a Welsh local authority, influenced the 1946 report of the Curtis Committee on the Care of Children. This revealed the inadequacy of childcare arrangements, awkwardly divided between local authorities and the voluntary sector, unevenly across the country. The Children Act, 1948, radically restructured children's services, bringing all childcare under local authority control. Authorities were obliged, and funded, to take into care all orphans and children under seventeen whose parents were judged unfit to care for them, and to supervise adoption procedures, prohibiting informal adoption. They were required to supervise children in foster-care and support them to age seventeen, through the transition to work.[31] Also in 1948, corporal punishment was abolished in the criminal justice system.

Local authorities were required to support unmarried mothers and their children, assisting them to stay together when possible. Many mothers lived with and were supported by their parents, as before the war, but many others lacked such support, still faced discrimination, difficulty renting a home and getting by, often forced into adoption as a result. Unmarried women giving birth in certain nursing homes, especially those run by religious bodies, continued, as they long had, to have their children removed for forced adoption. NCUMC still worked hard to help them avoid this.[32] Councils could fund voluntary organizations (including NCUMC) for this and other care work, including for older and disabled people, and supervised them. Again, there was no new building and people needing institutional care, whom authorities were obliged to shelter, were housed in former workhouses, the only available buildings, if there were no places in voluntary institutions. Residential and domiciliary social care, provided by voluntary organizations or local authorities required means-tested payments, unlike free healthcare, creating confusion, especially for older and disabled people for whom the dividing line between 'health' and 'social' needs was often unclear, a problem still unresolved in the twenty-first century.

Voluntary action

Voluntary organizations remained vital providers of social services. They faltered initially, uncertain of their roles as state welfare expanded and, partly as a result, donations declined.[33] Many Labour supporters were hostile to 'charity' which they thought 'patronizing' and 'demeaning', but Attlee, given his experience of voluntary work, was not. He and his colleagues realized that public funds could not meet all needs in current economic circumstances, and they encouraged collaboration between statutory and voluntary services especially at local level.[34] In 1948 Beveridge published another book, *Voluntary Action*, strongly supporting it, as he always had, and advocating state support and funding. The National Council for Social Services (NCSS) continued to coordinate the activities of voluntary organizations and to liaise between them and the state, believing strongly in the benefit to society of close collaboration between them.[35] Existing voluntary organizations found new roles, including advising clients on negotiating new statutory services. Citizens' Advice Bureaux (CABx), established just before the war to do just that, became even more active, supported by NCSS. During and after the war they received funding from local and central government and their numbers grew. The WVS unexpectedly continued after the war with government support, though many of its wartime volunteers resigned. Lady Reading was determined that it should continue, convinced it had a peacetime role.[36] It carried on its wartime activities, including settling European refugees in Britain and helping in emergencies, including the 1947 floods. It provided volunteers to support the NHS in hospitals and increasingly worked with local authorities as their services expanded, including recruiting and training 'home helps' to support older and disabled people and others in need with domestic work and delivering low-cost 'meals on wheels'.[37] This collaboration long continued.

Meanwhile new organizations emerged as gaps appeared in the welfare system.[38] Among others, the National Association for Mental Health (now MIND) formed in 1946 to campaign for improved services for mentally ill people, and new organizations supported the needs of older people.[39] In 1946 the COS was renamed the Family Welfare Association. It no longer assumed that poverty was the fault of the poor, but provided social work support to families, including advising them on access to necessary services.

Legal aid

An important new service, legal aid, was designed to assist poorer people to access the law. The Legal Aid and Advice Act, 1949, was introduced for this purpose, but it was introduced slowly to limit costs.[40] Aid, means-tested (by the NAB), to finance use of the high courts, including for divorce, was introduced in October 1950, but not until the 1960s was it available for representation in magistrates' courts, including for childcare proceedings. Legal advice was not state-funded until 1959 and then was limited. Free voluntary legal advice centres had been established since the 1890s, including by settlement houses such as Toynbee Hall. They often worked closely with CABx which could not themselves give legal advice but referred clients to the centres. The Local Government Act, 1948, empowered local authorities to provide information services to increase public awareness of public and voluntary services, including legal services, through their own offices or co-operation with voluntary organizations. Some local authorities established their own legal advice centres.[41]

Disability

Labour implemented another wartime measure, the Disabled Persons' Employment Act, 1944. Disabled adults had been neglected by the state, apart from small payments to contributors to National Health Insurance and a means-tested pension provided in 1920 for blind people from age 50. The 1944 Act arose from Bevin's attempts to maximize the workforce by including people disabled in the war, beginning in 1941 with retraining schemes. The act required employers of more than twenty workers to take, at normal pay, at least 3 per cent of their workers from a new, voluntary, Disabled Persons Register for those fit to work as effectively as non-disabled people, not in treatment under the Mental Health Act, or 'of habitual bad character'. Employers did not comply enthusiastically, and it was not rigorously enforced. After the war, Labour established rehabilitation centres and vocational training for disabled people, overwhelmingly male, and workshops for those unfit for regular work. From 1946, state subsidized 'Remploy' factories employed only disabled people, producing a variety of goods, some continuing until privatization in 2013. The needs of people too disabled to work were met, in limited ways, by the NHS, social services and the NAB. The changes were presented as equalizing opportunities and protecting disabled people from stigma. They greatly helped a minority of moderately disabled people but did little to improve opportunities for others.[42]

Outcomes

For all their limitations, Labour's social policies provided greater security for most people, at last a 'national minimum', a real if inadequate 'safety net' preventing the poorest falling too far behind the rising living standards of the majority. Poverty declined but was not eliminated, though systematic studies of poverty almost ceased between the 1930s and 1950s and the extent of decline is uncertain. The most severe destitution was certainly reduced. The reforms were only minimally redistributive and greatly benefitted many middle-class people, especially the lower middle classes on limited incomes who could not easily afford private education, healthcare or other benefits. The middle classes used health services more than poorer people, who were less accustomed to easy access to healthcare and took time to adjust. Middle-class children stayed in education longer. This was not an unintended consequence of universalism but conscious Labour strategy to win better-off voters while improving conditions for poorer people, recognizing that taxpayers would more willingly fund services benefitting themselves than supporting only the poorest. Labour hoped to remain in government long enough to expand social welfare as the economy recovered, as the Swedish Social Democrats constructed a comprehensive Welfare State during their long rule from 1931–76. Labour's social policies of 1945–51 were intended as a beginning not an end.

Full employment

National 'welfare' gained most from the achievement of full employment, certainly fuller employment for longer than at any time in modern British history. Unemployment hardly rose above 500,000 before 1951, mostly due to normal turnover, except in the crisis of 1947 when it reached 1,916,000 at the height of the freeze in February.[43] Beveridge defined full employment as allowing for 3 per cent 'frictional' unemployment due to turnover.[44] Full employment drew attention to productivity, which was lower than in competing economies, creating pressure to work more intensively which workers did not always welcome.[45] Pockets of above-average unemployment survived, particularly on Merseyside and Clydeside, along with labour shortages in some areas and occupations. Elsewhere, with work more readily available, workers fled poor conditions in dangerous industries, including mining. Given its importance, the government tried to attract workers by reducing the standard working week from six days to five and sanctioning house building in mining districts. Miners' meat ration was doubled in 1946.[46] Married women who were the traditional backbone of cotton textile production needed earnings less urgently when their husbands had regular work, and many left the industry. The labour market shrank further when the school-leaving age rose, and national service was introduced in 1947. Eighteen-year-old males were conscripted into the armed services in peacetime – unprecedented in British history – for eighteen months, extended to two years in 1950, continuing until 1961, to maintain the size of the British army and its capacity to respond to crises at minimum cost, including militant colonial independence movements in Malaya and Cyprus.[47] Many workers fled austerity and cold, particularly to Australia, encouraged by the Australian government's 'Ten Pound Poms' scheme: from 1947 ex-servicemen migrated free, other British adults for £10, children £5. A total of 175,138 UK citizens settled in Australia during 1945–50, considerably more than in any other country. Australia encouraged migration in order to remain 'white', preferably of 'British stock', and it was concerned about its low birth rate.[48]

The Ministry of Labour tried to encourage older workers to delay retirement and employers to keep them on, with little success. Few employers were persuaded that older workers were efficient and capable of learning new skills, despite growing evidence to the contrary. Research in the later 1940s and early 1950s by social scientists demonstrated that men (women were rarely studied) in their sixties and beyond were capable of learning new skills, despite the widespread myth to the contrary, had significant experience to contribute and were often more reliable than younger workers.[49]

Women's work

When Beveridge, Keynes and politicians discussed 'full employment' they meant male employment. They did not necessarily oppose women working but did not think it realistic to expect most women to work full-time all their adult lives. During the war, the government forecast a post-war labour shortage and planned to keep as many women at work as possible.[50] Many younger women gave up work after the war to start families, which the government encouraged, hoping to maintain the 'baby boom'. Psychologists argued that care of children other than by the mother was damaging, potentially causing 'juvenile delinquency'. Childcare experts challenged this, but mothers of young children experienced strong social pressure against taking employment and affordable childcare was scarce.

The Ministry of Labour encouraged older women to remain in or return to employment and many did, though rarely in conventionally male work. A strict gender division of labour revived. The expansion of social, health and education services created work judged suitable for women. The abolition of the marriage bar in most occupations – it survived in banking until the 1960s and the diplomatic service until 1973 – increased opportunities. The social prohibition against middle-class married women's employment declined, while more working-class women chose to stay home, at least while their children were small, as male employment and family incomes improved, relieved to escape the double burden of work in and out of the home. A new, cross-class, pattern emerged of women employed until the birth of their first child, taking a break for child-rearing, returning later, often part-time.[51] This was easier to combine with domestic responsibilities and suited employers who were not required to give part-timers paid holidays or other benefits. Employed women increased by 300,000 each year 1947–50, 11.5 per cent worked part-time in 1951, mostly 'returners' aged over forty.[52]

Equal pay remained rare despite continuous women's campaigns. The Royal Commission on Equal Pay reported in 1946. Following a thorough analysis of conditions across Britain it made a strong argument for 'equal pay for work of equal value' but concluded that speedy implementation could harm the economy. Three of the four female members of the Commission disagreed and recommended mandatory equal pay. Labour was supposedly committed to this by a vote of its annual conference but, repeatedly until 1951, spokesmen stated they supported the principle but, until the economy strengthened, implementation would delay recovery. Women continued to campaign.

Immigration

The labour shortage forced employers, including the government, to look abroad for workers. The first resort was always Ireland, which had long provided substantial numbers of immigrant workers. Women were especially encouraged to migrate for work as nurses, other hospital workers and teachers. A total of 50,000–60,000 Irish women and men entered Britain to work each year from 1946, but they could not fill all the vacancies.[53] The next option was continental Europe. About 120,000 Polish ex-servicemen stayed and worked in Britain after the war, and some Italian former prisoners of war.[54] Over 6 million people were homeless refugees in Europe, forced from their homes by the Nazis, living in camps for 'Displaced Persons'. Offering them employment reduced the costs for the government of supporting them in camps and, since they were not British nationals, the Ministry of Labour could control where they lived and worked. They often came to Britain reluctantly, feeling they had no option, hoping to return to their home countries. By 1949 many had done so or settled elsewhere, and the supply ended, though many settled permanently.[55] A total of 57,000 men and 20,000 women had worked in Britain, about 40 per cent of the women in domestic work in public institutions, 50 per cent in textile factories, the men around 50 per cent in agriculture, 20 per cent in mining. The largest group were Ukrainian.[56]

The last resort was the Commonwealth. West Indians were eager to migrate because of high unemployment at home, often having served in the UK armed services during the war, famously including the arrivals on HMS *Windrush* in 1948 – 492 men and 2 women from Jamaica. The Ministry of Labour was reluctant to recruit them due, they said, to the costs of transportation and doubts about their 'suitability'. They were particularly concerned that, as British citizens with rights equal to those of all native-born British people like everyone born in the Commonwealth at this time (a long-established right reinforced by the British Nationality Act, 1948), West Indians could not be controlled as the Europeans were, though nor could they be prevented from settling in Britain. Officials also expressed concern about stimulating racism, which was realistic, though it lurked in their own assumptions. The continuing labour shortage drove the Ministry of Labour to recruit West Indians, first, in 1950, women from Barbados to work as hospital domestics, then men to staff public transport. The NHS has always depended upon immigrant labour and expertise at all levels. About 1,000 men and women arrived from the Caribbean in 1951 and worked in a wide variety of occupations, mostly of low status and pay, whatever their qualifications. They supplied essential labour but often had difficulty finding accommodation and experienced racism at work and elsewhere.[57]

The family and population

Despite fears, the birth rate continued to rise. This was not due to many women having more children, average family size remained about two. Rather, a higher proportion of people now married and had at least one child. The reasons are uncertain, but after the war there was a more even gender balance due to rising male life expectancy and fewer men emigrating alone. Also, full employment and higher incomes may have encouraged more men to marry and perhaps influenced an unprecedented decline in the marriage age. Ages at first marriage fell to historically low levels from a norm over the previous 300 years of 27 for men, 25 for women to 22.6 for women, 24.6 for men in 1971.[58] Marriages lasted longer because they started earlier, average life expectancy lengthened and divorce remained difficult, though divorces and separations increased.[59] Infant deaths were low. In 1951, 14 per cent of all births within marriage were premaritally conceived, according to official statistics, more than before the war, suggesting that post-war Britain was less sexually repressed than sometimes suggested.[60] Births registered as 'illegitimate' in England and Wales fell from 6.6 per cent in 1946 to 4.8 per cent in 1951.[61]

But pessimism about the birth rate continued. The influence of eugenics had not gone away, including from the Royal Commission on Population, which reported in 1949. It warned of the risk that 'a disproportionately small number of the nation's children come from the higher income groups' creating a 'tendency towards lowering the average level of intelligence of the nation'.[62] A situation, they believed, potentially exacerbated by the recruitment of immigrant labour, for:

> the sources of supply of suitable immigrants to Great Britain are limited, as is also the capacity of a fully established society like ours to absorb immigrants of alien race and religion.[63]

It recommended higher family allowances and improved social services to encourage more births and help women combine childcare with the greater freedom and independence they aspired to, which the commissioners believed had driven the pre-war birth decline. Nothing changed.

General Election 1950

An election was unavoidable in 1950. Labour stood on its record, making few new promises. Its leaders were ageing and weary, and there were few younger people in prominent roles. The party manifesto, *Labour Believes in Britain*, was largely drafted by Morrison, promising nationalization of sugar, cement and water supply. A swing against Labour was expected. Continued rationing, controls and high taxes alienated many, though not all, middle-class voters. The Conservatives encouraged anti-austerity sentiment, though they too ran a low-key campaign promising no dramatic changes, not even ending rationing. Labour was well organized and still growing in membership. Its vote rose to 13.26m, but it held only 315 seats; the Conservatives gained 12.5 million votes and 298 seats, giving Labour an overall majority of five.[64] The turnout was 84 per cent, the highest of the century, suggesting that electors were engaged and evenly divided. Labour held its working-class vote, among women more firmly than men, while losing middle-class voters, male and female.[65] The overall swing from Labour was 3.3 per cent, in Wales only 0.3 per cent and in parts of rural England under 1 per cent.

Labour continued to govern, in a weak position, though the economy looked strong, with budget and balance of payments surpluses. Exports rose in value though imports rose faster. Britain's share of world trade grew.[66] But the Korean War from June 1950 increased defence costs. In October 1950 the fatally ill Stafford Cripps was replaced as chancellor by 44-year-old Hugh Gaitskell, bringing some younger blood into the Cabinet. A strong egalitarian, in his first budget in 1951 he raised the standard rate of tax to 9s.6d in £; the top rate was now 97.5 per cent. But he caused a crisis by introducing charges for false teeth and spectacles supplied through the NHS. Bevan – already opposed to Britain's development of nuclear arms and increased defence spending – resigned, with two junior ministers, Harold Wilson, future prime minister, and John Freeman, future TV personality. Attlee was in hospital; Bevin had just died. The generation of wartime Labour ministers was fading, literally dying out.[67] Labour, with its tiny majority, could not risk new or contentious policies. Nationalization of iron and steel was implemented as arranged before the election. Rationing and controls were gradually reduced while prices rose.

Election 1951

Attlee called another election in October 1951, hoping for a larger majority. Labour stood on its record since 1945, contrasting it with Conservatism in the 1930s. It had good reason, given its successful revival of the economy despite the unavoidable crises of the transition from war, while developing an exceptional, if imperfect, range of welfare measures.[68] A major issue again was housing. Labour promised to build more council homes, but its past failures lost working-class votes. The Conservatives were committed by their party conference to building 300,000 houses a year. They promised to reverse Labour nationalization, rationing, controls and high taxes, claiming they prevented economic growth, increased bureaucracy and eroded civil liberties.

Labour's vote rose to just under 14 million and 49.2 per cent; the Conservatives to 13.7 million and 48.68 per cent, but Labour won only 295 seats, the Conservatives 321. Again, the turnout was unusually high, 82.5 per cent, and the electorate deeply, closely divided, primarily by class.[69] Labour lost further middle-class support, due mainly to continuing high taxation and restrictions on consumption but gained a greater share of the working-class vote than in 1950. Again, it was a victim of the first-past-the-post effect, winning a majority of votes but concentrated in too few seats. Among women voters it almost returned to the high 1945 level.

Conclusion

Despite the setback of the Korean War, the economy had substantially recovered by 1951. This was not wholly due to Labour policies, also to worldwide demand and the creation of international institutions to prevent recurrence of the interwar crises. The Bretton Woods agreement of 1944, much influenced by Keynes, introduced almost thirty years of financial stability in the world economy when nations agreed to hold their currencies at stable exchange rates against the US dollar, while the United States kept the dollar stable against gold, reinforcing US hegemony. The International Monetary Fund (IMF) was established to facilitate international economic co-operation and assist nations through financial difficulties.

Labour's commitment to full employment and economic development contributed substantially to the recovery. The increased efficiency of key industries and improved supply of resources, including coal and electricity, assisted profitability, while improvements in healthcare, education and social security enhanced the quality and efficiency of 'human capital', while improving everyday life and diminishing social inequality. By 1951, investment had grown, output expanded, the balance of payments was restored, productivity improved, and the private sector was more closely regulated.[70] Labour's regional policy improved conditions in regions 'depressed' before the war.[71] Average real earnings rose, raising living standards amid full employment.

But business remained overwhelmingly private and business leaders resisted government 'interference', especially when they appeared to be doing well with unchanged methods. The gap between richest and poorest narrowed only slightly. In 1949 the top 10 per cent of income recipients received 27.1 per cent of total income after tax, the bottom 30 per cent 14.6 per cent.[72] Labour achieved much in six difficult years, but much remained to be done. Its ambitions for social democratic economic and social reforms were blocked by better-off voters resisting redistribution, not for the first or the last time.

CHAPTER 8
'NEVER HAD IT SO GOOD'? CONSERVATIVE GOVERNMENTS, 1951–64

Churchill returned to Downing St, aged seventy-seven, in poor health, promising, with no hint of 'consensus', to 'set the people free' from 'socialist controls'. His government and 'the people' benefitted from economic revival that owed much to Labour's 'controls' having delivered full employment, economic growth and improved living standards for many people. Beneath the rhetoric, Conservative election promises were cautious, as, following their small majority (17), were their actions. They were constrained by fluctuating world trade, the large defence budget (30 per cent of expenditure) boosted by the Korean War, conflict in Commonwealth countries seeking independence and development of the atom bomb, which was now public knowledge. The Cabinet was also cautiously constructed, mainly from Churchill's trusted wartime associates, favouring conciliatory reformers including R. A. Butler as chancellor of the Exchequer and Harold Macmillan placed, disappointed, at a new Ministry of Housing to fulfil the commitment to build more homes. Iain McLeod was appointed minister of health after impressing Churchill with his parliamentary attack on Bevan's handling of the NHS.

Social and economic policy

The Conservatives immediately faced a growing balance of payments deficit and pressure on sterling in an international downturn. The economy had recurrent problems through the 1950s and the government responded with alternating cuts and expansion- 'stop-go' as it became known – but no clear strategy other than, whenever possible, cutting taxes and reducing public ownership and controls. The economy grew at a reasonable rate by UK standards, averaging 2.42 per cent per year, 1950–73, but competitors grew faster, including Germany and France. UK productivity remained relatively low. Its main European competitors successfully implemented policies Labour supported, but Conservatives shunned: central planning and co-operation between management and unions bringing wage restraint in return for investment in technology, growth and job creation.[1] Labour successfully encouraged such co-operation in Germany during the occupation but failed to persuade British business and unions to follow. Its initiatives, including Development Councils to guide modernization and the British Institute of Management to improve the poor quality of British management, were discontinued, and the Conservatives had no alternative plans to modernize business.[2]

Butler – a less consensual chancellor than expected – attacked 'excessive' Labour spending and, obeying Treasury orthodoxy, cut social spending. Prescription charges of 1s (10p) were introduced and further dental charges. Treasury officials and some Conservative backbenchers proposed other charges, including 'hotel' fees for hospital stays, but the Ministry of Health and Cabinet resisted, fearing popular hostility.[3] NHS staffing was frozen. Macleod as minister of health and the Treasury wanted more cuts. An inquiry into NHS finances was appointed in 1952, chaired by Cambridge economist Claude Guillebaud.

In 1951 Rowntree published his third and final survey of poverty in York.[4] Slighter than the earlier surveys, by eighty-year-old Rowntree with an assistant, using a slightly more generous poverty measure, it concluded that poverty was almost eliminated: only 2.77 per cent of individuals, 4.64 per cent of working-class households, two-thirds retired, were now in primary poverty in York, still held to be a typical provincial town. They attributed the decline to post-war social legislation and price controls. But the methods of sampling and calculating living costs were faulty. Reworking in 1981 revealed that *c.* 12 per cent was a more accurate estimate of numbers in primary poverty, including more younger people.[5] Poverty had diminished, though by less than Rowntree suggested. At the time, his report entrenched the belief that poverty was now minimal and concentrated among older people.

In 1952 Iain MacLeod and another young Conservative MP, Enoch Powell, published *The Social Services: Needs and Means*, attacking the 'Welfare State', as they called it pejoratively, arguing, as Beveridge had feared, that it encouraged dependency on the taxpayer and reduced incentives to work. The NHS, particularly, was too costly and should be financed by private insurance. Social services and payments should be targeted on the neediest: 'the question . . . is not should a means test be applied to a social service, but why should any service be provided without a test of need?'[6] A long assault on universal services began, guiding Conservative social policy into the twenty-first century.

In December 1952, London vanished into the Great Smog, a fog so thick and polluted that about 4,000 people died, many more suffered breathing problems and travel and business were disrupted. Over decades, fogs had worsened as more steam trains belched smoke, domestic coal fires increased, steam-driven industry grew and three large, coal-fired power stations opened along the Thames. London was divided between inner areas inhabited by poorer people in overcrowded, polluted districts and smarter, more expensive districts, beyond the recognized 'smog line'. It was one of Britain's worst public health catastrophes, but the government was slow to respond. Then prize animals died at London's Smithfield Show. The press sounded the alarm, Labour MPs asked questions in the Commons and the National Smoke Abatement Society campaigned. The Conservatives resisted intervention, but in May 1953 appointed a committee which in 1954 recommended designated smokeless zones and smoke-controlled areas, with government subsidies for householders to convert to smokeless fuel. These were implemented in the Clean Air Act, 1956, the first significant attempt to control environmental pollution, with exclusion clauses for industrial emissions following pressure from industry. These limited its effectiveness and were much criticized, but pollution diminished in London and elsewhere, improving health and the quality of life.[7]

In 1953, following an upturn in world trade, Butler cut direct and indirect taxes, expecting to increase investment and consumption. Road haulage and steel were denationalized and controls on supplies reduced, while price controls remained. In another boost to private enterprise, in 1954 legislation permitted the establishment of commercial TV stations, financed by advertising, to rival the BBC. One area of public spending was too important to cut. Housing was a big issue in the recent elections and the Conservatives promised to build 300,000 houses each year. In 1952, 248,000 were completed, 212,000 in the public sector. In 1953, 327,000 were completed, 262,000 council homes, 65,000 private, the largest number of council homes built in any year of the twentieth century, except 1954 which matched it. The target was achieved annually until 1957: private building grew to 178,000 in 1963 while the public sector shrank to 130,000, despite continuing need among low-income households.[8] The target was achieved partly by reducing the size and quality of the standard 'people's house' and cutting the proportion of council homes with three or more bedrooms from four- to two-fifths. From 1957 councils were subsidized to build high-rise flats which were cheaper to construct but unpopular especially among families with children. Fewer amenities were provided for council estates or New Towns. In 1951, 53 per cent of housing was privately rented and rents remained controlled. Landlords protested that controlled rents left no margin for repairs. The Repairs and Rents Act, 1954, allowed them to raise rents if their properties were in good repair. Private rentals fell to 32 per cent by 1960, while owner-occupation rose from 29 per cent to 42 per cent.[9]

Election 1955

The Korean War ended in 1953, and the government could afford to end rationing in 1954. This was popular but stimulated imports, threatening the balance of payments, leading to further controls on spending. Churchill suffered a second major stroke and resigned in April 1955, succeeded by Foreign Minister Anthony Eden. An election was called for May 1955. Butler declaimed that

> We have burned our identity cards, torn up our ration books, halved the number of snoopers, decimated the number of forms and said good riddance to nearly two-thirds of the remaining wartime regulations. This is the march to freedom on which we are bound.[10]

It was not a march to a clear economic strategy, despite continuing evidence that Britain lagged behind faster-growing rival economies. The 1955 budget, a month before the election, further reduced the standard rate of tax to 8s.6d in £ and increased personal allowances, removing over two million people from direct taxation. Doubts were expressed about the wisdom of increasing purchasing power and, probably, prices, but the potential political advantage was irresistible. Ownership of TVs, cars and motorcycles grew. The value of hire purchase and other instalment purchases rose £208m–£461m, 1951–5.[11]

Labour had difficulty coming to terms with what was soon called the 'affluent society' after the US economist J. K. Galbraith's book of that name, published in 1958.[12] A party publication condemned 'the lifeless time-wasting of so many . . . people who find in TV almost their only pleasure'. Labour's failure to appreciate the real improvements brought to everyday life by modern gadgets, especially washing machines, alienated many working-class women especially. The Conservatives published pamphlets addressed to women, stressing the advantages of consumer goods and warning of controls and rationing should Labour return. They won female voters, attracting working-class women by building more houses and ending rationing, while full employment raised living standards and consumption. Women continued to campaign for equal pay with demonstrations and petitions to parliament, encouraged by the Labour-controlled LCC granting equal pay in 1952.[13] The Treasury remained hostile and the government prevaricated until in 1955, before the election, Butler announced equal pay in the public sector, where demands had been most insistent, to be introduced gradually over six years. Protests over private sector pay inequality continued.[14]

Labour was much divided, including over nuclear arms. Led by a weary Attlee, reluctant to retire, it offered no new policies, arguing again that full employment, stable prices and progress to greater equality required planning, controls and increased taxes on higher incomes. The Conservatives were helped by a newspaper strike lasting almost a month, a dock strike and threatened rail strike, all due to prices rising faster than pay, taking the opportunity to attack the unions. They secured a clear majority in the election, gaining 13,286,569 votes, 49.7 per cent, and 345 seats. Labour won 12,404,970 votes, 46.4 per cent and 277 seats on a turnout of 76.8 per cent. Voters remained quite evenly divided, but constituencies still were not. Labour's share of the non-manual vote and male voters increased slightly, while its share of female votes fell from 46 per cent to 42.5 per cent.[15] The swing to the Conservatives, 1.8 per cent, was fairly uniform across the country, lower in Scotland, where unemployment was high, and higher in the prosperous Midlands. Attlee resigned as Labour leader. Hugh Gaitskell was elected to succeed him.

1955–9: Decline?

Eden appointed an all-male Cabinet, all privately educated, most at Eton. In an autumn budget Butler clawed back twice the revenue given away before the election as the balance of payments plunged to a deficit of over £450m due to predictably increased imports. Local authority building was severely cut, purchase tax increased, two-thirds of the tax reliefs announced in April withdrawn. Gaitskell accused Butler of deceiving the nation. The reaction in the opinion polls (ever more influential as they proliferated in the 1950s) was so negative that in December 1955 Butler was replaced as chancellor by Macmillan, infuriating both. Macmillan was alarmed by the financial situation and in February 1956, after wrangles with Eden, announced more emergency measures: reduced bread subsidies to be followed by abolition, higher bank rate and further cuts to public spending.

Hopes of savings from cuts to the NHS were dashed when the Guillebaud committee reported in 1956. It concluded that costs had not soared as critics suggested but had fallen since 1948 from 3.75 per cent to 3.25 per cent of GNP. Capital spending on hospitals was only one-third the pre-war level; they ran with remarkable efficiency given that 45 per cent were built before 1891, 21 per cent before 1861. It recommended more spending on renovation. It found no evidence of waste, indeed that the NHS was highly cost-effective compared with healthcare in comparable countries, while charges for dental treatment and spectacles deterred people who needed them. This was not what the government or the Treasury wanted to hear and did not stop calls for cuts from the back benches, but it stopped the government from implementing them, especially in view of the popularity of the NHS with voters.[16]

On another major social policy issue, the government stressed the need to improve education and skills, given Britain's poor performance in technological innovation in business alongside rivals. Local authorities were encouraged to open technical colleges to enable younger workers to acquire skills. In 1957, eight technical colleges became Colleges of Advanced Technology providing degree-level training financed by central government. The advisory committee of the Ministry of Education produced successive reports proposing improvements. In 1954 *Early Leaving* stressed how many able children left school at fifteen without qualifications, recommending generous grants to help them stay on, which was not implemented. In 1959, the Crowther report on education at ages 15–18 proposed expansion of post-school education and training and raising the leaving age to sixteen, which was also ignored. Equally fruitlessly, in 1963 the Newsom report, *Half Our Future*, reinforced the message of *Early Leaving*, suggesting improvements to secondary modern schools, especially in deprived areas. In the same year, the Robbins report recommended expanding the universities, which still educated only 4 per cent of 18- to 21-year-olds, overwhelmingly upper and middle class and male, compared with 8 per cent in France, 20 per cent in the United States.[17] The Treasury slightly increased university funding. Some new universities were already planned, with philanthropic and local funds. Sussex opened in 1961, East Anglia in 1963, others soon after, despite pessimists, notably novelist and university lecturer Kingsley Amis warning, notoriously and wrongly, 'more will mean worse'.[18] The Conservatives did little to improve the education system.

Then came the Suez crisis in 1956, weakening Britain's international status and forcing Eden's resignation. He was succeeded as Conservative leader and PM by Harold Macmillan in January 1957. He was well aware of the economic as well as international difficulties. He stated in a speech in Bedford in July 1957:

Let's be frank about it; most of our people have never had it so good. Go around the country, go to the industrial towns, go to the farms, and you will see a state of prosperity such as we have never had in my lifetime-nor indeed ever in the history of this country. What is beginning to worry some of us is 'Is it too good to be true?' or perhaps I should say 'Is it too good to last?' For amidst all this prosperity, there is one problem that has troubled us . . . ever since the war. It's the problem of rising prices. Our constant concern is- can prices be steadied while at the same time we maintain full employment in an expanding economy? Can we control inflation? That is the problem of our time.[19]

Macmillan's much quoted, accurate, claim that most British people had 'never had it so good' was delivered as a warning about the state of the economy, not the triumphal message since remembered. It resonated with many people who were better off than before but felt insecure. But the government still had no clear economic policy and continued to alternate cuts with boosting taxes and public spending.

As promised in the election, the Rent Act, 1957, decontrolled rents on higher value property, on all properties when tenants left and allowed controlled rents to rise to twice the property's rateable value, arousing strong opposition. There were about six million private tenants, most on low incomes.[20] Controlled rents in London rose on average from 14s pw to 22s.4d, 1957–9, outside London from 9s.4d to 13s.1d. One result, especially in London, was unscrupulous landlords forcing out controlled tenants by making their lives intolerable, sometimes with loud music and all-night parties. This became a major scandal, labelled 'Rachmanism' after the most notorious perpetrator, Peter Rachman, when his tenants in deprived, multiracial Notting Hill complained of intimidation and extortionate rents for slum housing. Rachman, himself a Ukrainian immigrant who became very wealthy from his property dealings, later from owning fashionable nightclubs, died, unpenalized, in 1962.[21]

Labour attacked Conservative handling of economic and social policy, led by shadow chancellor Harold Wilson, while Gaitskell appeared to achieve consensus in the party. Future minister Anthony Crosland's *The Future of Socialism* (1956) argued that nationalization was outdated in the modern world of large multinational businesses. The way forward was acceptance of the mixed economy, controlled by Keynesian-style demand management, with social reforms promoting equality. Crosland believed that Labour should applaud the improved living standards of most working people, encourage pleasure, not grim devotion to duty, ceasing to condemn materialism.[22] And Labour must also tackle 'the more serious question of socially imposed restrictions on the individual's private life and liberty . . . the divorce laws, licensing laws, prehistoric (and flagrantly unfair) abortion laws, obsolete penalties for sexual abnormality, the illiterate censorship of books and plays, the remaining restrictions on the equal rights of women.'[23] Many party members disagreed, but he perceived major cultural changes in progress, presaging future Labour reforms.

Race and immigration

New social divisions became prominent. Commonwealth immigration helped resolve some socio-economic problems while creating others. The right of Commonwealth citizens, regardless of colour, to migrate to Britain, with equal rights with everyone of British nationality, continued. Immigrants increased, from a growing range of countries, but were outnumbered by emigrants, mainly to the white Dominions. Most immigrants, still, were Irish. By 1958 there were about 900,000 Irish-born residents in Great Britain, the largest number since the nineteenth century, with about 125,000 West Indians and 55,000 Indians and Pakistanis. The government feared racial conflict due to immigration from the Caribbean and South Asia, but official recruitment schemes continued due to labour shortages. Most West Indians, fleeing poverty and unemployment at home, came independently, aiming to better themselves, though regularly shocked by the restricted opportunities and racism they encountered. Smaller numbers came from Cyprus and Hong Kong, with an influx of refugees from Hungary following the Russian invasion of 1956. Most Europeans lacked automatic citizenship rights, but they were easy and cheap to acquire. There was significant immigration of white Commonwealth citizens and substantial internal migration. Around two million moved from insecurity in Scotland, Wales and Northern England to the Midlands and South, 1951–62.[24]

Black and Asian immigrants clustered in occupations short of labour, often at levels beneath their qualifications: Asians in northern textiles, engineering and foundry work in the Midlands, West Indians in the public sector, especially transport (mainly men) and the NHS (mainly women) which also relied on South Asian doctors. Chinese, Cypriot, Asian and Italian restaurants transformed the variety and quality of eating out across Britain, a lasting gain. Immigrants tended to cluster together, often severely overcrowded, for security and because discrimination by white landlords left them little choice. One such district was run-down Notting Hill, where serious race riots erupted in 1958. Like East London at the beginning of the century, racism emerged in a deprived community encountering significant immigration. A year later an Antiguan youth, Kelso Cochrane, was brutally murdered there, it was believed by white attackers, the worst of a string of white-on-Black attacks in London, Nottingham and elsewhere. The government faced pressures to restrict non-white Commonwealth immigration. Oswald Mosley marched again, through Notting Hill, leading what he now called a 'One Nation' movement, demanding 'Keep Britain White'; in the 1959 election he stood in North Kensington. That he lost his deposit suggests that extreme racists were a minority. Substantial, growing anti-racist movements emerged, campaigning for legislation against race discrimination.

Another growing social problem and dimension of inequality was expressed in complaints by Conservative backbenchers and others of 'moral decline' among young people, with rising panic about soaring 'juvenile delinquency', of which there was little evidence.[25] Fashionable psychologists, most influentially John Bowlby, encouraged the belief that mothers who abandoned daily care of their children for paid work created 'delinquency' among neglected children, and that schools no longer inculcated the 'traditional' values which allegedly prevented transgressions.[26] Others blamed the decline of religion or the influence of television.

'Affluence' was blamed for undermining the morals of young men who could now afford to patronize proliferating coffee bars and new clothing fashions. Young women could also enjoy modern fashion and, with young men, 'pop' music pouring out on vinyl records (seventy-three million sold in Britain in 1963[27]), film and TV. Much of the press believed youthful energy was enlivening dull British culture, but it was disparaged by cultural conservatives as creating American-style degeneration. The changing youth culture grew out of the greater economic independence of young people as more of them found decently paid work despite most leaving school without qualifications. In a full employment economy, parents needed less support, young people could afford to enjoy themselves and the market responded. But youth, like adult, affluence was not universal: there were real inequalities between regions of continuing unemployment, including Merseyside and Clydeside, and the rest.

Cultural change and cultural criticism

There was a growing tide of public social criticism from the later 1950s, from both progressives and cultural conservatives, signifying change and social divisions, facilitated by 'affluence' bringing the new mass medium of TV, more people with time and cash to buy magazines and books and a popular press eager for controversy. In the slowly expanding universities social science and cultural studies departments analysed social conditions and change, exposing multiple inequalities. Paperback publishers, still led by Penguin, mass-produced their commentaries. One highly successful Penguin/Pelican publication was *The Uses of Literacy*, first published in 1957, by the upwardly mobile, originally northern working-class academic Richard Hoggart. It was a passionate diatribe against what he called the 'candy floss world' of contemporary mass culture, abandoning, he believed, the self-improvement which had once characterized working-class patrons of the Workers' Educational Association (WEA) and Working Men's Clubs and the socially richer, more cohesive, working-class community he remembered in Leeds between the wars.[28]

Other critics, including Anthony Crosland, argued that cultural change was too slow, and prosperity had good as well as bad effects. Michael Young left his Labour Party post in 1951, becoming an independent social researcher, critical of the centralized state socialism he believed Labour had sponsored and seeking ways to enable everyone to enrich and control their own lives materially and culturally.[29] In 1952 he founded the Institute of Community Studies in Bethnal Green, East London, for research into the realities of everyday life of working-class people. One of its first publications was *Family and Kinship in East London* by Young and Peter Willmot (1957, Pelican 1962). They expressed surprise that, contrary to Hoggart's lament for the death of working-class community, it was flourishing in Bethnal Green. They challenged commonplace sociological assertions that formerly cohesive families were falling apart in the modern, affluent, mobile world, discovering in East London strong, supportive extended families. The chief threat to working-class community and family they identified was housing policy, demolishing East London 'slums' and moving tenants to distant estates, far from kin and familiar neighbourhoods. Another Institute of Community Studies publication, *The Family Life of Old People* (1957, Pelican 1963) by sociologist Peter Townsend, challenged another commonplace assumption, that families no longer cared for their older relatives. He demonstrated that family care was often more supportive now that families had social service support, were better off and had more time, hard and impoverished though many older peoples' lives were in other respects.

Continuing gender inequality was scrutinized, including by two female social scientists, Alva Myrdal and Viola Klein in *Women's Two Roles. Home and Work* (Routledge, 1956). They challenged Bowlby's belief that mothers of young children must be their full-time carers, describing this as 'a new and subtle form of anti-feminism'. Like many others, including social workers concerned with children, they accepted that young children needed supportive care but not necessarily full-time care by the natural mother.[30] Rather, like feminists for decades, they argued that women's work inside and outside the home, paid and unpaid, should be equally valued and women helped to choose, with maternity leave of one to two years, access to training before returning to work, better designed housing to assist housework, affordable day nurseries and shorter working hours for men and women, enabling couples to share domestic responsibilities. But one-third of men interviewed disapproved of married women working and most disapproved of mothers of young children 'going out to work'. Few gave much help around the home. Employers were unwilling to adapt to the needs of married women.[31]

Other surveys showed the limited work opportunities even of highly qualified women. Among women who graduated in science and engineering in Britain, 1954–6, (only 708) 74 per cent were employed in teaching or other public services, such as the NHS, because they despaired of their prospects in industry or scientific research.[32] A survey of young mothers at home in North London in the early 1960s found many feeling isolated and bored, keen to work as soon as possible, even if their husbands disapproved (as 27 per cent did), but no childcare was available and they were pessimistic about finding fulfilling work. Thirty-five per cent of the working-class wives and 21 per cent from the middle class regretted marrying too young, generally to escape their families or monotonous low-paid work.[33]

Sociologists also analysed and criticized secondary school selection. About 25 per cent of eleven-year-olds attended grammar schools in England, 30 per cent in Wales, still more males than females; fewer than 5 per cent entered the few technical schools; two-thirds attended secondary moderns. Selection was intended to grant equal opportunities to all regardless of background, yet research revealed that in England and Wales (more in England than Wales) three out of five children from professional and managerial backgrounds attended grammar schools, only one in ten children of unskilled manual workers. Middle-class children were more likely to stay on past fifteen. Secondary modern schools prepared most working-class children to leave at fifteen, without qualifications, for manual work. The proportions staying to eighteen and progressing to higher education in Wales was double that in England. Scotland had long had a more inclusive education system. Demand grew for comprehensive schools. By 1964 local authorities had established 200 in Britain, including the Labour-controlled LCC.[34]

Independent schools were attended by 5 per cent of UK children in the 1950s compared with 9 per cent in the 1930s. Some parents now preferred free grammar schools. One in eight middle-class children gained university places, fewer than one in 100 working-class children. Adequate means-tested maintenance grants were available for students from low-income families who performed well in national examinations, and no one paid fees. In 1960 only 25 per cent of university students were female, 15 per cent at Oxford and Cambridge, overwhelmingly studying arts subjects. A much higher proportion attended the predominantly female two-year teacher training colleges, to enter a traditionally female occupation.[35]

Inequalities in 1950s Britain were publicly revealed and challenged also on the stage and in literature by a disparate group of writers bundled together by the media as 'Angry Young Men'. Class inequalities were a major focus of the anger expressed in John Osborne's play *Look Back in Anger* (1956), Colin Wilson's widely cited essay *The Outsider* (1956), John Braine's novel *Room at the Top* (1957), in 1959 a highly successful film, and Alan Sillitoe's novel *Saturday Night and Sunday Morning* (1958), also a successful film in 1960, about a factory worker in Nottingham, showing how grim and alienating such work still was. A rare female contribution was nineteen-year-old Shelagh Delaney's *A Taste of Honey*, first staged in 1958, filmed in 1961, both immediately successful, about poverty, single motherhood and homophobia in Salford. This was staged a year after the official Wolfenden report recommended partial decriminalization of homosexual behaviour, though this was widely unpopular and the government ignored it. Another female contribution was Nell Dunn's novel *Up the Junction* (1963), about working-class life and sex in South London, portraying the lives of young working-class women amid shabby terraces, outdoor toilets and smoky air. But work was plentiful, if low-paid; the women could afford contemporary fashion and were not deferential to men. Dunn found life in Battersea a release from repression in wealthy Chelsea, where she grew up.[36] The London of the 1950s was not uniformly 'affluent', but it was very different from that revealed by Booth half a century earlier. These writers revealed the realities of social inequalities to audiences unfamiliar with them.

Journalists were another source of criticism. In 1962 Anthony Sampson, an *Observer* journalist, published *Anatomy of Britain*, blaming the 'white tribes' of the ruling-class for creating a 'living museum', holding Britain back from political and economic modernization. Economic journalist Michael Shanks made similar arguments in his Penguin *The Stagnant Society* (1961) alongside, among others, a collection of essays edited by the Hungarian novelist Arthur Koestler, dramatically titled *Suicide of a Nation*.[37] A new fashion for satirical comedy had similar targets. In 1960 a group of recent Oxbridge graduates, of differing social backgrounds (middle-class Peter Cook and Jonathan Miller, working-class Alan Bennett and Dudley Moore), launched *Beyond the Fringe* at the Edinburgh Festival, satirizing social class differences, politicians, the Church and established conventions. They became a lasting hit, performing at The Establishment Club in Soho from 1961 to 1964. The club took its name from an article by journalist Henry Fairlie in the right-wing *Spectator* magazine in 1955. He described how power worked in Britain through a matrix of loyalties forged through family connections, elite schools and universities, which he labelled the 'Establishment'. The term was embraced by social critics as representing all they opposed, including the fortnightly magazine, *Private Eye*, founded in 1961, and satirical TV shows. Such cultural criticism was widespread and growing under the Conservatives by the later 1950s, but by no means universal.

General Election 1959

Against this background Macmillan prepared for an election in October 1959. He persuaded the chancellor to deliver another generous pre-election budget, including bigger tax cuts than before the 1955 election, costing £360m. Labour and some economists argued these would harm economic recovery, but the Conservatives promoted them as signs of economic success, with enthusiastic press support. They launched an expensive poster campaign featuring families enjoying affluent consumption under the slogan, 'Life's Better with the Conservatives. Don't Let Labour Ruin It'. Labour still disparaged such celebration of consumer society and could not afford costly promotion, though they ran effective TV broadcasts assisted by a rising young MP with TV experience, Anthony Wedgewood Benn.[38] It was the most televised election so far and both parties were increasingly concerned with media presentation. Labour was now less visibly divided, and Gaitskell made a good impression. It focused on economic growth through planned investment, further public ownership and expansion of education, including development of comprehensive schools to improve opportunities for working-class children, stressing the need to reduce inequalities between rich and poor. It proposed ambitious pension reforms, raising pensions and linking them to earnings, as in much of Western Europe, to assist the largest group known to be poor.[39] The Conservatives, with no apparent sense of shame, accused Labour of bribing the electorate with unaffordable promises while remaining the party of rationing, controls and nationalization. They tried to steer delicately between cultural liberals and conservatives, emphasizing Conservative commitment to upholding moral standards and the family and strengthening the 'national character', while Butler represented the party as 'modern', adapting to change.[40]

The Conservatives won a third victory, increasing their majority to 100 seats with 49.4 per cent of votes, to Labour's 43.8 per cent from a 78.8 per cent turnout. The swing to the Conservatives was greatest in prosperous West Midlands and Greater London while areas of high unemployment including Clydeside and Manchester swung to Labour. Conservatives started a long decline in Scotland with its declining economy, remaining a minority in Wales. They had a strong hold on middle-class voters, better-off workers and, probably, women in all classes, though Labour gained slightly among women while losing among voters under thirty. Macmillan claimed class war was obsolete. Some Labour leaders feared affluence had so undermined its traditional support that it had no future. *Must Labour Lose?* in the new materialistic world, asked a sociological analysis of its performance, starting an anguished debate in the party.[41] The victory was widely attributed to the leadership of 'Supermac' and the economic revival.

1959–63: Crises

The boom peaked in 1959–60 with growth of 4–5 per cent, but the pre-election measures stimulated consumption and imports. Chancellor Heathcoat Amory wanted to reduce spending and raise taxes, but resigned when Macmillan, fearing justified criticism of the government's pre-election tactics, refused. Macmillan replaced him with the more reliable Selwyn Lloyd. But sterling weakened, exacerbated by a dockworkers' strike which widened the trade gap, and the bank rate rose to 7 per cent in 1961. Lloyd froze public sector pay, exhorting restraint in the private sector, noting that average incomes had risen 8 per cent in the previous year, productivity by only 3 per cent. He cut spending and raised prescription charges despite the conclusion, in 1959, of an official committee that 'the present charge is a tax which . . . is resented by patients and doctors as a tax on illness . . . [and] . . . has proved disappointing financially'.[42] Nevertheless Enoch Powell, minister of health from 1960, planned to redevelop hospitals. Civil servants in the Ministry, backed by the Guillebaud report and a Labour campaign, persuaded the Cabinet of the need for a major hospital building programme. In 1962 the Hospital Plan proposed ambitiously to build 90 new hospitals, drastically redevelop 134 and extend 360 at a cost of £500m over several years.[43] It was unclear how, or whether, funds could be raised, and the plan was not fulfilled when it was abandoned by a later Conservative government in 1973 amid economic crisis. But it protected hospitals from cuts and much-needed new hospitals were built, fewer than hoped but a significant improvement. There was growing criticism of the government's see-sawing fiscal policies in the Commons and the press.

Increasingly concerned about Britain's flagging competitiveness, the Conservatives sought a strategy for economic development. In 1960 they organized the European Free Trade Area (EFTA), with Denmark, Austria, Norway, Portugal, Sweden, Switzerland, to foster trade and growth with less regulation than the European Economic Community (EEC, formed 1958) and without its political goal to unify Europe, but it was less successful. British trade increasingly focused on the EEC as its colonial and world trading declined. Britain's share of world trade in manufactures fell from 16 per cent in the mid-1950s to under 13 per cent in 1960, while rival European economies expanded. In 1961 Macmillan persuaded the Cabinet that Britain must apply to join the EEC. The party was, and long remained, divided over membership. The government's popularity plummeted, and it lost a series of by-elections. In 1962–3 unemployment rose to the highest level since 1947, 878,000. It was an exceptionally hard winter, bringing power cuts. The government was blamed for not safeguarding energy reserves.[44]

Racial tensions continued. The election brought in new Conservative MPs from the West Midlands, with its high immigrant population, demanding immigration control. In 1962 the government introduced the Commonwealth Immigration Act, restricting immigration to those with 'special skills', or guaranteed employment, the first formal restrictions on immigration of Commonwealth citizens. Gaitskell attacked it in the Commons as 'a cruel and brutal anti-colour measure', but it was popular in polls.

De Gaulle, president of France, was already dubious about Britain's commitment to Europe and in January 1963 vetoed UK entry. Labour was divided about the EEC.

Gaitskell, surprisingly, announced his opposition to UK membership which, he told the party conference, would spell 'the end of Britain as an independent state . . . the end of a thousand years of history' and undermine the multiracial Commonwealth. This upset some of his colleagues, but he was supported by left-wing opponents of the 'capitalist club' as they labelled the EEC. Then, in January 1963, he suddenly died, aged fifty-six, following an apparently minor illness. Harold Wilson was elected to succeed him.[45]

The government was rocked further by a series of ministerial sexual transgressions.[46] Macmillan fell ill and resigned. He was succeeded by the relatively obscure Sir Alec Douglas-Home, who had abandoned his title as the fourteenth earl of Home. His premiership was a one-year campaign for the election due in 1964. Harold Wilson enjoyed the contest between an Old Etonian Earl and a man with a northern accent whose father was a works chemist, his mother a schoolteacher, though, like Home, he had studied at Oxford, gaining a first-class degree; Home achieved a third. Home's riposte to the '14th Mr Wilson' hardly undermined the contrast.

Election 1964

Wilson was younger, at forty-six, than any previous twentieth-century party leader. He represented the Conservatives as relics of the past when Britain urgently needed change and modernization, aiming to return the economy to modernization and growth and complete the Welfare State. He courted technocrats and scientists whom he believed could help regenerate the economy if business would use their skills. He supported joining the EEC with its large market for exports and competitive stimulus for producers. He drew the party together, sympathetic to the left but emphasizing continuity of policy with Gaitskell.

Labour's election programme, *Signposts for the Sixties*, promised renationalization of steel and a Land Commission to buy building land, but focused on stimulating innovation and growth by applying modern technology available in Britain but underused outside the defence industries.[47] Wilson presented it to the 1963 party conference in phrases which resonated through the election campaign and beyond:

> We are re-defining and we are re-stating our socialism in terms of the *scientific revolution* . . . the Britain that is going to be forged in *the white heat* of this revolution will be no place for restrictive practices or out-dated methods on either side of industry.

He called for a 'socialist inspired scientific and technological revolution releasing energy on an enormous scale . . . for enriching mankind beyond our wildest dreams', expressing concerns about Britain's industrial backwardness and poorly trained management. He criticized the 'stop-go' policies of the Conservatives as driven by short-term electoral considerations rather than economic strategy, deterring investment in British manufacturing. Labour published *Twelve Wasted Years*, 459 pages of exhaustive analysis of what they saw as the government's failings in all areas of policy. 'Thirteen wasted years' was an election slogan the following year.[48]

The Conservatives were driven to promote their version of economic modernization. Another upwardly mobile, lower-middle-class Oxford graduate, Edward Heath, contemporary with Wilson, became president of the Board of Trade, briefed to free the economy from what were represented as antiquated restrictions on competition. The chancellor, Reginald Maudling, faced with 878,000 unemployed, took the accustomed Conservative pre-election path: lowering the bank rate to stimulate demand. Growth rose from 4 per cent in 1963 to almost 6 per cent in 1964, but higher consumption raised imports and worsened the balance of trade. Pensions were raised but were still (at 33.7 per cent average earnings, compared with 30.5 per cent in 1948) inadequate for subsistence and many pensioners needed means-tested NAB supplements. Rather than raise state pensions further the Conservatives encouraged occupational and private pensions provided by commercial insurers, which mainly benefitted better-paid, mainly male, workers. Other national insurance allowances remained low.[49]

A hopeful sign for Labour, in April 1964, was victory in the first election for the new Greater London Council (GLC). Against Labour opposition, the government had combined London and Middlesex County Councils, expecting to end Labour's thirty-year control of London government through the LCC by merging central and suburban London. Labour made substantial gains in other local elections. In the general election, the Conservatives promoted the familiar message of self-congratulation about rising living standards and prophecies of doom about the return of socialism. In October 1964, Labour won narrowly, with 317 seats to the Conservatives' 304 and Liberals' nine. Labour gained 44.1 per cent of votes to the Conservatives' 43.4 per cent on a turnout of 77.1 per cent. Labour gained most in its strongholds of inner London, Lancashire, Yorkshire and Scotland. It had still to win the trust of many voters.

In the Midlands, the sitting MP for Smethwick since 1945, Patrick Gordon Walker, Labour's shadow foreign secretary, was defeated in a racist campaign featuring the slogan, 'If you want a nigger neighbour, vote Labour'. The successful Conservative candidate, local councillor Peter Griffiths, exploited anxiety over housing shortages, blaming immigrants. The national swing to Labour was 3.5 per cent; Smethwick swung to the Conservatives by 7.2 per cent. In the following year, Gordon Walker ran in a by-election in the normally safe Labour seat of Leyton, East London, and was defeated again in a campaign featuring opponents dressed as monkeys, brandishing the slogan, 'We immigrants are voting for Gordon Walker'. He won the seat in 1966. Elsewhere, race was not a major issue in 1964. Labour did not pledge to repeal the Commonwealth Immigration Act but committed to introducing anti-discrimination legislation.

Thirteen wasted years?

UK economic growth and living standards were both higher between 1950 and the early 1970s than before or later, despite fluctuations. But, throughout, competitors, including the renewed economies of Germany, France and Japan, outperformed it amid expanding international trade and finance. The UK government failed to diversify into new, modern areas of manufacturing and its share of world manufactured exports fell from 25 per cent in 1950 to 16.5 per cent in 1960, while imports grew. 'Stop-go' fiscal and budgetary policies, sometimes influenced more by the electoral cycle than the needs of the economy, had been damaging.

The Welfare State survived more or less intact with some erosion, including charges for health services and the lower quality of public housing, and it did not obviously improve. When possible, the Conservatives encouraged private rather than public provision including for pensions. The proportion of housing built for private ownership grew along with state subsidies for mortgage holders and providers. The belief that owner-occupation encouraged Conservative voting had not gone away. Aspirations to further privatization, notably in the health service, were restrained by public opinion and expert advice. State welfare remained popular.[50]

Poverty appeared to be at lower levels than at any time in the century so far, though no sound surveys appeared. Average living standards reached their highest ever level, although substantial inequalities remained. Income and wealth inequality did not change significantly. In 1949 the top 10 per cent of income recipients gained 27.1 per cent of personal after-tax income, the bottom 50 per cent shared 25.2 per cent. In 1964 they received 25.9 per cent and 24.2 per cent respectively.[51] Nor did gender inequality diminish in most respects including incomes despite women's continuing protests, while racial inequality and tension grew with increasing immigration in an insecure society. Most workers were still manual workers, while white-collar employment increased by 500,000 during 1951–7 with the growth of finance and the service sector, contributing more to social mobility than the education system.[52] The post-war social and economic situation is often described as a 'settlement'. By 1964, present and future trajectories in the economy and society were far from settled in a rapidly changing culture.

CHAPTER 9
HAROLD WILSON AND MODERNIZATION

In 1964 Britain led the world in pop music, with the Beatles and the Rolling Stones, and in youth fashion based in London's Soho, in Carnaby St, but not in manufacturing or politics. The Labour government focused on reviving the less successful features of the economy and society. Wilson worked to unify the party, giving his leadership rivals prominent roles, James Callaghan as chancellor, while a new Department of Economic Affairs (DEA), dedicated to economic planning, was created for George Brown, horrifying the Treasury. Optimistically, the departments were intended to co-exist in 'creative tension', the DEA focused on long-term planning for economic development, the Treasury on short-term finance. Wilson's closest allies, Richard Crossman and Barbara Castle, the only woman in the Cabinet, took the Ministry of Housing and Local Government and the new Ministry of Overseas Development (MOD) respectively. MOD signified the new postcolonial era and Wilson's personal commitment to aiding poorer countries, former colonies or not, and reducing global as well as national inequality.

Economic planning

Wilson aimed to expand Attlee's Welfare State while sharing Attlee's conviction that a prosperous economy was the best means to raise workers' living standards and fund support for those unable to work. But he was shocked to learn that Maudling's pre-election budget concessions had created an estimated £800m balance of payments deficit, the worst since the war.[1] Wilson was criticized for refusing to devalue the pound in response, but this was difficult politically for a government with a slim majority and Labour had suffered from devaluations in 1931 and 1949. Also, many poorer countries kept their reserves in sterling in London. Wilson, committed to overseas development, was 'not prepared to cut India's savings by 10 per cent'.[2] Instead, the bank rate was raised to 7 per cent, there was a temporary surcharge on imports and standard income tax rose to 41.25 per cent. Wilson sought a loan from the United States, now led by Lyndon Johnson. The United States was embarking on a war defending South Vietnam against Communist North Vietnam, a new front in the Cold War. Johnson wanted Wilson's support in return for a loan. Wilson refused to send British troops, which would have been unpopular and expensive, though he allowed the military to give strategic advice and expressed broad support for the war against communism, arousing left-wing criticism. Johnson agreed the loan, if only because British devaluation would have threatened the dollar and the Bretton Woods commitment to fixed exchange rates, which he wished to preserve. The

Treasury kept a tight grip on spending. In 1965 a National Board for Prices and Incomes was appointed to establish controls; the TUC agreed a voluntary incomes policy, setting increases at 3–3.5 per cent p.a. Through 1965 the bank rate eased, the economy grew slowly, unemployment averaged only 1.5 per cent. In 1966 prices were 9 per cent higher than in 1964, but average earnings 11 per cent higher.

Modernization and development of manufacturing to match overseas competitors was Wilson's main ambition. The financial sector prospered, but he and his advisers did not believe that it alone could sustain and enhance UK prosperity and competitiveness. In 1965 the DEA produced a National Plan, setting targets and providing advice for industries on investment, output and productivity. It aimed for annual economic growth of 4 per cent, compared with an average 2.9 per cent, during 1950–64. Actual growth during 1964–70 averaged 2.6 per cent.[3] In 1965 London and Manchester Business Schools opened, aiming to improve the quality of management, providing the first MA in Business Administration (MBA) courses in Britain, modelled on the Harvard Business School and successful French institutions.[4]

An essential complement to the Plan, the Ministry of Technology, was established to lead the drive for technological innovation in manufacturing.[5] It was headed by the left-wing leader of the Transport and General Workers Union (TGWU), Frank Cousins, who had no obvious experience in this field and was not an MP. Wilson apparently hoped he could emulate his predecessor, Ernest Bevin's, success in running the labour market and encourage worker participation in business management. Like Bevin, Cousins was soon elected to parliament in a by-election, but was less effective. 'Mintech' as it was known, absorbed and coordinated the responsibilities of existing departments for research and application of science and technology to industry. It gave limited funds to the private sector to develop new technologies and research and development were encouraged in the public sector leading to technological change and increased efficiency in postal and telephone services, mining and gas supply. Mintech particularly sponsored development of four key industries: computers, electronics, telecommunications and machine tools.[6] Labour's economic strategy and goals were clearly established in its first year.

Welfare planning

Average incomes, living standards and consumption continued to rise and income inequality gradually to narrow, but pockets of unemployment and deprivation survived. Since Labour believed that strong health, education and social security systems were essential underpinnings of a strong economy, it planned to expand state welfare so far as economic constraints allowed. Prescription charges were immediately abolished.

Crossman was disconcerted to be appointed Minister of Housing, rather than continuing responsibility for social security. Wilson persuaded him that housing was more important to voters. A White Paper in 1965 promised to deliver 500,000 houses a year by 1970, half in the public sector. This was never achieved but 400,000 were built each year, 1966–70, more than by their predecessors. There was a rising crisis of homelessness due to the previous government's slackening of rent controls and tenant security. The Protection from Eviction Act, 1965, aimed to increase security, while the Rent Act, 1965, reintroduced private sector rent controls, extended security of tenure and made harassment of tenants illegal, ending the scandals of Rachmanism. But furnished rentals were excluded, encouraging unscrupulous landlords to install minimal furnishings. Some of the worst abuses were eliminated but not all.

Anthony Crosland took charge of Education, long committed to equal access to good education and critical of the socially selective tripartite system. He issued a circular requesting local authorities to submit plans to reorganize secondary education on comprehensive lines, abolishing 11+ selection. They still could not be required to do so, but by 1970 most authorities complied. A Public Schools Commission was appointed to enquire into a major source of educational inequality but reached no satisfactory conclusion. In 1964, 76 per cent of Conservative MPs attended independent schools, 15 per cent of Labour MPs, 76 per cent of judges, 50 per cent of top civil servants, 60 per cent of directors of leading firms, all overwhelmingly male. Three-quarters of sixth formers attended this minority of schools. Crosland aimed to improve performance in the state sector.

Crosland also announced a 'binary policy' for higher education, funding the development of thirty degree-awarding 'polytechnics' out of local authority technical colleges, alongside the universities – thirty-eight by 1970, following the foundation of seven new universities in England and one, Stirling, in Scotland – while ten Colleges of Advanced Technology were granted university charters. Polytechnics focused on science and technology and, unlike most universities, provided part-time courses for people of all ages, developing the skills required in a modernizing economy and, hopefully, democratizing higher education. Part-time education, usually in the evening, after work, was the commonest means for people to compensate for an inadequate school education but opportunities remained limited at degree level. Crosland declared 'parity of esteem' between universities and polytechnics, though this was easier said than done in status-conscious Britain where 'polys' could be disparaged as second-class universities. Polytechnic student numbers rose from around 33,000 in 1962 to 215,000 in 1970/1971, mostly male.[7] Planning also began for a favourite Wilson project, a 'University of the Air', later named the Open University, designed to extend post-school opportunities and further democratize higher education by broadcasting part-time degree-level classes on radio and TV, supported by correspondence with tutors, printed materials and summer schools. It opened in 1969.[8]

The 1964 manifesto promised to raise all social security payments which 'have been allowed to fall below minimum levels of human need'. State pensions were immediately raised by 12s. 6d per week, the largest rise since pensions began. This was popular, given the extent of poverty among older people, but the pension remained insufficient to live on, worth only 21 per cent of average male industrial earnings. Also, the cost prevented the more ambitious reconstruction of pensions proposed by Labour advisers in 1957, linking contributions and pensions to earnings as elsewhere in Western Europe.[9] At least one million pensioners still needed means-tested NAB supplements. In 1966 the NAB was replaced by the Supplementary Benefits Commission (SBC), designed, with limited success, to introduce less stigmatizing methods of assessment, simpler administration and clarify rights to benefits. In 1965 redundancy payments were introduced, one-off payments linked to previous earnings paid by employers to workers made involuntarily redundant. In 1966 earnings-related supplements were introduced for sickness and unemployment benefits, funded by increased contributions, shifting from the flat-rate basis of social security. These measures were designed to encourage flexibility in the labour market, essential to the modernization programme.[10]

The rediscovery of poverty

But in 1965 shocking evidence exposed the urgent need to reduce poverty. On 23 December, to make maximum impact at Christmas, Brian Abel-Smith, from LSE, and his former colleague Peter Townsend, now Professor of Sociology at the new University of Essex, launched their research report, *The Poor and the Poorest*, revealing much more poverty than generally assumed, not confined to older people.[11] They aimed for a modern version of Booth and Rowntree, measuring what had changed from 1900 and alerting people to what had not. They measured poverty not by bare subsistence but by NAB benefit rates, set by the government as a basic minimum income related to average earnings. Townsend argued that, in the modern world, poverty should be defined relative to general living standards. Since most people now enjoyed high and rising standards the major problem was no longer absolute poverty, but 'relative deprivation' compared with national norms, which limited life chances from birth. By this measure, they found that 14 per cent of the UK population (7.5m people) were poor. A high proportion of these, as expected, were retired, 22 per cent in 1961, 62.55 per cent of all retired people. There was also extensive poverty among disabled people. But two million in poverty were children, mostly in larger families, 41 per cent with at least one full-time working parent, who were obviously also in poverty. This was the greatest shock. It was labelled 'the rediscovery of poverty' and made an international impact as the world was waking up to continuing international poverty. In 1964, Lyndon Johnson launched a 'War on Poverty', following similar findings in the United States,[12] while awareness grew of much greater poverty in what was increasingly called the 'third world' of 'underdeveloped' nations, terminology developed in the self-defined 'first' world of Europe, the United States and its allies, in contrast with the 'second' world of communist countries.

The UK findings were presented to Wilson and publicized on television and in the press, arousing shock and sympathy.[13] Public awareness of social problems was further promoted by a new generation of energetic, media aware, voluntary organizations, drawing on growing university research and the contemporary fashion for social criticism, mobilizing a young generation anxious to improve the world, hopeful after the election of a Labour government, their campaigns publicized by television and the ever less deferential, sensation-seeking, press. One organization grew directly from Townsend and Abel-Smith's research: the Child Poverty Action Group (CPAG) was founded in 1965 by social workers working with children and experiencing family poverty, supported by the two researchers, to campaign for support for families of poor children.[14] In the same year the Disablement Income Group (DIG) was launched by Megan du Boisson. Suffering from multiple sclerosis, she discovered that married women like herself, who were not employed and had not paid sufficient national insurance contributions, and all disabled people who had not paid contributions generally because their disability was severe and long-term preventing them from working, had no right to sickness benefits but had to apply for means-tested National Assistance. DIG campaigned for a non-contributory disability income, special allowances for those with exceptional needs, research into disability issues and, above all, greater understanding and respect for disabled people, exposing how neglected they were in the post-war Welfare State. DIG Scotland was formed in 1966 by Margaret Blackwood, who was in a similar position to du Boisson. The two organizations were new in being formed by and for the disadvantaged group concerned rather than by charitable others, stimulating the growth of similar institutions.[15] Shelter was founded in 1966 to help the growing numbers of homeless people. It built on the mass audience and publicity for the 1966 TV showing of Ken Loach's film about a homeless family, *Cathy Come Home.*

Established voluntary organizations still campaigned about persistent social problems, identified new problems, strove to help people in need and pressed government to act. They had all to adapt to the new world of high-profile media publicity, alongside the growing numbers of international aid organizations responding to 'third world' poverty. From 1963 five British-based organizations – British Red Cross, Christian Aid, Oxfam, Save the Children, War on Want – collaborated to raise funds for emergencies in poorer countries. They grew as colonialism declined, sometimes out of missionary organizations and/or staffed by former colonial administrators experienced in relief work. The five formed the Disasters Emergency Committee, using the new media boldness to spread stark images of human suffering, previously unseen by most people, seeking donations for victims of long-term poverty, too often worsened by famine, civil war and other crises.[16] Wilson was sympathetic, and their pressure contributed to the establishment of MOD. Concern about poverty at home and abroad was an important feature of late 1960s politics and culture.

Liberalization

Wilson was also under pressure to improve 'welfare' in other than strictly material ways, to develop a more open, tolerant culture, protecting certain stigmatized groups. By 1970 his government created an unprecedented series of laws which built upon and expanded ongoing cultural change, though much of it was controversial and divisive among voters and in the party and required compromise. Before the 1964 election he promised a free parliamentary vote on abolishing capital punishment, despite polls showing large majorities against it. He also supported action to improve race relations and women's rights and appointed Liberal Roy Jenkins to the Home Office in December

1965 to promote reforms. In 1964 a Labour private member's bill, supported by the government but amended to win Conservative support, abolished capital punishment for an experimental period of five years. It passed easily through the Lords, becoming law in 1965. Following the introduction of Life Peerages in 1958 the upper house contained more Liberals, many of them Labour nominees. Despite continuing opposition, parliament easily passed permanent abolition in 1969.[17]

The government responded to continuing racism and anti-racist protest with the Race Relations Act,1965. Also modified to satisfy parliament, it outlawed discrimination on grounds of race, colour, ethnic or national origin in public places or on public transport but overlooked the important areas of employment and housing. It established the Race Relations Board (RRB) to deal with complaints of discrimination, with local conciliation committees to consider complaints, secure conciliation or seek court proceedings. This was unwieldy and no successful prosecutions followed. Restrictions on immigration remained. It was an important beginning but criticized as inadequate by immigrant and anti-racist groups.[18]

In 1965 another backbench Labour motion proposed reducing criminalization of homosexuality, as recommended by the Wolfenden report in 1957. Ministers refused to support it given the small majority, the impending election and the extent of homophobia, but the Lords easily approved a Bill to decriminalize homosexual acts between adult men in private. It was delayed in the Commons by the election, along with legalization of abortion. The Abortion Law Reform Association (ALRA), founded in 1936, became very active again when Madeleine Simms was appointed leader in 1961, commissioning polls revealing higher than expected support for legalization. The press, popular and serious, discussed abortion more openly than before. The growing body of female columnists highlighted how illegal 'back-street' abortions damaged the health of women unable to afford private operations: 'As having an abortion has become so much a matter of having £200 and the right address, it seems grossly unfair that it should be denied to the have-nots' wrote Anne Batt in the *Daily Express* in 1965.[19] In 1965 National Opinion Polls (NOP) found 66 per cent of doctors supported legalization, only 10 per cent opposed; in 1966 that 75 per cent of women favoured it and only 20 per cent opposed.[20] But Catholic and other Christian opposition was increasingly organized and outspoken. The Church of England was officially opposed.

General Election 1966

The economy looked bright enough for Labour to risk an election in March 1966. Home resigned the Conservative leadership and Edward Heath was narrowly elected, the Conservatives' first 'lower-class' leader, son of a builder and a former parlour maid who, like Wilson, had made it to Oxford. Labour won a secure majority (266), with seats now more evenly spread around England. Some largely middle-class seats, including in the south, went Labour for the first time since constituency boundaries were re-drawn in 1949. More women voted Labour than Conservative.[21]

A seamen's strike for higher pay in May 1966 was unusual and disastrous for trade. Settling it destroyed Labour's policy of income restraint, provoked speculation against the pound on the international money markets and another sterling crisis in July. Supported by most of the Cabinet, Wilson again refused to devalue because he and the Treasury feared it would cause inflation, devaluations in other countries and worsening international relations, signalling Britain's weakness and decline, while harming people on the lowest incomes and poorer countries. Taxes rose, spending was cut, and a six-month pay freeze imposed, resisted by the TUC. Following a temporary recovery, the freeze ended, but, as incomes, consumption and imports rose again, the deficit recurred in early 1967 and a succession of crises followed. Labour considered another approach to the European Community (EC), as the EEC became in 1967. Some saw entry as a solution to the recurrent economic problems, especially as British trade with Europe's booming economy was growing while its share of Commonwealth and world trade declined, though the party continued to disagree on membership. Britain applied again in 1967, expecting de Gaulle again to say 'Non', as he did, though other members were well disposed.

Iron and steel were renationalized in 1967 and the nationalized industries performed well, though the economy remained in crisis through 1968. Cousins resigned from Mintech in July 1966 in protest at wage controls. He was replaced by Wedgewood Benn in what was seen as a key role in reviving British competitiveness. Mintech collaborated with France to build Concorde, a supersonic jet airliner capable of flying from London to New York in under three and a half, rather than the normal eight, hours. It operated successfully until 2003. In 1966 Mintech took over regulation of shipbuilding from the Board of Trade and in 1969 the Ministry of Power and its responsibilities for coal, electricity, gas, steel and oil. It oversaw mergers, modelled on the success of large companies in the United States, and assisted industry to adopt new technologies through a new National Computer Centre and an Engineering Advisory Service promoting the latest techniques.[22] But there were continuing concerns about the shortage of suitably skilled workers. An NEDC report in 1967 charted a 'brain drain' of qualified people from the United Kingdom especially to the United States, mainly scientists and engineers, due to higher starting salaries and better promotion prospects, urging comparable improvements in Britain.

Mintech's attempts to fund research and development in private industry had limited success. Its leaders remained conservative about new techniques.[23] Ambitious aims to make Britain a world leader in nuclear technology were unfulfilled. Britain spent more on R&D than many of its competitors, but it remained over-concentrated on defence and aerospace.[24] Mintech became 'the biggest state-directed complex of scientific and industrial power in Europe' with a staff of 38,900, including a high proportion of scientists and engineers.[25] It controlled a large defence procurement budget, though the nuclear weapons programme was cut back in the later 1960s.[26] It developed a regional strategy, to stop the drift of industry to the south and growing regional inequality, with some success. In 1966 five development areas were created covering almost half of Britain, where businesses were subsidized to expand. Public spending on roads increased. A

Selective Employment Tax (SET) was introduced in 1966 to fund improvements in manufacturing by taxing growing service industries to encourage them to shed labour which, hopefully, would shift to manufacturing.

These policies strengthened new industries, including computer, machine tools and electronics production, but they needed time to develop, and Labour was over-optimistic about short-term gains, though it deserved credit for thinking and planning long-term.[27] Many plans were abandoned by Heath's Conservative government which followed. Ministers and their advisers believed the conservatism of civil servants bore some responsibility for UK economic failures, that, too often, they were Oxbridge graduates trained in humanities or classics, lacking skills needed in the modern world like economics and reluctant to support progressive policies such as those of DEA. To compensate, ministers increasingly recruited expert special advisers from universities or business. The Fulton Committee on the Civil Service was established to investigate, concluding in 1968 that too little use was made of the skills of scientists, engineers and other professionals in policymaking.[28] One outcome was the establishment of a Civil Service College, planned under Wilson and opened under Heath, to broaden civil service training.

Expanding the Welfare State

Despite the economic crises, Labour continued its commitment to expand and improve the Welfare State. Voluntary groups kept up pressure, increasingly inspired by the 'welfare rights' movement, originating like much 1960s radicalism in the United States, to organize 'Claimants' Unions' advising and assisting people to claim benefits, fighting tribunal and court cases on their behalf when benefits were refused, training advocates and spreading information about benefit rules. Organizations, including CPAG, DIG, NCUMC, Shelter, adopted these tactics. They were prominent in the media promoting welfare campaigns, particularly in the influential weekly *New Society* (established 1962), which focused on social issues.[29]

Disability rights

DIG publicized the inequalities suffered by disabled people, demonstrating how lack of state support caused family breakdown, children orphaned or taken into care and the obstacles to living normal lives, including difficulty in accessing buildings or transport and preventable incarceration in institutions. It rejected the conventional pejorative language of 'cripples', 'handicapped', 'backward people', insisting that UK culture disregarded the dignity and human rights of disabled people. Crossman took over what became the Department of Health and Social Security (DHSS) in 1968 and announced in 1969 a National Insurance Invalidity Pension for the fully insured and a non-contributory attendance allowance for severely disabled people, £4 per week for those needing 24-hour care. He at last had the pensions reform proposed in 1957 embodied in draft legislation in 1969, together with the allowances for disabled people, but both were lost to the 1970 election. Most disabled people lived at home, cared for by family, friends or voluntary agencies. Local authority residential care was normally only available in homes for older people, though there were growing numbers of voluntary institutions. DIG helped shape the Chronically Sick and Disabled Persons Act, 1970, a private member's bill introduced by Labour MP Alf Morris, which the government prioritized to get it through before the election. Morris knew the impact of disability as one of eight children of a Manchester worker who was gassed and badly wounded in the First World War and died when Alf was seven. The Act required local authorities to register all disabled people in their district, inform them of available services and publicize these. It recommended, but did not adequately fund, expanded services, including home helps and day centres. It was implemented by the Conservatives, under further pressure from disability activists, creating some progress towards equal rights for disabled people.[30]

Housing

More homes were built during 1965–9 than in any five-year period since 1918, almost half council houses. Council housing subsidies increased, and the higher standards of construction, space and design recommended by the Parker Morris Committee in 1961 but ignored by the Conservatives became mandatory for public sector building in New Towns from 1967, for local authorities from 1969. In 1966 means-tested rate rebates were introduced and local authorities were encouraged to introduce rent rebates, though means-testing was unpopular. Still many people on low incomes could not afford council rents and experienced poor conditions in private rentals. In 1971, one-eighth of all dwellings, overwhelmingly privately rented, lacked at least one basic amenity: bath or shower (1.6m in England), indoor toilet (2m); 2.4m had no hot water supply to a kitchen sink or hand basin.[31]

A new generation of New Towns was launched as planned by the Conservatives, including Milton Keynes. Labour discouraged the high-density, often high-rise, building promoted by the Conservatives, especially after the dramatic collapse in 1968 of a poorly built tower block in East London, Ronan Point, after just two months' occupation, killing four residents. For the first time conservation and improvement of older buildings, including by local councils, was encouraged with subsidies for renovation rather than demolition and the introduction of conservation areas where development was strictly controlled. Whereas demolition had initially focused on decrepit 'slums', increasingly housing had been demolished merely because it was old and unfashionable, though much Victorian building, of which there was much in British towns and cities, was sounder than recent developments. The change was part of a revival of appreciation of Victorian culture after decades of disparagement, led by poet Sir John Betjeman and architectural historian Nikolaus Pevsner, following their campaign to prevent demolition of grand Victorian St Pancras station in London. It was saved in 1967 and renovated. This cultural shift was assisted by the Clean Air Act clearing pollution from inner cities. It encouraged owner-occupation by younger and lower-income buyers and the revival and 'gentrification' of older urban areas, especially following Labour's Option Mortgage Act, 1968, which subsidized lower-income house-purchasers who could also receive grants for renovation. By 1970 more than 50 per cent of households were owner-occupiers.[32]

Other schemes also sought to revive depressed inner cities. The 1967 Plowden Report on *Children and their Primary Schools* proposed 'educational priority areas' (EPAs) concentrating resources in poor areas, providing nursery education from children's earliest years and compensatory education for older children, with modest success. From 1968 the 'urban programme' focused aid on 'relatively small pockets of severe social deprivation' in cities and towns, working with councils, borrowing a model from the United States. In 1969 the Community Development Project placed teams in twelve areas and subsidized citizens tackling social, including racial, problems. They sought to reassure and help disadvantaged white inner-city residents who blamed immigrants for lack of jobs, poor housing and services, encouraged by sections of the popular press, though immigrants shared their difficulties and more, and most problems had other causes, mainly limited public resources. The project had hardly started in 1970 when Labour lost power, but some local initiatives continued-.

Social security

National insurance benefits were uprated again in 1967 and 1969. Following the revelations of poverty in larger families, in 1967 family allowances rose for fourth and subsequent children by 5s per week (25p). This did not satisfy CPAG, which campaigned for greater support to poorer families, but the chancellor refused to go further in an economic crisis. In November 1967 Callaghan exchanged posts with Roy Jenkins and moved, reluctantly, to the Home Office.[33] In 1968 the economy revived and Jenkins increased family allowances for all eligible children (first children were still excluded) by 10s (50p) pw, funded by reductions in child tax allowances. CPAG advocated abolition of tax allowances for the better-off to fund higher universal family allowances benefitting low-income non-taxpayers. Labour was cautious, partly because more manual workers now paid income tax as incomes rose. This caused bitter exchanges with CPAG, now directed by Frank Field, later a Labour MP, and the Chair, Peter Townsend, who claimed in a pre-election manifesto in 1970, with some exaggeration, 'the Poor get Poorer under Labour'.[34] But child poverty was rising partly due to growing numbers of families headed by single mothers following divorce or separation.[35] In 1969 Crossman appointed a committee on One-Parent Families to investigate their needs. It reported in 1974.

Health

Prescription and dental charges were re-imposed in 1968, following the crisis, to meet rapidly rising NHS costs and avoid cutting the much-needed hospital-building programme. Pensioners, children, Supplementary Benefit claimants and long-term sick and disabled people were exempted. A report by the Seebohm Committee on Personal Social Services in 1968 led to improvement in local authority services but criticism of their uneven quality and unequal outcomes continued.[36] Health and social services for older and mentally and physically disabled people living at home remained uncoordinated despite often uncertain boundaries between them. This became urgent following a series of scandals about the serious mistreatment of people in psychiatric hospitals, publicized in a book, *Sans Everything* (1967), by Barbara Robb, who formed Aid to the Elderly in Government Institutions to demand change, including improved community services to support older and disabled people at home. When Crossman took over DHSS in 1968, he visited hospitals, urging improvements which he worked hard to implement, de-institutionalization of patients where possible and improved services to assist them at home.[37] His proposals were partially implemented by the Conservatives.

Education

By 1970 about one-third of secondary pupils in England and Wales were in comprehensive schools, a ten-fold increase from 1964. The percentage staying past age fifteen rose from 27.3 in 1960/1 to 51 in 1970/1.[38] Plans to raise the school-leaving age to sixteen in 1970 were disrupted by the economic crisis and postponed to 1973, then implemented by the Conservatives. Among the crisis cuts, free milk for secondary schools was abolished. Yet education spending grew by 6–7 per cent each year, 1964–70; teachers in training increased by one-third, 1964–7.

Living standards

Labour expanded state benefits and services, 1964–70, despite economic crises and planned to go further had it stayed in government. From 1964 to 1970, GDP growth slowed slightly, to an average 2.6 per cent per annum, but the annual average growth of public expenditure was 5.9 per cent, much of it on health and social services. Poverty persisted, but average living standards improved, income inequality narrowed and consumption grew.[39] Demand for household appliances continued to climb, including colour TVs when they were introduced at the end of the decade. In 1965, 75 per cent of employees had two weeks paid holiday each year, 22 per cent two-three weeks and more took holidays away from home, most in Britain but increasingly abroad. Cinema, sport and other leisure activities continued to boom.[40] Car licences rose to 10.6 million in 1965; total vehicle licences from 4.4 million to 13 million 1950–65.[41] One unwelcome outcome was growing numbers of accidents due to drunken driving. Techniques emerged to test alcohol in the blood, and the Road Safety Act, 1967, introduced a blood alcohol limit for drivers; it became obligatory to provide specimens on request, using the newly invented breathalyser test. Publicans protested they would be bankrupted, but they survived. Road accidents in Great Britain fell from 292,000 in 1966 to 259,000 in 1976, road-deaths from 7,985 to 6,570, while vehicles increased to 17.5 million in 1975.[42]

The 'Permissive Society'

With a secure parliamentary majority, progressive politicians returned to promoting liberal legislation. The Criminal Justice Act, 1967, was designed to improve the treatment of the growing numbers of prisoners to encourage rehabilitation, including establishing a Parole Board to consider early release of short-sentence prisoners. Prisons worked to reduce re-offending, including providing industrial work experience modelled on factory conditions.[43]

The Lords again passed the Bill partially legalizing homosexuality, but leading ministers, including Wilson, resisted its introduction in the Commons, partly because, as Crossman put it, 'working-class people in the north jeer at their members at the weekend and ask them why they're looking after the buggers at Westminster instead of looking after the unemployed at home'.[44] The party was divided but there had been an influx of younger, more liberal Labour MPs in 1964 and 1966. The proportion of university educated Labour MPs rose from 39 per cent in 1959 to 46 per cent in 1964, 51 per cent in 1966 and surveys showed the close association between higher education and cultural liberalism.[45] Crossman supported homosexual and abortion reform and persuaded Wilson not to let these controversies drag on.[46]

The Wolfenden proposals to legalize homosexual acts in private (only) were modified to get the Bill through parliament and the government remained officially neutral. A couple could still be prosecuted for having sex when someone else was in the same building, and the armed forces and the merchant navy were exempted from the law.[47] The penalty for 'gross indecency' – effectively any visible act perceived as homosexual, such as kissing in public – rose from two to five years' imprisonment. The age of consent was fixed at twenty-one, as Wolfenden had recommended, not the heterosexual age of sixteen, for fear that young men would be seduced by older men, as though young women would not. The amended Sexual Offences Act passed the Commons by a clear majority and the Lords even more easily, becoming law in 1967. It applied only in England and Wales. There were campaigns to extend it to Scotland, which did not come until 1980. It was fiercely opposed in Northern Ireland, where the fundamentalist Protestant, Rev. Ian Paisley, led a 'Save Ulster from Sodomy' campaign. A gay man brought a successful case in the ECHR and the law changed in 1982. Campaigners were subdued but recognized the law was a start and that public prejudice remained so strong that it was wise not to criticize. Prosecutions for such 'acts of gross indecency' as men holding hands in public increased, from 420 in 1966 to 1,711 in 1974.[48] Activism for further change revived following the formation of the Gay Liberation Front in 1970.

Abortion

David Steel, a young, newly elected Liberal MP, cautiously accepted ALRA's persuasion to introduce a Bill to legalize abortion.[49] It passed its Commons second reading following a more explosive public debate than homosexual reform.[50] Following amendments, doctors could refuse to perform abortions on conscience grounds. The medical profession was divided. Many doctors with experience of the death and damage resulting from the large, and, it was suspected, growing, numbers of illegal abortions, supported legalization. It was opposed by disability activists who feared that easier abortion would prevent the birth of disabled people capable of viable lives. There was no question of women being allowed to choose: doctors must decide. The main issue was whether it should be allowed strictly on health or on broader social grounds. Health grounds won, including allowing abortion if the mother was judged likely to take her own life but not if she felt too overburdened to rear a child.[51] Abortion became legal in 1967, up to 28 weeks gestation, with permission from two doctors. As with the other liberal measures the legislation was an imperfect compromise, but it was a breakthrough, the first legal abortion in Western Europe. It was already legal in most communist countries.

Legal abortions increased from 22,100 in 1968 to 75,400 in 1970, evenly divided between married and unmarried women, most over 20.[52] The law applied in Scotland but not in Northern Ireland, where Catholics and Protestants united in opposition as on other liberal reforms. It was only permitted there when there was serious risk to the health and life of the mother and N. Ireland had the harshest criminal penalty for abortion in Europe: life imprisonment for a woman convicted of undergoing an illegal abortion. Women travelled to Great Britain for abortion but had to pay for it, they were not allowed on the NHS. Abortion was legalized in N. Ireland by the Westminster government in 2019 while the devolved government was suspended, but only limited facilities were provided.

Birth control

Birth control services were not available on the NHS and could still be provided free of charge by local authorities only if pregnancy put the mother's health at risk. Charities, notably the FPA, provided free services and demand was growing. The FPA worked hard in the 1950s and 1960s to publicize its work, improve public knowledge about birth control and increase state provision. The Church of England officially supported it; the Catholic Church did not. From 1960 the press was excited, and moralists alarmed, by the revolutionary new birth control pill, apparently more effective than other methods, and about the sexual liberation of women that could follow this easy, reliable form of contraception. The government held back from extending free services due to the extent of opposition. Then another Labour private member's Bill allowed, but did not require, local authorities to provide contraceptive advice and supplies free of charge to anyone regardless of age, marital status or any other limitation. The Family Planning Act passed easily through parliament in 1967, with little fuss even about supplying birth control to unmarried people, including teenagers, while sections of the press shrieked 'Sex on the rates!'. Fewer than 25 per cent of local authorities complied.[53] There was strong opposition to making it free on the NHS. Keith Joseph was reluctantly pressured in 1974 to integrate birth control within the NHS, providing free advice for all but free supplies only for those in 'special social need' or 'financial need'. Shortly after, Labour returned to government and Barbara Castle, as minister for health and social security, fulfilled Labour's election promise of free family planning on the NHS.[54] It remained hardest to obtain in Northern Ireland.

Fears that the change would encourage unaccustomed sexual licence, trashing 'traditional' conservative morals, were again challenged by official statistics of births within the first eight months of marriage: 14 per cent in 1951, 22 per cent by 1965.[55] Births to unmarried parents rose from 5 per cent of all births in 1950–2 to 8.2 per cent in 1971.[56] In 1971, 45 per cent of 'illegitimate' births were jointly registered by the parents, suggesting that they had stable, often cohabiting, relationships, another feature of cultural change.[57] Along with gradually easier availability of contraceptives and more women seeking independence, the birth rate declined from 1968 having risen steadily since the war.

Divorce

Divorce reform also followed decades of campaigning. Divorces in Great Britain rose from 25,672 in 1960 to 62,010 in 1970. It was still difficult and expensive, but more people could afford it. Women, especially, were less willing to tolerate failing marriages and readier to seek independence.[58] The Archbishop of Canterbury appointed a committee on divorce reform, whose report in 1966, *Putting Asunder*, accepted that divorce law could no longer be dictated by religious belief. It recommended 'breakdown of marriage' as the test for divorce, as reformers had long advocated. Women's groups insisted that reform must include sound financial provision for divorced partners, and it was generally agreed that divorce should only be granted when the court was satisfied that the settlement was adequate. There were outright opponents, including Labour feminist Baroness Summerskill vigorously attacking what she called a 'Casanova's Charter', enabling men to exploit women in short-lived marriages. A government Bill passed easily through parliament and came into force in 1971.[59] Applicants for divorce had to prove the marriage had broken down for one of five reasons: adultery, unreasonable behaviour, desertion, separation for more than two years if both agreed to the divorce, or for at least five years if they disagreed. Supporters of 'no fault' divorce were disappointed. Accompanying legislation allowed each divorced partner an equal share of family assets.[60] The laws applied only in England and Wales. Scotland retained its traditional system until a private member's bill by a Scottish National Party (SNP) MP brought the law into line with England and Wales in 1975. The English law was forced upon Northern Ireland in 1978 by the government, but divorce remained difficult to obtain. In Great Britain divorces rose rapidly, most initiated by women. An unknown number of couples could now divorce after 'living in sin', often for many years because they could not divorce under previous legislation.[61]

Censorship

Labour also abolished the Lord Chamberlain's duty to protect public morals by banning any 'unsuitable' play. It was held to obstruct experimental, innovative theatre and was easily evaded by staging plays at 'private' theatre clubs to evade censorship, and a play banned on stage could be shown to millions on television. No other non-communist country practised censorship, except Franco's Spain. An official committee recommended abolition which was achieved by another Labour backbench Bill in 1968.[62]

Race

Inequalities and tensions concerning race continued and were suspected to be growing along with the immigrant population. Non-white residents of Commonwealth origin in the UK in 1961 included 173,076 West Indians, 115,982 South Asians, in 1971, 302,970 and 462,125, in total populations of 52.7 million and 55.5 million.[63] Emigration still exceeded immigration every year during 1946–80.[64] In 1966 the RRB commissioned an investigation into discrimination, especially in areas not covered by the 1965 Act, revealing it to be widespread in employment, housing and services, causing low incomes, poor, often overcrowded housing and poor health. It was strongest against West Indians and as problematic for second as first generation Black or Asian residents. Employers claimed that employing 'coloured' people, especially in direct contact with 'white' clients, put them at a competitive disadvantage.[65] The RRB appealed for extension of the Race Relations Act.

The formation of the National Front, an anti-immigrant, nationalist party, in 1967 raised tensions. So, even more, did an explosive, much publicized, speech by Enoch Powell in April 1968, one of several he made about immigration. Following a reference to 'wide-eyed, grinning piccaninnies', the former professor of classics proclaimed, 'As I look ahead, I am filled with foreboding. Like the Romans I seem to see "the river Tiber foaming with much blood"', referring to a passage of Virgil's *Aeneid*, as, understandably, few realized. It was well received in his Midlands constituency, Wolverhampton, which had the highest immigrant population outside London. A Gallup poll found that three-quarters of respondents agreed with Powell and London dockers marched in his support.[66] He was dismissed from the Shadow Cabinet. Resistance to racism also continued and grew, by people of many backgrounds, inspired by the activism of the civil rights movement in the United States.

Labour disappointed anti-racists when it introduced the Commonwealth Immigrants Act, 1968, which further limited immigration by restricting entry of citizens who obtained their British passports overseas and had no guaranteed employment in the UK, unless they had at least one white British grandparent. Immigrant numbers were severely limited. All white Commonwealth citizens retained entry rights. It was a panic measure rushed through parliament to limit the entry of Asians fleeing persecution in Kenya following the Africanization policy of the newly independent country. It was strongly criticized by civil liberties groups and other liberals. Immigration from Asia, Africa and the Caribbean fell by half in the next ten years.

To soften the impact, also in 1968 a second Race Relations Act covered discrimination in employment and housing and strengthened the RRB's powers to investigate complaints and initiate proceedings. It established the Community Relations Commission (CRC) to promote good race relations and advise the Home Office. But sanctions remained weak, and many members of minority groups were unaware of the legislation or had little faith in it. The police successfully put on pressure to be exempted. Gallup polls found that nine-tenths of respondents approved of the immigration restrictions, a bare majority believed that 'coloured' immigrants should compete equally for work with the rest of the population or vote in British elections.[67] The law at least signalled government opposition to discrimination, providing a moral lead, if more limited than some wished. Immigrants continued to suffer substantial disadvantage.

In 1968, for the first time, the law acknowledged the inequalities and discrimination faced by another minority group, Gypsies and Travellers, after they rebelled. Their itinerant lifestyle and irregular employment excluded them from essential services, including education, access to a GP, national insurance. If they tried to settle, they faced discrimination from local authorities and landlords. If they did not, their caravan sites aroused hostility, harassment, and eviction, with some local authorities declaring their districts 'no-go' areas for travellers. Pubs displayed 'No Gypsies' signs. In 1965 Crossman commissioned a national survey which recorded 15,500 Gypsies and Travellers in England, Wales and Scotland, a probable underestimate. Only twelve local authorities had established caravan sites, just one-third of families had access to on-site water, children's education was severely deficient. The findings were circulated to local authorities with 'strong and detailed advice' on providing sites, requesting reports on action taken. In 1966 the Gypsy Council formed to campaign against eviction and for equal status and respect with the settled population. By 1968 300 complaints were made against pubs under the Race Relations Act, but none went to court: Gypsies and Travellers were not recognized as a 'race' under the Act. The Caravan Sites Act, 1968, was initially a private member's Bill from Liberal MP Eric Lubbock, which the government supported. It required local authorities to provide sites for Gypsies and Travellers, though with no deadline; they could evict them from unauthorized sites. By 1973 between one-fifth and one-quarter of the required sites were established. The needs of this excluded group were becoming recognized though equality remained remote.[68]

Equal pay

The government's final reforming breakthrough, following another long campaign, was the Equal Pay Act, 1970. It was initiated by Barbara Castle, as minister for employment and Productivity from 1968. Women in the Labour Party, trade unions and women's organizations campaigned for it with increasing intensity in the 1960s, before the Women's Liberation Movement (WLM) took off from 1969. Seventy per cent of new union members during 1964–70 were female, and unions took notice. There was a flurry of strikes for equal pay and equal treatment at work in the mid-1960s. During the 1966 election campaign, an alliance of women's organizations demanded equality at work, in taxation, pensions and other benefits.[69] The EC, in its founding Treaty of Rome, 1957, committed member states to 'maintain the principle of equal remuneration for equal work as between men and women workers', following pressure from women across Europe. Labour leaders were anxious to meet EC standards where possible to increase their chances of admission.

When Castle became the responsible minister, she faced two strikes which, she later commented, 'fired my determination to force the macho male chauvinists in the Treasury to accept the principle of equal pay'.[70] The first was the strike of women sewing machinists at Ford's factory at Dagenham in June 1968, the subject of a film, *Made in Dagenham*, in 2010. Castle intervened and the women gained something closer to equal pay – a rise from 85 per cent to 92 per cent of the men's rate. The strike led to the formation of the National Joint Action Committee for Women's Equal Rights among women's groups and trade unionists. It adopted a charter calling on the TUC to campaign for equal pay and equal opportunities. The second dispute arose from a pay demand by male engineers which disadvantaged women. Castle 'knew then that left to themselves the unions would never do anything serious about equal pay and that the government had to legislate'.[71] In spring 1970, when the election had been called, women Labour MPs tabled an amendment to the government's Prices and Incomes Bill demanding that pay controls should not prevent moves towards equal pay. Castle pointed out that the government was likely to be defeated on the amendment unless she announced equal pay legislation. The Cabinet felt forced to agree. She rushed the Equal Pay Bill through parliament before the election, later admitting, 'It was far from perfect, but it established the principle on which later refinements could be built. I knew that if we lost the election our Tory successors would be forced to proceed with it.'[72] It required equal rates of pay for the same or similar work, to be assessed by job evaluation schemes. Compliance would be voluntary until 1975 to allow time for evaluation. Claims of non-compliance would be made to an employment tribunal and successful claims compensated by up to two years' back-pay. The act overlooked women's unequal access to promotion or appointment to higher paid work.

Women remained concentrated in low-status, low-paid work. Employers still argued that they were not victims of discrimination: it was rational to withhold training or promotion when women would leave to raise a family. The law was evaded in various ways. In 1970 the median earnings of adult women full-time workers were 54 per cent of males', by 1983 66 per cent, following further legislation.[73] The struggle continued.

Youth

Changing youth culture brought other legal changes. With growing affluence more people were marrying, buying property and making other contracts at earlier ages but legally could do none of these things without parental permission until age twenty-one. In 1968 the legal majority was reduced to eighteen. The voting age fell in consequence. There was no sign of pressure for this from young people. Wilson's hope that young voters would support Labour may have helped. There was stronger youth support for relaxing the law on the use of drugs, but very strong popular and political opposition. After an investigation, a Misuse of Drugs Act was drafted which relaxed penalties for use of cannabis, the most popular drug, but not for producing or supplying it. This was passed by the Conservatives in 1971.

Election 1970

In 1970 the economy was recovering aided by an upturn in world trade; unemployment averaged 2.5 per cent during 1966–70. By May 1970 Labour had a seven-point lead in the polls and Wilson led Heath by 21 points on personal popularity. He called an election. The polls were even on which party could best manage the economy, but up to the election they predicted a Labour win.[74] Labour issued a cautious manifesto, but, on a lower turnout than in 1966 – 72 per cent – lost the election, losing fifty-eight seats on a swing of 4.7 per cent, the highest since 1945. Race probably played a part: the Conservatives targeted marginal constituencies where it was a particular issue. Labour was not helped by the announcement, two days before the election, of an unexpected balance of payments deficit, nor by conflict with the unions and growing 'Troubles' – conflict between Catholics and Protestants – in Northern Ireland. The liberal reforms may have alienated some voters but, asked by Gallup why Labour had lost, one in four voters replied, 'the cost-of-living'; no other reason came close. Support among men, especially manual workers, fell more than among women, from 69 per cent in 1966 to 58 per cent.

Conclusion

The liberal reforms were seen by supporters as introducing a more open, equal society where excluded groups had equal rights. Most were tentative beginnings, compromises attacked by Labour's many radical critics for not going far enough, but signs of cultural progress, building on changes through previous decades. For many they contributed to improved life satisfaction and living standards, but change was unequal across the UK, like much else, and slowest in Northern Ireland. They stimulated the emergence of the Women's Liberation Movement and the Gay Liberation Front at the end of the decade demanding more reform, together with anti-racist groups and others. In the eyes of opponents, they ushered in a 'permissive' society, destroying established values, undermining 'traditional' morality. Still in the twenty-first century the legislation was blamed for the growth of single parenthood, youth crime and most of society's ills.

By 1970 Labour could claim substantial achievements. Despite economic crises, income inequality was gradually narrowing, though relative poverty persisted.[75] According to official estimates, in 1964 the top 10 per cent of income earners, after tax, had 25.9 per cent of total earnings, the bottom 50 per cent 25.2 per cent. In 1970 the numbers were 23.9 per cent and 26.1 per cent respectively.[76] Peter Townsend calculated that the percentage of UK households in relative poverty (i.e. with incomes below 60 per cent of the median, which became the internationally accepted measure) in 1968–9 was 10.6, with 29.5 'on the margins of poverty'. Poverty was greatest in Northern Ireland, least in parts of Greater London, greater among women than men and among over 65s and children above other age groups, in large families and ethnic minorities.[77] Major inequalities of gender, race, disability and homosexual rights were confronted and modified, though far from eliminated. There were substantial, if incomplete, welfare reforms and significant legal reforms, though never enough to satisfy the growing body of radical critics.

CHAPTER 10
THE 1970s

'DISMAL DECADE'?

The 'Seventies' is commonly described as a decade of turbulent discontent and decline, terminating the post-war 'golden age' of progress. It was indeed a time of recurrent economic crises, national and international, more severe than in the 1950s and 1960s, with increased industrial action, inflation and unemployment. The UK again became more divided between regions of decline and unemployment and prosperity and consumption as manufacturing and Britain's share of world trade continued to decline relative to its competitors, while finance and services flourished. Growing inequalities due to decline of long-established industries stimulated nationalism in Scotland and Wales and deepening 'Troubles' divided Catholic and Protestant communities in Northern Ireland.

It is less often noticed that also in the 1970s income inequality in the UK reached its narrowest point of the century and the Welfare State its peak level and quality of services and benefits. There were further advances towards gender and race equality. The liberating sexual and cultural practices derided by cultural conservatives as 'permissive' – divorce, separation, cohabitation, open homosexuality – continued to spread, increasing personal 'welfare', alongside 'new social movements', including the Women's Liberation Movement (WLM), the Gay Liberation Front (GLF) and anti-racism, all working actively and with some successes, along with the older trade union movement, to reduce continuing inequalities.

Heath in power

Heath appointed one woman to his eighteen-member Cabinet, Margaret Thatcher. In the contemporary culture he believed he needed a token woman, placed in charge of the suitably female terrain of Education. Fifteen ministers were privately educated, four at Eton.[1] Heath and Thatcher were exceptions, both upwardly mobile, via Oxford, from the borders of the working and lower middle classes, her father a shopkeeper. They had little else in common. She married a millionaire businessman; he was unmarried. He believed in firm policies and aimed for close control of the party. He excluded Powell from the Cabinet and others with whom he disagreed. His decidedly un-consensual programme, launched in March 1970, advanced the policies of his Conservative predecessors, including curbing unions, making social security benefits more 'selective', that is, means-tested, ending incomes policies and liberating business from government 'shackles'.

Economic policy

Reversing the relative weakness of the economy compared with Britain's competitors was central for Heath as for Wilson, though their approaches were very different. Unlike Wilson, he had the advantage of inheriting a large budget surplus, with revenue exceeding expenditure by over 5 per cent of GDP. Heath believed the state could assist growth in a free enterprise economy, if its institutions were suitably reformed, though intervention should be limited. Several Labour controls were removed. MinTech was merged into a new Ministry for Trade and Industry under John Davies, Director-General of the Confederation of British Industries (CBI), 'the bosses' trade union', and its commitment to industrial modernization terminated. Davies announced that taxpayers' money should not assist 'lame duck' industries. Then, early in 1971, a formidable lame duck emerged: internationally prestigious Rolls-Royce, Britain's leading manufacturer of aero-engines and luxury cars, faced bankruptcy. It was too important to lose, and, to Labour's glee, it was nationalized. The motor manufacturing arm was privatized in 1973. This was one of several Conservative U-turns when free enterprise did not always succeed.

In the 1971 budget Chancellor Anthony Barber sought to encourage investment and demand with tax cuts, with little effect. By summer 1971 urgent action was needed to avert crisis. A large programme of public works in deprived areas, increased house improvement grants and capital allowances for industry were introduced, with further tax cuts, and the Bank of England cut interest rates to encourage borrowing. Unemployment rose to 900,000 in early 1972, heading to the symbolically dangerous one million, while prices rose internationally, in the UK by 7 per cent. By early 1973 most industrial nations experienced inflation and slower economic growth, the UK more than most. The Bretton Woods system of fixed exchange rates collapsed, and the pound slipped badly. Inflation increased union pressure for wage rises.

Welfare

Social security

The government sought cuts to state welfare. Crossman's pensions reforms were abandoned because they were costly and threatened the increasingly powerful private pension sector. The pledge to extend 'selectivity' was implemented. CPAG still campaigned for higher universal child allowances. Sir Keith Joseph at DHSS introduced a cheaper alternative, Family Income Supplement (FIS), a means-tested benefit for low-paid working families. It was designed to tackle the growing problem, highlighted by

CPAG, of the many full-time workers too low-paid to support their families, but, as ever with means-tested benefits, take-up was low, only 50 per cent of eligible claimants, leaving many in poverty. FIS subsidized low-paying employers and created a disincentive for low-paid workers to earn more for fear of exceeding the means limit and losing benefit, making a net loss, known as the 'poverty trap'.[2] On another issue raised in the late 1960s, Joseph was reluctantly pressured in 1974 to integrate birth control services into the NHS, providing universal free advice, but free supplies only for those receiving means-tested benefits.

Housing

The 1970 Conservative manifesto attacked Labour's failure to build as many houses as promised, despite their building more than any other government in the twentieth century.[3] It pledged to build more, especially owner-occupied, homes. Housebuilding then declined from a total of 378,000 in 1969, mostly public sector, to 280,000 in 1974, about 60 per cent private sector.[4] The major policy change was the Housing Finance Act, 1972, which required council rents to rise to 'fair rent' (i.e. local market rent) levels, aiming to end government subsidies. Labour's means-tested rent-rebate scheme, which was optional for councils, was extended to private tenants, supported by government funds, subsidizing landlords and extending the 'poverty trap'.[5] The Act was strongly resisted by Labour-controlled councils, but they were forced to comply. It did not apply in Scotland.

Education

Margaret Thatcher became notorious for withdrawing free milk from primary schoolchildren over age seven, lampooned by Labour as 'Margaret Thatcher, milk snatcher', despite having itself withdrawn milk from secondary schools. She raised the cost of school meals. By 1970 most local authorities had adopted comprehensive secondary schooling. Thatcher withdrew Crosland's circular recommending this, but authorities of all political persuasions continued to switch. More comprehensives were established during her period of office than in any other. There was little enthusiasm among voters or education professionals for returning to the inequities of grammar schools and 11+ selection. The school-leaving age was raised to sixteen in 1973, as planned by Labour. Education spending rose faster than in 1964–70, largely due to implementation of Labour policies. The expansion of universities, polytechnics and teacher training colleges continued: 13 per cent of 18- to 21-year-olds entered some form of higher education in 1972 compared with 8.5 per cent in 1962, though expansion slowed when the Conservatives cut means-tested grants.[6] The university student population remained predominantly middle class and male, though numbers of female and lower-middle-class students slowly increased. Older students had access to the Open University and other HE institutions.

Strikes

Meanwhile, living conditions declined for many people, sparking protest from unions. The government introduced restrictions on the right to strike, stimulating further militancy. Days lost in strikes in 1972 were the highest since 1926 and union membership rose from 47.7 per cent to an unprecedented 49.6 per cent of the workforce, during 1970–4. Public support for the unions rose in the polls. Mining declined as other sources of power, mainly oil, replaced coal. Its workforce shrank from over 700,000 in 1961 to under 300,000 in 1971.[7] This was achieved calmly, through natural wastage, under former Labour minister, Lord Alfred Robens, at the NCB. But miners' earnings fell behind other workers' and the cost of living. They were reluctant to protest, fearing job losses, but officials of the National Union of Mineworkers (NUM) demanded a 40 per cent wage-rise. The NCB, no longer led by Robens, directed by the government, offered only 6 per cent, below inflation. With majority approval in ballots made obligatory by the government, with high turnouts, in January 1972 the miners began their first national strike since 1926. It lasted six weeks, with widespread popular support, causing power cuts and closures in other industries. The government declared a state of emergency, placing industry on a three-day week to conserve energy. An enquiry was appointed under Lord Justice Wilberforce. With unusual speed, within two days it endorsed the miners' case for higher pay, with state subsidies, due to the industry's importance to the economy and the exceptional working conditions.[8] The miners gained an average 17 per cent rise plus subsidized travel to work, more paid holiday-time and overtime and improved pensions.

Defeated again, the government sought, unsuccessfully, to negotiate an incomes policy with the TUC. The 1972 budget made large cuts to income tax and purchase tax to stimulate demand. In November 1972, pay, prices, rents and dividends were frozen, continuing for the rest of the government's time in office, achieving lower inflation. Output grew by 10 per cent and unemployment fell to *c.* 500,000 at the end of 1973, but the balance of payments ran into deficit as consumers bought imports. There was a run on the pound, and in mid-1973 the bank rate rose. Disillusion was growing, including in the Treasury, with Keynesian methods of controlling demand because they could not control import prices.[9] Heath hoped the economy would revive when the UK finally joined the EC in January 1973, long his ambition. Pompidou had replaced de Gaulle as French president, removing the main obstacle to UK entry.[10] But it was a bad time to join, shortly before the 'oil shock' ended the three decades of post-war growth in Western Europe.

The price of Middle East oil quadrupled following the October 1973 Arab–Israeli war. Arab oil-producing countries cut supplies to Western supporters of Israel, including Britain, by 25 per cent. Oil prices doubled.[11] The flow of cheap Middle Eastern oil was a major source of growth in Western Europe. It caused a severe crisis, labelled the 'oil shock'. Coal again became an essential source of power. A state of emergency was declared followed in December by another three-day week for all industries. The bank rate rose to an unprecedented 13 per cent. The government planned to cut public spending in 1974–5 by an exceptional £1,200m. Eighty per cent of miners voted for another strike from 10 February, due to the cost of living.

Heath called an election for 28 February 1974, declaring as the central issue 'Who Governs Britain?' claiming the unions were challenging government power. The miners continued their strike but kept it lower-key than the last for fear of harming Labour in the election.[12] They were not the Conservatives' biggest problem. The inherited budget surplus had been transformed into deficit and tax revenue fell as a proportion of GDP by at least 7 per cent, due to the oil shock and tax cuts.[13] Amid a three-day week, power cuts and petrol shortages disrupting business and everyday life, polls indicated that most voters believed the Conservatives had mishandled the economy, lacking consistent policies. Cuts to welfare did not increase their popularity.

General Election February 1974

Labour was not optimistic about the election. They feared that, as Heath hoped, they would not win an election fought over union power. There was no clear winner. Labour won 301 seats, the Conservatives 297 though they were just ahead on votes: 11.8 million to 11.6 million on a 78.7 per cent turnout. The Liberals held the balance with fourteen seats. Voters were closely divided particularly over economic conditions and policy, with many prospering while others suffered. The results expressed growing national divisions. The Welsh Nationalist party, Plaid Cymru, won an unprecedented two seats, in mainly Welsh-speaking areas with high unemployment. The Scottish National Party (SNP) won a record seven seats for similar reasons. Heath tried but failed to negotiate a coalition with the Liberals.

Wilson returns

Wilson returned to Downing Street with no overall majority. Despite radical criticisms of his previous government and Labour divisions, with the left growing stronger, he remained secure as leader, still the pragmatic conciliator, reflected in the title of Labour's manifesto, *Let Us Work Together*. Labour was committed, supported by the party conference, to 'a fundamental and irreversible shift in the balance of power and wealth in favour of working people and their families' via a wealth tax, capital gains tax and nationalization of development land and mineral rights. It promised higher pensions and renegotiation of the terms of entry to the EC. A National Enterprise Board (NEB) would buy into and seek to improve the performance of private firms, still a central Labour aim. A 'social contract' was agreed with the TUC, exchanging pay restraint for price controls, welfare reforms and repeal of Heath's restrictions upon unions. Denis Healey became chancellor and Callaghan foreign secretary, while Jenkins returned to the Home Office. Crossman was seriously ill and died in April 1974. There were more left-wingers among the new Labour MPs, and more were union sponsored.[14]

Determined to call and win another election, Labour settled the miners' strike with a 29 per cent pay rise, ended statutory pay controls and the three-day week, and repealed the trade union restrictions, supported by the CBI, since business did not gain from industrial turmoil. Healey recalled, 'My predecessor left me with an economy on the brink of catastrophe.'[15] Again, developing the economy was a priority. Value Added Tax (VAT), the EU's preferred consumption tax introduced into the UK by Barber, which everyone paid, was reduced from 10 per cent to 8 per cent and income tax rose. While Labour was in power, until 1979, income tax reached a peak at 83 per cent for the top rate. Basic foods were subsidized: bread, flour, butter, cheese, milk, tea. Council rents were frozen, and the Housing Finance Act replaced by legislation restoring local authorities' power to fix rents and increasing subsidies to stabilize rents. Government spending rose from 39 per cent to 46 per cent GDP, during 1973–5, mostly funded by overseas borrowing, already exceptionally high under Heath.[16] Earnings outstripped prices and unemployment remained around 500,000 in 1974. Renegotiation of Britain's relationship with the EC began, as Wilson had promised its, mainly left-wing, opponents in the party, to be followed by a referendum on membership-.

General Election October 1974

Wilson judged it safe to call another election in October 1974. Polls suggested most voters again believed the cost of living their greatest problem and Labour best equipped to handle it. Labour won 319 seats, the Conservatives 277, the Liberals 13. Plaid rose to three. The SNP gained eleven seats and 30.4 per cent of the Scottish vote, more than the Conservatives. Labour's overall majority was only three, but the minority parties were unlikely to support the Conservatives.

After losing another election, Heath resigned, reluctantly. Margaret Thatcher was decisively elected to succeed him, to everyone's surprise including her own. For the first time a British political party was led by a woman. The Conservatives immediately went ahead of Labour in Gallup polls. Feminist campaigning was at a height, but few feminists supported Thatcher's politics or believed she was sympathetic to them, as she was not, though some believed her victory signalled progress for women, a hopeful sign for the future.

EC referendum

The promised referendum on EC membership came on 5 June 1975. Debates about the EC centred almost wholly upon the likely economic effects of membership. Wilson and

Callaghan negotiated minor concessions for Commonwealth imports and modification of Britain's budget contribution. The party remained divided. Wilson allowed ministers a free vote in the referendum. The UK outcome was 67.2 per cent for remaining, on a 64.5 per cent turnout.[17]

Economic policy

Labour returned to the mission of reversing the decline of British manufacturing and trade relative to expanding economies including those in the EC. In January 1975 the National Enterprise Board (NEB) was established. Its main function became supporting and aiming to modernize 'lame ducks', including the car manufacturer Chrysler, to save jobs. The once-vibrant motor industry was failing against overseas competition and ailing British Leyland was part-nationalized in 1975. British Aerospace was nationalized in 1977. There were successes including the British National Oil Corporation (BNOC), nationalized in 1976 following the welcome discovery of oil in the North Sea which came on stream through the rest of the decade. It produced a financial surplus in 1977–8 and by 1980 oil exports and imports balanced.[18] Labour revived the attempted technological revolution, though not MinTech, revitalizing the Ferranti electronics company and funding the establishment of Inmos in Bristol, which successfully developed advanced computing technology.

It was less successful at reviving established industries. Manufacturing decline continued. Compared with its main competitors it suffered from too little long-term investment, especially in new technology and skilled workers, due to management weakness and the preference of the financial sector for short-term gains. The most successful economies – notably Germany – benefitted from coherent, consistent industrial policies and government support, especially for research, development, innovation and training, in mostly coalition governments arising from their Proportional Representation (PR) election systems. The UK, with its first-past-the-post election system, suffered from the lack of consensus on industrial policy between competing parties and governments through the post-war decades and the consequent absence of long-term planning.[19]

In 1975 the largest industrial sector, metals and mechanical engineering, employed 4.2 million people, compared with 1.5 million in banking, insurance and finance. Over the next decade and a half, the balance shifted, and the service sector, including retail, hotels and catering, grew to dwarf the industries as the consumer market continued to expand and finance, focused on the City of London, flourished. White-collar jobs increased in the public and private sectors, while manual work contracted, increasing the demand for graduates, and providing opportunities for social mobility for young people from working-class backgrounds, as state education improved and more gained qualifications. But unemployment also grew, including among young people.

Inflation soared, still propelled by the oil shock. It rose above 19 per cent in UK in December 1974, peaking at 27 per cent in August 1975, falling to 21 per cent in early 1976 while averaging only 10 per cent in comparable countries.[20] Labour avoided serious industrial conflict due to the social contract and the Employment Protection Act, 1975, largely drafted by the TUC. This extended employee rights to appeal against unfair dismissal and trade union rights to recognition by employers, and established an Advisory, Conciliation and Arbitration Service (ACAS) for neutral settlement of disputes. In victories for growing female trade union activism, demanding rights already normal in the EC, it became illegal to dismiss a woman because she was pregnant (previously commonplace, and it continued) and statutory maternity leave was introduced for full-time workers, granting eleven weeks' leave before the birth and twenty-nine weeks after, at 90 per cent of normal pay for six weeks, then statutory sick pay. Mothers were guaranteed reinstatement in similar, though not necessarily the same, work on return.[21] These were imperfect, but real, improvements to women' rights and incomes.

High wage settlements increased workers' security but prolonged inflation, while public spending and the budget deficit rose. In the 1975 budget Healey cut spending severely and raised taxes, prioritizing inflation reduction over full employment. In July 1975 the unions reluctantly agreed a one-year pay freeze. Unemployment rose from 628,000 in January 1974 to 1.4 million in January 1976, passing the symbolic one million for the first time since 1947. It was concentrated in the areas of traditional manufacturing and mining as both declined further: South Wales, Southern Scotland, Belfast, Northern England and parts of the Midlands, further increasing regional inequalities.

But for those in adequately paid, generally non-manual work, spending on comfortable lifestyles grew. More installed central heating. The first huge shopping centres opened. More could afford colour TV, cinema-going, eating out as restaurants increased and improved, and holiday travel abroad with the growth of affordable package holidays.

Prime Minister Callaghan

In March 1976 Wilson expectedly retired. It later emerged that he was suffering from the early stages of dementia. Callaghan was elected to succeed him and worked hard to hold the party together. Labour declined in the polls and lost by-elections to the Conservatives due to the cuts, inflation and growing nationalism in Scotland and Wales, losing its parliamentary majority. Callaghan told the party conference in September 1976: 'We have been living on borrowed time . . . We used to think that you could spend your way out of a recession', but this stimulated inflation 'which hit hardest those least able to stand [it]'. He insisted that it was essential to reduce labour costs and make Britain more competitive.[22] Labour appeared to have abandoned Keynesianism. After a brief revival, UK output was lowest since the 1930s. In September 1976 over 1.25 million were unemployed. The balance of payments deficit approached £1bn, inflation was 16 per cent, the bank rate 15 per cent, sterling was worth an exceptionally low $1.66 and falling.[23] Public spending (including supporting the unemployed) and government borrowing remained high. Raising taxes was now harder for Labour politically since, as incomes rose, workers on average incomes or less paid income tax as most previously had not.

Healey tried to increase international confidence in sterling with extensive further spending cuts. When this failed, he acceded to pressure from the Treasury to request a loan from the International Monetary Fund (IMF), the first request from a major industrial nation. This caused a further crisis of confidence in sterling. The loan, $39bn, was the largest the IMF had ever made. A prolonged battle ensued in the Cabinet over the up to £1bn expenditure cuts required in return.[24] In December Healey announced cuts mainly to housing and education, though less than the IMF requested, and the deficit fell. He sold 15 per cent of the government's shareholding in British Petroleum (BP) while oil share prices were booming, retaining a 55 per cent majority holding.

Healey revealed much later that the Treasury had 'grossly overestimated' the deficit and the loan had been unnecessary, arguing that the main problem when managing the economy was lack of reliable data, which perhaps helps to explain the failings of successive government policies.[25] Most cuts were restored the following year and borrowing was much lower than forecast. Healey drew on only half the loan and it was fully repaid before Labour left office in 1979. But this was unknown at the time and Labour's reputation for financial management suffered, assisted by hostile media. The *Sun* (previously on the left but since 1969 a right-wing tabloid owned by media baron Rupert Murdoch) screamed, '3 Million Face the Dole Queue', though just 1.3 million were unemployed. IMF support did much to restore international confidence in the economy, assisted by increasing North Sea oil flows.[26] By late 1977 the pound was worth $1.91, causing concern about export prices. Following Healey's 1978 budget the balance of payments achieved a £1bn surplus. Inflation fell to 7.45 per cent, along with an improved balance of trade amid international economic revival, though GDP growth remained slow.

Despite panic at the time and negative memories, kept alive by Labour's political opponents, the IMF crisis was minor compared with other twentieth-century financial crises, with no severe economic outcomes, but perceptions of it, encouraged by the growing neoliberal right, damaged Labour politically.[27]

The Welfare State at its peak

Pensions

Despite the economic crises, the post-war Welfare State reached its peak under this government in terms of expenditure and range of services. Healey's 1974 budget raised taxation, social security payments and total social spending. Labour committed to raising pensions and other allowances regularly in line with earnings or prices, whichever was higher. Barbara Castle at DHSS withdrew the Conservatives' pension scheme and revived that of the previous Labour government.[28] The Social Security Pensions Act, 1975, introduced State Earnings Related Pensions (SERPS) for implementation in

1978. Pensions would accumulate over twenty years, fully funded by contributions, both earnings-related, supplementing the flat-rate basic pension which would increase annually in line with average earnings. Based on the best-paid twenty years of working life, SERPS would yield around half-pay for those on average earnings, comparable with pensions elsewhere in Western Europe and a massive improvement on the still inadequate basic pension. Unpaid carers for children at home or for older or disabled relatives, counted as contributors. Widows inherited their husbands' pensions. Women with interrupted working lives gained from the best-paid twenty years rule. It was the most advanced state pension in the world in providing equal rights for women and carers. Workers could contract out into occupational schemes providing equivalent benefits, if they were transferable, inflation proofed and strictly quality controlled.[29]

Family poverty

Labour's February 1974 manifesto promised 'a new system of CHILD CASH ALLOWANCES for every child, including the first, payable to the mother', replacing FIS. The Finer Committee on One Parent Families, appointed by Labour in 1969, produced in July 1974 a comprehensive survey of the incomes, social conditions, housing and employment conditions of this population, which was growing mainly due to increasing divorce, making up 8 per cent of all families in 1971, 10 per cent in 1975. It documented their relative poverty, recommending a Guaranteed Maintenance Allowance for all one-parent families, introduction of Child Benefits for all children with 'the utmost priority', and expansion of day-care services, prioritizing lone parents. None of these would be means-tested. It criticized the discrimination which effectively excluded single mothers from council tenancies, proposing that local authorities take responsibility for those in housing need. Since single parents were overwhelmingly mothers on low incomes, it urged faster progress to equal pay and equal opportunities for women in employment, education and training, equalization of employment rights between full- and part-time workers and extended maternity leave. Unfortunately, these expensive proposals appeared when the economy was in 'oil shock' crisis and rising unemployment, inflation and cuts to public spending, including on day care, worsened the situation of many families. Castle admitted that 'my heart sank' when she read them, since, already, 'my spending demands were making me unpopular in the Cabinet'.[30]

Castle focused on increased child allowances, which reappeared in the October manifesto. Child poverty remained at similar levels to the mid-1960s (around 13 per cent of all children), not higher despite rising unemployment and single parenthood, but still too high. The Cabinet preferred to help all families in hard times rather than risk unpopularity by singling out lone parents, and universal Child Benefits became law in August 1975, replacing family allowances and child tax allowances with a more generous weekly cash benefit for every child, payable to the mother, as originally proposed by CPAG. Under Treasury pressure to delay payment, Healey announced a start date of April 1977, but to satisfy campaigners introduced a tax-free 'Child Interim Benefit' from 1976, granting £1.50 pw to the first child in all single-parent families. He raised the income single parents could earn without losing benefits. Callaghan was hostile to the costly plan, dismissed Castle and tried to amend and delay it, but a vigorous 'Child Benefits Now' campaign supported by CPAG, other NGOs, trade unions, the Church of England, women's organizations and academics, forced a climb-down.[31] The full Child Benefit of £4 pw for all children was paid from 1979, with an additional 50p for children of lone parents, greatly assisting low-income families.[32]

The Housing (Homeless Persons) Act, 1977, gave local authorities responsibility for housing the 'unintentionally homeless', improving single mothers' access to council housing. The increasingly strident right-wing tabloids, especially the *Sun* and *Mail*, accused women of becoming pregnant just to obtain a council home, a slur which continued, though repeatedly disproved by research.[33] Throughout the 1970s, tabloids agitated about widespread benefit fraud, though official evidence showed it was minimal. Rising numbers of one-parent families and unemployed people aroused unsubstantiated attacks on an 'over-indulgent' welfare system encouraging 'shirkers' and 'scroungers'.

Health and social services

In February 1974 Labour pledged 'to phase out private practice from the hospital service' because it absorbed too many NHS resources. It established a Royal Commission to review the future of the NHS which did not report while it was in power. Castle extended free NHS family planning services to all, including vasectomy, previously free only for medical reasons. She continued Crossman's attempts to improve and integrate health and social services for the neglected groups of physically and mentally disabled and frail older people, though they remained inadequate despite repeated complaints and campaigns.[34] She set funding priorities for the NHS to allocate resources to neglected groups and aimed to reduce local inequalities in resources and health outcomes. A Resource Allocation Working Party (RAWP) produced a funding formula based on regional population and health needs which for a decade prioritized deprived areas quite successfully. But inequalities in health and life expectancy were due not only to unequal services but to socio-economic, including ethnic, differences. In April 1979 Castle's successor, David Ennals, appointed a committee of medical and social scientists to analyse these inequalities, which reported after the 1979 election.[35]

Weaknesses in local social services were revealed by the death in 1973 of eight-year-old Maria Colwell from abuse by her stepfather. Neighbours reported her being beaten and she was visited by social workers, doctors, and other officials, but no action followed. She was taken to hospital by her mother and stepfather and pronounced dead, with severe bruising, internal injury, and brain damage. Her stomach was empty. Her stepfather was sentenced to eight years' imprisonment, but it was halved on appeal. The case received massive publicity, bringing into public discourse abuses which were not new but long suppressed. In 1974 Castle established firmer guidelines for local social services, but over the next twenty years forty similar cases of child deaths by family violence came to public notice.[36]

Education

Labour was dissatisfied with the incomplete spread of comprehensive schools. The 1976 Education Act allowed the education secretary to compel local authorities to submit proposals for comprehensive reorganization. By 1981 about 83 per cent of children in state secondary schools in England, 96 per cent in Scotland and 96.6 per cent Wales were in comprehensives, compared with 69 per cent, 87.6 per cent and 88.5 per cent in 1975.[37] More children stayed on to later ages, more gained qualifications than ever before, while more students entered higher education.[38]

Housing

High rents and homelessness were severe enough by 1974 to trigger a 'squatting' movement. Young radicals moved into empty buildings to provide shelter for themselves and others, remaining for variable lengths of time before eviction. Homelessness fell, following Labour's rent controls and the 1977 Act, but did not disappear and squatting continued. Fewer homes were built than under the Conservatives, but improvements to older housing continued, assisted by improvement grants. During 1971–81 homes lacking basic amenities fell in England from 1.6 million to 0.5 million without a bath or shower, 2 million to 0.6 million lacking an indoor toilet, 2.4 million to 0.7 million without hot water supply to the kitchen.[39]

Women's liberation?

Campaigns for other equalities continued. What is sometimes presented as a period of growing individualism saw a striking growth of collective organization by groups, mainly of younger people, co-operating to promote their own and others' interests including concerning gender, sexual preference and race, choosing what was later called 'identity politics' over formal political organizations, though not always wholly rejecting them.

Persistent gender inequalities were challenged by feminists in a revived women's movement, the so-called 'second wave', a label which mistakenly implied that women had been quiescent since the 'first wave' before 1918. They certainly had not, but much remained to campaign about. Like other contemporary radical movements, feminists preferred direct, public action to patient lobbying. It was a movement mainly of younger women. Similar movements were emerging in other countries, including the United States. In 1969 there were seventy local women's liberation groups in London and the numbers grew nationally.[40] Feminism became public and flamboyant again, notably when women dramatically interrupted the televised Miss World beauty contest at the Royal Albert Hall, London, in 1970, shouting, 'We're not beautiful, we're not ugly, we're angry.' The right-wing tabloids responded with hostile images of feminists as 'bra-burners', ugly, dungaree-wearing man-haters.

The international character and impact of women's activism was signalled in 1977 when the UN instituted an annual International Women's Day to promote women's rights. The movement in Britain brought hidden issues into public view and new groups of women into activism, reflecting and advancing cultural change. Black and Asian women created organizations around the UK campaigning against restrictive immigration laws, virginity tests imposed on women immigrants, domestic and sexual violence, discrimination including in employment which they experienced due to both race and gender. They resisted marginalization by male-dominated organizations and by the white-dominated WLM, increasing its sensitivity to race.[41]

Labour introduced the Sex Discrimination Act, 1975, tackling some inequalities by outlawing discrimination in employment, education, advertising and provision of housing, goods or services. At last married women no longer needed their husband's agreement to undertake hire purchase or other financial arrangements even when they had independent earnings. The Equal Opportunities Commission (EOC) was established to investigate complaints and support women claiming discrimination. The act was partly a response to WLM, partly completion of unfinished business from the 1960s resulting from previous women's campaigns, partly conformity with the expectations and practices of the EC. It forced medical schools to remove the quotas restricting women's entry: by the early 1990s women grew from a small minority to over 50 per cent of medical students. Most male Oxford and Cambridge Colleges at last admitted women and women students at Oxford and Cambridge increased from 15 per cent and 10 per cent, respectively, to over 50 per cent by the 1990s. Female lawyers increased from 4 per cent in 1971 to 27 per cent in 1990.[42] In 1975 also the Equal Pay Act came fully into force; the average gender pay gap narrowed only from about 50 per cent to 40 per cent during 1970–80.[43]

More women were employed, though a high proportion, mainly mothers, still worked part-time with fewer employment rights than full-time workers. About 45 per cent of married women were employed in 1970, 60 per cent in 1980. In 1977, 5 per cent of mothers of children under five were in full-time employment, 22 per cent part-time.[44] Women protested that the workforce remained heavily gender-divided with unequal pay and opportunities, with women from ethnic minorities especially disadvantaged. Women's trade union membership and activism grew. In 1975 the TUC adopted the Charter for Working Women, a sign of growing numbers and influence of women in unions. It demanded equal pay, equal opportunities at work, eighteen weeks paid maternity leave, a minimum wage, increased family allowances and an end to discrimination against women in social security and tax, some of which Labour delivered under this or later governments. In 1976 a widely supported strike by Asian women about pay and conditions at Grunwick, a photo-processing business in London, publicised race and gender discrimination at work, but after three years it was unsuccessful due to intransigent opposition from an employer who refused to recognize the union, part of the rising international neoliberal tide.

More women were ambitious for careers while others were driven to work by inflation, especially of housing costs, and single motherhood. Childcare remained scarce and expensive. The better-off two-thirds of households owned washing machines by 1972 which eased housework. But domestic standards and expectations rose and the time women, employed or not, spent on housework hardly changed between the 1930s and 1970s.[45] Most men still contributed very little. Gender roles in marriage were gradually shifting but Gallup in 1973 found that only two in three women even knew their husband's take-home pay.[46]

Women's opportunities were limited partly by their continuing under-representation in higher education. Still, more girls than boys left school without qualifications, though the proportion of female university students rose from 28 per cent in 1971 to 38 per cent in 1979.[47] They remained concentrated in arts and social sciences, few in natural sciences, fewer still in engineering and few in academic posts especially at the higher levels. Women remained the great majority of students in teacher training colleges.[48] It became a little easier to retrain on returning to work after childcare and more older women attended universities, especially the Open University, but women still had fewer opportunities than men to gain further training at work.

A newer cause of protest, domestic violence, had been exposed intermittently since the 1860s when feminists campaigned against 'wife torture'.[49] Still in the 1970s upholders of the justice system, including police, refused to take it seriously, insisting that 'domestic disputes' were private, beyond their powers to intervene. Public resistance was sparked from 1971 by Erin Pizzey whose concern grew partly from her personal experience of violent parents, partly by hearing victims reveal their experiences. She founded and raised funding for refuges for mothers and children who were trapped in abusive relationships because they could not afford to live independently. She publicized the plight of 'battered wives', as they became known, and the failure of the police to support them, and gained a grant from DHSS in 1974 to support the families. Her book, *Scream Quietly or the Neighbours will Hear*, brought further publicity, and the Women's Aid Federation (WAF) was formed by feminists to promote the campaign.[50]

Pizzey was not a feminist and left the movement due to her tense relationship with WLM and increasingly with WAF. Their supporters founded and staffed refuges throughout the country, raising funds from charities, private donors, central and local government, revealing the shocking dimensions of a long-hidden problem, a serious and growing cause of poverty as more women, with their children, left abusive marriages. By 1980 there were about 200 refuges. WAF campaigned for legal reform. In 1974 a Bill introduced by Labour MP Jo Richardson led the Commons to appoint a Select Committee on Violence in Marriage. This noted that the law allowed courts to grant injunctions prohibiting men from molesting their female partners (and occasionally vice versa), on pain of imprisonment, and they could order them to leave the family home, but it was rarely implemented. Women did not always seek protection from the justice system, fearing reprisals from their partners. Police were reluctant to act. The Domestic Violence and Matrimonial Proceedings Act, 1976, made domestic violence a specific offence. Courts could punish violence against a partner, married or unmarried, or child, and exclude violent partners from the family home; from 1978 magistrates' courts could issue personal protection orders and exclusion orders, though not to unmarried partners.[51] The law was imperfect but better than anything before. The 1977 Housing (Homeless Persons) Act removed a barrier to victims leaving violent partners by obliging local authorities to house them if they became homeless. But still in 2008–10 one in four women in UK was estimated to experience domestic violence at some point in their lives; on average, two women, and occasional men, were killed each week by partners or ex-partners.[52] Still, police did not always take complaints seriously and WAF and women's refuges continued, though they were severely reduced following public spending cuts from 2010.

WLM also raised awareness of rape, another long-standing form of violence rarely publicly discussed, mainly against women, though GLF publicized attacks on gay men. The extent was unknown but appeared high. Victims often failed to complain, fearing reprisals from the perpetrator, feeling shame or that they would be disbelieved and denigrated. Realistically enough. Police and the courts did not always treat reports seriously but blamed the victim, for drunkenness or wearing 'provocative' clothing, rather than the perpetrator.[53] The first Rape Crisis Centre opened in North London in 1976 providing counselling, refuge and support, established by feminists, funded by charities and a supportive local authority. Sixteen centres, plus rape crisis phone lines, were established by 1981. From 1977 women's 'Reclaim the Night' marches paraded through streets at night asserting their right to walk unmolested at night. The Sexual Offences (Amendment) Act, 1976, introduced by a Labour backbencher, guaranteed anonymity for victims alleging rape, not for the perpetrator.[54] But still in the early twenty-first century 167 women were reported to suffer rape in the UK every day; only one attack in five was reported to the police because the victims were traumatized, feared reprisals or publicity, uncertain of support and fearing blame from police or the courts. Women still felt unsafe in the streets at night since molestation, rapes and deaths continued.

WLM also campaigned for men to share domestic work, for 24-hour nurseries for parents required to work 'unsocial' hours, such as low-paid women night-time office cleaners, and they protested about such work conditions. Also, for abortion on demand, without the obligatory agreement of two doctors, which was hard to obtain in some, especially strongly Catholic, areas. But some important inequalities were overlooked by this predominantly young women's movement, notably high levels of poverty among older women and their inadequate pensions compared with most men.

There was no gender revolution in the 1970s, but steady if incomplete improvements in women's material and cultural welfare, in pay, education, work and welfare support, in legal rights and protection against physical and sexual violence. Many young women grew up with higher expectations, encouraged by parents who could no longer assume that marriage was their only future as divorce increased. Aspiration to greater equality appeared increasingly realistic, but still more women were in poverty than men.

The permissive seventies?

Partly due to the new movements many aspects of sex were more openly discussed, continuing earlier trends. The cultural and legal changes of the 1960s affected many peoples' lives. Divorces shot up when the 1969 divorce reform was implemented in 1971, from 285,449 in England and Wales in 1966–70 to 812,403 in 1976–80, in Scotland 20,280 and 45,340, most following petitions by wives, who could now expect greater financial security following divorce.[55] It had long been argued that easier divorce would reduce cohabitation; the opposite occurred, and it grew. Marriages fell from 82.3/1000 men, 97.9/1000 women in 1971 in England and Wales to 46.6/1000 men and 64/1000 women in 1981. As divorces made marriage appear precarious, people perhaps became more cautious, delaying marriage or choosing a trial period of cohabitation before commitment, though others consciously rejected official sanction for a committed partnership.[56] The birth rate continued to decline from 16.9/1000 population in 1966–70 in England and Wales to 12.2 in 1976–80; in Scotland 17.9 to 12.7; 21 to 17.5 in Northern Ireland, while life expectancy continued to rise.[57] More births outside marriage were registered by both parents, 45.5 per cent in England and Wales in 1971, 58.2 per cent in 1981, suggesting larger numbers in stable relationships.[58] There were more unconventional households, including gay couples and complex families of divorced and re-partnered parents, increasingly openly acknowledged and accepted.

Race

A lively Black youth culture continued to flourish and expand. This helped mobilize a popular anti-racist movement uniting Black and white youth. In 1976 activists in the Marxist Socialist Workers' Party, incensed when rock star Eric Clapton supported Enoch Powell, organized Rock against Racism (RAR), running events where Black and white bands played under anti-racist banners. Within a year they arranged 200 concerts. But throughout the 1970s there were conflicts between white and Black youths particularly in districts with rising unemployment. Some white youths supported the National Front which tried hard to attract them. Surveys showed considerable racism among younger, like older, white Britons, though anti-racist movements remained strong.[59] The National Front declined into insignificance by the mid-1970s, while new organizations, including the Anti-Nazi League (ANL), formed 1977, drew wide support from prominent people and organized successful demonstrations and carnivals with RAR.

Resentment among immigrants of all ages was fuelled by the Conservative Immigration Act, 1971, which restricted the right to remain to British passport-holders or people whose parents or grandparents (or those of their husband- not their wife) were native-born British subjects, effectively excluding most non-white Commonwealth citizens, increasing the sense of racial exclusion. Though in 1973 Heath's government accepted more than 20,000 Ugandan Asians fleeing President Idi Amin's Africanization drive.

Labour gained more support for its Race Relations Act, 1976, which outlawed discrimination in employment, training, education and provision of goods and services and it became an offence to incite racial hatred. The CRC and RRB were amalgamated into the Commission for Racial Equality (CRE) which gained powers of investigation and to assist individuals taking complaints to court. This followed pressure from anti-racist organizations, including the Campaign Against Racial Discrimination (CARD), the West Indian Standing Committee and the Indian Workers Association, which increasingly co-operated, supported by backbench MPs.

Still, few Black or Asian people were employed in management or the professions, other than the NHS to which South Asian doctors and Caribbean nurses remained indispensable, though rarely in the highest levels or more prestigious specialisms. More were in skilled manual work: one-fifth of men with university degrees equivalent to British standards were manual workers in 1974, unimaginable for white British graduates. Many Asians, particularly, were self-employed, often in small shops and restaurants. Minorities still lived mainly in segregated areas of inner cities with poor amenities. People of Black Caribbean origin were now owner-occupiers and council tenants in similar proportions to white people, more often in poorer properties. Only 4 per cent of Asian households were council tenants and 75 per cent were owner-occupiers, also often of poor-quality homes. The numbers and geographical concentration of immigrants and their increasing tendency to vote made them potentially decisive in certain constituencies; polls showed they inclined strongly to Labour who they believed more supportive. They became increasingly active in local politics, especially in London where the Labour-led Greater London Council (GLC) and some borough councils were active in anti-racist campaigning, working with voluntary organizations created by and for minorities and providing support services.[60]

On behalf of the most forgotten minority, the Gypsy Council kept campaigning, nationally and internationally, against exceptional inequalities. It pioneered mobile caravan-schools: it was estimated in 1971 that, of 6,000–8,000 school-age children in the community, only about 2,500 attended school and attainment was low. Labour's 1968 Act was not delivering enough sites, causing problems for settled and travelling communities. Public prejudice and sometimes violent hostility continued. Following an official investigation, Labour introduced 100 per cent grants for local authorities to build sites, which grew substantially after implementation in 1980, though other inequalities continued.[61]

Nationalisms

Northern Ireland remained tense and nationalism grew further in Scotland and Wales whose economies continued to decline. Callaghan promised devolution. In 1978 parliament agreed to make devolution in both countries subject to referenda in which a minimum 40 per cent of each electorate voted 'Yes'. These took place on 1st March 1979. Scotland voted 'Yes' by 33 per cent to 31 per cent on a 64 per cent turnout, too small a majority to conform with the legislation; 59 per cent of Welsh electors voted 'No' by 47 per cent to 12 per cent, overwhelmingly even in strongly Welsh-speaking areas, driven by fears that devolution would further harm the Welsh economy.[62]

Election 1979

The outcome of the referenda contributed as much to destroying the government as industrial conflicts. Callaghan delayed the general election expected in October 1978 because he believed the economy was recovering, which he hoped would benefit Labour. But the cost of living rose leading to more pay demands and strikes in what the irrepressible *Sun* labelled the 'Winter of Discontent'. There were strikes and overtime bans by lorry drivers, railwaymen, water workers, NHS workers, ambulance drivers, refuse collectors, local government employees, including school caretakers which closed some schools. Militancy among these workers in essential public services was rare, suggesting desperation at worsening conditions, especially the cost of living. In 1979 trade union membership reached its highest-ever point, 50 per cent of workers, thirteen million, most in the public sector. There were rumours of shortage of medical supplies and other essentials due to strikes. The tabloids carried pictures of cancer-stricken children and older people suffering hypothermia. Union leaders pointed out that essential supplies always got through, 98 per cent of establishments had no dispute during 1977–9, and more days were lost through sickness and accidents than strikes.[63] But Conservatives and the press highlighted unburied bodies in cemeteries and places where uncollected rubbish piled up in the streets, claiming the unions were out of control.

Inflation fell but unemployment rose to 1.36 million in December 1978.[64] The upheavals put the Conservatives twenty points ahead in the polls by February 1979. Callaghan reluctantly surrendered to the unions. Government and TUC agreed to maintain essential services during strikes. Wage settlements were higher than before, without the disastrous consequences forecast by the hostile media. The agreement helped Labour stabilize the economy, though the long-term problems of declining manufacture and trade and poor productivity remained. But following the referendum the government lost SNP support. Nationalists supported an opposition no-confidence motion which the government lost by one vote. A general election was called for May. Thatcher's Conservatives made much of the 'winter of discontent', with a prominent poster of a lengthy dole queue captioned 'Labour Isn't Working'.

They won and entered government with a clear majority (forty-three seats). More starkly than any time since 1945, the Conservatives represented the prosperous South of England and Labour the declining industrial regions. Welsh and Scottish Nationalists won two seats each. Conservatives won 44 per cent of votes to Labour's 37 per cent, their lowest share since 1931, with a 76 per cent turnout. Liberals took 14 per cent and eleven seats.

Conclusion

It was a turbulent decade, but for many British people one of improvement. Despite international economic crises, inflation, rising unemployment, manufacturing decline, most people enjoyed improving living standards and more leisure. The mid- to late-

1970s have been estimated as the period of narrowest income inequality of the twentieth century, though substantial inequalities remained.[65] Atkinson calculated that in 1949 the top 10 per cent of income holders after tax held 27.1 per cent of total UK income, the bottom 50 per cent 25.2 per cent. In 1975/1976 the figures were 22.3 per cent and 27.4 per cent respectively.[66] Households in relative poverty by the measure of incomes below 60 per cent of the median were estimated as fairly stable through the 1970s at about 13–15 per cent.[67] Most were households headed by single mothers or retired people, child poverty was at similar levels.[68] In 2004 the New Economics Foundation think tank devised an index of national economic, social and environmental well-being, and concluded that for most respondents to a survey Britain's best year since 1950 had been 1976.[69] Not everyone flourished but unemployed people and others in need were protected by adequate, if not generous, state welfare. Unemployment benefits rose from £8.60 per week in 1974 to £15.75 in 1978,[70] compared with average manual wages of £43.60 and £89.70 but adequate for subsistence.[71] Food banks were unheard of. Gender inequalities continued gradually narrowing owing much to feminist militancy. Victims of domestic violence and rape were supported as never before by voluntary and statutory services. Equality for homosexuals progressed still more slowly, for racial minorities hardly at all, despite advances in anti-discrimination legislation and anti-racist protest. A generation that had grown up since 1945, mostly better-educated, better-off, more confident, and less deferential than older generations, challenged established values, seeking to transform the culture, not just for themselves but for everyone. Public tolerance of unconventional lifestyles appeared to be growing, along with greater willingness especially of younger people to embrace them, which to some signified just how 'benighted' society had become – a cultural division which showed no sign of decline. It was turbulent decade: the peak of (limited) post-war social and economic progress and the beginning of its end as neoliberal opposition to state-directed moves towards equality became increasingly influential nationally and internationally.

CHAPTER 11
THE 'IRON LADY', 1979–90

More determinedly than any previous Conservative premier Margaret Thatcher aimed to dismantle the Welfare State and collective social responsibility, minimizing state direction of the economy, maximizing private enterprise in all areas, 'rolling back' advances in state action since 1945 – in practice by utilizing and often strengthening central state mechanisms. She believed that inequality was the natural and desirable state of society, incentivizing the disadvantaged to aspire and strive, but she thought the word 'inequality' unacceptably pejorative and banned it from official discourse, preferring the more ambiguous 'variations'. Strongly individualist, she sincerely shared the Poor Law principle that poverty was caused by personal failings and people should be incentivized to adopt the commitment to self-help and family support she believed had been destroyed by the Welfare State, as previous right-wingers had believed it was destroyed by philanthropy, despite strong evidence to the contrary. People should work rather than expect support from the state or the community, as in reality overwhelmingly they did, or, if they could not, look to their families for support, as, again, very many did. The economy, she believed, was similarly crippled by the state 'feather bedding' business and/or strangling it with official 'red tape'; businesses also should be freed to shape their own futures and succeed.

The first woman premier was intensely hostile to feminism, and she permitted few, reluctant, moves towards gender and racial equality or gay rights, again because she believed unequal outcomes were due to lack of effort not to discrimination. She told a group of children in a TV programme in 1982:

> I think most of us got to our position in life without Women's Lib and we got here, not by saying 'you've got to have more women doing so-and-so' but saying 'look we've got the qualifications, why shouldn't we have as much chance as a man?' And you'll find that so many male bastions were conquered in that way, whereas Women's Lib, I think, has been rather strident, concentrated on things that don't really matter.[1]

Only one woman was appointed, briefly, to the Cabinet throughout her eleven years in office, Baroness Young as Lord (*sic*) Privy Seal, April 1982–June 1983. Just 19 women had been elected among 635 MPs, the fewest since 1951: 8 Conservative, 11 Labour. Under her premiership women voters shifted from Conservatism, dividing between the opposition parties, part of a growing international 'gender gap' in voting, as men were more attracted to neoliberalism while women resisted its effects, particularly welfare cuts. Thatcher strongly promoted her vision of the 'traditional family' based on lifelong marriage. Yet divorce rose to unprecedented levels, more children were born to unmarried, cohabiting parents, more openly gay partners, female and male, lived together, increasingly with children. Much changed in the 1980s, not always in directions chosen by Margaret Thatcher.

Thatcher cautiously chose a Cabinet balancing relatively progressive Conservatives - 'wets' she called them- and those closer to her convictions. It was deeply split between old, 'One Nation', relatively Liberal, Conservatism and newer neoliberalism and between 'grandees' and self-made men. Ninety-one per cent were privately educated, 27 per cent at Eton.[2] The party was changing rather more. Fewer MPs came from public schools, Oxbridge, landowning and inherited wealth, more from grammar schools and provincial universities, business and professions. This partly explains her relatively cautious policymaking in her first term.

But Thatcher did not abandon all principles. She was convinced that civil servants, indeed all public employees, depleted rather than created wealth, burdening the economy with regulatory 'red tape', lacking the skills essential for the modern world, shielded from real life by excessive job security and pensions. She made severe cuts: civil servants were reduced by 142,515, 1980–90. Departments delivering services, including vehicle licensing, publication of official documents (HMSO) and highway management, were transferred to semi-autonomous 'agencies', still under tight central budgetary controls but not responsible to ministers.[3] Exceptional numbers of policy advisers were appointed, often at higher cost than senior civil servants, mainly businessmen or academic economists who shared her views.[4]

Another priority was to 'reform', that is, crush, the unions.[5] In 1979, under Labour, miners received a 20 per cent pay rise and the pay of public sector workers rose significantly. This was followed by tight limits and real terms decline under Thatcher. Trade union demands for higher pay were represented as 'selfish', those of businesspeople as fair rewards for effort. Trade union rights were restricted in Employment Acts in 1980 and 1982 while the Social Security (No 2) Act, 1980, restricted Supplementary Benefits for strikers' families to £12 pw while average earnings of male manual workers were £111.7 pw.[6] There was no immediate union response. Days lost in strikes fell by almost 75 per cent by 1983, partly because unemployment rose from 1.2 million in May 1979 to 3.2 million in January 1983, by far the highest since the war, highest in manufacturing and mining which continued to decline, weakening the unions. Union membership fell from 13.2 million in 1980 to 11.3 million in 1984.[7] A total of 5,000 factories closed during 1979–82.[8]

The economy

The 1979 budget of Chancellor Sir Geoffrey Howe reduced the basic rate of income tax from 33 per cent to 30 per cent, the top rate from 83 per cent to 60 per cent, while VAT, which hit the lowest incomes hardest, rose from 8 per cent to 15 per cent. Prices soared. Howe abolished controls on currency exchange transactions, which benefitted and delighted City of London financiers. Restrictions on bank lending were eased, though the bank rate remained 14 per cent in 1980. National insurance contributions rose. By 1990 all state contributions to the national insurance fund were withdrawn; for the first time since 1911 pensions and other contributory benefits were financed entirely by employer and employee contributions, reducing the redistributive element of social insurance. The government was committed to cutting total public spending while raising it on defence and law and order and keeping it level on the popular NHS. Gallup found the 1979 budget 'one of the least popular budgets, proposed by one of the least popular Chancellors of the past 27 years';[9] a majority claimed, with good reason, that the government only helped the well-off. The government and premier had consistently bad ratings.[10] A letter to the *Times* from 364 economists in 1981 argued, presciently, that 'present policies will deepen the depression, erode the industrial base of the economy and threaten its social and political stability', as unemployment continued to rise and manufacturing output to fall. Economic growth was only 0.6 per cent in 1980–3, well below the average 2.4 per cent pa since 1950.[11]

Manufacturing output fell 14 per cent in 1979–80. International oil prices rose, benefitting North Sea oil. By summer 1980 inflation was above 20 per cent and two million were unemployed, the deepest slump for fifty years. The government was driven into retreat: North Sea oil revenues were taxed; in 1981, a 'once and for all' levy was imposed on banks, raising £400m, on the grounds that 'peculiar circumstances' had generated 'windfall profits' in both sectors.[12] Employment growth in the 1980s was concentrated in low-paid work and insecure self-employment. Women experienced less unemployment than men mainly because so many were employed in low-paid, often part-time, work in the growing service sector, selling fast food, clothing and household goods or staffing call-centres. More women now expected employment, more needed it when household budgets were under pressure, more were single parents.

Despite the economic problems, Thatcher stood by her policies, telling the party conference in October 1980: 'You turn if you want to. The lady's not for turning.' 'Wets' who opposed her were sacked from the government and replaced by supporters. More businesses were privatized.[13]

Rolling back the Welfare State – Part I

Housing

An early example of privatization was the Housing Act, 1980, giving council tenants of at least three years' standing the right to buy the freehold of their house, or a 125-year lease of a flat, at heavily discounted prices. Council house sales had always been possible, at local authority discretion, which was now withdrawn. Discounts of up to 30 per cent of the market value were introduced by Heath's government, then withdrawn by Labour. Tenants were now entitled to discounts of 33–50 per cent depending on their length of tenancy, to a maximum of £25,000, later increased to a maximum 70 per cent and, from 1989, up to £50,000 in some areas.

More houses sold than flats, especially sounder, more attractive older houses. Buyers were mainly middle-aged couples from better-paid, skilled working-class backgrounds in more prosperous parts of the country, further increasing social and regional inequality. More homes were council-owned in Scotland than in England, but fewer were sold. By 1995 1.7 million tenants in Great Britain had bought a quarter of the 1980 stock. Councils were forbidden to spend income from sales on housebuilding, so the stock shrank: council housing fell from almost one-third to one-fifth of total housing, 1979–94. Housing was the area of government spending that dropped furthest, but, unlike many other Conservative policies, council house sales were popular, at least with better-off people. In 1987 40 per cent of owners of former council houses voted Conservative, as Thatcher hoped, 25 per cent of tenants. Government subsidies to non-profit housing associations increased to help cover the growing lack of affordable rentals. By the 1990s these were the main suppliers of what was now called 'social' housing for lower-income people.[14]

The 1980 Housing Act assumed that local authorities would replace subsidies by raising rents for the remaining tenants. By 1986 rents rose by 50 per cent on average .[15] As real incomes fell and unemployment rose, more households could not cope. In 1982/1983 a means-tested Housing Benefit was introduced to assist them, amalgamating Supplementary Benefit rent support and rate rebate, available to council and private tenants at considerable public cost. It was paid directly to landlords, creating an incentive to raise rents. Sixty per cent of council tenancies received it in 1984/1985.[16] For the first time, council tenants were predominantly on low incomes, in contrast to the original ideal of socially mixed council housing, as a reduced stock provided only for those in greatest need.[17] Clearer divisions were emerging between working people who prospered and increasing numbers feeling 'left behind'. The outcome was a lasting shortage of housing affordable by people on low incomes and increasing homelessness.

Tax relief on mortgages rose from £1.6m to £5.5m during 1979–89, stimulating house price inflation, while subsidies to local authority housing fell from £1,258m to £520m.[18] Prices rose also due to the removal in 1982 of restrictions on personal credit, facilitating larger mortgages. Previously, substantial deposits (generally 25 per cent of the price) were required and mortgages were fixed in proportion to the income of the mortgagee(s). Less responsible mortgage selling, credit and debt grew. New UK housing loans increased from £6bn to £63bn during 1978–88; non-housing loans by UK banks from £4bn to £28bn.[19]

Social security

Thatcher believed that,

> Welfare benefits, distributed with little or no consideration of their effects on behaviour, encouraged illegitimacy, facilitated the breakdown of families, and

replaced incentives favouring work and self-reliance with perverse encouragement for idleness and cheating.[20]

Thatcher was encouraged by poll evidence of declining public support for social spending and high taxes, from 44 per cent to 22 per cent since 1969, though support for the NHS and other universal services remained high.[21] She proceeded to remove the 'safety net' which since the late 1940s had protected those on lowest incomes from falling too far behind the rest. The first target for cuts was social security, the largest, fastest rising social spending programme, mainly due to unemployment. Income-related, short-term unemployment and sickness benefits were axed, claimed to encourage idleness. From 1983 sickness pay was no longer paid from public funds but by employers, who were expected to police and discourage sickness leave, potentially deterring hiring of workers with health problems. From 1982 benefits were uprated in line with prices not earnings, ensuring lower rises. Pensions fell from over 23 per cent of average male earnings in 1981 to 15 per cent in 1993, cutting the cost by one-third but increasing the numbers of pensioners needing means-tested supplements, while the value of Supplementary Benefits fell from 61 per cent median earnings in 1978 to 53 per cent in 1987.[22]

Education

Labour's legislation requiring local authorities to abolish selective secondary education was repealed. It had almost disappeared in Wales and Scotland. A few English authorities, including Kent and Lincolnshire County Councils, never abandoned it. Very few reintroduced it. By 1995/1996 only 5 per cent of pupils in UK secondary schools attended grammar schools, the highest proportion in Northern Ireland where selection prevailed in schools strictly divided by religion.[23] The 1980 Education Act introduced 'Assisted Places', funding initially 5,300, later 35,000, means-tested places at independent schools. In 1992, 7 per cent of all pupils attended private schools, 5 per cent of them with free places.[24]

The second term

By 1983 economic growth headed towards a more encouraging 4 per cent, but unemployment was 3.2 million. The government stressed falling prices, which affected more people and more potential Conservative voters. Howe's 1983 Budget increased the mortgage tax relief limit to £30,000 and raised Child Benefit. Following victory in saving the Falkland Islands from Argentinian invasion in 1982, Thatcher judged it safe to hold an election in May 1983.

Thatcher was encouraged also by divisions in the Labour Party. Callaghan resigned and left-wing Michael Foot was elected to succeed him. Jenkins and other right-wingers left and formed the Social Democratic Party in 1981. Labour's lengthy election manifesto – described as 'the longest suicide note in history' by a shadow minister – was rushed out with too little preparation. It promised to reduce unemployment by increasing public spending, introduce a five-year economic plan, restore trade union powers and promote industrial democracy, renationalize privatized industries, increase spending on education and welfare, end gender and race discrimination and withdraw from the EC.[25] The Conservatives were so convinced that the unrealistic promises would damage Labour that party officials bought and distributed 1,000 copies.[26] Foot did not present a strong leadership image. Labour slumped to under 28 per cent of votes and 209 seats to the Conservatives' 42.4 per cent and 397, winning slightly fewer votes than in 1979. The Conservatives benefitted from the Falklands victory and economic growth, probably still more from the SDP breakaway splitting the Labour vote.[27] Foot resigned and was replaced by Neil Kinnock, who sought compromise and party unity.

Thatcher's self-confidence grew, and she was ready for another battle with the miners. The industry had stabilized, benefitting from high oil prices and Labour subsidies. By 1980 oil prices had fallen, coal subsidies were cut and pit closures proposed. Strikes in areas most affected forced the government to maintain subsidies. Thatcher ordered building up of coal stocks against future strikes and chose tougher negotiators. The NUM had a new, uncompromising, president, Arthur Scargill. In April 1984 he called a strike over pit closures but failed to call a national ballot, relying on each district to do so. Many miners were dubious due to loss of pay but supported the strike. Other unions were too concerned for their members in precarious times to support them. Substantial coal stocks prevented serious shortages, and past successful union tactics, especially secondary picketing, were now illegal. A sum of £200m was invested in a mobile police force drawn from forty-three forces to maintain access to the collieries. They made 11,000 arrests and were accused of excessive violence, especially when police horses charged pickets at Orgreave (Yorks) coking plant in June 1984 and more than 120 pickets and police were injured. Polls indicated less public support than in 1974 but substantial sympathy. The Labour Party kept its distance. The strike lasted a year until privation drove many miners back to work. The NUM was bankrupted by court rulings against mass picketing. There was no prospect of a negotiated settlement since neither Thatcher nor Scargill would back down. She won. Pit closures accelerated and NUM membership fell from 200,000 in 1984 to 105,000 in 1986, 53,000 in 1990. By 1994 there were only seventeen deep mines in the country and 11,000 miners.[28] Trade union membership fell to under 9.5 million in 1991, the lowest since 1940.[29] Thatcher had successfully crippled the 'enemy within', as she called unions.

Unemployment rose to 3.4 million in 1986, possibly over 4 million following changes to official statistics designed to reduce the numbers. It became more difficult to qualify for unemployment benefit and older unemployed people were, whenever possible, transferred to disability benefit, while official statistics included only those 'unemployed and claiming (unemployment) benefit', as not all unemployed people did. From 1979 to 1996 the basis for calculating unemployment was adjusted thirty-one times, always in a downward direction.[30] The official numbers fell to 1.5 million by June 1990.[31] For those in work, job insecurity grew as protection of less organized workers was dismantled.

Closing the GLC

Thatcher was less restrained in her second term. Local authorities faced greater controls. Like the unions, many of them were perceived as socialist enemies of government principles. None more so than the Greater London Council (GLC), the largest council in the country, headed from 1981 by Labour's Ken Livingstone. In 1986 it was wound up, with the other seven Metropolitan Counties, all Labour-controlled. Thatcher opposed Livingstone's use of GLC income to regenerate the London economy, reduce transport costs and aid radical groups, including feminist and anti-racist campaigners in the increasingly culturally diverse capital. Livingstone did not help to save the GLC by posting London's rising unemployment figures on large signs outside County Hall, across the river from parliament, with defiant political slogans. Many GLC powers were taken over by central government, some, including housing and education, by the London boroughs, others by new semi-independent 'agencies', including the London Regional Transport Authority. All local transport was deregulated by the Transport Act, 1985, enabling private companies for the first time to run bus and other public transport services.[32]

Rolling back the Welfare State – Part II

Social security

There were more fundamental reforms of social security. Norman Fowler, minister for social security, aspired to what he called its most profound overhaul since Beveridge, aiming to cut costs and simplify a system that had become increasingly complex. Benefits were complex due, not just to bureaucracy as Fowler implied, but to the complexity of many peoples' lives and incomes, increased by the extension of means-testing. The UK now had one of the most 'targeted', complex social security systems in the world. Fowler introduced the Social Security Act, 1986. Income Support (IS) replaced Supplementary Benefit (SB), introducing new benefit scales applied to all means-tested provision, categorizing claimants into broad types rather than assessing individual needs. The universal Child Benefit was frozen and supplemented by a means-tested Family Credit for low-income families with a parent working less than twenty-four hours per week. Most discretionary SB payments – for example, for furniture or special dietary needs- were replaced by cash loans from a new, limited, Social Fund. The 'poverty trap' became still more severe and more people in need were excluded by failure to apply for means-tested benefits. The numbers in poverty rose due to the benefit changes, unemployment and growing numbers of single-parent families, from about 5 million living below the official poverty line of 60 per cent of median household income in 1980 to over 11 million in 1990.[33] Despite the aspiration to cut costs, social security spending rose from £49.9bn pa to £61.4bn 1979/80 to 1990/91 due to growing numbers in need and administrative costs.[34]

Fowler's Review also proposed cutting public spending by abolishing Labour's SERPs pension reform and shifting responsibility for pensions to individuals, employers, and the market. This was opposed by the CBI and the pensions industry, which did not want to provide for low-paid people with poor job prospects, while actuaries were rightly concerned that most people lacked the financial skills to choose private pensions and risked becoming victims of unscrupulous mis-selling. Instead SERPS was amended, becoming less generous especially to those with low earnings and interrupted work histories, mostly women, increasing inequalities in later life. Despite the actuaries' warnings, workers were encouraged with increased tax relief to take out private pensions which were deregulated.[35] At least 400,000 people were sold disadvantageous pensions, often persuaded to leave better public sector schemes, creating a mis-selling scandal reversed, at considerable cost in compensation, by the next Labour government.

Health

In 1982 Thatcher assured her party conference, 'The National Health Service is safe with us. . . . The principle that adequate healthcare should be provided for all regardless of the ability to pay must be the function of any arrangements for financing the NHS. We stand by that.'[36] This followed press reports of her plans to privatize and charge for health and social services, and negative responses. The NHS survived the first term relatively unscathed, but severe inequalities in services and outcomes continued. The committee of medical and social scientists appointed by Labour to investigate these inequalities reported in 1980.[37] The government circulated 260 duplicated copies of this very thorough, damning, report, over August Bank Holiday weekend, with limited press access. It concluded that people on low incomes had poorer health throughout their lives and lower life expectancy than better-off people for reasons connected more with social and economic conditions than with the NHS. The health and life expectancy of men and women in classes I and 2 had improved in the previous 20 years, while those in classes 4 and 5 had changed little or deteriorated, a difference probably greater than in comparable countries.[38] Black and Minority Ethnic groups had worse health outcomes than British-born white people.[39] There was a press furore, but the government refused to act, claiming that the recommendations for improved health services targeted at deprived people were too costly.[40]

The 1983 manifesto 'welcome[d] the growth in private health insurance in recent years'. Lawson aspired to privatize the NHS, but Treasury officials argued that it was cost-effective, comparing well with other countries. Sir Roy Griffiths was imported from Sainsbury's to advise and proposed professional managers to replace medical professionals to increase efficiency. His recommendations increased central supervision and management costs with no obvious increase in efficiency or quality of services. Prescription, dental and ophthalmic charges rose. Hospital catering and cleaning services were 'outsourced' to private providers and private medical services were encouraged and deregulated; consultants' opportunities for private practice grew and tax exemptions were introduced for employer-provided medical insurance.[41]

The effects of unemployment and erosion of health and welfare services aroused much concern, including among Anglican clergy encountering poverty in their parishes. In 1981 the Archbishop of Canterbury, Robert Runcie, appointed a commission which visited more than thirty towns and in 1985 published a highly critical report, *Faith in the City*. It exposed the 'two nations' they found of 'shabby streets, neglected houses, sordid demolition sites of the inner city . . . [and the] . . . busy shopping precincts of mass consumption'. It urged the government to act, and the Church established a fund to help the inner cities, improved training for urban clergy and support for Afro-Caribbean Anglicans who were especially deprived. An unknown Cabinet member leaked the report to the press, labelling it 'pure Marxist theology', greatly increasing its public impact.[42] A shortened version sold over 60,000 copies. In 1986 the Church published *Not Just for the Poor: Christian Perspectives on the Welfare State*, a vindication of Beveridge's principles as fair, humane, and closer to Christian ideals than those behind current government policy. Anglicans forcefully opposed Fowler's Social Security Act, arguing that it reintroduced Victorian notions of 'deserving' and 'undeserving' poor.[43] Thatcher had grown up as a Methodist and was now a church-going Anglican, but she believed the clergy shared the narrow-minded traditionalism of all professionals and ignored them.

Freeing the economy

The government pursued privatization of the economy more determinedly. Until 1983 annual receipts from privatization never exceeded half a billion pounds. After 1983 they were never less than £1bn pa, peaking in 1988–9 at £7.1b.[44] Shares in British Gas were promoted in 1986 in a major advertising campaign featuring 'ordinary' people urging others to buy the bargain shares and 'Tell Sid' to do likewise. More than four million small investors applied for the shares which were over-subscribed five times. By 1990, 40 companies, employing 600,000 people, were sold. City financiers gained from arranging the sales and buying and selling shares. Seven per cent of British people held shares in 1980, 29 per cent in 1990.[45] Many small shareholders sold quickly at a profit; the greatest beneficiaries and biggest shareholders were pension funds.

Privatized companies did not obviously become more efficient to the benefit of consumers. Most became private rather than public monopolies, cutting workforces and raising the salaries of senior management, increasing inequality. They were not entirely free of state control but subject to new 'arm's length' regulatory offices – 'Ofgas', 'Oftel'- empowered to regulate prices to reassure consumers.

Finance

The financial sector, above all its apex, the City of London, was increasingly successful and internationalized as regulation declined. More foreign banks bought into the city, especially from the United States, fleeing stricter regulation at home. The gentleman's club atmosphere of the city changed to a more competitive, profit-seeking culture, with fewer leisurely lunches and longer working hours. Salaries – 'compensation' in less vulgar city terminology – rose fast enough to shock even Thatcher. She told BBC TV in 1985, 'Top salaries in the City fair make one gasp, they are so large.'[46] The average income of directors of Morgan Grenfell investment bank rose from £45,000 in 1979 to £225,000 in 1986, salaries of bankers and brokers in their twenties and thirties from £25,000 to £100,000 pa, while profits boomed.[47] In 1982 it made headlines that a leading Lloyds underwriter earned over £320,000.[48] The beneficiaries were overwhelmingly male. There were few women above the level of secretary and, despite gradual change, the city was notorious into the twenty-first century for sexual harassment and extreme gender differences in employment and pay.

Financial reform affected the wider population. Hire purchase controls were abolished in 1982, regulation of bank charges for loans was relaxed leading to increased use of credit cards, first issued in 1962. Credit card holders increased during 1980–90, from 11.6 million to 29.8 million.[49] Personal debt rocketed from £7m in 1979 to £52.5m in 1990.[50] A growing amount was owed by low-income families to new payday loan companies at high interest rates, another sign of growing poverty and inequality.[51] Loans also fuelled consumption among the better-off: from 1978 to 1988 households with telephones increased from 62 per cent to 85 per cent, with central heating from 54 per cent to 77 per cent, more people took package holidays abroad, bought clothes, leisure, household goods. Pension funds profited from high interest rates, encouraging some businesses to raid them to restructure the business, raise salaries or pay shareholders, instead of building the fund for future rainier days. A champagne-quaffing branch of celebrity culture emerged from the huge salaries, cars, yachts and (multiple) homes of financiers and other high-paid businessmen, often primarily resident in low-tax havens like Monaco, to the disadvantage of the UK Treasury. Deregulation enabled unprecedented tax evasion; one of the fastest growing occupations of the 1980s was accountancy. The city underwent fundamental changes, with some fraud and corruption, but it boomed, and the government talked of the UK's economic future as based on services, especially financial services, rather than manufacturing.

The growing inequalities sparked protest. From 1983 'Stop the City' demonstrations challenged financiers' profits, gained from investing abroad while British industry declined. A merchant banker asked by a journalist why he did not invest in a high unemployment area like Liverpool, replied, 'Would you invest there? In a lot of bloody-minded Liverpudlians?'[52] The gap between the wealth of the top 1 per cent of wealth-holders in the UK and the remaining 99 per cent narrowed from the Second World War to the late 1970s, then widened. In 1950 the top 1 per cent held about £300bn, the bottom 99 per cent about £600bn, in 1975 about £259bn and almost £1,000bn, respectively, by 2000 *c*. £700bn and £2,400bn.[53]

The third term

With the economy apparently reviving and unemployment falling, Thatcher called another election in June 1987. The Conservatives won 20 fewer seats than in 1983 but an overall majority of 101, benefitting again from Labour's split. Shortly after the election, in which it won just six seats, the SDP merged with the Liberals, becoming the Liberal Democrat Party in 1989. Again, the Conservatives swept southern England, but in Scotland, still suffering from unemployment and industrial decline, they fell from 21 to 10 seats, while Labour gained 50, its highest number ever. Among skilled workers only 36 per cent voted Labour, 40 per cent Conservative.[54] Some doubted whether Labour would ever be elected again as the manufacturing working class dwindled, and Conservatism attracted survivors. Before and after the election, Thatcher faced opposition to privatization and cuts to the public sector from her secretaries of state for Scotland, Wales and Northern Ireland, following the negative impact on these countries, all with high proportions of public sector jobs and high unemployment. Subsidies to Northern Ireland, where the 'Troubles' were still severe, rose from £100m in 1972 to £1.6b in 1988–9, not including the costs of the army stationed there, aiming to ease economic decline and conflict.

Nigel Lawson, chancellor from 1983, in his 1988 budget cut the basic rate of income tax from 27 per cent to 25 per cent, top rate from 60 per cent to 40 per cent, below 50 per cent for the first time since 1945. Those earning median annual male incomes (£12,750) now paid a slightly higher proportion of their income in taxes, rates and national insurance; those earning five times the median paid 15 per cent less. The budget was criticized for encouraging spending and inflation, which reached 8.3 per cent in January 1989. It stimulated imports, creating a massive balance of payments deficit. Interest rates rose to 15 per cent in October 1988. House prices fell, while mortgage costs rose, causing some to lose their homes.

Rolling back the Welfare State – Part III

In her third term Thatcher was even more determined to shrink the public sector and 'dependence' on the state, sparking more opposition, including among Conservatives. She told *Woman's Own*,

> I think we've been through a period where too many people have been given to understand that if they have a problem, it's the government's job to cope with it . . . they're casting their problem on society. And, as you know, *there is no such thing as society*. There are individual men and women, and there are families, and no government can do anything except through people, and people must look to themselves first.[55]

This conviction soon permeated all areas of social policy.

Education

The government described the Education Reform Act, 1988, as 'the most important change in the administration of schools since 1944'.[56] It followed minimal consultation with education professionals, like most of Thatcher's initiatives. Again, it increased central control over the professionals, increasing financial accountability to central government while theoretically extending 'consumer choice' in a 'quasi-free market'. Schools could opt out of local authority control, with central government funding, if most parents approved. The remaining local authority secondary and larger primary schools would control their own budgets, managed by school governors, now required to include parents, local community representatives and teachers, further reducing local authority control. The notoriously progressive Inner London Education Authority was abolished, and its powers devolved to London boroughs. The Act introduced Britain's first 'National Curriculum' for 'core' subjects (English, Maths and Science) and 'foundation' subjects (History, Geography, Technology, Music, Art, P.E., Modern Languages) specifying curriculum content and attainment targets and tests for children aged seven, eleven, fourteen and sixteen. Schools were required to provide religious education 'reflecting Britain's Christian character', while religious diversity grew and church attendance fell. The curriculum was compulsory for state schools, discretionary for private schools, limiting teachers' freedom to shape course content. Teachers criticized the constraints, confirming Thatcher's conviction of their inflexible traditionalism. There was more support for a single General Certificate of Secondary Education (GCSE) for sixteen-year-olds replacing the socially divisive O levels and CSEs. Exam results were published in league tables of school attainment, designed to stimulate school performance through competition, though they did not take account of intake and tended to increase social selection, as better-off parents used them to determine where to live. House prices rose fastest close to schools high in league tables.[57]

Such dramatic changes were not justified by declining school performance since well-qualified school-leavers had increased with comprehensives. Scotland, where the 1988 Act largely did not apply, retained its distinctive educational structure, the national curriculum was not introduced, local authorities retained most of their powers over state education and outcomes continued to improve. School-leavers in England & Wales with at least 5 O levels/GCSEs rose from 18.1 per cent in 1970/1971 to 21.8 per cent in 1980/1981 to 32.7 per cent in 1990/1991.[58] Girls had long shown greater ability than their exam results and employment patterns suggested.[59] As their opportunities for work and further education expanded, they had incentives to match ability with performance and increasingly outperformed boys. The shift was widely interpreted as a 'problem of underperformance' by boys, as the previous lesser performance of girls was not. Children from minority ethnic backgrounds also performed better than 'white' children, on average, with differences among and within minority groups: girls of Black Caribbean origin outperformed boys, children of Pakistani and Bangladeshi origin included some of the best and worst performers, while those of Indian and Chinese origin outperformed all others.[60] There was a certain narrowing of class differences, though poverty was still seriously disadvantageous.[61] Pessimists attributed improved school performance to falling exam standards, without convincing evidence. Comprehensive education had generally improved outcomes, though independent schools, with smaller classes and greater funding outperformed most state schools in exams and university entrance.

Public spending on education fell from 5.2 per cent GDP, 1979/1980, to 4.8 per cent, 1989/1990, after rising for three decades, the biggest cut of the century.[62] By 1990 concern rose about large class sizes, shortages of books and equipment, the declining real pay and increased workload of teachers, whose morale sank like that of other professionals disparaged by the premier. The annual, independent British Social Attitudes Survey (started 1983) revealed demand to 'increase taxes and spend more on health, education and social benefits' rising from 32 per cent of respondents in 1983 to 58 per cent in 1994, with particular concern about education. Nevertheless, more young people stayed longer at school (rather fewer in England than in Wales and Scotland), probably because the introduction of GCSEs enabled more to gain qualifications, while HE expanded, and the job market contracted especially for the less qualified. Eighteen- to 21-year-olds in HE in Great Britain rose from 12.7 per cent to 20.3 per cent between 1977/1978 and 1990/1991.[63] Female students increased from 28 per cent to over 50 per cent from 1970 to the mid-1990s, though courses remained gender-segregated, with females still concentrated in the Arts and Social Sciences. The higher social classes were over-represented among male and female students, while ethnic minorities were under-represented.

But higher education was squeezed financially. In 1981 university funding was cut by 18 per cent over three years despite rising student numbers. Class sizes grew and investment in libraries and other facilities fell. Overseas students' fees rose. In 1984 Keith Joseph proposed fees for home students, but withdrew following opposition from Conservative backbenchers, alarmed at the likely reaction of their constituents. In 1988 student grants were reduced and loans introduced, repayable when the graduate's income surpassed 85 per cent of median earnings, further reducing incentives for working-class students to attend university, particularly universities away from home which would increase their costs. The 1988 Education Act transferred university funding to a Universities Funding Council, replacing their previous financial near autonomy with government control, and shifted polytechnic funding from local authorities to central government. It also abolished secure tenure of university posts from appointment to retirement, another blow to professional security.[64]

Housing

Council housing continued to contract. The Housing Act, 1988, aimed to further reduce the role of local authorities by allowing non-profit housing associations and profit-making landlords to take over council housing. Tenants and councils resisted, and estates of poorer tenants were unattractive to both sectors, but by 1995 diminishing resources drove more than fifty councils to transfer their entire housing stock to housing associations, whose share of 'social' housing rose from 5 per cent in 1978 to 19 per cent in 1995, while their government grants were cut, leading to higher rents and more Housing Benefit claims.[65] SB rent payments in 1980/1 cost £2.8bn; in 1995/6 Housing Benefit cost £12.2bn.[66] The 1988 Act abolished rent controls for new private tenants, while landlords received generous tax incentives to expand the private market. Social housing was increasingly residualized and stigmatized. Council tenants in the bottom two income quintiles increased from 51 per cent in 1979 to 76 per cent in 1994, with similar proportions among housing association tenants.[67]

Homelessness grew. From 1979 to 1992 households statutorily homeless under the 1977 Act increased from 70,000 to 180,000.[68] Homeless families placed in bed and breakfast accommodation due to lack of council housing – a costly, inadequate solution – increased to 12,000 in 1991.[69] Desperate people sleeping on streets were not included in the official homeless figures, which excluded single people. A survey of sleepers on the streets and railway stations of London on a cold night in April 1989 found 789, three times the number detected in December 1965 and a probable underestimate. The April 1991 census recorded 1,197 rough sleepers in Greater London, 2,852 throughout Great Britain. Shelter estimated over 8,000 in 1993. Thatcher failed to persuade the Charity Commission to withdraw Shelter's charitable status due to its 'political' attacks accusing her housing policies of increasing homelessness.[70] An independent survey in 1981 concluded that rough sleepers were rarely criminals or wasters as often claimed, but mostly homeless for medical or other reasons beyond their control, including lack of support after leaving local authority care.[71] Thatcher dismissed the report but the situation became so desperate that in 1990 the DoE funded the 'Rough Sleepers Initiative' providing hostel places and attempting to improve access for single people to permanent housing, initially only in London, from 1996 in other cities and towns.

Housing suffered most from cuts to social spending, from 3 per cent to 1.8 per cent GDP in 1980–90.[72] Council house building in Great Britain collapsed from 146,000 in 1975 to under 2,000 in 1995. Total housing completions were about 200,000 pa during 1980–95, mostly for owner-occupation. Renovation of older properties continued in all sectors and there were fewer severely substandard homes.[73] During 1971–91, dwellings in UK lacking one or more standard amenities (bath or shower, kitchen sink or washbasin with hot and cold water, indoor toilet) fell from 17.4 per cent to 1 per cent. The worst conditions were still in the private rental sector.[74]

Social services

Labour's guidelines for improved local services were abandoned, council budgets cut, the rate cap restricted spending and central government sought to shift services to the private or non-profit sectors or to families. The Local Government Act, 1988, required local authorities to put services out to competitive tender, theoretically to increase efficiency and cost-effectiveness. Too often it led to deteriorating services and rising costs under private, profit-making providers.[75] Disabled activists campaigned still more vigorously for improved support. In 1981 Disabled Peoples International was formed, then in 1985 Voluntary Organizations for Anti-Discrimination coordinated UK disability charities, later renamed Rights Now! The Disabled Persons (Services, Consultation and Representation) Act, 1986, required councils to assess the needs of all disabled people requesting services and provide help in accessing telephone, TV, radio, libraries, holidays, recreation, education and transport to and from services and occupational, cultural and social facilities. Cuts to local authority funding hampered implementation, while demand grew as the population aged and higher living standards and improved medical care enabled more disabled people to live longer.

Voluntary organizations still provided essential services, under growing pressure from government to replace public services, with subsidies. Aware of their limited resources and fearing dependence on government funds and the controls attached, they often felt they had little alternative in the interests of people in need. Contrary to Thatcher's convictions, most care was still provided by families and neighbours, increasingly as public services deteriorated. The Office for Population, Censuses and Surveys (OPCS) reported in 1992 that 16 per cent of British adults had caring responsibilities for disabled or frail people, often at considerable personal cost. Few could do more without expert support, which dwindled, but government policy was still driven by the assumption that modern families neglected needy relatives and family care must be enforced by withholding services when relatives were available.[76]

From 1948 local authorities could charge for residential care at their discretion. From 1983 they were obliged to charge means-tested fees, also for home care including home helps and meals on wheels, at discretionary, highly variable, rates. In 1995 a meal cost £1.65 in Kent, 35p in Derbyshire.[77] The uncertain boundary between need for free healthcare and chargeable social care remained deeply problematic. The extent and standard of residential and community services declined. Fewer older and disabled people resided in local authority institutions, more in voluntary and, especially, growing numbers of profit-making institutions. Fees rose in the latter; social security funding for residential care for those unable to pay rose from £10m to £2,072m pa during 1979–91.[78] Consequently public spending on social services rose while service users paid more and services declined in quality.[79] In 1990 responsibility for funding was shifted from IS to local authorities to reduce central costs, another charge on shrinking local budgets causing further cuts to services. There was growing concern at the low pay of care providers, affecting their numbers, quality and skills.

Health

The 1987 Conservative manifesto promised to 'improve' the NHS. The third term began with protests by NHS staff about cuts. Waiting times for treatment grew, highlighted in the press. Thatcher believed, she wrote later, that 'the NHS had become a bottomless financial pit'.[80] She had no solutions other than, as ever, to extend private practice and business practices and discipline the professionals. She leaned strongly towards private health insurance, but the Treasury still believed it created costlier healthcare, citing the US example. Private medical insurance policies increased from 1.3m in 1979 to 3.3m in 1990, encouraged by tax incentives, but were still widely unpopular. Thatcher introduced a White Paper, *Working for Patients* (1989), pledging that the NHS would 'continue to be available to all, regardless of income . . . financed out of general taxation'.[81] It proposed radical changes incorporated in the Health Service and Community Care Act, 1990, following modifications after strong opposition from the BMA. Under a new 'internal market', hospitals became independent 'trusts', non-profit organizations, within the NHS but with greater freedom to arrange pay and service delivery, including with private providers. They were encouraged to seek 'efficiency savings' as cuts were described. GPs received spending limits, forcing them to prescribe cheaper drugs when possible. More managers and administrators were required; their salaries cost £158.8m in 1990, £609.6m by 1994.[82]

Still greater local inequalities in treatment, outcomes and funds followed. By 1996, thirty-four NHS trusts were in deficit and there were fewer NHS beds.[83] Hospital-acquired infections, previously rare, became a serious problem as hygiene deteriorated when cleaning and other services were 'outsourced' to low-paid workers for private companies. Opposition grew. Ambulance crews struck for higher pay, the first strike for years to win wide popular support, especially when the new minister of health, Kenneth Clarke, described them as 'glorified taxi drivers'. Spending on older patients and mental illness fell, while average life expectancy rose, and mental illness did not decline.[84] Dental charges rose to a point where fewer dentists thought NHS practice worthwhile and NHS provision shrank. Prescription charges rose from 20p per item in 1979 to £5.65 in 1997, though the proportion of free prescriptions for pensioners, children, and people on benefits, rose from 65 to 84 per cent, and they raised little revenue.[85] Respondents to Social Attitudes Surveys giving health as the highest priority for government spending rose from 36.7 per cent to 60.7 per cent during 1983–9, surpassing any other item, reinforcing evidence of the continuing strong popular commitment to the NHS.[86]

An ageing population

The birth rate remained historically low. More people lived longer. Over-60s were 17 per cent of the UK population in 1960, 20.7 per cent in 1990. In 1981 average male life expectancy at birth was 71, at age 65, 78. Women could still expect longer lives, at birth to 77, at 65 to 82. More people remained healthy longer: men aged 65 to age 75, on average, women to age 77.[87] The averages, as ever, masked inequalities: the poorest died on average 10–15 years earlier than the richest and experienced poorer health. Through the 1980s inequality between rich and poor increased among older and younger people, with women of all ages still more at risk of poverty than men. Older workers were especially vulnerable to unemployment. Employment among men aged 50–64 fell from 88 per cent in 1973 to 63 per cent in 1995. They suffered especially from the decline of manufacturing. Once unemployed they were unlikely to work again due to employers' age discrimination. More well-paid senior managers retired early with generous pensions as businesses sought to cut costs, short-sightedly taking advantage of surpluses in their pension funds due to high interest rates.

The international improvement in average life expectancy in higher income countries followed unprecedented improvements in living standards, diet and healthcare. But, as in the 1930s, the dominant response was panic about the growing 'burden' of ageing populations requiring healthcare and pensions funded by a shrinking younger generation. The fears were, again, reinforced, by assumptions that low birth rates and lengthening lives were now permanent features of modern societies. That immigration of younger people helped offset birth-rate decline was rarely noted. The healthcare costs of older people were relatively high mainly because many fewer younger people now suffered serious illness or death, and rising costs owed more to the high costs of drugs, technology and salaries than to older people.[88] It was rarely noted that older people made major, growing, contributions to the care of family, friends, neighbours and others, much needed as services declined, at substantial savings to the public purse, while contributing more to the economy through taxes and spending than they received in benefits and services.[89] The 'burden' of ageing was invoked by the government to justify cutting the real value of pensions and the costs of healthcare. In response older people, like other excluded groups, became more assertive, campaigning against inequality, inadequate pensions and discrimination, including the formation in 1988 of the Campaign against Age Discrimination in Employment (CADE).

Family policy

Reviving the 'traditional' family was a persistent Thatcher mission. In 1982 a Cabinet Family Policy Group was appointed.[90] A leaked paper suggested that its brief included 'what more could be done to encourage families, in the widest sense, to assume responsibilities taken on by the state, for example responsibility for the disabled, the elderly, unemployed 16-year-olds'. It asked 'Do present policies for supporting single parents strike the right balance between ensuring adequate child support to prevent poverty and encouraging sensible and self-reliant behaviour by adults.'[91] Thatcher later recalled:

> There was great pressure, which I had to fight hard to resist, to provide tax reliefs or subsidies for childcare. . . . I did not believe that it was fair to those mothers who chose to stay at home and bring up their families on the one income to give tax reliefs to those who went out to work and had two incomes.[92]

Childcare remained inadequate and expensive, deterring many women, especially single mothers, from working, unless their parents could help, as grandparents, mainly grandmothers, increasingly did, sometimes giving up their own work to do so.

Support for families declined. From 1980 councils were no longer required to provide school meals. In 1986 benefits were reduced for 18- to 25-year-olds, on the assumption, often mistaken especially concerning the poorest, that they had families to support them. Young people in care lacked family support and ceased to be the responsibility of local authorities at age 16. In 1988 IS was withdrawn from 16- to 18-year-olds and Child Benefit from those not in full-time education or training. Student loans and withdrawal of students' right to claim benefits during vacations increased their dependence on their families or on part-time work. Many families could not afford to support their children unaided. Thatcher became

> Increasingly concerned . . . that . . . we could only get to the roots of crime and much else besides by concentrating on strengthening the traditional family. All the

evidence- statistical and anecdotal- pointed to the breakdown of families as the starting point for a range of social ills.[93]

There was no such evidence. Research indicated that the major cause of problems among younger, and older, people, including 'family breakdown', was poverty.

Polls suggested that most British people were more optimistic and realistic. In 1984 responses to Gallup challenged narratives of social decline. Only 21 per cent ascribed poverty to lack of effort, 32 per cent thought unemployment benefits too high, discouraging work, but 41 per cent thought them too low, causing hardship.[94] The British Social Attitudes Survey found high levels of contact and mutual support within families and changing expectations of gender roles. In 1984, 43 per cent of respondents agreed that 'A husband's job is to earn the money; a wife's job is to look after the home and family'. By 1989 only 25 per cent agreed.[95]

Families were certainly changing. More unconventional families lived openly together, gay and heterosexual.[96] Births outside marriage rose from 11.5 per cent of all UK births in 1980 to 28 per cent in 1990, 33.6 per cent in 1995. In 1995, 78 per cent were registered by both parents, often living together. In 1980 there were 940,000 single-parent families, 1 in 8 families with 1.5 million children, rising to 1.3 million, 1 in 5 families with 2.1 million children, in 1992, overwhelmingly headed by mothers, 60 per cent divorced or separated, 33 per cent never married, 7 per cent widowed, 66 per cent received IS. They clustered in poorer districts.

In 1983 leaked government papers described supporting one-parent families as 'subsidizing illegitimacy and immorality'. Thatcher repeated the persistent, baseless, slur about the 'growing problem of young girls who deliberately become pregnant in order to jump the housing queue and gain welfare payments'.[97] Teenage pregnancies fell slightly through the 1980s, and any woman desperate enough to become pregnant to gain a council home was likely to be disappointed. As the stock declined, she would be allocated, at best, a substandard dwelling or a bed- and -breakfast room. Thatcher became convinced that 'feckless fathers' were to blame for poverty among single mothers. She 'was appalled by the way in which men fathered a child and then absconded, leaving the single mothers- and the taxpayer- to foot the bill for their irresponsibility'.[98] In the late 1980s only one in three lone mothers received regular maintenance from the fathers, but non-payers were not all 'feckless' but unemployed, very young, low-paid or had a second family to support. Social security policy had long assumed that a father's primary responsibility was to the family with whom he lived. Thatcher vowed to make fathers responsible for all their children, partly in the improbable hope of dissuading them from forming new families they could not afford.

The outcome was the Child Support Act, 1991, drafted in a hurry with little research or consultation and rushed through parliament under pressure from Thatcher before she lost office in 1990, assisted by Treasury officials keen to cut the benefits bill.[99] It established the new principle that the needs of first families took priority over second even when the father lived with the latter. Officials could initiate maintenance procedures even if claimants wanted no contact with the father, often due to domestic violence.

Refusal to name the father 'without good cause' could lead to benefit reduction of up to 40 per cent. 'Good cause' was initially defined as the child having been conceived due to rape or incest, despite evidence that 1-in-6 divorced and 1-in-10 single or separated women gave domestic violence as the cause of separation. An amendment allowed that 'risk to her or any child living with her suffering harm or undue distress' must be considered. The act was implemented in 1993, after Thatcher left office. It proved costly and inefficient.

Social movements

Activists continued to demand greater equalities. Refuges and helplines continued, often supported by Labour-controlled councils. Gay activism grew as HIV-AIDS emerged as a serious crisis. The first death in Britain occurred in July 1982 – the Terence Higgins Trust was founded in the dead man's name to support other victims. Three more were known to have died by 1983 and what the tabloids labelled a 'gay plague' unleashed panic-stricken homophobia. Gay men were portrayed not as innocent victims of a new disease but as deviants spreading fatal illness through their disgusting practices. Self-help and support groups were established. Deaths rose to around 1,000 per year by the early 1990s. Partners of victims suffered the additional trauma of lacking legal rights even to visit the sick person in hospital, stimulating calls for formal partnership rights for gay couples.

The DHSS and Chief Medical Officer recommended leaflets and advertisements advising on safe sex, but Thatcher was reluctant. In late 1986 heterosexuals were diagnosed, and panic surged. An unprecedented £20m health education campaign followed. Media advertising proclaimed, 'Don't Die of Ignorance' and leaflets were delivered to 23m homes. Thatcher cut the campaign when no heterosexual AIDS epidemic materialized.[100] Gay organizations, including the Higgins Trust, played a major role in promoting safe sex. But homophobia was rampant. To combat prejudice and discrimination, some Labour-controlled London boroughs promoted positive images of gay people through sex education in schools, which were publicized and often caricatured in the media and opposed by morality groups. Sex education was not compulsory, and pressure grew in the Conservative Party to let parents withdraw their children. In her post-election conference speech, Thatcher attacked 'positive images', claiming that 'children who need to be taught traditional moral values are being taught that they have an inalienable right to be gay'.[101] Section 28 of the Local Government Act, 1988, forbade local authorities promoting 'the teaching in any maintained school of the acceptability of homosexuality as a pretended family relationship'. It aroused widespread protest and demonstrations, further stimulating gay and lesbian organization.[102] Stonewall was founded in 1988 to lobby against it and for equalizing the age of consent, gay adoption and parenting and partnership recognition. In January 1989 the AIDs Coalition to Unleash Power (ACT-UP) was formed to protest at health authorities denying treatment to infected people.[103]

Section 28 was never enforced, but councils and schools became cautious about sex education. Gay rights campaigners believed it intensified police activity which grew with the AIDS epidemic: arrests of gay men reached record levels in the late 1980s.[104] The Social Attitudes Survey found that in 1983, 49.6 per cent of respondents thought 'sexual relations between two adults of the same sex' 'always wrong'; in 1990, 55.5 per cent.[105]

Women

Gender equality also progressed slowly. The EOC, firmly led, with closer relations with trade unions and support from the EC, became more effective. Thatcher's waning enthusiasm for the EC was not enhanced when in 1983 she was forced by a decision in the European Court of Human Rights (ECHR) to revise the Equal Pay Act, replacing equal pay for 'like work' with 'work of comparable value'. It followed a successful case brought by women cooks at a Merseyside shipbuilding firm, aided by the EOC, arguing that their work was comparable with that of male painters and others employed by the company and should be paid equally. Another European court ruling in 1983 judged unlawful Britain's exemption from the Equal Treatment Directive of people employed in private households and businesses with fewer than five employees. The Sex Discrimination Act, 1986, outlawed discrimination in collective bargaining agreements and extended anti-discrimination law to small businesses.

Feminist activists engaged more in formal politics, local and national, and in unions, as potentially more effective than public campaigns for challenging a hostile government. In Scotland nationalism grew in opposition especially to welfare cuts, privatization and the erosion of local government, and Scottish feminists campaigned for gender equality in local government employment. They became active in the growing movement for devolution, determined to be fully represented in any elected Scottish government.[106] More slowly, similar movements emerged in Wales where the 1970s women's movement was weaker.[107]

Race

Racial inequalities and resistance to them continued. 1981 brought riots in deprived inner-city areas, Toxteth in Liverpool, Brixton in London, later in parts of Bristol and Birmingham, partly responses to racism and aggressive policing, including stopping and searching young Black men, disproportionately, on suspicion of intended crime, often unjustified. The riots were also provoked by unemployment and poverty which were especially acute in minority ethnic communities. A report following an investigation by Lord Justice Scarman acknowledged widespread discrimination and inequality but denied accusations that 'institutional racism' pervaded the police, recommending recruiting more police from ethnic minorities. Partial implementation of the report did not prevent further demonstrations challenging police behaviour, most seriously in Tottenham, North London, in 1985, where a policeman was killed. This led to substantial investment in the area and improved relations between police and community.

Immigration declined. The British Nationality Act, 1981, further restricted the rights of Commonwealth citizens to British nationality to those with a British-born grandparent, while high unemployment made the UK less attractive. Anti-racist groups remained active. By the mid-1980s Bernie Grant (Tottenham), Linda Bellos (Lambeth) and Merle Amory (Brent), all of Afro-Caribbean origin, led Labour-controlled London councils. Four Black MPs were elected for Labour in 1987, including Bernie Grant. In 1992 the first Asian Conservative MP was elected.[108]

Gypsies and Travellers were still profoundly excluded, though they gained from Labour's reforms. Settled sites increased, but mainly for permanent settlement which not all travellers wanted. The reforms improved access to education, health and welfare services but there was no security of tenure and tensions with local residents and police harassment continued. In 1985 there were an estimated 9,900 Gypsy and Traveller caravans in England. The 1989 Local Government and Housing Act secured grants for permanent sites but problems continued.[109]

Downfall

Cuts to public services, especially the NHS, and continuing economic problems increased opposition to Thatcher in the country and her party. Then came the 'poll tax', a fundamental reform of local taxation, another blow to local government. A persistent source of frustration for a government seeking to control local authorities was their capacity to raise local rates and spend the income as they wished. For centuries rates had been fixed according to the valuation of each property. Thatcher first capped rate-income, then rates were abolished and replaced by a 'community charge', a regressive, flat-rate tax on all individuals living in a local authority area regardless of income or assets. It was dubbed a 'poll tax' by its many opponents, causing riots and large demonstrations. It passed through parliament, with significant Conservative as well as Labour opposition, in 1987. It was not implemented in Northern Ireland, where there were troubles enough. In Scotland it was introduced in April 1989, a year earlier than in England and Wales, and strongly opposed. It was evaded throughout Britain as rates had rarely been. It was opposed by many Conservative voters, complaining about varying tax levels in different districts and because, for many people, it increased their tax liability at a time of rising prices and financial pressure.[110]

Thatcher sank in the polls while Labour recovered, and senior Cabinet ministers resigned. Michael Heseltine challenged her for the leadership in November 1990. In the first round she failed to win outright, insisted she would fight on, but was dissuaded by ministers, fearing that her evident weakness and the divisions in the party would lose them the next election. She resigned in style with a high-spirited speech in the Commons. John Major won the vote to succeed her, probably because he was less divisive than others, more emollient amid party tensions. He was the son of a former music hall performer who ran a small garden ornaments business. He left grammar school at sixteen, did not attend university and trained in banking, working his way up from the cashiers' desk, also becoming a councillor in Lambeth, South London.[111]

Conclusion: 'Thatcherism'

Margaret Thatcher's name became a slogan, an 'ism', because her thinking and actions challenged important cultural currents, remaining influential after her demise, creating long-term changes in politics, the economy and society. The shopkeeper's daughter rejected the *noblesse oblige* sentiments of the old Conservative elite, but espoused other 'Victorian values', as she put it, especially the 'traditional family' and self-help, reviving the language of blaming the poor while encouraging popular ownership of property and shares. She challenged institutions and professionals she believed protected established structures and practices at the public expense, including her own university, Oxford, whose academic staff refused her an honorary degree in 1985 because her policies were doing 'deep and systematic damage to the whole public educational system in Britain'.[112]

She was prime minister for eleven and a half years, the longest since Lord Liverpool retired in 1827. Income tax cuts during 1979–90 increased incomes of £10,000 by £320 pa, those of £70,000 by £36,310.[113] Poverty increased, among children from 8 per cent in 1979 to 28 per cent in 1992 by the official measure.[114] Average real incomes rose 37 per cent during 1979–92, but those of the poorest 10 per cent fell 18 per cent, while the richest 10 per cent were 61 per cent richer.[115] Unemployment reached its highest level since 1940, manufacturing dwindled, while finance boomed. This deepened social divisions and the sense of exclusion of unemployed people in Northern England, Wales, Scotland and Northern Ireland, often, though not always, expressed in the language of class. Urban areas, including council estates, became more socially divided following rising house prices and council house sales. Though Thatcher banned use of the word 'inequality', under her rule inequalities – economic and cultural – grew spectacularly after narrowing since 1945.

Thatcher would never acknowledge it, but under her premiership the post-war Welfare State was slashed, and state-guided economic growth terminated. The skeleton of state welfare survived, but the quality of healthcare, social security benefits, social services and state education declined. Where the private market replaced the public sector, it challenged belief in its superior efficiency. People proved overwhelmingly unwilling to adopt private health insurance or private pensions partly due to cost, primarily because they had experienced superior, less costly public services. Contrary to Thatcher's ambitions, through the 1980s public social spending shot up, funding inferior services under more complex, often inefficient, administration by a government publicly hostile to 'red tape', failing to meet the growing needs of an increasingly impoverished population. This was indeed a 'dismal decade' for very many people.

CHAPTER 12
JOHN MAJOR

John Major's supporters included Conservatives who expected him to modify Thatcher's more extreme and unpopular policies, in particular the poll tax, but not to abandon her broad neoliberal trajectory. Initially he appeared more progressive, but increasingly his actions seemed hardly distinguishable from hers, and there was little sign of an alternative vision. Meanwhile income inequality continued to widen, poverty to grow, unemployment remained high, personal debt increased and average living standards stalled. Expressions of discontent multiplied until Labour's resounding victory in 1997.

The first term

Major was the youngest, least experienced premier of the century so far, born in 1943, from an unprivileged background. He tried initially to distance himself from Thatcher's unpopular policies and appeal to disaffected groups. He ordered Lamont (still chancellor) to unfreeze Child Benefit; then in 1991 it was increased and index-linked, as CPAG proposed. Compensation was awarded to haemophiliacs infected with HIV during blood transfusions. He met gay rights campaigners and in 1991 launched Opportunity 2000, initiated by businesspeople to achieve gender balance at all levels of employment by 2000. But with scant support from most employers little changed. Equalities for women, homosexuals and ethnic minorities did not advance noticeably under Major.

The poll tax was replaced with council tax for implementation in 1993, a local tax levied on the value of broad 'bands' of properties, with discounts for residents living alone, only with children or carers or with low incomes. It did not revive the right of local authorities to alter the tax rate at their discretion. In England and Scotland its valuation remained unchanged in 2023, despite sharply rising property values in the intervening thirty years, to the advantage of owners of expensive properties. Wales revalued in 2003 and plans another in 2025. Under Major – the first premier since Attlee to have been a local councillor – central control of local government increased further. The spending cap was extended to smaller councils, and all councils faced intensified pressure to privatize remaining services. The Conservatives continued to lose heavily in local elections, especially in Scotland.

Major's big idea to establish his distinctive identity was the 'Citizen's Charter', launched in July 1991, notionally to improve the increasingly privatized public services and support the 'ordinary person' against 'faceless bureaucrats', in response to growing criticism. By 1996 forty-two charters listed standards for services, independent inspectorates monitored performance, league tables were published, complaints and redress procedures established, but without enforcement processes. Privatization, contracting out and competitive tendering for public services continued with little obvious improvement to services.[1]

Reduction of civil servants and their powers continued. By 1991, fifty semi-autonomous 'Next Steps' agencies were established, employing 50 per cent of all civil servants. Whitehall's role was restricted to formulating policies, while the agencies provided the services and ministers could avoid responsibility for all-too-frequent failed outcomes. By 1997 there were 137 agencies, including the Benefits Agency created in 1991 to administer social security payments, Her Majesty's Revenue and Customs (HMRC) handling taxes, the Crown Prosecution Service, and the Serious Fraud Office, together employing almost 384,000 staff. Agencies employed their own staff and were responsible for their own budgets. Their CEOs were mostly appointed by open competition, 35 per cent from outside the service.[2] Performance did not obviously improve.[3] The Child Support Agency was a costly shambles due to the poorly designed Child Support Act, and the Prison Service Agency faced riots and breakouts by prisoners. The CEO of the CSA resigned, and the CEO of the PSA was sacked by the Home Secretary. The Benefits Agency was criticized for inefficiency by the National Audit Office, and it lost costly appeals by claimants against its decisions, including to the European Court of Justice. In 1991 this ruled UK social security law guilty of discrimination because, since 1984, married or cohabiting women, not men, claiming disability allowances had to prove they were incapable of performing both paid work and 'normal household duties'. Almost 300,000 had been disqualified.

Catering, cleaning, estates management, security, financial, legal and IT support were 'outsourced' from civil service departments as elsewhere in the public sector, generally worsening the pay, benefits, security and working conditions especially of lower-level staff. In 1995–7 more agencies were wholly privatized, including Her Majesty's Stationery Office (HMSO), the long-established government publishing arm, and the Recruitment and Assessment Service, responsible for recruiting to the civil service elite fast-stream. This was strongly, but unsuccessfully, opposed by senior civil servants and some politicians. Civil servants' morale declined and resignations increased as they perceived few efficiency gains but felt serious concern about the decline of accountability and commitment to public service. Increasingly, senior appointments, including permanent secretaries, were filled by external advertisement rather than traditional internal promotion, and budgets and staff were cut further. There was continuing criticism of politicization of the service and of ministerial preference for advice from the many special advisors appointed from outside the service.[4]

Election 1992 and after

When an election was unavoidable in April 1992 inflation had fallen to 4 per cent but unemployment was close to 3 million, GDP had declined and interest rates remained above 10 per cent. In his campaign Major spoke a different language from Thatcher, of creating a 'classless society', while upholding popular features of her policies. He attacked the 'Socialists', appealing to voters who had bought their council houses and shares in privatized industries not to 'let Labour ruin it'. He challenged the prospective Labour budget outlined by John Smith, the shadow chancellor, which promised higher direct taxation to fund improved services, labelling Labour the 'tax and spend party'.[5] He won a clear, but reduced, majority of thirty-eight seats.

After gaining a higher proportion of female votes than Thatcher, Major appointed two female Cabinet ministers, following none in his previous Cabinet: Gillian Shephard at Employment, Virginia Bottomley at Health. He supported establishment of a Sex Equality branch at the Department of Employment and Shephard initiated an investigation into the difficulties of working women. But these were exacerbated by the government's continuing deregulation of the labour market, including the abolition in 1993 of Wages Councils (established by Churchill in 1909) which minimally safeguarded mainly female pay. There were few obvious improvements.

Major favoured joining the EU's Exchange Rate Mechanism (ERM), designed to stabilize exchange and interest rates, when it was established in 1990, but the UK joined at too high an exchange rate, which increased trading costs and inflation. The pound threatened to sink below the minimum level set by the ERM, causing large sales of sterling on international markets on 16 September 1992 – 'Black Wednesday' as it became known. The Bank of England sold over £15bn of its reserves, the largest sale in its history, interest rates rose to 15 per cent and Britain left the ERM that evening in an atmosphere of severe crisis. The pound was devalued by 10 per cent, which assisted exporters and the balance of payments, but the deficit of government revenue over expenditure was over 10 per cent of GDP in 1993–4, the highest figure recorded in peacetime.[6] Lamont was sacked as chancellor. His successor, Kenneth Clarke, cut public spending and increased indirect taxes, while reducing income tax by 1 per cent in 1995 and again in 1996, hitting the lowest-paid hardest. Interest rates fell to around 6 per cent, inflation declined and economic growth rose to 4.7 per cent in 1994, but the government never recovered from what were seen as misjudgements leading to Black Wednesday.[7] Labour established a lasting lead in opinion polls.

At the 1993 party conference Major appealed to the nation to 'get Back to Basics' and unite behind 'common sense British values'. Echoing Thatcher, he pledged to end 'permissiveness' and promote 'accepting responsibility for yourself and your family and not shuffling it off on the state. . . . It is time to return to those old core values'. These included emphasizing the '3Rs' in education, which he believed were neglected by 'trendy teachers'.[8] This was enthusiastically received but soon undermined by a series of sexual and financial scandals among members of the government. Plans to privatise the Royal Mail were shelved in 1994 due to backbench and popular opposition. One of the few other publicly owned undertakings remaining to be privatised was British Rail, for which there was also little obvious public enthusiasm, but it was rushed through before the 1997 election.[9]

Social policy

Education

From 1992 Major sought voter support with more ambitious social policies, which also largely continued those of Thatcher. The 1992 Education (Schools) Act required schools to publish exam results, arousing such hostility from teachers, including threatened boycotts, that the tests were simplified. It established a new Funding Agency for Schools, allowed to remove state schools from local authority control and fund private schools opting into the state sector. Sex education became voluntary: schools were advised not to emphasize sex but 'the value of family life'. Polytechnics were removed from local authority control and re-designated as universities. All university funding was now channelled through new Higher Education Funding Councils (HEFCs) in each country of the UK, further increasing government control over once-autonomous institutions. Unprecedented regular national assessment of the quality of university teaching and research was introduced, and league tables encouraged. Universities could now admit as many students as they wished, with little additional funding, but could boost income by charging overseas students what fees they chose. The government still dared not risk alienating voters by charging fees for home students, despite rising numbers and costs. It announced a target of one-third of the age group to enter universities by the end of the century. This was reached by 1994/1995, when numbers were again capped. As student numbers grew faster than funding, class sizes grew and facilities deteriorated.

Further education colleges were removed from ever-dwindling local authority control. Teacher training colleges were amalgamated with universities or became independent universities and training was extended from two to three years, leading to a degree, though ministers proposed that training should occur in schools, as increasingly it did, providing practical skills rather than theoretical knowledge which, they argued, encouraged left-leaning teaching fashions. Suspicion of public sector professionals and increased central control of all levels of education continued, while salaries were limited, as elsewhere in the public sector.[10]

Housing

Housebuilding fell from 203,000 in 1990 to 189,000 in 1996, overwhelmingly in the private sector. Council house construction shrank further, to 10,200 in 1991, 1,900 in 1995.[11] Tax relief on mortgage payments was progressively reduced from 1991, mainly to offset rises in other housing costs, especially Housing Benefit. This soared due to unemployment and low pay combined with rising private rents and the shortage of local authority housing. High interest rates caused mortgage arrears, repossessions and the newly prevalent phenomenon of negative equity: houses valued at less than the owners' mortgages. More positively, homeless people requiring local authority housing declined 172,000–135,000 during 1990–5, while households placed in bed-and-breakfasts fell,

12,200–4,500, as councils leased cheaper private accommodation and provided hostels, including refuges for women homeless after fleeing domestic violence.[12]

Health

In 1991 the Patients' Charter included three new 'rights' to healthcare: information on local health services, including on quality and waiting times; guaranteed treatment within the hardly reassuring period of two years from joining a waiting list; complaints about the NHS to be properly investigated. Seven national standards were listed, including that ambulances should arrive within fourteen minutes in urban areas, nineteen in rural; patients in outpatient clinics would receive specific appointment times and be seen within thirty minutes, those in hospital accident and emergency departments immediately. All were desirable and in many areas much needed, but they were not enforceable or fulfilled by health authorities under increasing financial pressure. The Conservatives' regular device to achieve improvement through competition, as with schools and universities, annual Performance Tables, was employed in the NHS from June 1994 without obvious benefits.

From 1992 specific health conditions were targeted for improved treatment: cancer, heart disease, stroke, mental illness, HIV/AIDS, sexual health, accidents. Targets were set for reducing death rates and behaviours known to increase risk, including smoking. Some serious health, especially mental health, problems were overlooked, and it was unclear how, or whether, targets could be achieved, or the source of funds to pursue them. Inequalities in NHS expenditure and numbers and availability of GPs across English regions grew and there were continuing inequalities between rich and poor and between ethnic groups in expected years of life and good health.[13] In 1993 Thatcher's 'care in the community' initiative was implemented, continuing local authorities' responsibility for chronically sick, aged and disabled people living at home, but obliging them, since they had no further funding, to purchase 'care packages' from private or voluntary providers rather than providing their own services. Fragmented, less publicly accountable, services resulted.[14]

'Child support'

Thatcher's Child Support Act, 1990, was implemented by the Child Support Agency (CSA) from 1993. The regulations, like the legislation, were drafted hurriedly and administered by inexperienced officials. The CSA took over the courts' powers to assess, collect and enforce maintenance payments for all single parents receiving benefits (527,000 in 1993) and new claimants, on the assumption that many claimed benefits from the state because 'feckless fathers' failed to pay due maintenance. IS was reduced by the full amount of maintenance payments. A large backlog quickly developed because most cases were more complex than anticipated. The system was intended to cut benefit costs but, remarkably, it was not foreseen that because the CSA prioritized fathers' responsibility for first families it disadvantaged many second families, who needed benefits. Or that many fathers were not evading maintenance but were unable to afford it because they were unemployed or low-paid. Fathers who believed they were doing their best for both families were infuriated, and some fathers, not always the most deserving, staged dramatic, much-publicized protests in prominent London spaces. Most single mothers struggled rather than protested. The Inland Revenue was expected to pursue fathers who failed to pay maintenance, but grew tired of hounding them, often fruitlessly, for small sums and the CSA added this to the tasks for which it was unprepared. It was ordered to cut £530m from the benefits bill in the first year but undershot by £112m, while successfully arranging maintenance in fewer than one-third of eligible applications. It was a widely criticized fiasco. The CEO resigned after a year. The system was modified in the Child Support Act, 1995, but little improved, leaving single-parent families in poverty.[15]

To convey his understanding of the difficulties of single mothers, Major revealed that his sister and mother-in-law had raised children alone, but to justify cutting benefits he and his ministers, like Thatcher, blamed state welfare for encouraging partnership breakdown and single motherhood. At the party conference in October 1992, Peter Lilley, Secretary of State for Social Security, intoned a widely publicized pastiche of Gilbert and Sullivan, announcing he 'had a little list' of:

Benefit offenders who I'll soon be rooting out . . .

Young ladies who get pregnant just to jump the housing list.

And dads who won't support the kids of ladies they have kissed.

And I haven't even mentioned all those sponging socialists.

He later argued in the *News of the World*, without evidence, that the rise in violent crime was due to growing numbers of fatherless families. John Redwood, Secretary of State for Wales and a strong supporter of Thatcherite neoliberalism, visited an estate in Cardiff which, he claimed, was 50 per cent populated by one-parent families including many young, never-married mothers. Only 17 per cent of the 3,500 families were headed by single mothers, 60 per cent of them over 24, most previously married or in long-term relationships.[16] Redwood later proposed withholding benefits from single mothers until the father moved back, to provide 'the normal love and support that fathers have offered down the ages', presumably abandoning any second families.[17] The vice-chair of Cardiff social services committee, a social worker, commented that the main problem for the families was poverty, in an area of high unemployment; most mothers were loving and supportive and wanted to work if they could. A senior police officer commented: 'as the police had exclusion orders for violence against half the men involved, the last thing they wanted was to see women and children forced to allow the fathers to return'.[18]

But Redwood's pronouncements were enthusiastically received by sections of the press. *Daily Mail* columnist Keith Waterhouse attacked the

Single Parent State . . . the single mum can rake in over £100 a week in state benefits . . . she can jump the housing queue and raise her family in one of those lovely tower blocks. … Then there is the Unmarried Mothers' Union – the single parents' militant wing where having a baby is not so much a happy event as a political statement. You cradle the little mite in your boiler suit and carry a placard demanding crèche facilities at the bingo hall.[19]

Unrecognizable but increasingly commonplace stereotypes.

Single mothers did not receive priority for council housing. Department of the Environment researchers discovered that over 40 per cent of unmarried mothers under twenty lived with their parents.[20] The Liberal *Independent* pointed out how many single-parent families were in bed and breakfast accommodation, while the *Guardian* commented that it was indeed desirable to reduce teenage pregnancies, so it was unfortunate that one in four family planning clinics had closed following government cuts.[21] A DSS source stated that Redwood's comments did not represent government policy.[22]

Amid widespread media denigration of 'scroungers' on benefits, the 1996 budget announced the freezing of One Parent Benefit and abolition for new claimants. As the 1997 election approached, John Redwood proposed, in the name of 'family values', that single mothers should give their children up for adoption.[23] Single mothers faced the most sustained attack from the government and the media of the twentieth century. But denigration was not universal: 53 per cent of respondents to a national poll believed women capable of bringing up children alone.[24] Never before had so many children been born outside marriage or so many unmarried couples openly lived together, facing little evident disapproval from family, friends and neighbours. Cutting benefits did not get more mothers into work but made families poorer, worsening the already high levels of child poverty – about 24 per cent in Great Britain in 1995/1996.[25] Many mothers wanted to work but were hampered by lack of affordable childcare and high unemployment.[26]

The government attempted to deal with one genuine cause of partnership breakdown. The Family Homes and Domestic Violence Bill, 1995, strengthened and simplified the law criminalizing domestic violence, for the first time treating married and unmarried couples equally, but 'pro-marriage' Conservative MPs were strongly opposed, and it was withdrawn. An amended version returned in the Family Law Act, 1996, which also made legal aid available for mediation preceding, hopefully averting, divorce, and provided for divorce only following mediation, for which £2m was granted to the voluntary marriage guidance service, Relate.[27] In the Lords, Baroness Patricia Hollis (Labour) successfully inserted an amendment allowing partners, normally wives, to claim 50 per cent of the other's pension rights as part of the divorce settlement.

'Selectivity'

The shift to 'selective', means-tested, payments targeted on the poorest, but relatively costly and inefficient, continued under Major. In 1996 contributory, universal unemployment benefit and means-tested IS were merged into 'Job-Seekers' Allowance' (JSA). The right to the contributory benefit was halved to cover six, rather than twelve, months' unemployment, thereafter means-tested and reduced by 20 per cent for 18- to 25-year-olds. Claimants had to sign a 'job seekers' agreement' to seek work, risking penalties if they failed even in areas of high unemployment. The Social Security (Incapacity for Work) Act, 1994, replaced long-term Invalidity Benefit with Incapacity Benefit. Previously claimants had to prove unfitness for any available work for which they had appropriate skills and aptitude. They must now prove unfitness for *any* work, as assessed by a doctor appointed by the Benefits Agency rather than, as before, their own GP. Increasingly conditions for payment of benefits were tightened, causing severe hardship for many claimants and many successful appeals, costly to the government. The reason, Peter Lilley explained, was that 'The number of people receiving Invalidity Benefit has doubled in the past ten years, although the nation's health has been improving', implying extensive, unproven, fraud.[28] Through the previous decade, older unemployed people had been encouraged to claim Invalidity Benefit in order to lower the unemployment statistics, moving them from relatively generous insurance-based allowances onto lower, means-tested, payments, under pressure to seek work, though older jobseekers rarely succeeded in a discriminatory labour market.

Disability

Similar changes made the lives of disabled people still harder. In 1992 Nicolas Scott, minister responsible for disabled people, admitted they experienced discrimination at work, breaking with the Conservative stress on the burden on employers of ensuring equal treatment of disabled workers. From 1982 to 1993, fifteen unsuccessful Private Members' Bills sought equal rights for disabled people, while EU pressure to resolve this and other forms of discrimination grew.[29] In 1992, a Labour Civil Rights (Disabled Persons) Bill was supported by an unprecedented thirty-three Conservative MPs. During the debate, 2,000 demonstrators descended on Parliament, a building exceptionally poorly adapted to the needs of disabled people. Scott's disabled daughter was a leading campaigner, but the government circulated anonymous press briefings suggesting that reform would cost employers at least £17bn. Ministers did not openly oppose the bill but worked hard to destroy it. They fixed the final stage for the day Labour MPs were attending the funeral of their latest leader, John Smith, who had died suddenly. The bill fell when there were too few votes to be quorate. Disabled activists, invited by Labour MP Denis Skinner, were refused access to parliament for five hours, causing further protests, including attempts by disabled people to haul themselves over the parliamentary threshold.[30]

Following a media furore, with images of wheelchair protesters, Scott was replaced by William Hague. A compromise Disability Discrimination Act, 1995, in principle increased protection against discrimination in employment, provision of services and sale of land, though not in education. It established the National Disability Council to advise government on disability issues, without powers to act against discrimination. It defined as 'disabled', 'someone who has a physical or mental impairment that has a substantial and long-term adverse effect on his or her ability to carry out normal day-to-day activities' and defined 'impairment' more precisely than before but imperfectly, learning difficulties were excluded, among others.[31] Applicants for disability benefits continued to be harshly treated and severely sanctioned.

The 1996 Community Care (Direct Payments) Act allowed local authorities to fund essential services for disabled people. This followed growing criticism of community services for sick and disabled people released from institutions, especially following the murder in 1992 of Jonathan Zito by a paranoid schizophrenic man who had been released but unsupported in the community. But local authority funds remained depleted and services poor, despite Zito's family and others campaigning for improvement.[32]

The social policy changes started under Heath, taken further under Thatcher, and continued under Major seriously increased hardship for many disadvantaged people, replacing their right to support when in need for no fault of their own, which Beveridge and Labour had established, with dependence on, often unskilled, assessments. The post-war Welfare State was continuously eroded. Where possible, responsibility for social welfare was transferred from the state to profit-making private providers and non-profit voluntary organizations at no significant saving to the taxpayer. Voluntary organizations, including CPAG, Citizen's Advice Bureaux, and One Parent Families (OPF, formerly NCUMC), campaigned against the changes, with little effect, though they supported claimants' legal appeals against harsh decisions and perhaps prevented further cuts.

Age discrimination

Discrimination against older people had rarely been openly acknowledged. It was widespread and taken for granted, like other forms of discrimination, until victims protested which occurred later than among other groups because many older people regarded it as normal and protest a younger persons' activity. Life expectancy continued to rise. By 1995 at sixty-five, a man could, on average, expect to live a further fifteen years, a woman eighteen years, though large socio-economic and ethnic inequalities continued. More people were healthy and active to later ages which partly explains their growing assertiveness against discrimination in healthcare, employment and much else. The international panic continued about the growth of 'dependent' older age groups while younger workforces shrank along with the birth rate.

Though more people were fit to work later in life, in the early 1990s one-third of workers in Britain and elsewhere in Western Europe retired, often reluctantly, earlier than had long been normal, before age sixty. A fortunate minority retired on comfortable company pensions, as employers reduced costs by pensioning off expensive senior workers; others were forcibly retired by the decline of manufacturing and faced survival on deteriorating state pensions.[33] About 40 per cent of UK pensioners lived in poverty by the official measure.[34] Earlier retirement was often represented as unavoidable due to technological change and the presumed incapacity of older workers to adapt and retrain. Workers even in their forties might not receive training, despite decades of research demonstrating that many in their sixties could outperform average 25-year-olds, helped by their greater experience, and most older people could learn new skills including using modern technology.[35] In the 1990s they increasingly protested. The Campaign against

Age Discrimination in Employment (CARD) was formed in 1988; then in 1992 the Scottish Pensioners' Forum was created by the Scottish TUC, 'to allow pensioners to speak on behalf of pensioners'.[36]

But they faced further problems. After the body of media tycoon Robert Maxwell was found floating in the Atlantic in 1991, it emerged that £400m had been diverted from the pension funds of Maxwell's Mirror Group to support his failing companies. Employees, past and present, lost their pensions, highlighting the insecurity of the occupational pensions successive Conservative governments had encouraged. It also became clear how many suffered because the Thatcher government's deregulation enabled, indeed encouraged, private finance companies to persuade people with secure public sector pensions to transfer to more expensive, less advantageous, private schemes.

In 1990 the ECHR upheld a man's contention that the lower UK pension age for women, sixty, discriminated against men. The government announced the gradual rise of the female age to sixty-five from 2010 to 2020, though it failed to warn women. Many were shocked when the change arrived, and they had to work five years longer than they expected or retire without a pension. There was no evident public protest at the time, including from women's organizations, who continued, like the rest of society, to marginalize older women.[37]

Income inequality

Cuts to benefits, including pensions, contributed to the continuing increase in income inequality, though it rose more slowly than in the 1980s.[38] Income inequality was a reality in most OECD countries, but from the late 1970s was greatest in the United Kingdom; by 2000 it was greater only in the United States, Portugal and Mexico.[39] By 2000/2001 in the UK *c.* 10.4 million individuals received below 60 per cent of median income, mostly adults of working age, many in low-paid work.[40] Single parent families were most likely to suffer poverty and 40 per cent of pensioners. Top incomes continued to soar. Businessmen were increasingly joined by sports stars. The rewards of successful male (only) footballers, tennis-players, golfers and so on rose to previously unimaginable heights as sports became increasingly commercialized. Household debt continued to grow. From 1960 to 1980 individuals declared insolvent in England and Wales averaged under 4,600 pa; by 1990 almost 14,000, in 2000, 30,000.[41]

Race

Some ethnic minority communities suffered more deprivation than others. Immigrants became increasingly diverse as the UK attracted political refugees and economic migrants from more countries, fewer from former colonies. By the 1990s the small Chinese and African-Asian populations had on average similar incomes and employment opportunities to the white population and higher educational attainment. At the other extreme, more than four in five Pakistani and Bangladeshi households had incomes below half the median, four times as many as white households.[42] By 1999 unemployment among all minority ethnic groups was double that of white people, reinforcing disadvantages in health, education and housing.[43]

Racism continued to be pervasive. This became especially evident in 1993 when a Black teenager, aspiring architect Stephen Lawrence, standing harmlessly at a bus-stop in South London, was murdered in a clearly racist attack. The failure of the police to conduct serious investigations caused outrage among the Black Caribbean community and more widely and was much covered in the media. Five young white men were arrested and acquitted, though two were re-tried and convicted in 2012. Public anger and persistent campaigning by Stephen Lawrence's parents and their supporters led the next Labour government to appoint an investigation into the failure of the police to conduct an effective investigation, which reported in 1999.[44]

Organization within and across minority groups grew. The 1990 Trust grew out of Black community and lobby groups formed in the 1970s and 1980s, a research and networking organization coordinating campaigns on local and national issues and for individuals experiencing discrimination or other forms of mistreatment. In 1996 it established Operation Black Vote, urging minority communities to campaign, register and vote on equality issues.[45] In the 1980s the government refused to grant Muslim schools voluntary-aided status equally with Jewish, Catholic, Methodist and Anglican schools, despite the growth of the Muslim population in the UK (600,000 in 1980, 1 million in 1990, 1.2 million in 1995[46]). This further stimulated minority organization. The Hindu Council was formed in 1994, the Muslim Council of Britain in 1997, when Britain's first Muslim MP was elected, Mohammed Sarwar, Labour, in Glasgow, Govan.[47] They provided services and support for their communities, aiming to increase understanding of their faiths and improve the living and working conditions of their followers.

Gypsies and Travellers remained the most excluded minority group. The Criminal Justice and Public Order Act, 1994, removed local authorities' duty to provide permanent caravan sites, introduced under Labour, cancelling their grant aid. This was designed to encourage (or force) Gypsies and Travellers to move into permanent housing, while introducing tougher measures to remove them from unauthorized sites. The moves were widely criticized, described as 'ethnic cleansing'. Save the Children was concerned about the impact of insecurity and evictions on children's health and welfare and there was strong opposition in parliament, mainly from Labour. But travelling or stopping in groups of more than six vehicles became a criminal offence, and harassment and eviction of Gypsies and Travellers increased. About 90 per cent of planning applications for sites, even on land they owned, were rejected. Anger and supportive organizations increased, but the tentative moves towards greater equality for Gypsies and Travellers since the 1960s went into reverse in the 1990s.[48]

Gender

Women's employment and educational opportunities continued gradually to improve, partly due to EU influence, but gender equality remained distant. In 1991, 67.6 per cent of working-age women were employed, 70.3 per cent in 2001, many still in low-paid, often part-time, work.[49] In 2000 the weekly pay of women in full-time work averaged only 76 per cent of that of men. The gap for part-time workers was even greater. It was narrowest for women working full-time in the professions, who earned 93 per cent of male salaries in 2000. It was widest for both full- and part-time manual workers.[50] The Thatcher and Major governments resisted the Equal Opportunity Commission's calls for stronger legislation on equal pay and sex discrimination, arguing that regulation hampered the free market.

The growing numbers of single mothers had an especially hard time in the labour market as elsewhere. The 1992 Conservative manifesto promised to 'encourage the development of childcare arrangements in the voluntary and independent sectors', and some funding was provided for pre-school and after-school care, enabling some mothers to work. From 1990 employers could offset against tax the cost of workplace nurseries, which increased, while local authority nursery places declined following funding cuts.[51] In 1993 Major declared he wanted 'over time to move to universal nursery education' but John Patten, education secretary, opposed this and nothing happened. An inadequate childcare allowance of up to £28 per week was introduced, to help single parents and other low-income mothers work full-time.[52] The EU recommended accessible childcare services and flexible leave arrangements to help parents, including fathers, fulfil their family and work obligations, and extending employment rights to part-time workers, who were overwhelmingly female. In 1994, responding reluctantly and incompletely to an EU directive, the government ruled that fourteen weeks' maternity leave should be available immediately a woman took a job, rather than after two years as instituted in 1975, and extended to part-timers. After two years in the same employment, it was extended to twenty-eight weeks, improving maternity rights to the standard long established elsewhere in Europe. But Michael Portillo, employment secretary, refused to introduce paternity leave, which was also Europe-wide. Britain still had the worst provision for working parents in the EU and trailed in most areas of gender equality.

Election 1997

Following the 1992 election, Labour leader Neil Kinnock resigned and was replaced by Scotsman John Smith. Smith was somewhat more progressive than Kinnock on issues of welfare and equality and keen to unify the party, but two years later he died suddenly of a heart attack, aged fifty-four. Tony Blair won a clear majority in the leadership election. Aged forty-one, a lawyer from an independent school and Oxford, he emphasized his youth and distance from traditional 'Old Labour'. He spoke respectfully of Thatcher, but called for a 'modern', post-Thatcher agenda, appealing to the left and centre against neoliberalism. He appointed working-class former trade unionist John Prescott as deputy-leader to help unite the party. He presented his own middle-class background as an asset, shifting Labour from identification with a dwindling working class to promoting the aspirations of 'middle England', as he called the now dominant middle class. At his first party conference as leader in October 1994, he launched the concept of

'New Labour', calling successfully for rewriting Clause 4 of the party's 1918 constitution, eliminating its commitment to nationalization. Party membership grew.[53]

Major failed to unite the Conservatives but held on for the full five years of the parliament. By 1997 unemployment remained close to 2 million, the economy was not flourishing, middle-class people were suffering particularly from rising prices, public sector workers from pay restraint and cuts, and the party from successive scandals. The election was fixed for 1 May 1997. Blair's campaign stressed the contrast between 'New' and 'Old' Labour. The shadow chancellor, Gordon Brown, underlined this by abandoning 'tax and spend', promising for the first two years in office to adhere to Clarke's stringent public spending guidelines and not to increase direct taxation.

Labour won 419 seats (44.5 per cent of voters) in the biggest electoral swing against the Conservatives since 1945, though the turnout, 71.5 per cent, was the lowest since 1935, especially low in some of Labour's traditional heartlands where unemployment was high and the appeal to 'Middle England' made many working-class voters feel their problems were ignored. The Conservatives won only 165 seats, their worst performance since 1906, with none in Scotland or Wales. Remarkably, 120 women MPs were elected (of 659). 102 were Labour, 13 Conservatives with 3 Liberal Democrats, 2 for the Scottish National Party. This followed Labour's introduction of All-Women-Shortlists (AWS) in a proportion of seats, proposed by John Smith, who supported gender equality.

Labour had an exceptional majority following the weak Major administration and exceptional opportunities to achieve change, which was widely supported. It was much needed. Major resigned as Conservative leader and was replaced by 36-year-old William Hague, the youngest party leader since Pitt the Younger.

CHAPTER 13
NEW LABOUR

Blair was conscious of the extent of change since 1979, determined to avoid Labour's conflicts of the 1980s and to work with many, not all, of Thatcher's policies. He believed they were popular with voters, especially in 'middle England', that he wished to attract, and that reversing all the profound changes would be difficult. He would accept some privatization and build good relations with business. He recognized that the decline of manufacturing, trade unionism and the public sector had eroded Labour's traditional voting base and it must appeal to a changed culture where old class boundaries were blurred and questioned. He also challenged certain legacies of Thatcher: inequality between richest and poorest had grown unacceptably and must be reduced, especially the extent of poverty and insecurity, and services, particularly the NHS and education, which mattered to most voters, had declined too far. However, like Thatcher but to a lesser degree, he believed inequality was unavoidable and, up to a point, desirable because it encouraged aspiration to better lives. This was the 'New' Labour vision that drove him.

Blair was, at forty-four, the youngest-ever UK premier until matched by Conservative David Cameron in 2010, from more middle-class origins than the three recent Conservative leaders and a committed Anglican, later Roman Catholic like his wife Cherie, a successful lawyer. As MP for Sedgefield, County Durham, from 1983, he encountered working-class people, many of them not working following the decline of the major local industry, mining. Polls recorded Blair as the most popular premier since 1945 and expectations of his government were high, indicating the extent of disillusion with the Conservatives. Blair was as determined as Thatcher to subvert established institutions, but different institutions in different ways. He sought to centralize and control policymaking, though he met resistance particularly from Gordon Brown, chancellor of the Exchequer, previously his rival for party leadership, with whom relations were tense. Cabinet meetings were short and relatively infrequent.[1] Blair preferred 'sofa government', informal discussion with chosen advisers. Too often policies were impatiently changed before they had time to work through, with no consistent vision behind the restless innovation.[2] Media presentation became indispensable. Blair was acutely responsive to the new 24-hour news cycle and proliferating media outlets as the internet expanded and newspaper circulation declined. He held regular, televised press conferences. 'Spin' (news management) became a word indissociable from Labour's political presentation, controlled by the Director of Communications and Strategy, former *Mirror* journalist, Alastair Campbell.

Blair was increasingly criticized for isolation from public opinion (except as represented in the media), including in the Labour Party, from which he was distant and also sought to control. Individual party membership rose from 265,000 in 1994 to 405,000 in 1997, then sank to 248,294 in 2002, 198,026 in 2005, the lowest since 1918, as disillusion set in intensified by opposition to the unpopular, unsuccessful war in Iraq from 2003. Membership of the other main parties also declined. Popular discontent with formal politics seemed confirmed by falling election turnouts. In 1997 it was the lowest since 1935. The next election, in 2001, produced the lowest, 59.4 per cent, since 58.9 per cent in the unusual circumstances of 1918. Labour won more middle-class and Southern English votes, as it hoped, but there were signs that working-class voters felt neglected and alienated. New Labour made little obvious effort to attract them. Turnouts were especially low in some traditionally working-class Labour constituencies, especially in North-West England and Glasgow. The divided Conservatives offered them no alternative.[3]

Economic policy: The first two years

Ultimately Labour received less credit than it deserved for real improvements to the economy and public services, bringing higher employment, declining poverty, low inflation, and sustained GDP growth. It was surprisingly reticent in public about these successes, perhaps fearing accusations of overspending. Brown at the Treasury was highly influential in domestic policy and led on social policy, in which Blair had less interest. He was fortunate to inherit an economy in better shape than in 1990 or 1993, though far from ideal. Unemployment fell to what now seemed a moderate 1.5 million in mid-1997. Brown was determined to achieve stability and practice what he called financial 'prudence'. One of his first, unexpected, moves was transferring control of interest rates to the Bank of England, which established an independent monetary committee, of bank officials and external members, to set interest rates, aiming to control inflation to a target of 2.5 per cent; it fell to 1.5 per cent in 1999. This was designed to stop the previous government manipulation of interest rates for short-term political motives and was popular in the city. Brown established the Financial Services Authority (FSA) for closer control of financial institutions excessively deregulated by the Conservatives.

Prudent Brown paid off the inherited deficit by 1998 and, more gradually, much of the national debt, helped by increasing tax revenues and £22bn from the sale of digital channels in 2000.[4] He pledged to dispel Labour's 'tax and spend' image by accepting the spending and income tax limits set by Kenneth Clarke for 1997–9. But no limits were set for indirect taxes which increased, including fuel taxes which protected the environment by discouraging motoring as well as raising revenue, though raising them aroused hostile demonstrations. Environmental protection was a Labour commitment as it became more salient internationally and a subject of growing campaigns.

Tax-rises funded some redistribution, though the word was largely banned by New Labour lest it disturb 'Middle England'. It included Brown's introduction in 1999 of the Working Families Tax Credit (WFTC), a means-tested supplement to low pay paid through the tax system, designed to eliminate the serious problem of poverty in families where one or more full-time workers received inadequate pay in the deregulated labour market. It helped many families but had the usual problem of means-tested payments that about 500,000 eligible workers did not apply by 2000/2001; and it effectively subsidized low-paying employers.

Inflation remained low and unemployment fell below one million in 2001. Reducing it was another of Brown's commitments, and a manifesto pledge, especially to reduce youth unemployment. 'Work is the best welfare' was another New Labour mantra- as Labour had argued from its foundation, though its current leaders seemed unaware of this.[5] It was also a Conservative belief, but this government provided positive assistance to find work, rather than 'incentivizing' by punitive withdrawal of benefits. Brown imposed a 'windfall tax' on the privatized utilities, including water and energy, which were accused of exploiting their monopoly positions to impose excessive prices. It yielded £5bn which was dedicated to advice and training, a 'New Deal', for unemployed 18- to 25-year-olds. By 2005, 500,000 long-term unemployed young people had work. New Deal 50+ was introduced in 2000 to help over-50s find work; 120,000 succeeded by 2004. Unemployed single mothers were also assisted to find work or training, with free childcare, with positive results. Official unemployment figures had never fallen below 5 per cent of the workforce in eighteen years of Conservative rule; by 2001 they were 2.5 per cent.[6]

Blair was a strong supporter of the EU and largely adopted its Social Chapter, which Major had rejected. Hence Labour introduced the first universal minimum wage in UK history in 1999 (following New Zealand in 1894, the United States in 1938, then most other developed countries). It was set at a cautiously low level: £3.60 per hour for workers aged 22+, £3 for those aged 18–22. A total of 1.9 million workers were expected to benefit. An independent Low Pay Commission was appointed, of academics and trade union and employer representatives, to recommend annual upgrading. Business leaders forecast catastrophic effects, which proved unfounded.

Other items of the Social Chapter delivered an exceptional framework of new workers' rights, particularly helping women. Blair sought to persuade business that a more secure workforce would benefit production. The UK remained opted out of the EU's preferred maximum 48-hour working week, but introduced equal rights for part-time with full-time workers including to holiday and sickness pay, especially benefitting women; universal paid maternity leave was extended from 14 to 26 weeks; unpaid paternity leave, of only two weeks, was provided after one year's service; women gained the right to return to their previous job, or a suitable equivalent, after maternity leave and could not be dismissed for any reason connected with pregnancy and maternity, as was all too common; parents could request flexible working hours to match their childcare responsibilities, though employers could refuse; all workers gained the right to 'reasonable' unpaid leave for deaths, accidents or serious illness among close family or friends, increased protection against, and compensation for, unfair dismissal, and four weeks annual paid leave, excluding public holidays; night-working was restricted to eight hours; minimum rest periods were established; discrimination at work on grounds of gender, age, race, disability, sexual orientation, union membership or part-time working was prohibited; processes for trade union recognition were established and strengthened, giving all workers the right to representation by a union when supported by most of the workforce.[7] These were significant improvements to working and living conditions especially for the lower-paid.

Also in the first two years, Labour put £800m into renovating some of the poorest, most neglected remaining council estates, raised Child Benefit by over 20 per cent and increased international aid and development funds by 25 per cent. They increased spending on art galleries and museums also by 25 per cent. This had been severely cut by Thatcher, who introduced the first entry charges. Labour abolished them. Visitors greatly increased. Blair believed strongly in social responsibility, that there was such a thing as society and an obligation on all its members to contribute to social stability, cohesion, well-being. He rejected the social injustices of the previous period while embracing the market, as did Brown, without the rhetoric.

Devolution

In 1997 Wales and Scotland were allowed to hold devolution referenda. Both were successful and devolved governments were elected in 1999 allowing Scotland substantial, Wales rather less, control over social policy. Unlike Westminster, both were elected by forms of proportional representation (PR), partly due to pressure from women who internationally gained more seats under PR. In the first devolved elections in 1999, 41 per cent of representatives elected to the first Welsh Assembly were female, 37.2 per cent in Scotland, compared with 18.2 per cent in Westminster. The second election in 2002 returned 51.7 per cent female representatives in Wales, the first elected assembly in the world to achieve gender equality.[8]

Local government

Labour promised to restore elected government to Greater London if approved by a London referendum. In May 1998 this succeeded. The first election, in May 2000, returned Ken Livingstone, now a Labour MP, to his former role as Mayor of London, also by the Single Transferable Vote PR system. He was an Independent since he was opposed by Blair and Brown as excessively Old Labour. He comprehensively defeated their candidate, a reluctant Frank Dobson, Secretary of State for Health. Livingstone proved moderate – his limited powers left him little choice – and at the next election, in 2004, Blair, also with little choice given Livingstone's popularity, let him stand for Labour. He did his best, within the limitations, to improve social conditions in London. He had most control over roads and transport and introduced Britain's first Congestion Charge, limiting traffic and pollution in central London by charging for entry during working hours. He improved bus services and held transport fares steady and relatively low, but he could not prevent Brown insisting upon a complex and ultimately costly

Public Finance Initiative (PFI) arrangement for much-needed improvements to the underground. PFI had been introduced by Major in 1993 but relatively little used. It enabled public institutions to contract out construction work to private firms, since Treasury concern about public spending prevented much necessary construction. It was extensively used, and much criticized, under Brown's Chancellorship, proving highly profitable to private business at high long-term public cost.

Labour also promised elected mayors in other cities and revival of local authority powers lost since the 1980s. The Local Government Act, 2000, recommended larger councils to elect executive mayors and cabinets, paid, for the first time, for their increased responsibilities; fewer than twenty councils chose elected mayors (also elected by PR). Central control persisted, sometimes in new forms. Labour aimed to improve the quality and effectiveness of services, which Blair believed could be achieved by targets and performance indicators. From 2000, each authority had to produce a performance plan and a ceiling was placed on the level of council tax they could raise. They did not receive significantly greater government funding.

Many authorities, including those Labour controlled, disliked the targets and indicators and wanted more devolution. But increasingly education funding was centrally determined. More 'social' housing was transferred to housing associations and local authorities were granted no housebuilding funds despite the shortage of low-cost homes. Private builders were required to provide a proportion of 'affordable' housing as a condition of receiving planning permission, but the definition of 'affordable' was uncertain and it was not enforced. The supply of social housing slipped further behind demand and need. Total housebuilding fell to one of its lowest points since 1947 with just 179,160 units completed in 2000/2001, 25,527 publicly owned. House prices continued to rise. The number of statutorily homeless people in England grew from 44,000 in 1997 to 75,000 in 2002, 12,000 in bed- and- breakfast accommodation. Labour established a Rough Sleeper Unit which provided hostel accommodation and support and numbers gradually fell.[9] Response to housing need was the greatest social policy weakness of the three New Labour governments.

Constitutional reform

More positively, the Human Rights Act, 1998 (HRA), embedded the European Convention on Human Rights in UK law from 2000. This led to legal changes including the Gender Recognition Act, 2004, enabling transgender people to be legally recognized in their new gender. Also, to the establishment of the Equality and Human Rights Commission (EHRC) in 2007 to protect and promote all equalities in England and Wales. It merged the Equal Opportunities Commission, Commission for Racial Equality and Disabilities Rights Commission and took responsibility to protect and promote equalities for gay and transgender people and prevent discrimination due to age. In Northern Ireland a statutory Human Rights Commission with similar responsibilities was established in 1998, when Blair played a major role in ending thirty years of 'Troubles' with the Good Friday Agreement. Scotland used its devolved powers to appoint a similar commission.

From 1997, the changed composition of the Commons reflected the wider, gradual shift towards greater equalities, with more women than ever before and an unprecedented nine Black and Asian MPs, though it was still distant from representing the demographic structure of the population. Blair's first Cabinet included five women (among twenty-three), more than ever before. But before the election, too late to influence most candidate selections, disappointed men made a successful court challenge to AWS under sex discrimination legislation. The leadership did not challenge it – Blair was not strongly committed to AWS – and shifted to 50/50 male/female shortlists. Labour had six fewer female MPs in 2001 (95, 23 per cent of the parliamentary party), while Conservative women increased to fourteen, the Liberal Democrats to five. The Sexual Discrimination (Election Candidates) Act, 2002, freed all parties to take positive action to increase female representation, enabling Labour to revive AWS, with little obvious response from other parties. The 2005 election returned 128 women (98 Labour, 17 Conservative, 10 Liberal Democrats, UUP and Sinn Fein one each), a record 20 per cent of MPs.

Under John Smith Labour had promised a Ministry for Women to conduct gender audits of legislation, responding to the commitment to 'gender mainstreaming' promoted by the EU since the 1980s. Gender equality was to be integrated within all policies and programmes. Blair was unenthusiastic, and no ministry emerged. A junior minister, Joan Ruddock, was appointed Under-Secretary for Women in the Department of Social Security. A Women's Unit was established in the Cabinet Office, to pursue gender mainstreaming. It conducted useful research, but its remit was ill-defined and its influence limited. Equality Units were instituted by the devolved Scottish and Welsh governments.[10]

Employment policies

Blair and Brown believed that the state could best stimulate economic growth and social improvement by constructive co-operation with business and investment in education and training to improve skills. In April 1997 Brown declared: 'It is business not government that creates lasting prosperity. . . . The job of government is not to tell people how to run their businesses but to do what it can to create the conditions in which business can thrive and opportunities for all can flourish.'

Blair pledged to re-establish trade union rights, within limits, stating in 1997 that he would not wholly repeal Thatcher's anti-union laws: 'there will be no return to flying pickets, secondary action, strikes with no ballots or the trade union laws of the 1970s.' Union membership declined still further to 16 per cent of the workforce by 2006, overwhelmingly in the public sector, where they were constant irritants to Blair and Brown, opposing their adoption of Thatcher-style managerialism and targets. Blair regarded unions as 'Old Labour' relics and refused to meet the TUC in his first six months in office. John Monks, the TUC general secretary, described their relationship as like 'embarrassing elderly relatives at a family reunion.'[11]

But Blair and Brown shared 'Old' Labour's commitment to full employment and Brown's 'New Deal' increased employment at all ages, assisted by economic revival.[12] It was harder to improve skills and business did little to help. In 2006 it was estimated that one-third of working-age adults were low-skilled, despite Labour funding workplace training schemes and other initiatives. Productivity still trailed behind Germany, France and the United States. In 2005, 20 per cent of young people aged 16–24, almost 1 million, were not in education, employment or training – NEETS, as they became known. The skilled working-class continued to shrink and the economy suffered from sluggish research and development in the private sector.[13] This led the government to open the labour market to well-educated, trained immigrants from poorer countries of central and Eastern Europe, welcoming free movement within the EU, while immigration continued from elsewhere.

Social policy

Labour's 1997 campaign made little direct reference to social welfare issues, though it did promise to reduce educational disadvantage, introduce the minimum wage and get 250,000 under-25s off benefits and into work, as it did. After the election, Blair gave his first major speech outside parliament on a Peckham (S. London) housing estate, promising there would be 'no forgotten people and no no-hope areas'.

Child poverty

In March 1999, in a lecture commemorating William Beveridge at Toynbee Hall, (where the Child Poverty Action Group formed in 1965[14]) Blair unexpectedly announced: 'Our historic aim [is] that ours is the first generation to end child poverty forever . . . it is a twenty-year mission, but I believe it can be done.'[15] He promised to end child poverty by 2020. There was no sign of a strategy to fulfil the pledge, though Brown – as surprised as anyone by the announcement- worked on it. In September 1999 the Department of Social Security issued the first of a series of annual audits of poverty and exclusion, *Opportunity for All*, much influenced by Brown. It promised an 'integrated and radical policy response' to childhood deprivation, worklessness, health inequalities, crime, poor areas, poor housing, pensioner poverty, ill-health and isolation and discrimination on grounds of age, ethnicity, gender or disability. A list of policies included a comprehensive 'Sure Start' programme for children under four in deprived areas; substantial increases to health and education funding, especially favouring poorer areas; targets for improved employment, education, health and housing and reduced crime in the most disadvantaged areas, with another ambitious aim that 'within 10-20 years, no one should be seriously disadvantaged by where they live'. It also announced Educational Maintenance Allowances (EMAs) to enable young people from low-income families to stay in education to eighteen; improved benefits for disabled adults and children; action to reduce inequalities in income

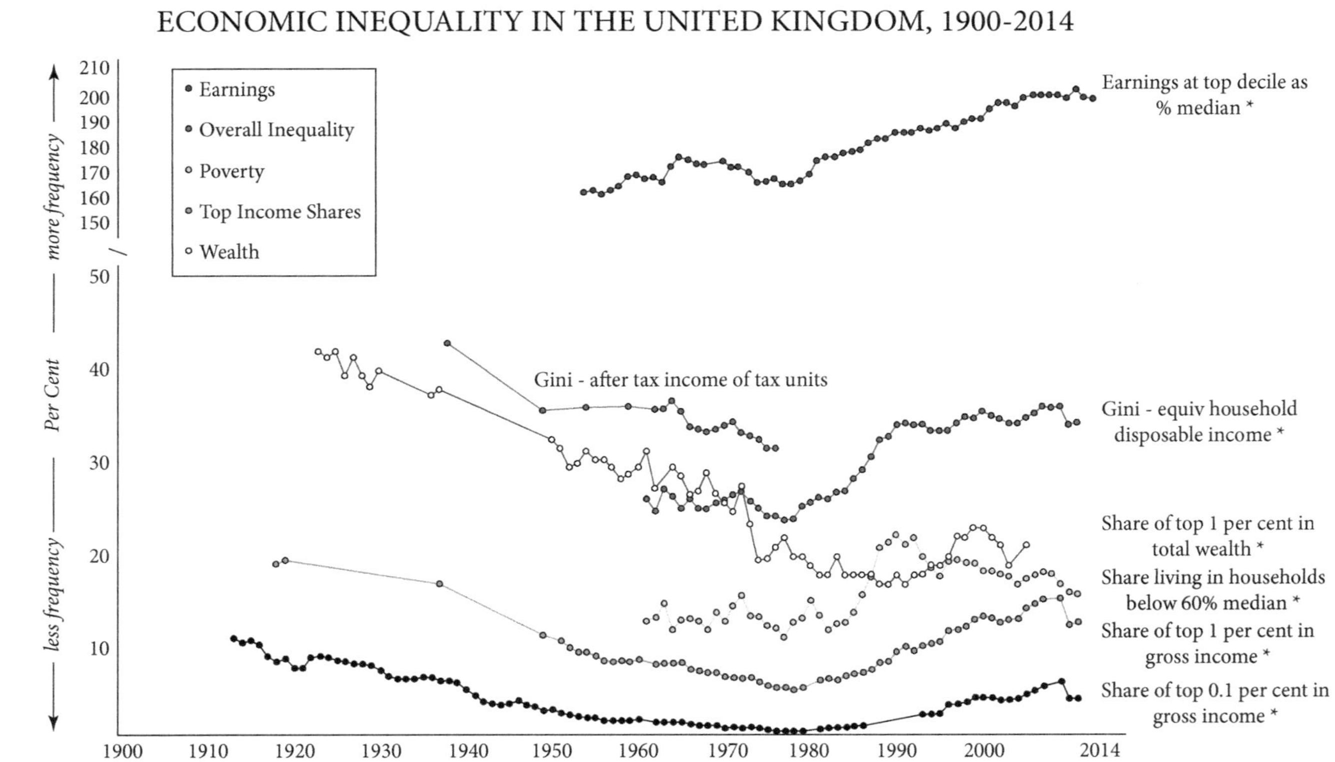

Figure 1 Relative child poverty rates, 1961–2014 (GB) Note: Poverty line is 60 per cent of median income. Years up to and including 1992 are calendar years; thereafter years refer to financial years. Incomes are measured before housing costs have been deducted and equivalized using the modified OECD equivalence scale. Authors' calculations based on Family Expenditure Survey and Family Resources Survey, various years. *Source*: Jonathan Cribb, Robert Joyce, David Phillip, *Living standards, poverty and inequality in the UK: 2012* (IFS, 2012), p. 84. Updated from recent IFS data: www.ifs.org.uk/tools_and _resources/incomes_in_uk

between ethnic groups, including grants to local authorities to improve and equalize educational attainment. All were implemented.

By 2010 about 1.1 million children had been removed from poverty, not meeting Blair's target of halving child poverty since 2000, but a substantial improvement. This was partly due to the strong underlying economy, which owed much to Brown's management. The WFTC, the minimum wage, increased Child Benefit and the increased length and generosity of maternity pay raised family incomes, while the employment New Deals reduced the number of workless families. Children under sixteen in workless households fell from 2.4 million in 1996 to 1.7 million in 2006. Forty-five per cent of single parents were in work in 1997, 57 per cent in 2008.[16] (See Figure 1.)

Support for the youngest children improved dramatically. By 2002, 93 per cent of three- and four-year-olds from social classes IV and V received nursery education compared with 17 per cent in 1997. In 500 of the most disadvantaged districts Sure Start centres provided parenting support, childcare, play and learning opportunities, healthcare and advice and support for children with 'special needs', as the various forms of childhood disability were now known. Outcomes were positive and Sure Start was popular with parents. In 2006 it came under local authority control and centres spread through England and Wales, beyond deprived areas. There were 1,000 by 2006.[17] Similar centres were adopted in Scotland and Northern Ireland.

Pensioner support

Annual winter fuel payments of £100 to everyone over sixty were introduced in 1997, raised in 2008 to £250, £400 from age eighty, to protect their health. In 1999 means-tested income support for poorer pensioners was rebranded as Minimum Income Guarantee (MIG), with an above-inflation rise and future increases linked to the more generous measure of earnings rather than prices. The universal state pension increased by less, remaining linked to prices and still inadequate for subsistence without a supplement. Anti-poverty groups complained that Labour, like the Conservatives, focused on raising means-tested rather than universal benefits, though Labour's increases were greater. In 2003 MIG was renamed Pension Credit (PC). The maximum means-tested PC plus pension rose to the highest level ever, though still only just above the official poverty line. In 2008 Brown introduced free travel on public transport buses for over-60s throughout England. This was already available in Scotland, Wales and some English towns, including Greater London where it covered all forms of public transport and Livingstone introduced it also for 11- to 15-year-olds on buses. Free TV licences were provided from age 75 and free eye tests and increased income tax allowances for all pensioners. Universal free travel and winter fuel allowances were criticized for benefitting rich as well as poor but means-testing was costly and inefficient while universal benefits were sure to reach the poorest. As with all means-tested benefits, up to 30 per cent of eligible pensioners, often the neediest and most isolated, failed to claim PC, unaware they were eligible, deterred by the complexity of the process or fear of stigma.[18]

Cash benefits

In 2003, WFTC was extended to low-wage households without children and renamed Working Tax Credit (WTC), while a new Child Tax Credit (CTC) amalgamated means-tested IS and tax credits for children, particularly benefitting low-income families and significantly reducing child poverty. Take-up increased but remained incomplete. The Welfare Reform Act, 2007, provided greater support for Incapacity Benefit (IB) claimants who joined in work-related activity and training, but it rose only in line with retail prices, as did Jobseekers Allowance and IS, and they declined in real value.[19] Other benefits for disabled people increased, but so did means- and fitness-testing and sanctions for those failing the tests; disabled campaigners criticized poor information, severe conditionality and difficulty in accessing benefits. Unemployed and disabled people of working age (other than single mothers) – both unpopular, polls suggested, with many voters and with the tabloids, who accused them of idleness and fraud against all evidence – were less favourably treated than pensioners, children and workers.

Education

While means-testing or restricting some cash benefits, Labour substantially increased spending on education and health services, used by most families in all classes. Another Blair rallying cry on entering office was 'Education, Education, Education!'. The share of education funding for deprived areas grew from 1999. Initiatives included Excellence in Cities, funding learning mentors and other provision for talented pupils in the most deprived third of LEAs, and grants to schools with high concentrations of ethnic minority students, both successfully improving outcomes, especially in London. School performance targets were adjusted to take account of socio-economic intake. By 2006 the performance at GCSE of Black, Pakistani and Bangladeshi compared with white pupils improved as did the relative performance of children receiving free school meals in every ethnic group, though the gap with more privileged pupils remained substantial especially at older ages.[20]

A Standards and Effectiveness Unit was established in what became the Department of Education and Employment, to stress the government's determination to raise workplace skill levels. Ambitious targets were set for literacy and numeracy at age eleven, measured by national tests, supported by David Blunkett, secretary of state for education, 1997–2001, who was blind, the first minister ever with such a disability. Targets were introduced for the percentage of pupils per secondary school gaining five or more GCSEs, as a measure of success, and league tables to advertise these differences. The Scottish and Welsh governments rejected league tables for all public services.

Labour retained the city technology colleges and 'specialist' secondary schools introduced by the Conservatives, partially funded by private sponsorship in the (dubious) belief that this raised standards. A special adviser to Blair, former journalist Andrew Adonis, elevated to the House of Lords and appointed minister for education, 2005–8, branded them 'Academies', effectively state-funded independent schools, free from local authority control, with 10 per cent capital funding from private sponsors who controlled boards of governors and owned the land and buildings. Local authorities lost more education powers. The schools employed their own staff and set their own admission requirements. Blair was enthusiastic about them and admired independent schools, like the one he had attended, encouraging their co-operation with state schools. From 2000, schools with fewer than 15 per cent of pupils gaining five A*–C grades at GCSE in three successive years were considered for closure or conversion to Academies. There were fifteen Academies in 1997, forty-six in 2006/7.

To promote equality, many disabled children were moved from special to mainstream schools, where mentors, learning support units and pupil referral units were established to improve performance among all disadvantaged children, reduce truancy and keep pupils in school to age eighteen.[21] In 2003, following the brutal neglect and murder of eight-year-old Victoria Climbie by the aunt to whose care she had been entrusted by her parents in Africa, the government established the 'Every Child Matters' strategy, ideally providing integrated support for everyone from birth to age nineteen. The Children's Act, 2004, required schools, hospitals, local social services, police and voluntary groups to cooperate for this purpose. To help disadvantaged children, tests were introduced for five-year-olds, to identify needs, and for all ages extended schooling from 8 am to 6 pm, after-school and school holiday clubs, help with study and referral to specialist services including speech therapy were established. Schools were encouraged to open centres combining early years' care, education and healthcare. Healthy Eating guidelines were devised for school meals by popular TV chef Jamie Oliver. The changed expectation of schools, from preparation for employment to child and family welfare, was expressed in another name-change for the responsible department in 2007 to Children, Schools and Families.

A problem was shortage of teachers, especially as class sizes fell. Successful students from elite universities rarely entered school-teaching as they commonly had until the 1950s, as opportunities widened. Pay rises had little effect. Unqualified teaching assistants were recruited to support teachers.[22] It was harder to recruit heads, despite substantial pay rises, as the pressure of targets, league tables and other demands grew. Changes to the curriculum had uneven effects. At secondary level, compulsory citizenship, social, health and careers education were introduced. Some established subjects, including foreign languages, became optional from age fourteen and take-up fell. The focus on exams and testing arguably narrowed education. Vocational diplomas were introduced alongside A-levels, to improve work skills, but were underfunded and it was hard to attract suitable staff. £19bn more was spent on schools, 1999–2002, a further 60 per cent by 2005–6, much of it on 'initiatives' and consultants, with mixed results.[23] Many school buildings needed expansion and renovation and spending rose from £1.26bn in 1997–8 to £3.02bn in 2005–6. To restrain it, Labour adopted PFI for schools as for NHS and transport developments at significant long-term cost, generally twice that of direct public funding, causing the services concerned major future financial problems.

Blair's main contribution to higher education was the introduction of tuition fees in 1998. He recalled this in his resignation speech as 'deeply controversial and hellish hard to do' but he believed he had been 'moving with the grain of change around the world', though fees were not levied elsewhere in the EU.[24] In 1997/1998, 5,853,000 students were in full-time higher education in UK, compared with 2,165,000 in 1981–2, as it moved belatedly from an elite to a mass system.[25] The Major government appointed an enquiry into university funding, chaired by former civil servant Lord Dearing, which reported in 1997, after the election, that the system was overstretched but maintaining standards. It proposed that students should pay 25 per cent of their tuition costs, but maintenance grants should continue. But Blunkett, under Treasury pressure, announced their abolition and the introduction of fees of £1,000 p.a., with means-tested loans for lower-income students to pacify opposition, expressed in the biggest backbench revolt of Blair's first term. Students demonstrated and some occupied university and Department of Education offices. Following costly means-testing, one-third of students did not pay fees. Universities received £40m for hardship funds for students who exhausted their loan entitlement. Blunkett fought hard to prevent fees rising further and the 2001 manifesto promised they would not, but after the election and Blunkett's departure from Education, universities were allowed to charge up to £3,000 p.a. from 2006.[26] More student demonstrations followed. Charles Clarke, education secretary from 2001, modified the policy: payment of fees was deferred until graduates earned £15,000 p.a. and a more generous package of grants and bursaries was introduced. This scraped through the Commons by only five votes, opposed by Liberal Democrats, some Conservatives and many Labour backbenchers.

The government was concerned about unequal social access to universities, especially Oxbridge. The gender balance improved but 50 per cent of places at Oxford and Cambridge went to independent school pupils, female and male. Universities became subject to 'performance indicators' including proportions of entrants from state schools, lower socio-economic groups and districts with low HE participation. Those meeting the targets received 5 per cent additional funding, laggards were named and shamed. Critics feared that fees and loans deterred low-income candidates. Their numbers did not rise, and mature student numbers fell, often unable to support both themselves and their children through university, especially damaging the Open University. Blair did not help with another public promise, in 1999, that by 2010, 50 per cent of the population would receive higher education by age thirty. The current figure was 43 per cent. There was controversy about whether university education really was best for 50 per cent of people or for the economy, given the shortage of skilled tradespeople. But, overall, universities were in a better state by 2007 than in 1997.

Health and welfare

'There are twenty-four hours to save the NHS' was another Blair rallying cry on entering office. Problems included long waiting times for operations, underfunding and poor outcomes by international standards, including for cancer and heart disease. Targets were introduced for waiting times and a national framework for treating heart disease. Prevention was emphasized, a minister for public health appointed and cutting smoking prioritized.

It was banned in enclosed public spaces in England, including pubs and restaurants, from July 2007, following bans in Scotland in 2006, Wales and Northern Ireland in April 2007, all remarkably calm and successful. The National Institute for Health and Clinical Excellence (NICE) was established in 1999, an independent regulator of NHS standards. The changes were positive, but there were demands for funds to improve services.

During the 2001 election campaign, Blair had difficult exchanges with patients in Birmingham, then took greater interest in health, convinced that NHS performance would improve through competition, internally and from the private sector. Hospitals were transformed into Foundation Trusts, comparable with academy schools, managing their own budgets and services, competing in an 'internal market'. The cost was criticized by the Audit Commission and the Commons Public Accounts Committee.[27] NHS funding grew from £30bn to £90bn, during 1997–2007, raising NHS investment to the EU average, and more went to deprived areas. It was not always well managed but outcomes and patient satisfaction improved, staffing rose by 25 per cent, especially at senior levels, waiting times fell. Hospitals became cleaner and fewer patients suffered hospital-acquired infections. Medical students increased by 50 per cent, nursing students by 30 per cent, GPs by 9 per cent.[28] Buildings improved, but mainly through PFI, bringing long-term costs. Mental health was still relatively neglected and socio-economic inequalities continued. In 2005, 66 per cent of the most deprived areas had over 10 per cent fewer GPs than the average.

Life expectancy continued to rise, unequally due to unequal access to improved living standards and healthcare: in 2010 life expectancy of males born in wealthy Kensington and Chelsea, London, averaged eighty-eight years, in poorer, mixed-race Tottenham, seventy-one.[29] It was lowest in poorer parts of Glasgow: seventy for males, seventy-seven for females. Sixteen per cent of the UK population was aged sixty-five or over, the highest proportion ever.[30] Obesity was a growing problem and cause of ill-health, partly because American-inspired cheap fast food was widely available and attractive to those on low incomes, despite campaigns to improve diet from school onwards. Widespread abuse of alcohol was another concern.

More health advice and services in schools and increased emphasis on sex education probably contributed to a 10 per cent fall in pregnancy among under-18s, during 1998–2003. From 2000, the morning-after (abortion) pill was available from pharmacies without prescription, amid accusations of government-sponsored promiscuity and failed court challenges by anti-abortionists.[31] They tried again to limit the law on abortion, but the government's Sexual Health and HIV Strategy from 2001 prioritized improved abortion services and equalizing and speeding access.[32] Abortion remained illegal in Northern Ireland; around 1,500 women each year travelled to Britain for private abortions.[33]

The ageing society

Many pensioners gained from Labour reforms and pensioner poverty declined but continued. In 1997, 20 per cent of pensioners were poor by the official measure, 14 per cent in 2005–8, while many lived barely above the poverty line. Others were comfortably off, benefitting from high pay while working, good occupational pensions and the unprecedented rise in the value of homes bought before prices boomed. Older women of all ethnicities, on average, still outlived men and were still more likely to be poor than men, especially if they were widowed, divorced, separated, or never married. Older male and female members of minority ethnic groups, including Gypsies and Travellers, were poorer on average than white people. They received lower state pensions if they had not been in insurable employment for at least forty years, were less likely to receive occupational pensions or they were low, due to low earnings and/or fewer working years.

Some commentators, including future Conservative minister David Willetts, constructed from the good fortune of the largely male minority a narrative of generational conflict, with a wealthy 'baby-boomer' generation, born *c.* 1945–1960s, living in luxury while younger people suffered rising housing costs, declining pensions and paying through taxes for the healthcare and pensions of their selfish elders.[34] This overlooked both substantial continuing pensioner poverty and the considerable financial and personal support provided by better-off older to younger people and to society through work and taxation.[35] Inequalities within the older and younger generations were at least as great as between generations, in the UK and other high-income nations.[36] Also, contrary to caricatures of 'baby-boomers' as selfish, dependent burdens, they contributed significantly to society and the economy by voluntary action: in 2001, 27 per cent of over-65s volunteered regularly with NGOs or helped sick and frail family, friends and neighbours, a pattern repeated in annual official surveys until 2010.[37] In 2008, 28 per cent of volunteers with Voluntary Service Overseas (VSO), established in 1958 to encourage young people to volunteer in poorer countries, were aged over fifty compared with about 3 per cent twenty years earlier. Older people offered more useful skills and experience – of medicine, teaching, engineering and much else – than younger volunteers. Also, by 2010 one in three working mothers relied on grandparents, mostly but not exclusively grandmothers, for childcare, some giving up their own employment to help their daughters work as childcare became more costly. Thirty-one per cent of grandparents helped their grandchildren buy a home. Far from selfishly hoarding their assets, 'baby boomers' who could shared with younger people, and continue to do so to the present in all the respects listed above.[38]

A commission chaired by financial expert Adair Turner pointed out in reports in 2004 and 2005 that UK state pensions remained among the least generous in the developed world. It recommended uprating them in line with earnings, raising the pension age to match average life expectancy and requiring workers to join occupational pension schemes or a state-provided alternative, to supplement the state pension.[39] The Pensions Act, 2007, helped by reducing the qualifying period for state pensions to thirty years and introducing credits for long-term disabled people, unpaid carers for children and disabled and older people. It proposed gradually raising the state pension age to sixty-eight from 2024 to 2046 due to longer lives and longer years in good health on average. The timing was distant to stem protest, though the TUC, and an official report in 2010, pointed out that about 20 per cent of workers, generally the poorest, were already forced to retire before state pension age due to ill-health and would suffer from the change.[40]

Increasing numbers of older people already worked to later ages, because they wanted to or needed the income. Some employers regretted the loss to their businesses following over-enthusiastic dismissal of higher-paid, experienced older workers since the 1980s to increase profits, and the government encouraged later retirement to cut the cost of pensions and compensate for the declining number of younger workers and taxpayers due to the low birth rate. This was expected to continue but, unexpectedly, births rose from 2001, continuing into the twenty-first century, probably due to improving living standards, though it took some time to be recognized and for policies to adjust.

Older people increasingly resisted inequalities and discrimination, no longer accepting them as a normal fact of later life. More were educated, confident and active than previous generations and more willing and able to assert themselves – the rebellious '1968ers' were ageing. In 1998, the voluntary Third Age Employment Network was founded to advise on finding work and training and lobby for more.[41] The government responded with an Age Positive campaign, and in 2000 an EU Directive on Equal Treatment in Employment specified age as a dimension of inequality for the first time. The UK implemented it slowly and incompletely. From 2006 workers could request to work past fixed retirement ages, but employers could refuse without explanation. Following protest, Labour abolished fixed retirement ages, implemented in 2011. Employers could then insist on retirement only by workers demonstrably unable to work efficiently.[42] But discrimination at work continued, experienced by women at earlier ages than men, including in high-profile occupations. In 2011 Miriam O'Reilly successfully brought a much-publicized case for age discrimination against the BBC when she was sacked as presenter of a TV show, aged fifty-three, on grounds of age, while her visibly older, male co-presenter continued. She then campaigned on behalf of other victims.

Discrimination in healthcare was also nothing new, but older people and their families were less willing to tolerate it. Women were routinely called for screening for breast cancer only to age seventy, although breast cancer was most common past seventy. There was still insufficient coordination of health and social care for frail older and disabled people. Discrimination in health and social care became illegal under the Equality Act 2010, one of New Labour's last measures; few cases followed. Casual ageism continued in many areas of life. A national survey for Age Concern in 2005 found more people (29 per cent) reporting discrimination on grounds of age than any other cause. Almost 30 per cent of respondents believed it was growing; one-third thought people over seventy 'incompetent and incapable'.[43] From 2007, the EHRC took responsibility for researching and monitoring age discrimination at all ages. Old age was at last recognized as a significant dimension of inequality, though the EHRC was accused of giving it low priority.

Immigration

Immigration was not a major issue in the 1997 or 2001 elections. Polls showed only 3 per cent of voters rated it among their top three concerns. Labour's 1997 manifesto promised 'firm control' but offered no clear vision. The Conservatives had quietly increased work permits for immigrants to meet skill shortages including in the NHS, which still depended heavily upon immigrants at all levels. Labour, also concerned about labour shortage in key jobs, eased the controls further, enabling highly skilled people to enter the UK without job offers. Labour shortages in hospitality, food processing and seasonal agricultural work (all unattractive to British workers because low-paid, but important to the economy) led to an entry scheme for low-wage work. Visa restrictions were eased for international university students, and they were allowed to work while studying. By 2004 the UK had captured 24 per cent of the world English-speaking student market and income from overseas student fees grew from £622m in 1997–8 to £1,275m in 2003–4, valuably raising university incomes.

In the 2004 EU elections the new, anti-EU, United Kingdom Independence Party (UKIP) won 28 per cent of votes and twelve of the UK's seventy-eight seats, on a 34.19 per cent turnout.[44] The EU was enlarged from 2005 to include Central and Eastern European states, granting their citizens the right of free movement within the EU. This increased opposition to the EU in Britain, especially when the government imposed fewer controls on migration than some other countries. UKIP, with its slogan 'Take Back Control of our Country', spread panic about impoverished East Europeans invading Britain, seizing welfare and work, and it attracted working-class voters who felt abandoned by the Labour Party and feared immigrant competition for homes and services. UKIP's main appeal was to the dispossessed, mainly in England. It won few votes and no seats elsewhere in the UK.

A total of 630,000 EU citizens registered in the UK between May 2004 and March 2007. A Worker Registration Scheme recorded their employment and monitored their highly restricted access to benefits. Most were young and migrated to work. Their work and tax payments contributed substantially more to the economy than they took in social services, while often experiencing poor pay, working and living conditions.[45] Local authorities receiving large numbers of immigrants had no funding to expand services to meet the increased demand. Immigrants were unfairly blamed for overstretched education and health services and housing shortages – due to Conservative policies – and hostility grew. The poor treatment and low pay of migrant workers led to a trade union campaign for improvement, partly from realistic fear it would drive down standards for all workers. This was reinforced by the tragedy in Morecambe Bay in 2004, when at least twenty-one illegal immigrant Chinese workers were drowned by an unexpected sea-surge while collecting cockles for sale, for which they were unlawfully employed below the minimum wage. The Gang Masters (Licensing) Act, 2004, attempted, without total success, to regulate employment agencies to prevent exploitation of migrant workers, especially in agriculture and fisheries.

Immigration was swelled by growing numbers of refugees from crisis-hit countries seeking asylum. In 1997 Labour promised to reduce a backlog of 52,000 asylum applications, largely due to Conservative staff cuts. Staff were not replaced, and the asylum queue grew to 125,000 by 1999 as refugees fled wars in Kosovo, Sierra Leone, later Iraq and civil war in Sri Lanka. The Immigration and Asylum Act, 1999, increased penalties on traffickers of illegal incomers, and the number of countries from which a visa was required for entry grew from nineteen in 1991 to 108 in 2005.[46] Persistent media assertions that asylum seekers were undeserving economic migrants masquerading as refugees, attracted by Britain's welfare system, ignored the heart-breaking experiences of many of them, the ungenerous level of British benefits compared with many other West European countries, and evidence that these were not significant motives for undergoing the stress and dangers of travelling for asylum. Immigrants were now forbidden to work to support themselves and their families for at least six months after arrival. The 1999 Act replaced cash payments to often destitute people with vouchers for essential supplies, lest cash be spent on drink and drugs as some alleged. The Black trade union leader Bill Morris led protest against this 'cruel' system, which 'deepened the misery of those in need', leaving them without cash for essentials like public transport.[47] They were then allowed cash payments of 70 per cent of ungenerous IS. A National Asylum Support System was established to manage the dispersal of asylum seekers from crowded South-East England, often to areas where housing was vacant because there were few jobs, receiving minimal support in unfamiliar environments, though faith groups and voluntary agencies did much to help. Still, local authorities received little help to meet their needs.[48]

Polls showed increasing concern about immigration while asylum seekers declined to 49,000 in 2003, 23,500 in 2006, partly due to greater controls, probably more to the end of the Balkans war and peace in Sri Lanka. Some rejected asylum seekers vanished and could not be traced and removed. Some employers readily employed illegal workers willing to work hard for low pay. Fears of terrorism increased tension around immigration, intensified by 9/11 in New York then the London bombings on 7 July 2005 (7/7) when three British Muslim suicide bombers exploded bombs on London transport killing 52 people and injuring over 700. Blair promised that any asylum-seeker involved in terrorism would be denied refugee status, though the bombers were all British citizens. This was enacted in 2006, with still tighter checks on foreign nationals entering and leaving the UK.[49]

The increasingly large and diverse UK population of immigrant origin often experienced the same hostility as refugees and significant social and economic disadvantage.

The government established an enquiry into the death of Stephen Lawrence in 1993 chaired by the former High Court Judge Sir William Macpherson, which reported in

Table 3 Multi-Cultural Britain 2001

Identities Recorded in 2001 Census, % UK Population
Indian 1.8%
Pakistani 1.3%
Bangladeshi 0.5%
Black Caribbean 1%
Black African 0.8%
Chinese 0.4%.
Total minority ethnic population 7.9%.
660,000 people in England and Wales identified as mixed-race, the first time this question was asked in a census.

Source: Census April 2021. Office for National Statistics. http://www.statistics.gov.uk.

1999. It was a damning indictment of what Macpherson described as 'institutional racism' among the police, causing their failure to investigate the killing adequately. Still, no one was convicted of the crime.[50] The Race Relations (Amendment) Act, 2000, placed a new, enforceable duty on public authorities, including the police, to promote equal opportunities and eliminate discrimination. Police forces appointed more Black and minority ethic officers, some of whom complained of their colleagues' racism.

In 1999, unemployment among ethnic minorities averaged twice that of white people, deepening inequalities of income, health, education, housing. Disadvantage was greatest among Bangladeshis and the small Somali population, mostly recent refugees from conflict in their home country. A report in 2000, *The Future of Multi-Ethnic Britain* commissioned by the Runnymede Trust, an NGO devoted to promoting racial harmony founded in 1968, described diversity in educational attainment. Five-year-olds of Black Caribbean origin started school performing at national average standards, but by age ten fell behind, boys performing worse than girls. Indians achieved above the national average throughout their school careers. Pakistani and Bangladeshi children started below average but steadily closed the gap: they were well represented among university entrants but over-represented among school pupils with the poorest qualifications; more girls took A-levels than white females. National attainment levels on entry to university were exceeded by Indian, Pakistani and Black Caribbean women and Indian, Pakistani and Bangladeshi men, despite the disadvantages many of them experienced.[51]

Occasional conflicts erupted, with riots in May 2001 in Oldham, then in Burnley, Lancashire, causing extensive damage, arising mainly from unemployment and police treatment of Black and Asian youths. Professor Ted Cantle, a specialist in community cohesion, was appointed to investigate. He criticized the separation of people of different ethnic backgrounds at home, school, work, worship, leisure and cultural activities, proposing an 'open and honest' debate on how to increase cohesion and equalize opportunities. He recommended that no school should have more than 75 per cent pupils of one ethnicity and proposed training local officials and citizens in the realities of a diverse society and in means of fostering cohesion. The government then required local authorities to consult minority groups about their plans, but change was slow. More clashes followed in Birmingham in 2005 between Black Caribbean and Pakistani residents. London, with the most culturally diverse population, experienced no serious conflicts. Minority ethnic groups were poorly represented on the staff of media organizations, including the BBC and national newspapers, which perhaps influenced their representation in the media. They were similarly under-represented in all high-profile occupations, including parliament and senior business management.[52]

Following 9/11 and 7/7 Muslims faced attacks and heightened discrimination. The HRA for the first time gave all faith groups legal recognition and rights to practice their beliefs, but in 2001 a Home Office report, *Religious Discrimination in England and Wales*, revealed that one-third of Muslims, 25 per cent of Jews and 16 per cent of Christians reported discrimination at work. The Employment (Religion and Belief) Regulations Act, 2003, outlawed discrimination on grounds of religion or belief in the workplace. The Race and Religious Hatred Act, 2006, created the offence of 'inciting religious hatred'.

Despite the tensions, even after July 2005 polls suggested that most people – 68 per cent, 74 per cent of Muslims – supported a society which valued all cultures. A 2005 poll for Stonewall showed 35 per cent of respondents feeling 'less positive' towards Gypsies and Travellers, 34 per cent to refugees/asylum seekers, 18 per cent to ethnic minorities, including Black and Asian people, 17 per cent to gays and lesbians. The polls were not inconsistent but expressed the diversity of views.

The number of minority ethnic MPs crept up: twelve in 2001, all Labour. In 2002 Paul Boateng became the first Black Cabinet minister, as Chief Secretary to the Treasury. He left parliament in 2005 to become UK's High Commissioner in Mandela's South Africa. In 2005 thirteen Labour and two Conservative minority ethnic candidates were elected, in 2010 sixteen Labour (including the first three Muslim women) and eleven Conservatives, as parties strove to increase their diversity and appeal to minority voters.

Gypsies and Travellers gained further advances, as under previous Labour governments, though far from full cultural acceptance and equality. Helped by sympathetic MPs they achieved greater toleration of unauthorized encampments, improved access to healthcare and voting rights. The HRA helped some defend their right to live on land they owned, but others failed. In 2004 Housing and Planning Acts required local authorities to provide for the needs of local Gypsies and Travellers. A *Sunday Express* poll found that 75 per cent of householders believed they should pay lower council tax if Gypsies camped nearby. In 2007 they were included in the remit of the EHRC, but they continued to experience the greatest disadvantages of any social group (Table 3).[53]

Gender and inequality

Poverty among younger women increased with the numbers of single mothers. In 2006 there were 1.8 million single-parent families, overwhelmingly headed by mothers, caring for almost 3 million children. Forty-two per cent of children in poverty were in single-parent households. Only 3 per cent of single mothers were teenagers. Twelve per cent were from ethnic minority groups, with major differences particularly between households of Black Caribbean origin where single parenthood was widespread and Muslims for whom it was unacceptable.[54] Inflation, including of housing costs, contributed to shorter career breaks for most working mothers: by 2000 most mothers of children under five were employed, often part-time, despite the continued inadequacy and cost of childcare, hence the need for grandparents.

Girls in all ethnic and socio-economic groups now outperformed boys at all levels of education. By the mid-1990s more than half the university intake was female, though courses remained heavily gender-segregated: still few women studied sciences and engineering.[55] Women, young and old, married and unmarried, with and without children, still trailed men in employment opportunities and pay. In 2007/8, 11 per cent of directors of the top FTSE 100 companies were female, up from 8.3 per cent in 2003. In the same period female editors of national newspapers rose from 9.1 per cent to 13.6 per cent, senior judges from 6.7 per cent to 9.6 per cent, top civil service management from 22.9

per cent to 26.6 per cent, secondary school heads from 30.1 per cent to 34.10 per cent.[56] The average gender pay gap was 27.5 per cent in 1997, 16.4 per cent in 2010, 19 per cent in 2014. It remained especially stark in finance, where women still reported discrimination.[57] Most women workers were still concentrated in low-paid, low-status work.

There was similar very gradual narrowing of the inequalities experienced by gay and trans people, often following campaigns and appeals to the ECHR.[58] In 1999 National Opinion Polls (NOP) found 66 per cent of respondents supporting equality, though homophobic incidents continued, including in 1999 a nail bomb exploding in a gay pub in Soho, killing three people.[59] Section 28 was repealed in Scotland in 2000, in England and Northern Ireland in 2003, and same-sex couples gained the right to adopt children.[60] In 2003, Employment Equality (Sexual Orientation) Regulations made workplace discrimination illegal.[61] In 2004 the Civil Partnership Act granted registered same-sex couples the same rights and responsibilities as married, heterosexual couples.[62] In 2005 the first gay civil partnerships were registered. The 2006 Equality Act outlawed discrimination on grounds of sexuality in provision of goods and services. In 2008 incitement to homophobic hatred became an offence. Polls indicated high levels of public support for the reforms, from 68 per cent for civil partnership to 93 per cent for protection of gay people from discrimination and harassment at work.[63]

In 2002 the ECHR found Britain in breach of the rights of trans people to marry and receive respect for their private lives. In 2004 the Gender Recognition Act gave them the legal right to live in their acquired gender, when they had done so for at least two years with medical support. In 2005 the first gender recognition certificates were issued, and the first transsexual marriages celebrated, but trans people still experienced discrimination.[64]

Income and wealth inequality

Income inequality continued to increase though more gradually than before. Wealth inequality grew faster: the share of the richest 10 per cent (excluding housing) rose from 57 per cent to 63 per cent in the two decades to 1996, to 71 per cent by 2003. Blair and Brown built close links with finance and the city continued to boom, attracting more foreign businesses and overseas investors. Incomers bought London property for investment or, at most occasional, residence, inflating prices further. Pay and bonuses continued to soar. The *Sunday Times* described 1997–2007 as a 'golden age' for the very rich, estimating that in 1997 the wealth of the UK's wealthiest 1,000 totalled £98.99bn; by 2007, £359,943bn. Blair, who amassed a considerable fortune after resigning as premier, never criticized this burgeoning of wealth. He wrote in the 1997 manifesto, 'I want a country in which people get on, make a success of their lives. I have no time for the politics of envy', and later, 'We favour true equality; equal worth and equal opportunity, not an equality of outcome focused on incomes alone',[65] telling BBC TV *Newsnight* in 2001, 'It's not a burning ambition of mine to make sure David Beckham earns less money.'[66]

Labour fulfilled the pledges in the manifestos for Blair's three elections not to raise income tax, though other taxes rose. Policy focused on improving opportunities at the bottom and reducing the income gap between the bottom and the middle, not on the growing gap between the middle and the top. From 1997 to 2008 poverty fell among pensioners and families with children but rose among childless unemployed and working-age people. Long-term poverty diminished, from 12 per cent of the UK population and *c.* 16.5 per cent of all children in 1998, to 8 per cent and 10 per cent in 2003, though following the 2008 financial crisis it returned to 2000 levels.[67] Tax and social security changes under New Labour were more redistributive than any since 1979 but Britain remained one of the most unequal societies in the developed world.[68] Among the thirty-one richest countries, UK income inequality was now outstripped only by Chile, the United States, Israel and Portugal.[69]

Election 2005

Following the unpopular Iraq War from 2003, Blair's already declining poll ratings plummeted and never recovered. Labour crashed in local and European elections in 2004, winning just 23 per cent of the European vote, 26 per cent of local votes, though in the general election of May 2005 it gained from the weakness of successive Conservative leaders. Blair fought the election on a programme emphasizing 'diversity and choice' for providers and consumers of public services, which market research suggested appealed to Middle England, while appealing to working women and trade unionists by pledging to extend maternity pay and protect the rights of workers transferred from public to private employment. The turnout rose to a still low 61.2 per cent, while Labour slipped to 356 seats and 35.2 per cent of votes compared with the Conservatives' 198 and 32.4 per cent, an overall majority of 65. Turnout in working-class constituencies remained low, and hostility to the Iraq War was widespread. Blair was the first Labour leader to win three successive elections, but celebrations were muted. In 1997, 6 per cent of poll respondents thought Blair out of touch with ordinary people, by 2007, 51 per cent. In 2000, 46 per cent thought him 'trustworthy', in 2006 29 per cent, largely due to his arguments for the war.[70]

Following the election, the Conservatives changed their leader for the fourth time since 1997. Hague was succeeded by Iain Duncan Smith, followed by Michael Howard, who both failed to impress. They were followed by the relatively inexperienced 39-year-old David Cameron, the first Old Etonian leader since Home. He claimed privately to aspire to be 'heir to Blair' and to support many Labour policies, promoting a moderate, 'compassionate Conservative' image, also seeking as wide an appeal as possible.

From Blair to Brown: Financial crisis

In June 2007 Blair resigned, replaced by Brown. Before resigning, Blair rushed through a series of measures designed to secure his 'legacy', including expansion of academy schools and renewal of the Trident nuclear weapons programme purchased from the United States by Thatcher. Both passed the Commons only with Conservative votes after Blair's governments received more defeats in parliament than any other since 1945.

On taking power Brown proclaimed outside No 10, 'Let the work of change begin.' But soon his plans were stalled by attempted terrorist attacks in London, then Glasgow, with one death. Then by major floods and a serious epidemic of foot-and-mouth disease among cattle. Brown handled the crises calmly and effectively. Even the *Mail* conceded that 'Brown could be a great Prime Minister'.[71] In the polls he was well ahead of the Conservatives on managing the economy, and as party leader ahead of Cameron. Then, in September 2007, a serious financial crisis emerged in the United States, where banks had granted too many insecure mortgages. Confidence collapsed and banks stopped lending to one another. The British bank Northern Rock experienced a run on its deposits until the government guaranteed all bank and building society savings ultimately up to £50,000. It then nationalized Northern Rock to prevent its collapse causing chaos.

By autumn 2008, after a succession of US bank collapses, British bank shares plummeted and the government nationalized Bradford and Bingley building society to save it, while the crisis hit other European countries. In October the Treasury, now headed by Alastair Darling, outlined a £500bn international bank rescue plan which Brown persuaded EU leaders, then G7 finance ministers, to accept. In Britain it entailed costly part-nationalization of three big, failing banks: Royal Bank of Scotland (RBS), Halifax and Lloyds. The Bank of England cut interest rates to 3 per cent then to an unprecedented 0.5 per cent in 2009 and announced £75bn of 'quantitative easing', printing money to subsidize the still collapsing banks. Darling temporarily reduced VAT to encourage consumer demand and raised the top rate of income tax from 40 per cent to 45 per cent on incomes over £150,000.

Brown again took the lead, persuading a meeting in London in April 2009 of the G20 richest world economies to pledge £1.1 trillion to the IMF to prevent another collapse, while declaring a crack-down on tax havens and hedge funds, which did not evidently occur. Economic meltdown was averted, but the effects on the British economy were acute because it was exceptionally dependent on financial services for employment and tax revenue and many households were in debt. Banks tightened lending to businesses and consumers. Unemployment rose past 2 million in early 2009 for the first time since 1997, and retailers were hard hit. Woolworths went out of business in the UK, after trading for almost 100 years, shocking the nation. Brown deserved credit for averting the international crisis but got less than he merited. He was blamed by the opposition for the national economic problems, which would have been worse had he and Darling not acted. Popular sympathy declined as executives who had led their banks into chaos received big pay-offs, starkly illustrating income inequality. The banks seemed to have learned nothing and repented not at all.

Brown was clearly exhausted by the financial crisis. He lacked lightness of touch in public. The Tory lead in the polls grew, and he faced pressure to resign. An election was unavoidable in 2010 and came in May. It would have been hard for any government to survive the financial crisis, however deftly handled. The Conservatives relentlessly, often unfairly, attacked Labour's responses, including the bank bail-out, while encouraging voters' concerns about immigration, crime and the EU. Brown entered the campaign under the slogan 'A Future Fair for All', stressing Labour's successful handling of the recovery, pledging to support jobs, not to increase income taxes or VAT, to protect services, work for economic recovery and halve the deficit, though he underplayed many real achievements of Labour's years in power. The campaign focused upon him rather than other Labour figures, probably mistakenly given his poor public image. Labour was short of funds and ran a poor campaign. The Conservatives spent four times as much.

Brown was attacked by the *Sun* as 'Prime Sinister', waster of taxpayers' money, 'deceitful'. Polls, however, suggested that, unpopular as Labour was, voters were unconvinced by the Conservatives and a close result was likely. The turnout rose slightly to 65 per cent. The Conservatives gained 36 per cent of votes and 307 seats, Labour 29 per cent and 258; Labour suffered in areas of highest unemployment, though it remained strong in Scotland, Northern England and inner London and among ethnic minority voters, including Muslims. The Conservatives agreed to form a coalition government with the Liberal Democrats. Brown resigned as Labour leader, and Ed Miliband, previously minister for energy and climate change, was elected to replace him.

Conclusion

New Labour did much to reduce inequalities, though some gains were eroded by the financial crisis. Poverty declined and lower incomes rose, but income inequalities grew, more slowly than in the 1980s, as top incomes grew faster, peaking in 2009–10 following the financial crisis.[72] Education and health services improved; effective measures got more people into work and improved the life chances of children in low-income families, though the social security system became more selective and punitive particularly of the long-term unemployed and some disabled people.[73] Regional inequalities persisted, with highest incomes concentrated in London and South-East England, the lowest in Northern Ireland, North-Eastern England and parts of Scotland and Wales, though Northern Ireland had reason to be grateful to Blair for ending the Troubles.[74] Conditions for some low-income families deteriorated due to Labour's greatest failure: to reverse the decline since the 1980s in the supply of affordable housing. The economy grew but productivity remained poorer than in comparable countries.

Inequalities of gender, race, age, sexuality continued gradually to narrow, assisted by government action, but did not loom large in Labour's public campaigns, for fear of alienating 'Middle England'. Historically low election turnouts suggest Labour may instead have alienated much of its traditional support among working-class people, who felt it no longer spoke for or to them. Fewer people identified as working class with the decline of manufacturing, but more than New Labour appeared to believe. Their resentment, at being 'left behind', continued to harm Labour electorally for some time ahead.[75] Another, smaller, traditional source of support, radical intellectuals, had been alienated by the Iraq War. Blair's 'legacy' was, at best, mixed, Brown's rather better, but unjustly scarred by the international financial crisis which he received little credit for helping to alleviate.

CHAPTER 14
2010–23, 'AUSTERITY'

The coalition government continued until 2015, effectively controlled by the Conservatives. Cameron and the chancellor, George Osborne, established a regime they called 'Austerity', with low taxes and a shrinking state. Under successive Conservative governments public spending fell from 42 per cent of GDP in 2009/2010 to 35 per cent in 2019/2020; in the least deprived 20 per cent of districts in England by 16 per cent, in the most deprived 32 per cent. Further declines followed, with increasing numbers of local authorities facing bankruptcy by 2023. The lower the household income, the more they lost in tax and benefit changes.[1] Cameron argued that this was essential to repair a Britain 'broken' by Labour's supposed irresponsible spending. He proclaimed a desire to improve social conditions, but not through state welfare: rather a 'Big Society' must replace the 'Big State'. He appeared to mean that voluntary action had been undermined by state welfare and must be revived to replace it. In fact, as we have seen, it had been continuously active in the post-war Welfare State, increasingly as it strove to maintain services cut by Conservatives and keep the Welfare State alive. It was an important feature of UK culture.[2] Cameron soon went silent on the issue, while he and Osborne revived negative assaults on people in poverty. He stated in October 2010: 'Taking more money from the man who goes out to work long hours each single day so the family next door can go on living a life on benefits without working – is that fair? . . . If you can work but refuse to work, we will not let you live off the hard work of others.' Governments persistently ignored evidence of the large, growing numbers of working people in poverty.

Severe cuts to public services were announced in the June 2010 budget, more in the five-year plan of October 2010, which also cut grants to voluntary organizations, totalling £11bn 'welfare reform savings'. Benefits, including pensions, were linked to the Consumer Prices Index (CPI), a lower measure than the Retail Price Index (RPI) used by Labour, causing real cuts. Housing Benefit was reduced. The plan was described by the respected, independent Institute for Fiscal Studies (IFS) as 'the longest, deepest, period of cuts to public services since at least the Second World War.'[3] In 2014 Osborne announced a freeze on benefits for two years. It was extended to April 2020, cutting the real value of benefits by 6 per cent from 2015, pushing 400,000 people into poverty. An estimated £37bn was cut from benefit spending by successive Conservative governments, 2010–21.[4] CPAG calculated that Child Benefit lost almost 25 per cent of its value in that time.

Privatization revived. Public sector pay was frozen. Whitehall costs were cut by one-third, local authority funding by 30 per cent: Sure Start Centres, social care, youth and other services contracted. Childcare in England became scarcer and more expensive than in any comparable country. In Scotland it was still provided by local authorities, much cheaper, with better trained staff. Educational Maintenance Allowances (EMAs) were abolished only in England. Most benefits were frozen and reduced in value, except those of pensioners, who had voted substantially for the Conservatives and were guaranteed an increase in state pension and Pension Credit of at least 2.5 per cent p.a. From 2014 less predictable younger voters faced the rise in the state pension age to sixty-six planned by Labour for 2026 brought forward to 2020, along with the planned equalization of women's pension age. Women were still not informed in time to prepare and formed the Women Against State Pension Inequality (WASPI) protest group, which failed to achieve change.

The further rise to sixty-seven for men and women was brought forward to 2026–8, to rise again to sixty-eight in 2044–6, later changed to 2037–9. This aroused opposition from NGO Age UK, among others, concerned that the rise to sixty-six already further disadvantaged the growing numbers of people who before age sixty-six, or even sixty-five, were in poor health, had difficulty finding work or were full- or part-time unpaid carers. They advocated improved benefits for these people and in 2023 persuaded the government not to bring forward the rise to sixty-eight, but they remained concerned about growing poverty in later life.[5] In 2021 the government proposed scrapping free NHS prescriptions for over-60s, requiring them to pay until they qualified for the state pension, but as the cost of living rose, it was not implemented.[6] Wales abolished prescription charges in 2007, Scotland in 2011. Northern Ireland phased them out in 2008/2010. All three countries charged less for dental and optical care than England, where charges rose and NHS care became harder to access.

The Conservatives aimed to eliminate local authority schools, planning to convert all remaining state schools to Academies. Sixty-six per cent converted by 2015, without evident improvement in standards. Local authorities running successful schools opposed further conversion, supported by parents. Government control of the English school curriculum tightened. State-funded 'free schools' could now be established, controlled by parents, charities, teachers and others, regardless of local need. Scotland and Wales introduced neither free schools nor Academies, retaining local government control. Universities were allowed to raise fees to £9,250 pa in England, £9,000 in Wales, and did so gradually. Grants and loans to students were cut. For the substantial numbers of overseas students, fees now averaged £13,500 p.a. By 2015 under 20 per cent of university income came from government, but it continued regular assessments of teaching and research.

NHS spending rose, much of it on administration, while pay of nursing and allied hospital staff was frozen and need for services rose in an ageing, increasingly impoverished, unhealthy society. In England (only) the Health and Social Care Act, 2012, encouraged outsourcing of NHS services to the private sector. Public spending on private healthcare rose by £1bn during 2014–19. Staff numbers declined along with conditions, nurses in England from 408,000 in 2008 to 333,000 in 2013, 322,637 in 2022; GP numbers also fell, all driven by increased stress at work and decline in the real value of pay, many taking early retirement or emigrating to work in Australia, Canada or elsewhere where work conditions and pay were better. Many European immigrants left following Britain's vote to exit from the EU in 2016, still more when it finally left in January 2020. Hospitals fell into deficit and poor care caused a succession of scandals in maternity, mental health and other services. Waiting lists grew and 'non-essential' operations were reduced and delayed, including for cataract removal or joint replacement – not life-threatening conditions but seriously hampering the independence especially of many older people and increasing their need for other services.

But the number and quality of residential and community services for older and disabled people in England and Wales (services for which Wales had less autonomy than Scotland) dwindled as local budgets were cut and private providers' profits fell when local authorities could no longer afford to subsidise them or clients to pay higher charges, causing declining conditions in care homes and other services and many closures. In Scotland personal care at home or in institutions was largely local authority controlled and free. A government commissioned report chaired by economist Andrew Dilnot in 2011 recommended more government funding in England and Wales and a limit to individual lifetime costs for care. It was welcomed by the government, but little changed. Persistently to the present (2023) governments have promised improved funding for social care, but no action has followed. From 2010 to 2016 in England and Wales, 30 per cent fewer people received publicly funded care and growing numbers of older people 'blocked' hospital beds, staying in them longer than they needed because care they did need was unavailable elsewhere.

Disability benefits were progressively cut, while claimants faced stricter work-capability assessments conducted by private contractors without medical or other relevant skills, designed to force them into work, often inappropriately. Many appeals followed, two-thirds successful and costly to public funds. Conditions, including pressure to work, were further tightened in the chancellor's 'Autumn Statement' in November 2023 as the numbers unemployed due to sickness and disability kept rising. He suggested that this was due to fraudulent preference for life on the country's inadequate benefits. The fact that in many cases it was due to delays in treatment by an overworked, understaffed NHS was ignored.

By 2016 only 7 per cent of households occupied council houses, often of poor quality, better housing having been sold since the 1980s. The lack of official concern for council tenants, and leaseholders of former council property, was evident from the Grenfell Tower fire disaster in London in 2017, when seventy-two people died due to poor fire protection and maintenance of a tower block in prosperous, Conservative-controlled, Kensington, despite residents' complaints. It caused widespread publicity and public horror. The government promised funding for removal of unsafe flammable cladding from tall blocks and improved safety measures, but both advanced slowly and controversially. The shortage of affordable homes continued to grow along with homelessness. Another sign of falling living standards was that owner-occupation declined from 71 per cent of homes in 2003 to 64 per cent in 2021/2 while private rentals and rents increased, unaffordable by many.[7] Increasingly, high-priced private rentals were in poor condition, often damp and endangering residents' health, even causing deaths, ignored by owners. Much publicized was the death of two-year-old Awaak Ishak in Rochdale in 2020 due to damp and mould in the family flat and a landlord who ignored their persistent complaints. He was not alone. Underfunded local authorities could not afford repairs or to house the homeless. Rough sleeping increased.

'Universal discredit'

The coalition and its Conservative successors encouraged the notion relentlessly promoted in the popular media of benefit claimants as irresponsible 'shirkers', defrauding an over-generous system funded by hard-working 'strivers', that is, taxpayers. Post-war notions of welfare as the right of all citizens in need in a caring society had vanished from political and popular discourse. On this basis, means-tested Universal Credit (UC) was introduced in the Welfare Reform Act, 2012. A single payment replaced six means-tested benefits: Income Support, Jobseeker's Allowance, Employment and Support Allowance, Housing Benefit, Child Tax Credit and Working Tax Credit. Its main objective was to force anyone judged capable into work- any work – a return to ancient Poor Law principles. The Work and Pensions secretary, Iain Duncan Smith, was mainly responsible for the innovation and claimed, 'A life on benefits is a poor substitute for a working life but too much of our current system is geared towards maintaining people on benefits rather than helping them to flourish in work; we need a reform that tackles the underlying problem of welfare dependency.'[8] This was not the core problem. From the start, a high and rising proportion of UC recipients were in work, but too insecure and low-paid in what was becoming known as the unregulated 'gig economy' to avoid poverty. All benefits were capped below average wages, at low levels.

Supporters argued that the previous system was too complex, and the single UC benefit was simpler and cheaper to administer. A complex system had developed because work, family and personal lives are complex. Previously, if circumstances changed for reasons beyond individual control – unemployment, sickness, accident, rising or falling pay or rent – only the relevant benefit was reassessed. Now one change required reassessment of the whole package, halting all payments for at least five weeks, often longer because it was inefficiently administered, neither cheaper nor more efficient than the previous system, causing starvation, rent arrears and debt, increasing already severe poverty. Claims could only be made online, though many low-income people lacked access to the internet or expertise in using it. Partners in abusive relationships were especially hard hit because UC payments were made monthly into one household bank account, often giving the abusive partner total control. Previously they were made to the relevant claimant e.g., Child Tax Credit normally to the mother. The Scottish government divided all UC payments between partners and paid fortnightly. In 2014 the high costs of administration caused Osborne as chancellor to reduce UC benefit further, pushing even more people into poverty. Another notorious feature of the Welfare Reform Act became known as the 'bedroom tax'. People living in 'social' housing had their Housing Benefit reduced by 14 per cent if they were judged to have a spare bedroom, 25 per cent if they had two or more. It ignored the possibility that the spare room was needed by a disabled family member or for any other necessary use. It further increased poverty.

Under another clause of the Welfare Reform Act, households with at least two children were allowed no further UC payment for additional children born after 6 April 2017, excluding twins and triplets. One academic expert described it as 'the worst social security policy ever'. A collaborative academic research project into the impact of the policy reported in July 2023 that it had resulted in more than 1 million children living in poverty and damaged their mental health. It did not lead to fewer births, as policymakers apparently hoped, and more than half the households involved included workers.[9] Nevertheless, a spokesperson for the DWP responded to critics: 'families on benefits are asked to make the same financial decisions as families supporting themselves solely through work'. The Children's Commissioners for Scotland, Wales and Northern Ireland called for it to be scrapped, without success; this lay outside their devolved powers. Scottish powers over social security spending were partially extended in 2016. It abolished the two-child limit and established a new weekly payment of £10 for each child up to age 16 in families on UC, rising to £25 in November 2022. It mitigated the bedroom tax by introducing discretionary housing grants.

In 2017 the leading food bank charity, the Trussell Trust, stated that demand for free food had risen by 30 per cent in areas where introduction of UC was most advanced. In 2018 the National Audit Office reported that it cost more to administer than the benefits it replaced. Also in 2018 the UN Special Rapporteur on Human Rights and Extreme Poverty, Philip Alston, made an unprecedented tour of the UK. In 2019 he reported with horror on the extent of poverty and the contribution of the scheme, 'fast falling into Universal Discredit' as he put it, to the terrible conditions when, 'Social support should be a route out of poverty'.[10] His excoriating report was dismissed in Westminster but welcomed by the Scottish government.

The Conservatives proclaimed their policies a success because official unemployment figures were the lowest since 1975. But, unlike in 1975, increasing numbers of workers were in insecure, low-paid work, keeping their families in poverty, without trade union protection due to union decline. In an effectively unregulated labour market, some employers ignored the minimum wage (renamed the 'living wage' by Osborne, which it was not) and workers' rights to sickness and other benefits, treating employees as self-employed and therefore ineligible for benefits, or placing them on insecure 'zero hours' contracts with uncertain daily or weekly hours and pay. In 2014 about half a million workers in UK were on these contracts. By 2020 the number doubled as the 'gig economy' expanded, ignored by successive governments. In 2023 the TUC described how intensification of working hours was another feature of this unregulated economy. Fifty-five per cent of workers surveyed, including schoolteachers, care workers and postal workers, reported that working hours had increased while pay had not and they had lost control over their working time, required to respond to emails outside working hours and facing constant surveillance, causing exhaustion.[11] The Health and Safety Executive, a government agency theoretically 'responsible for the encouragement, regulation and enforcement of workplace health, safety and welfare', created by Labour in 1974, had its budget halved over the previous decade and its enforcement declined. Public sector pay rises were frozen at 1 per cent from 2011 to 2017, then in 2020 at 1.4 per cent, lagging far behind the private sector, stimulating an unusual number of strikes in 2022-3 by public sector workers who had hardly ever, or never, gone on strike, including nurses, doctors, teachers, ambulance drivers. The 'living' wage was raised in 2023 but remained inadequate to protect families from poverty. In 2023 the independent Institute for Employment Studies published a report concluding from consultation with business groups, work seekers, work coaches and others that a policy of forcing jobseekers into any job, however inappropriate, led to high turnover and poor performance. Official policy should rather provide access to training.[12]

Poverty

A striking number of independent expert institutions revealed that the numbers in poverty rose from 2011/2012, after falling through the 2000s. Surveys by the Joseph Rowntree Foundation (JRF, founded in memory of Seebohm Rowntree) found that in 2015–16, 20 per cent of the UK population lived in poverty, 60 per cent in households including an inadequately paid full-time worker. CPAG estimated that 30 per cent of children in the UK (4.1 million) were in poverty in 2016–17, 67 per cent in households with at least one full-time worker.[13] The IFS supported this estimate and stressed regional variations: in 2016–17, 24 per cent of children in Scotland were in poverty, 37 per cent in London, the difference driven mainly by housing costs. They found similar numbers in poverty with similar causes in 2018.[14] As described in the reports, all these findings were derived from comprehensive official government surveys of reported household incomes, including the UK-wide Family Resource Survey conducted annually from 1992 by the Office of National Statistics (ONS) in collaboration with the Northern Ireland Statistical Agency and sponsored by the DWP. Official findings were supplemented by comprehensive large-scale surveys by each institution. The data was far more comprehensive and scientific than that available to Booth and Rowntree or to interwar researchers. The reports all employed the measure of relative poverty now accepted internationally in high-income countries: incomes below 60 per cent of the national median. As the 2023 JRF report put it, 'Being in poverty is when your resources are well below what is enough to meet your minimum needs, including taking part in society', a standard very similar to that employed by Booth and Rowntree.[15]

There was unprecedented use of food banks by families who could not otherwise afford to eat. Food banks were almost unheard of in Britain before 2010, successors to early twentieth-century soup kitchens, unseen since 1945, significant examples of voluntary action responding to welfare crises. In 2017/2018 the largest national food bank, the Trussell Trust, distributed 1.3 million food parcels, and the number rose thereafter at least to 2023 (1.5 million).[16] There were also hundreds of small, local food banks run by faith institutions, community centres and other groups and total provision is unknown. Some ministers applauded this extensive voluntary action rather than seeking to eliminate the deprivation that made it necessary.

In October 2022 Alston's successor, Olivier de Schutter, repeated his warning about the disturbing extent of poverty in the UK, compared with other high-income countries.[17] He repeated it even more firmly a year later, stating that UK poverty levels were 'simply not acceptable' and the government was violating international law. The UK had signed the international covenant on economic and social rights which created a duty to provide a level of social protection that ensured an adequate standard of living, but this was being broken. About to visit the UK, in an interview with the *Guardian* he described the UC as a 'leaking bucket', the £85 per week payment for single adults, 'grossly insufficient'. He stated 'It's simply not acceptable that we have more than a fifth of the population in a rich country such as the UK at risk of poverty today. . . . The policies in place are not working or not protecting people in poverty and much more needs to be done for these people to be protected'. Increasing UC, he said, would be 'the single most important step the UK could take towards meeting its international obligations'. He stressed that the UK was not alone in failing to tackle poverty: 'we need to stop thinking that economic growth will lift all boats . . . in most of the OECD countries growth of GDP has been going hand in hand with increasing inequalities and a failure to reduce levels of both absolute and relative poverty'. 'We should focus instead on providing support to low-income households, providing access to work for all people . . . and creating a much more inclusive economy-rather than one that creates wealth for the elites and particularly for the shareholders of the largest corporations.'[18]

The government responded, as it had to Alston, with denial, arguing that there were 1.7m fewer people in 'absolute poverty' in 2021–2 than in 2009–10.[19] Under the coalition government the DWP had labelled its preferred definition of poverty as 'absolute poverty' and fixed its measure at household income below 60 per cent of the median in 2009/2010, after housing costs and allowing for inflation. This conveniently presented lesser, or no, increases in poverty over time compared with the internationally accepted measure of relative poverty, hence its rejection by De Schutter and other experts.

Child poverty continued to be a major concern. It was driven by the effects of UC, low family incomes and the rising cost of housing. According to the relative poverty measures and sources discussed above, in 2018/2019, 31 per cent of children in England were in poverty, 28 per cent in Wales, 24 per cent in Scotland, 25 per cent in Northern Ireland. Deprived, mixed-race East London boroughs including Newham (50.3 per cent) and Tower Hamlets (55.4 per cent) had the highest levels, but from 2014/2015 the greatest increases were in Middlesborough (41.1 per cent in 2018/2019, 28.69 per cent five years earlier), Newcastle-upon-Tyne and parts of Birmingham (41.6 per cent, the highest level outside London). Most poor children lived in working households.[20]

Housing costs were a major driver of poverty. Northern Ireland had the highest levels of unemployment and low-paid work, but the lowest house prices, lower mortgages, the lowest proportion of renters and the lowest rents for social and private housing. In 2019/20 they averaged £74 and £97 respectively, compared with £99 and £131 in the rest of the UK. Scotland had the lowest proportion of households paying rent and a higher proportion of tenants in social, mostly council, housing, 57 per cent compared with the 45 per cent UK average.[21] The Scottish government controlled social rents from shortly after devolution, and controls were established in Northern Ireland. From 2016 it became almost impossible for landlords in Scotland to evict tenants without good cause. In 2022 Scotland froze private rents for six months due to rising inflation. Northern Ireland could not because it lacked a functioning government, due to deep political divisions. The English government announced in 2022 a 7 per cent cap on social rents to be confirmed in 2023, and controls on no-fault evictions, which were extensive. A Renters Reform Bill was presented to parliament in May 2023 and expected to be debated, but this was uncertain and it included only limited controls on eviction and none on rents, which continued to rise. It was delayed and still not implemented in December 2023.

Rising poverty and inequality caused life expectancy to fall for poorer people after rising for over a century. Through the 2000s the gap in average life expectancy and healthy life expectancy between the poorest 20 per cent of areas and the rest narrowed. From 2011 to 2018 among women in the most deprived areas of England, life expectancy fell fastest, by several months to just above age seventy-eight, while in the least deprived it rose above eighty-six.[22] In 2023 average life expectancy for men in the most deprived areas was 73.5, for women 78.3, in the least deprived 83.2 and 86.3 respectively. Years of healthy life also declined in deprived areas.[23] Births declined again after rising since 2001, in England and Wales by 12.2 per cent during 2012–19, probably also due to lower incomes and poorer services, again arousing fears about the impact on the economy.

Another outcome of health inequalities exacerbated by poverty was a rising number of maternal deaths during pregnancy or childbirth with 9.6 mothers on average dying within six weeks of childbirth for every 100,000 births. By 2022 deaths were most frequent in the most deprived areas and among Black (especially, 34 in 100,000 maternities in England) and Asian (c 16 deaths/100,000) mothers.[24] There were comparable rises in deaths of babies. A senior World Health Organization (WHO) doctor commented that 'other countries with similar levels of economic development are faring better in terms of their maternal mortality'. She attributed the rise to poor health, including high levels of diabetes and obesity, and the failure of antenatal care services to reach women from Black, Asian and minority ethnic backgrounds and those in deprived areas. She considered maternal deaths a 'warning signal for the entire UK health care system'. In 2023 maternity services were reported to be the most inadequate services in the NHS.

Brexit

Meanwhile another crisis developed as Conservative hostility to EU membership mounted. David Cameron had little experience of foreign affairs. He decided that to restore the economy Britain's international position must be strengthened, requiring a close relationship with the United States and active membership of the EU. Despite 'Austerity', he insisted on keeping Trident and building costly aircraft carriers, planned by Brown, as essential, expensive, symbols of Britain's international status. In 2011 he co-operated with France in an assault against President Gaddafi's repression of Libya, leading to a long civil war. In 2013 he wished to join the intervention against the use of chemical weapons in Syria, but parliament refused, and his foreign policy ventures ended.

Conservative hostility to the EU was encouraged by UKIP. There was growing pressure for a referendum on membership. Cameron promised that, if the Conservatives won the election due in 2015, he would renegotiate the UK's settlement with the EU and hold a referendum. Conservatives won the election with a 12-seat majority, ending the coalition and forcing Cameron to call the referendum. UKIP won only one seat but came third in votes with 12.9 per cent. Miliband had not made a strong impact and resigned. Jeremy Corbyn was elected Labour leader. He was an MP from 1983, never a minister, well known as a left-winger, active in anti-war organizations, dubious about EU membership in a party much divided about it. Labour membership increased substantially following his election, especially among younger people.

Certain he would win, Cameron ignored warnings from officials against a simple majority vote in the referendum, despite the closeness of the sides in opinion polls. Anxious to unite the party, he made little effort to defend EU membership and promised a substantial cut to immigration as its opponents demanded. A bitter campaign included much misrepresentation by the 'Brexiteers', as they became known, in their demands to 'Take Back Control', which overlooked the fact that Britain had, and had always exercised, control over the EU directives it adopted. Their well-funded campaign blamed the size of British contributions to the EU budget and immigration from the EU for the weaknesses of public services, including the NHS, which were actually due to Conservative cuts. It ignored the positive contributions of European workers, including in the NHS, and the benefit to deprived areas, including South Wales and North-East England, of substantial EU subsidies. UK voters overall rejected the EU with a narrow majority of 51.9 per cent to 48.1 per cent from a turnout of 72.2 per cent, but with clear majorities for 'Remain' in Scotland and Northern Ireland. In England younger and better-educated voters were strongly pro-Remain. Altogether just 37.5 per cent of qualified UK voters voted to leave. Cameron resigned.

Leading Brexiteers, including the most prominent, Boris Johnson (mayor of London – which overwhelmingly voted Remain – until 2016, a Conservative MP from 2015), appeared as unprepared for the result as Cameron. No-one had addressed the difficulties separation from the EU, the UK's largest market, would bring, including on the Irish border. Cameron was succeeded by Theresa May, previously Home Secretary, a low-profile Remainer with little experience of foreign affairs. She mistrusted civil servants as too uniformly pro-Remain and relied upon a small circle of inexperienced advisers to negotiate leaving the EU. Over three years of uncertainty before Britain finally left the EU on 31 January 2020 business investment stalled. Brexiteers believed a strong relationship with Washington would secure Britain's world influence, but President Obama thought leaving the EU made Britain a less useful partner. He built close links with Germany instead. The election of Donald Trump to the US presidency in 2016 added to the uncertainty. He had no interest in Britain.

May called a sudden election in June 2017, perhaps hoping to boost her status and power in the country and the party since the Conservatives were well ahead in polls. But the poll lead dropped as the campaign progressed, and she lost her overall majority. Labour under Corbyn won more votes, 12.8 million, than in any election since 1997 – to the horror of his many opponents in the party who thought him too left-wing – just 789,225 votes but 56 seats behind the Conservatives because Labour piled up votes in its traditional heartlands. UKIP gained no seats, only 1.8 per cent of the votes and declined thereafter, soon replaced by the Brexit Party, also led by Nigel Farage. The Conservatives remained weakly in government following a deal with the Eurosceptic Democratic Unionist Party (DUP) of Northern Ireland, which favoured stronger barriers between the Republic (in the EU) and the North, where divisions were reviving.

One week after the election May responded to the Grenfell Tower fire crisis indecisively and with her characteristic lack of social skills. Then in April 2018 the *Guardian* exposed what became known as the 'Windrush scandal'. As Home Secretary May had developed a policy of seeking out and punishing illegal immigrants, creating what she described as 'a hostile environment'. The *Guardian* revealed that many people who had moved to Britain wholly legally from the Commonwealth, often as young children accompanying their parents, were being punished as illegal migrants if they could not provide documentary evidence of their right to remain in Britain, which until 1973 was the right of anyone born in the Commonwealth. A high proportion of victims had migrated from the Caribbean, and it was called the 'Windrush scandal' recalling the arrival in 1948 of one of the first substantial groups of immigrants from the Caribbean aboard HMS *Windrush*. Many who had not kept documents confirming their long-ago arrival were detained, deported or lost their rights to work, benefits and healthcare, driving them into destitution, sometimes death. May and the Home Office faced severe criticism.[25] In December 2018 a compensation scheme was established for victims, but in 2023 many were still uncompensated and suffering exclusion.

May proposed a compromise EU deal to the Cabinet in July 2018. Leading Brexiteers, Johnson and David Davis, resigned. Leaving Europe, planned for 29 March 2019, was delayed while negotiations continued, amid division in the party. May failed to get a compromise agreement past the Commons. In the election for the EU parliament in May 2019, the Brexit Party gained the largest share of votes with 31.6 per cent, the Conservatives only 9.1 per cent, Labour 14.1 per cent. May resigned. Boris Johnson won the party leadership promising to leave the EU with or without a deal. He called an election in December 2019, boasting of Britain's 'Return to Greatness'. The campaign exposed Labour's divisions. The Conservatives gained an 80-seat overall majority, winning a substantial number of traditional, mainly Brexit-voting, Labour seats in Northern England – labelled the 'red wall' – perhaps helped by Johnson's (unfulfilled) promises to 'end austerity,' and the Conservative practice of blaming immigrants for growing difficulties of accessing work, healthcare, education, affordable housing, all due to Conservative 'austerity'. Labour slumped with 203 seats, its worst result since 1935. Corbyn resigned and the centrist Sir Keir Starmer, former director of Public Prosecutions, politically inexperienced, was elected to replace him. Johnson signed a withdrawal agreement which failed to solve the Irish border problem, and Britain left the

EU on 31 January 2020. Poverty and inequality had grown during the years that Brexit dominated politics, disrupting economic life.

Covid

Disruption and poverty grew further with the unexpected emergence of the Covid-19 pandemic shortly after Brexit. The UK was slower than many other countries to impose restrictions when it started, and when it revived in autumn 2020, the government argued that the priority was to keep the economy going. Perhaps Johnson was preoccupied with Brexit and other matters, though he was hospitalised with Covid in April 2020. Thereafter his government lacked consistent policies and the devolved governments followed different, often more effective, approaches. The first 'lockdown' covered the whole UK from March to June 2020. The UK economy has never in modern history shut down so extensively for so long, with closure of 'non-essential' shops and businesses, including restaurants, pubs and flower shops, while supermarkets flourished. This caused high unemployment especially among the lowest-paid, further increasing poverty, use of food banks and homelessness. The Trussell Trust distributed 89 per cent more food parcels than in the same period in 2019, almost 100 per cent more to families with children. Domestic violence, mental illness and suicide increased due to household lockdown and financial stress.

Nor had schools previously closed for so long. Disrupted education exposed inequalities between richer children with greater access to computers and other devices for distance learning, more space and more parental support for home learning, with potentially harmful effects on the futures of poorer children, including from the loss of free school meals.[26] In 2020/2021 the government provided vouchers for meals for starving children in school summer holidays, then in Christmas holidays, following a campaign by well-known Black footballer Marcus Rashford, who had himself grown up in poverty with his lone mother. It improved children's lives but did not reduce poverty. There were further disruptions when schools and universities temporarily reopened and Covid spiked again, infecting teachers and students. Further lockdowns followed.

From the start of lockdowns people suffering from health conditions making them vulnerable to infection were required to self-isolate at home. Initially the government ordered everyone over age seventy to do so, until prominent septuagenarians complained of age discrimination, pointing out that they were healthier than many younger people. The government then required isolation based on health, not age. Working people expected to self-isolate after contact with Covid victims were eligible for sickness benefits of only £95.95 per week, the lowest in the thirty-eight developed nations of the OECD, worth just 18 per cent of average earnings. But at least two million insecure, low-paid workers lacked access to sick pay. Better-paid workers could mostly work from home on full pay. Many on low incomes lacked this option and felt they must go to work to avoid destitution, risking sickness and infecting others, causing deaths. Despite the difficulties, lockdowns were generally carefully observed – except, it was later revealed, by the Prime Minister who attended parties in Downing Street, gatherings that were banned for everyone else. Largely due to widespread condemnation of this thoughtless behaviour, and a police fine, he resigned in July 2022, followed by two prime ministers in quick succession, Liz Truss and Rishi Sunak, a period of considerable confusion in government and persistent economic decline.

The UK had high infection rates and, a year into the pandemic, one of the highest death rates per head of population in the world, according to the ONS the highest in Europe, 169 per 100,000 by February 2021.[27] Testing for the virus and tracing contacts of victims was highly inefficient. It was allocated, at huge cost (£12bn), to inexperienced private companies with close personal links to the Conservatives due to the government's preference for the private sector. Johnson stated in a speech to the Conservative Party conference in October 2020 that this was 'a moment when the state must stand back and let the private sector get on with it'. 'Test-and-trace' could have been managed more successfully at much lower cost by local public health departments, despite their severe cuts. The Welfare Reform Act, 2012, abolished regional public health authorities, run by the NHS, transferring them to underfunded local authorities, much restricting their activities and cutting their budgets by 40 per cent by 2019/20.[28] The devolved governments placed greater trust in the public sector with better outcomes. From early 2021 England used public health departments for a more intensive and effective testing service in areas experiencing new variants of the virus.[29] Throughout, publicly funded NHS staff played the central, indispensable role of caring for Covid patients. And from early 2021 the government allowed them, assisted by volunteers, to manage a very efficient system of vaccination which reduced infection and deaths. The NHS was widely praised and thanked.

From March 2020 the government funded 80 per cent of the normal wages of many people temporarily unemployed due to lockdown, known as the 'furlough', expecting employers to pay the remaining 20 per cent. Eighty per cent of an inadequate wage increased poverty, and many – at least three million – low-paid and (often theoretically) self-employed workers were excluded from the scheme. UC was raised by £20 a week in April 2020. IFS reported that, even while the uplift was in progress, out-of-work households received £1600 per year less in benefits than they would have received in 2010.[30] And the JRF estimated that of the 13.4m people in poverty in 2020/2, 46 per cent were on UC.[31] Despite much pressure to retain it, the uplift was removed in October 2021, pushing an estimated further 840,000 into poverty. The government argued that it was too expensive to retain. It continued to be harshly administered. In January 2022 almost 40,000 claimants had their benefits stopped or cut, usually for failing to keep a Jobcentre appointment concerning their benefit, even when they had a good reason such as illness or traffic holdups.

The workers suffering most from pandemic-induced conditions included young people aged 16–25 and older workers in their fifties. They were most likely to be unemployed as businesses cut staff or closed due to reduced demand and rising costs. The JRF found that people already struggling before March 2020 were hardest hit by the lockdowns. An estimated 2 million families, including 1 million children, struggled to feed themselves, stay warm or keep clean even before Covid. Destitution was greatest in the North-East and North-West of England and parts of inner London, affecting over one in 100 families in these regions. In-work poverty was greatest in London, least in Scotland. Poverty and Covid death rates were greatest in parts of Northern England and London. London has long had the richest and some of the poorest communities in the UK. Recent immigrants, many ineligible for welfare support, were disproportionately destitute in the pandemic. Disabled people were even more severely disadvantaged than before. By 2022, 30 per cent of disabled people in the UK (3.8 million adults, 300,000 children) were in poverty due to cuts to benefits and increased charges for services following cuts to local authority funds.

Covid did not evidently worsen the gender gap in pay which was 15.5 per cent in April 2020 compared with 17.4 per cent a year earlier.[32] But women were more disadvantaged than male workers in other ways. Working mothers – rarely fathers – needed time off to care for their children and supervise their education during school closures, and they lost pay. More female workers suffered the ill-effects of closure of businesses and furlough. Women's groups including those representing ethnic minorities, campaigned for the government to provide adequate, affordable childcare, close the gender pay gap, introduce flexible working for all when needed and raise benefits, without evident effect.[33]

Black and Minority Ethnic communities, particularly those originating in Bangladesh and Pakistan, experienced high Covid infection and death rates, mainly because they had low incomes, worked in environments with poor protection against infection and often lived in overcrowded homes. In December 2020, 34 per cent of Pakistani and Bangladeshi workers' families were in poverty, compared with the 25 per cent average of white families.[34] Covid made certain long-standing race inequalities more public, but the most disadvantaged minority group, Gypsies and Travellers, were ignored during the pandemic as before. In 2023 a survey of more members of this community than any previous study found that 62 per cent had experienced a racial assault, more than any other ethnic group. Gypsy/Traveller men were 12.4 times more likely to suffer from two or more physical health conditions than white British men, the highest of any ethnicity. They suffered the most severe socio-economic deprivation. Fifty-one per cent had no educational qualifications, had extensive financial difficulties and benefit dependency. They were least likely to be employed during the pandemic and, at the time of the survey, 85 per cent were in precarious employment.[35] In 2022 a much higher proportion of Gypsy and Traveller children (60 per cent) had free school meals than of any other social group.[36]

Social care

Covid deepened and raised awareness of many social problems, including the inadequacy of social care for older and disabled people in residential homes and their own homes, and the low pay and poor working conditions of care workers. They were in the bottom

10 per cent of UK workers' pay in late 2022. The situation was poor before Covid but became worse when, early in the pandemic, to free hospital beds for Covid victims, the government ordered removal into care homes of the many occupants of hospital beds who no longer needed treatment but could not find the care they needed elsewhere. They were not tested for Covid before transfer and added to sickness and deaths as well as overcrowding in an already overloaded sector. At least 36,000 people died from Covid in care homes. Another example of official lack of concern for the needs of older and disabled people, indeed of persistent discrimination against them, was the government's slowness to provide care services with protective equipment, further raising infection and death rates. Residents suffered also from the ban on visits from family and friends during lockdown.

In 1979 two-thirds of residential care was NHS or council-run, by 2020, 84 per cent was run by for-profit companies. They raised fees to levels individuals, families and councils could not afford. Availability and quality of care declined further during Covid. Many private homes went bankrupt and closed. An investigation by the *Guardian* in 2023 revealed that in the previous four years almost £500m of taxpayers' money was spent on places in below-standard care homes in England, many deemed 'not safe' by the regulator, the Care Quality Commission, while some private operators earned millions in profits.[37] A total of 380,000 people in Britain lived in care homes, more than a third funded by taxpayers. Private homes were too often staffed by untrained, underpaid workers, who failed to deliver proper nutrition and medicines in dirty, dangerous properties. Residents experienced serious abuse in some private homes. Councils tried to avoid placing residents in inadequate homes, but often had no choice. A woman described her grandfather's treatment in an NHS-funded care home in North-East England:

> His room was dirty, smelled of pee, the bedding and towels were dirty and ragged. One member of staff was sacked for the way they treated my grandad. They dragged him out of bed and wouldn't listen when he said no . . . it has been devastating to watch his life end this way. I'm heartbroken.[38]

The Local Government Association warned of a £13bn annual shortfall in funding to meet rising care costs and growing demand from an ageing population. When Boris Johnson became premier in 2019, he promised 'to fix the crisis in social care once and for all'. Nothing changed. In March 2023 a 'fair cost of care' survey commissioned by the Johnson government reported a £2.3bn per year 'black hole' in funding for older people in care and nursing homes, due to inadequate funding of councils to pay for those unable to afford private home fees, leading to closures or poor conditions in homes. Staff resigned due to pressure, exhaustion and poor conditions, causing severe staff shortages. At least £650m, probably more, was missing from funding for carers for people living in their own homes.[39]

The decline of public social care increased pressure on families, normally women in families (six in ten unpaid carers[40]) to provide care. The 2021 census revealed that five million people, including children as young as five, provided long-term unpaid care to people with severe health conditions or problems related to old age. The Carers Trust reported in 2022 that 41 per cent of unpaid carers surveyed had given up paid work, 23 per cent had cut their hours. More than 25 per cent were cutting back on food, heating, leisure, while a third said their mental health was harmed. They estimated that carers withdrawing from work cost society £1.3bn p.a. The CEO of Carers UK stated, 'Without the support provided by unpaid carers, our health and social care systems would simply collapse.' They estimated in 2023 that 10.6 million people in the UK were unpaid carers. 1.5 million people in England and Wales gave more than fifty hours per week, with limited public help. Carers Allowance was the lowest state benefit and required a complex application process.[41]

In 2023 there were 165,000 social care staffing vacancies in England and Wales and millions of hours of unmet care needs. The government promised £500m investment in the workforce in England. In March 2023 it halved this amount but by December 2023 it had not been provided. In June it announced the launch of a joint NHS and Social Care programme to recruit a volunteer army to take medical equipment and drugs, shopping and prescriptions to people's homes, aiming to free hospital beds which were again becoming 'blocked' by people no longer needing hospital care. Volunteers would also tackle loneliness at home with support by phone. The Director of Care Rights UK, which represents residents and relatives, said it 'feels like a desperate measure to try and save a system that is crumbling'.[42] The government was perhaps building on volunteers' indispensable contribution during the pandemic, bringing food and medical supplies to people in self-isolation, managing and contributing to food banks and much more. But it was far from certain that volunteers would be available or willing to take over government responsibilities as normal working life resumed and the outcome was unclear late in 2023.

Similar problems of deteriorating care arose from privatization of children's care homes. In 2005 there was a *c.* 50/50 division between public and private placements in England and Wales. In 2023 *c.* 80 per cent were privately owned. There was strong evidence of harm to children, not least because they were frequently moved to unfamiliar places. Scottish and Welsh governments were committed to moving away from for-profit homes; Northern Ireland was reviewing it. There was no sign that the English government planned reform.[43]

The NHS

The NHS experienced increased demand for its services before and still more during Covid, following funding cuts and growing shortages of doctors and nurses. European immigrants left due to uncertainty about their future after Brexit, while others resigned from exhaustion and overwork, retiring early or migrating to work with better pay and conditions in Australia, Canada and elsewhere. These problems, plus prioritization during the pandemic of the many Covid cases, delayed treatment of conditions including cancer and heart disease, causing further deaths. GP surgeries closed to avoid transmission of infection. Consultations were available only online or by telephone, causing failure to diagnose serious conditions.

Some older people were denied life-saving treatment for Covid because it was judged that, because they suffered from other conditions, there was 'no clinical benefit'. Age discrimination was suspected. Some hospitals refused life-saving treatment to people above a certain age; the proportion receiving it above age sixty fell by half at the height of the pandemic. This was not new, but it was exacerbated by Covid. A study by the Royal College of Surgeons and Age UK in 2012 stated that 'Whilst a patient's health needs-including conditions that could be treated by surgery-increase with age, planned (elective) surgery rates decline steadily for people as they grow older'. Hence, 'many older people are missing out on potentially life-saving treatment'. They also reported in 2014, based on analysis of surgery rates across England's 211 clinical commissioning groups for 6 procedures known to be effective for older people, that a number of CCGs operated on very few people over 75 for breast excision, gallstones, hernia or knee replacement, much restricting their lives and life spans.[44] During the pandemic their access to treatments was even more restricted. Even fewer women over 70 were treated for breast cancer, though more than three times as many women over 75 than aged 45–49 were diagnosed with the condition, as had long been the case. Deaths of poorer women in pregnancy and childbirth also increased further during the pandemic.

Poverty and inequality

In early 2020 Boris Johnson claimed that poverty had fallen since 2010, perhaps using the DWP's preferred 'absolute poverty' measure. He was reproved by the Office for Statistics Regulation for using statistics 'selectively, inaccurately and misleadingly'.[45] The pandemic and the cost of living crisis that followed deepened already severe inequalities. JRF found that by 2022 total poverty had fallen in Scotland, reaching 18 per cent compared with a 22 per cent average in England, 24 per cent in Wales, 17 per cent in Northern Ireland, but that the number of people in 'very deep' poverty (households with less than 40 per cent of the national median income) in Scotland had markedly increased over the previous two decades, as it had throughout the UK, where it rose from 37 per cent of those in poverty in 2002/2003 to 47 per cent in 2018/2019.[46] Most were single adults, from ethnic minorities, disabled or in low-paid work. In 2021 the Scottish government committed to developing a 'minimum income guarantee' setting a floor below which nobody could fall, when it became affordable.

The report of the ONS for the financial year ending 31 March 2020 stated that the richest 1 per cent of households in Great Britain (263,000 households) each had fortunes of over £3.6m. The poorest 10 per cent had £15,400 or less, almost half with more debts than assets. ONS calculated that the income inequality gap between richest and poorest had widened since 2010 to 36.3 per cent. The wealthiest 10 per cent held 45 per cent of all wealth in Great Britain, the bottom 50 per cent only 9 per cent. The investment bank

Credit Suisse calculated that in 2021 more than 258,000 UK people became millionaires, the total reaching a record 1.5 million. Its Global Wealth Report showed that the richest 0.00004 per cent of the world's adult population benefitted from 'almost an explosion of wealth' 'due to the surge in the value of financial assets during the Covid-19 pandemic'. The richest 1 per cent increased their share of the world's wealth for a second successive year from 44 per cent to 46 per cent. More than a third of the world's millionaires, 24.5 million, lived in the United States, with China in second place (10 per cent) followed by Japan (5.4 per cent), the United Kingdom (4.6 per cent) and France (4.5 per cent). UK adults had a median wealth of $142,000, putting it in ninth place in the world.[47]

The rich grew richer during Covid, while the poor became poorer. Households of white ethnicity were four times more likely to have wealth above £500,000 than Black Africans. Median wealth was 2.5 times higher in South-East England than in the North-East, mainly due to house prices. Big inequalities continued within each age group, among younger people fuelled by inheritance and parental support. The IFS estimated that in the early 2020s the children of homeowners were three times more likely to buy a home, assisted by funds from parents, than the growing numbers struggling to pay rising rents. Members of white families were more likely to receive these transfers than those of Black, Pakistani or Bangladeshi families.[48]

Where the head of household was aged 55 or above and in work, average household wealth was £553,400, while very many older people remained in poverty.[49] In September 2022 IFS reported that people aged 65+ taking new employment rose by 173,000 in the first quarter of 2022. They attributed this to the rising cost of living, with inflation at 9 per cent, while the state pension rose by only 3 per cent in 2022 combined with the rise in pension age to sixty-six in 2020, leaving many 65-year-olds in 'absolute poverty' when they could not keep or access employment for the additional year. Increasing numbers were unable to work to pension age due to poor health; the working-age benefits for which they qualified were inadequate. Occupational pensions declined in value as they ceased to be fixed to final salary, but to average working-life salary, for new pensioners. Women suffered from the lack of warning about the rising state pension age and most women received lower occupational pensions than men due to lower pay and working lives interrupted by caring responsibilities. On average women received £11,581 pa in occupational pensions, compared with the male average of £16,034.[50] In 2021 the Scottish Widows pensions company calculated that the average woman in her 20s could expect to have £100,000 less in her pension pot by retirement at age 68 than a man of the same age. The gap was widened by the pandemic which most affected incomes in work mainly performed by women and more women had their working lives interrupted by Covid-related responsibilities including for children.[51]

Further research by Rest Less, an online community advising workers over 50, showed that in 2022 446,601 were working past age 70, compared with 227,926 in 2021. Most were men but the rise was steepest among women, 66 per cent compared with 58 per cent. Most were struggling especially as prices rose, with inadequate savings. The CEO of Rest Less said that 'Employers have begun to recognize the valuable contribution of older individuals in the workplace and the huge benefits of multigenerational teams, though there is still a long way to go'.[52] ONS data showed that in 2023 there was a nine-year gap in life expectancy and an eighteen-year gap in healthy life expectancy between the most and least affluent 10 per cent.

Poverty was increased by termination of the UC uplift in October 2021. The government promised payment of at least £1,200 to low-income families in 2022, but this did not cover the cost of inflation in food and energy prices following the Russian invasion of Ukraine in early 2022 and the impact of Brexit on Britain's extensive food imports from Europe. In 2022 child poverty rose in Wales to 34 per cent from 31 per cent in 2019.England averaged 29 per cent, North-East England 38 per cent, Scotland and Northern Ireland 24 per cent. It continued to be highest in East London, in Tower Hamlets 51 per cent in 2020/2021, down from 56 per cent in 2019/2020, Bethnal Green and Bow 56 per cent.[53]

The Trussell Trust reported that 95 per cent of people using their food banks in early 2020 were 'destitute', unable to afford to eat or to stay warm. Sixty-two per cent of working-age people helped in 2020 were disabled, three times their proportion in the population. Eighteen per cent of households needing food were headed by single parents, overwhelmingly single mothers, more than twice their percentage in the population.[54] At their best these and other food banks, including one that former premier Gordon Brown helped establish in his former constituency in Fife, Scotland, continuing his mission to eliminate poverty, provided not only food but clothes, bedding, toiletries, nappies, and made essential repairs to homes and gadgets. In 2023 Brown described how 'Families with children are sleeping on the floor under one sheet. Four children are taking it in turns one night in four to sleep on a settee'.[55] This was not only true in Fife.

In April 2023 the Trussell Trust announced that in the past year it had donated a record 2,986,203 food parcels from its 1,646 outlets, 37 per cent more than in 2021–22, more than during the pandemic, as the cost of living drove more than 750,000 people to use them for the first time. One in five was in work. More than a million children lived in households receiving Trussell food parcels, more than ever before. Donations declined due to rising prices and Trussell spent £7.5m (£4.5m more than the previous year) replenishing stocks. The biggest increase was in North-East England, 54 per cent; in no region or nation of the UK was it below 28 per cent.[56] Simultaneously a UK-wide survey by the Warm Welcome campaign reported that more than half a million people visited 'warm rooms', otherwise known as 'warm banks', during the winter because they could not afford to heat their homes. These were an unprecedented, growing voluntary innovation due to high energy prices and an impoverished population.[57]

IFS calculated that 49 per cent of children in lone parent families were in poverty in March 2020, compared with 25 per cent in two-parent families, due to 'reductions in the real value of state benefits in the years from 2011 to 2019'. Lone-parent families were most affected by the benefit cap, the four-year freeze on benefits from 2016, the two-child limit and lowering of the age of the youngest child when single parents were required to enter employment.[58] Before 2008 they could claim income support until their youngest child was sixteen or nineteen if in full-time education. Following a series of changes the limit fell to age three. The high costs of childcare combined with inflation made things worse. JRF reported in 2022 from a survey of 4,000 low-income families that 70 per cent of lone parents skipped meals to feed their children, 50 per cent of dual parents. Forty per cent could not keep their homes warm compared with 31 per cent of two-parent families.[59] In April 2023, based on a survey of over 3,000 parents, CPAG calculated that the two-child limit for benefits was now affecting 1.5 million children, more than a million were living in poverty. Its effects were exacerbated as more families struggled to pay for energy and food. Parents skipped meals; children could not join school clubs and outings. Fifty-eight per cent of families affected had a working member. CPAG calculated that abolishing the limit would cost £1.3bn a year, lift 250,000 children out of poverty, leaving 850,000 in less profound poverty.[60] Childcare costs prevented many low-paid mothers from working. In 2023 the government announced expansion of the scheme allowing thirty hours per week of free childcare for children of working parents aged nine months to three years, but it would not be introduced until 2025 and the New Economics Foundation reported that richer families were almost six times more likely to benefit than poorer families in real need due to strict rules on parents employment and scarcity of care centres in poorer districts.[61]

An Oxford study in 2022 found that death rates of women in pregnancy, childbirth and early maternity were rising especially among women suffering multiple disadvantages, made worse by the rising cost of living and reduced access to NHS healthcare due to Covid and funding cuts. It concluded that the UK must invest more in health support.[62] In January 2023 the Care Quality Commission reported 'concerning decline' in maternity services over the past five years due to shortage of staff.[63] Child deaths in England, traced by the National Child Mortality Database, fell during the pandemic mainly due to decline in infectious illnesses among children who were not in school, but they rose in 2022 due to unsuitable accommodation, unheated homes and malnutrition.[64] The Database also showed that from 2020 death rates of white babies were stable but among Black and Black British infants deaths rose from just under 6 to 9 per 1000 live births. Among Asian and Asian British babies it rose by 17 per cent.[65] Other research found the rising cost of living damaged mental health throughout Great Britain, especially among those on lowest incomes.

Housing costs continued to be a major contributor to poverty and inequality. In April 2023 private landlords in England were earning £1.6bn annually in Housing Benefit, too often for high rents for 'non-decent' homes. London was worst affected with £500m in 'benefit' going on privately rented homes in disrepair, cold, damp, lacking modern facilities or failing to meet health and safety standards, according to analysis by City Hall described by the London mayor, Labour's Sadiq Khan, as a 'scandal'. He called on the government to reform the private rented sector as promised in their 2019 manifesto and empower him to raise standards and freeze rents. More than £250m a year was spent on similarly poor homes in North-West England. The 2021 census showed five million households renting from private landlords in England and Wales, up 28 per cent in a decade. There was also terrible overcrowding. The National Housing Federation found that in early 2023 310,000 children in England shared a bed with parents or siblings and two million – one in every six children – lived in cramped conditions. In an estimated

180,000 families, parents slept in a living room, bathroom, hallway or kitchen.[66] In 2022 Michael Gove, the minister responsible for housing and 'levelling up', announced plans for a bill to 'slash' the amount of Housing Benefit given to landlords letting non-decent homes and ban 'no fault' evictions since fear of eviction often prevented renters from complaining about substandard homes. But the Renters' Reform Bill, 2023, was much weaker than Gove suggested and in late 2023 it was unclear when it would be implemented. Meanwhile the Ministry of Justice reported that the number of no-fault evictions rose 38 per cent on the previous year.[67] Homelessness continued to rise. The Department of Levelling Up, Housing and Communities reported that in January–March 2023 the number of households in England in temporary accommodation, 104,510 including 131,370 children, was the largest since records began in 1998, 10 per cent more than in 2022.[68] Most were in hotels or bed-and-breakfasts, at considerable cost to local authorities. The main cause was eviction from a private tenancy following steep rent rises or landlords selling up due to increased mortgage interest. The numbers of people sleeping rough in London rose by 12 per cent – 4,000 people – in the twelve months to summer 2022.[69]

In February 2023 the JRF and Trussell Trust called for a permanent increase in UC because basic benefits were at least £140 a month below the real cost of food, energy, transport, internet use, toiletries and other essentials. The real value of benefits had fallen to a forty-year low following cuts and freezes, even for those claiming their maximum entitlement, from which many were excluded by caps and deductions. They estimated that raising benefits to cover all essentials would cost £20bn a year, which politicians were likely to resist, but it would pull 1.7 million people out of poverty including 600,000 children, and over time would bring savings by reducing demand for NHS and other services and benefits. They argued that benefits should always be linked to the actual cost of low-income households' basic needs. A 'government spokesperson' responded that work was the best way to raise income, again ignoring how many very poor people were working.[70]

Poverty continued to be exacerbated by non-take-up of means-tested benefits. In 2022/2023 Policy in Practice, a think tank working with councils, government and community organizations to analyse the impact of social policies, advise on policy change and help people access benefits to which they were entitled, reported that £19bn was unclaimed in UK each year. Families could be forgoing up to £4,000 a year. The main reasons were the complexity of the system, lack of awareness of eligibility and fear of being perceived as 'benefit scroungers'. They estimated that 1.3 million households did not take up UC, with £7.5bn unclaimed each year. Almost three million families failed to claim council tax relief (£2.9bn) and five million support for water, energy and broadband bills (£2bn). Around 850,000 pensioner households failed to claim £1.8bn a year in Pension Credit. Advisers helped a pensioner couple in Kent living on £280 a week secure an extra £222 a week in PC; a Coventry pensioner living on £55 a week was found to be eligible for a further £138 a week. Policy in Practice urged the government to provide positive messaging about benefits, so that people were not put off.[71] Nothing changed.

In 2023 the NCVO surveyed 7,000 adults and found the proportion participating in voluntary action, including raising funds, had fallen from 11 per cent to 6 per cent since 2018.[72] The CEO of NCVO suggested, 'People who were lifelong volunteers broke their habit during the pandemic and haven't yet got back to it.'[73] Many pre-pandemic volunteers were older people who were prevented from contact with others during lockdown. Younger people who took up volunteering because work was suspended during the pandemic had returned to work. The *UK Giving* report by the Charities Aid Foundation (CAF) found that most volunteers were still older people. Only 6–7 per cent of people aged 16–44 volunteered in 2021/2022, 5 per cent of 45- to 54-year-olds and at least 10 per cent of over 65s, though fewer than before the pandemic.[74]

The Institute for Government in late 2023 reported that key public services were performing worse than before the pandemic, having previously declined steadily since 2010, due to funding cuts. Worst affected were the NHS, where waiting lists for treatment stood at an unprecedented 7.75 million in England and were predicted to rise, and law courts which faced a backlog of almost 90,000 cases. Schools were experiencing a widening attainment gap between children from better- and worse-off homes, declining attendance and a shortage of trainee teachers. Childcare provision had been reduced, privatized and become more costly. Increasing numbers of libraries, day centres, luncheon clubs had closed, community transport cut, public conveniences mostly closed, waste collection reduced to fortnightly or less, grants to voluntary and community groups and support for rough sleepers cut.[75] There was no sign of likely improvement.

Sad news kept pouring in. The government attempted to help consumers with rising fuel costs. In early September 2023 campaigners from the End Fuel Poverty Coalition and National Energy Action (NEA) told the parliamentary Energy Security and Net Zero Select Committee that excess winter deaths caused by living in cold, damp homes climbed by almost 50 per cent in the previous winter after more than one million vulnerable households missed out on energy bill support provided by the government but inadequately administered and publicized: 4,706 deaths compared with 3,186 the previous year despite relatively mild weather. The CEO of NEA said that vulnerable households had been forced to turn off their heating or not wash or eat due to 'impossible levels of debt', leading to 'an explosion in the mental health crisis'. More than £400m in government funds earmarked to help the vulnerable pay their energy bills was unspent. The head of energy at Citizens' Advice said it had received almost 130,000 calls for emergency help, 'up significantly from the previous winter' and expected numbers to rise further in the following winter. The previous year's 'string' of government schemes had failed to reach all intended households: *c.* 750,000 households eligible for the £400 winter energy bill discount had not received it because they were not billed directly by an energy supplier, missing out on over £300m. They included Gypsy and Romany communities and those in multiple occupancy households. About 300,000 homes eligible for the £150 energy bill rebate through the warm home discount scheme missed out on £45m. A total of 250,000 households using prepayment meters missed £98m in support vouchers.[76]

Conclusion

The UK suffered more than comparable countries from poverty and poor economic growth following Austerity, Brexit and the pandemic. The Resolution Foundation reported in 2022 that, following the financial crash, from 2010 incomes in France grew by 34 per cent, in Germany 27 per cent, while in the UK they fell by 2 per cent, because Cameron and Osborne made cuts at a time of recession when they could have invested. In Europe only Greece and Cyprus did worse. In 2016 the UK economy was 90 per cent the size of Germany's, by 2022, 70 per cent. Since Brexit, trade with the EU had fallen by 16 per cent. In July 2022 the average British household was £8,800 poorer than its equivalents in France, Germany, Australia, Canada and the Netherlands, particularly due to Britain's relatively low economic growth combined with its greater inequality. The top 10 per cent of British households were richer than those in many European countries, the poorest fifth were more than 20 per cent poorer than their equivalents in France and Germany.[77] In April 2023 the IMF estimated that the UK economy was the weakest in the G7 and among the weakest in the G20. However, towards the end of the year they were predicting that Germany would be weakest in the G7, 7 per cent below its pre-pandemic level, as industrial production fell and energy costs rose. In August 2023 the National Institute for Economic and Social Research forecast that the UK was 'heading towards five years of low economic growth'. They calculated that the poorest tenth of the population would need an income boost of £4,000 pa to achieve the living standards they had experienced in 2019. The poorest households would be 17 per cent worse off than in 2019, the richest 5 per cent worse off.[78] The Resolution Foundation saw no sign of hopeful government plans to strengthen the economy or end the growth of poverty and insecurity, a view shared by the CBI and the Commons Treasury Select Committee, both of whom urged policy change.

CHAPTER 15
THE FUTURE?

Poverty in the UK is now at similar levels to 1900, with similar causes: too much insecure, low-paid employment, inadequate public support for people suffering involuntary deprivation, poor housing and poor public services. Surveys then described starving, ill-clad children, parents skipping meals to feed them, families sleeping on floors in desperately overcrowded homes, their health endangered by damp, with minimal access to healthcare – all disturbingly similar to the revelations of surveys in the twenty-first century. Free healthcare has not dwindled to anything like the levels of a century ago, but it has become harder to access, including dental care.

Such conditions did not persist from then to now. Their decline was gradual and relatively recent, and it must surely not persist in a now much richer, though similarly unequal, nation. A major difference between then and now is that, at the time of Booth and Rowntree's surveys, state welfare provision had always been very limited. Concern at their findings led to effective demands for its gradual growth leading to improved economic and social conditions. Now, as a result, state services are still more substantial than in the 1900s, but they have undergone severe decline since the 1980s, especially since 2010 – another major cause of severe poverty. Another disturbing contrast between the effects of the poverty surveys of Booth and Rowntree and those of today is the absence now of comparable levels of public concern and fewer widely reported proposals from influential sources of changes to eliminate these terrible conditions. Conservative politicians advocate economic growth and incentivizing people to work as the answers, overlooking the large and still growing inequalities been rich and poor, the numbers of hard-working people in severe poverty, and reasons, including poor access to healthcare and costly childcare, why many do not work. They do not appear to share the recognition which became influential then that state measures to improve health and welfare can facilitate economic growth by building a stronger, fitter more committed workforce, despite the fact that, now as then, the UK economy is declining relative to its competitors. Labour promises stricter regulation and improvement of the labour market, construction of good, affordable housing, improvement of the benefit system and a new race equality act should it win the election due in 2024. This is a hopeful sign since over the past century Labour has been the main promoter of improved state welfare, though it is understandably cautious about policy details due to uncertainty about the state of the economy if it takes over. And another difference between then and now is that then various forms of socialism were growing internationally, while now right-wing politics, hostile to redistribution from rich to poor, are much stronger and very influential in the UK as elsewhere. It is also important that the politics of comparable countries with more favourable social and economic conditions are determined by proportional representation voting systems, leading to co-operation, coalition and compromise, however reluctant, between competing political parties. In the UK, with its first-past-the-post voting system, extreme party policy divisions over economic and social policies, lack of policy continuity between successive governments and, hence, effective long-term planning have been evident, and harmful, through the past century. There is no sign that this will change.

The response to revelations of poverty in the 1900s included demands for state-led reform from trade unions, the Labour Party, women's groups and other voluntary organizations. Now the unions and NGOs, including CPAG, Shelter, Age UK and many more, and women's organizations, support and propose reforms but have much less influence upon government. The first key measures of state welfare by the post-1906 Liberal government followed the Liberals' success in the 1906 election facilitated by their secret alliance with Labour, a collaboration which seems unlikely to be repeated. This led to the gradual expansion of state welfare and reduction, though not elimination, of poverty, stimulated by two world wars, moving faster after 1945, peaking in the 1970s, as described in the preceding chapters.

Is it realistically possible to reverse the decline of the Welfare State that followed and the revival of poverty since the 1980s? Thomas Picketty asks, after studying the emergence of what he calls the 'social state' in most high-income countries and its subsequent late twentieth-century decline: 'can we imagine a twenty-first century in which capitalism will be transcended in a more peaceful and lasting way or must we simply await the next crisis or the next war?'[1] He concludes convincingly that 'a market economy based on private property if left to itself . . . contains powerful forces . . . which are potentially threatening to democratic societies and to the values of social justice on which they are based'.[2] The very rich 'never fail to defend their interests'.[3] He points out how in many countries, including the UK, the 'explosion of high incomes' from the 1980s increased the political influence of very high earners because of their interest in keeping taxes low and ability to 'use their windfall to finance political parties, pressure groups and thinktanks'.[4] Low taxation necessitates minimal state provision of services and regulation of the economy, urged also by the right-wing press and social media, whose influence also grew from the 1980s, and it remains prominent in Conservative statements and policies in 2023.

So are there realistic options for reversal of the current situation? If so, how quickly could it be achieved and what should it entail? Previous chapters have shown that major drivers of the rise of poverty since the 1980s have been abandonment of labour market regulation and the undermining of trade unions, reducing their power to negotiate on behalf of workers, combined with government cuts to welfare benefits, services and taxes. The post-1945 Labour government not only instituted the modern Welfare State but also raised taxes and regulated the economy more closely than before, controlling wages, prices and supplies, achieving full employment for the first time in peacetime and improved economic growth. Full employment continued to the 1970s, and many labour market controls survived or were revived and extended by New Labour in the early 2000s, following modifications by Conservative governments, which intensified after 2010. It has been estimated that if in 2023 'the same share of GDP was paid out in wages as in 1976 the average working-age household would have an extra £9,744 a year'.[5] In 1976 the unions were at their peak and negotiated agreements with the Labour government, maintaining work conditions and the real value of wages at a time of financial uncertainty and inflation, supported by sound public services and benefits. Poverty was never eliminated but it was massively lower than in the 1980s and since 2010.

State welfare and the regulated labour market were shattered by Margaret Thatcher's governments in the 1980s at a time when anti-state, finance-driven neoliberalism was growing internationally. She believed that economic growth could be fostered by instituting a 'flexible labour market', freeing employers from controls over working conditions while crippling the unions and cutting public spending. Conditions improved somewhat when New Labour from 1997 introduced the UK's first minimum wage and adopted some EU-inspired improvements to work conditions as well as improved public services. But under Conservative governments from 2010 the value of the minimum wage (never high) declined and insecurity at work increased to levels similar to those described by Booth and Rowntree, in what was now known as the 'gig economy'. Government regulation of the workplace severely declined and poverty grew, owing much to extreme policy differences between the ruling parties.

An obvious starting point for the elimination of working poverty in the twenty-first century is to establish and enforce a genuine living wage which covers all the essential needs of households, supervised and adjusted by a body like the Low Pay Commission, established by New Labour for this purpose when it introduced the minimum wage, but no longer effective. It should be supported by effective regulation of work conditions, including eliminating zero hours contracts and fake self-employment, ensuring that all employees have full rights to sickness, redundancy and other benefits and a regular working week with fixed hours that employers are required to observe. These improvements should not be costly to the government, apart from the limited costs of regulation. Employers will no doubt claim they will be ruined, as they did when the minimum wage was introduced, with no evident losses. Such pressures can be, and have been for several decades, very effective in influencing Conservative policies.

Households must be further supported by high-quality public services, including for health, education and transport, all of which would also benefit the economy. Households vary in size, age and gender structure, have diverse needs and costs vary regionally and across the countries of the UK, whose policies have diverged increasingly since devolution. Housing costs are a major cause of poverty, especially in England. This can be resolved by increasing the stock of local authority housing at affordable rents, devastated by Thatcher's sale of council houses, and reintroducing quality controls, rent controls and security of tenure for private tenants, also eliminated in the 1980s. This requires replenishing local authority funds, restoration of their control overspending and their capacity to respond to local needs, also severely diminished since the 1980s, indeed leaving a substantial number of authorities, large (including Birmingham) and small, in bankruptcy in 2023. Local authorities themselves demand such changes. Reform could be funded, at least partially, by revaluation of council tax for the first time in England since it was instituted in 1993, raising the tax on higher value properties together with a system of redistribution between richer and poorer authorities. This would also assist the very necessary return to public ownership and funding and improvement of much deteriorated essential services, including social care for children and older and disabled adults.

Adequate child, disability and other benefits can help to cover household needs, plus public provision of affordable childcare at the level of other high-income countries to enable more parents to work, which England lags far behind. These reforms would raise government costs as, still more, will other essential reforms including restoring standards of health and education services and raising state pensions for the first time to an adequate level. But improved health, education, social security, social care and childcare, together with improved pay and working conditions, can be expected to increase the numbers and quality of workers, contributing to economic growth and tax revenue. And funding is potentially available from redistributive wealth taxes and 'windfall taxes' on high profit businesses. Picketty points out that the frequent objection that 'high taxes will make top earners flee the country' conflicts with all international evidence.[6]

The reform proposals suggested so far revive policies which contributed successfully, if slowly, to the rise of state welfare and the decline of poverty in the past. Are there possible new approaches? Various proposals have been made in recent years. One suggestion is for a Universal Basic Income (UBI), a regular payment by government to all adult citizens with potential to achieve rapid change, designed to alleviate need and replace payment of other benefits, removing the need for costly administration of the latter. Similar ideas have been proposed in Britain since the eighteenth century, including the Webbs' campaign in the 1900s for a 'national minimum', and they have the advantage of eliminating means-tested benefits with their associated stigma and inefficiency. As state welfare has declined and insecurity grown internationally since the 1980s UBI has attracted interest in most high-income countries and inspired experiments in Finland, India, South Korea. Their outcomes indicate that UBI was generally wisely spent by recipients on necessities, diminishing poverty, increasing independence, hard work and good health, not wasted, as critics fear. Wales is currently (2023) paying an unconditional £1,600 a month for two years to young people leaving care, with outcomes as yet uncertain. The only place to introduce such a scheme long-term is Alaska where since 1982 annual payments have been made to everyone who has lived there for a year and intends to stay, funded by royalties from oil companies and state oil revenues. In 1980 Alaska was the most unequal state in the United States, in 2018 the most equal. Implementation of UBI has been resisted elsewhere due to the cost above all, despite likely savings on other benefits, and fears that it would disincentivize work, which the pilot schemes appear to contradict.[7]

A possible cheaper, modified form of UBI could be provision of benefits fixed at the same level as an adequate 'living wage', which might not cover all in need but would protect most from poverty, especially if it was fairly, not harshly, administered.

A similar proposal by the New Economics Foundation, a moderate left-of-centre UK think tank, recommends a 'Social Guarantee'. This aims to guarantee everyone's right to life's essentials, including education, healthcare, a decent home, food, energy, social care and childcare. It includes three key elements: a living wage paying adequate rates for secure jobs with good hours and trade union recognition; a living income provided by a reformed social security system delivering a decent quality of life with a sufficient minimum income and supporting those who can into work; universal, high-quality services including free healthcare and education, affordable housing built to green standards, social care and childcare affordable or free when needed, all funded by a combination of national and local taxation. All the proposals incorporate consultation with users to ensure high standards and co-operation in administration with local authorities who are best informed about local needs.[8]

There is no sign of a prospective government taking up this or any similar proposal and the influence of the very rich on the Conservative Party, and to some degree the Labour Party, opposing such reforms, remains strong, with little sign yet of strong competing pressures comparable with those in the 1900s. There were growing numbers of strikes about pay and work conditions especially in the public sector, including by teachers, doctors, nurses and railway workers, in 2022/2023, but with limited success, and there is little sign of government policy changing.

However, there is an encouraging growth of proposals for change from well-informed independent bodies. In February 2023, in response to continuing high and rising poverty levels, the JRF together with the Trussell Trust advocated a relatively modest proposal that the government provide an 'essentials guarantee' granting needy claimants legal entitlement to the 'essentials' of life, including food and energy, with the level of benefits set by an independent body. The JRF estimated that, at current prices, the standard allowance should be £120 per week for a single person, compared with the current £85 on UC. This won the support of more than twenty health bodies including the BMA and the Royal College of Nursing, all concerned about the impact of poverty on health. The Liberal Democrats agreed in a pre-conference manifesto that that the level of UC should be decided by an independent body. The *Guardian*, which reported the proposal in an editorial, argued that raising the local housing allowance (frozen since 2020) and removing the two-child benefit cap were arguably more urgent priorities, but that the advocacy of such 'bold longer-term ideas' by civil society organizations was a 'relief'. It also reported survey findings that most respondents believed benefit claimants deserved to afford more than basic food and utilities, including such additional comforts as haircuts, celebrations and internet connections, suggesting some popular support, at least on the centre-left, for a more generous benefit system.[9]

The Poverty Strategy Commission which aims optimistically to forge a national political consensus on reducing poverty, and includes former ministers from the three main parties, argues in a report published in September 2023 that millions of low-income families are 'surviving not living' and are forced to endure unacceptable levels of poverty.[10] The Commission was established in 2021 and chaired by Philippa Stroud, former adviser to Iain Duncan Smith when he was Minister of State for Work and Pensions,

2020–16, driven by concern at the high and rising levels of poverty. Former ministers involved include Tory former welfare secretary Stephen Crabb, former Liberal Democrat coalition minister David Laws and Labour former Treasury minister Stephen Timms. Academics and think tanks to the left and right of centre are also members, including the New Economics Foundation, and charities including Trussell Trust.[11] The Commission estimates that increasing hardship affects six million families and that it would cost £36b to provide them with £6,000 a year in benefit and wage rises plus investment to lower housing and energy costs and improve health services. Their current recommendations include a 5 per cent uplift in benefits, to rise with inflation, with provision for housing and childcare costs, the additional costs of disability and energy and travel costs, all fundable by higher taxes. The Commission was still in February 2024 considering and consulting on full proposals, seeking to put poverty back on the political agenda before the general election. It is concerned at the lack of urgency from the two main parties over the scale and nature of poverty and by the failure to offer adequate protection to the poorest. It is perhaps a hopeful sign that proposals for state action to relieve poverty are coming forward increasingly, including from the political centre-right, but it is hard to be optimistic about change in the near future, as Picketty also is not from his much wider international historical survey. A Labour election victory in 2024 might arouse some hope. Action is urgently needed to relieve the intolerable conditions in which too many people are barely surviving in a rich country, but when and how it might emerge remains unclear.

NOTES

Chapter 2

1. Robert Humphreys, *Sin, Organized Charity and the Poor Law in Victorian England* (London: Macmillan, 1995).

2. Deborah Dwork, *War is Good for Babies and Other Young Children: A History of the Infant and Child Welfare Movement in England, 1898–1918.* (London: Routledge, 1987).

3. Patricia Hollis, *Ladies Elect. Women in English Local Government, 1865–1914* (Oxford: Oxford University Press, 1987).

4. E. P. Hennock, *The Origin of the Welfare State in England and Germany, 1850–1914* (Cambridge: Cambridge University Press, 2007).

5. Quoted in Jose Harris, *Private Lives, Public Spirit. Britain 1870–1914* (London: Penguin, 1994), p. 199.

6. Parliamentary Papers, 1904, (Cd2175) XXXII quoted in J. Burnett, *Plenty and Want* (Aldershot: Scolar Press, 1978), p. 272.

7. Pat Thane, 'Government and Society in England and Wales, 1750–1914', in *The Cambridge Social History of Britain 1750–1950*, Vol. 3, ed. F. M. L. Thompson (Cambridge: Cambridge University Press, 1990), pp. 1–62.

8. Charles Booth, *Life and Labour of the People. Vol 1. East London* (London and Edinburgh: Williams and Norgate, 1889), p. 6.

9. Ibid., p. 598.

10. Charles Booth, *Life and Labour in London*, First series, Vol. 1 (London: Macmillan, 1901), pp. 166–7.

11. Ibid., 2nd series, Industry, Vol. 5, pp. 294–5.

12. Ibid.

13. Booth, *Life and Labour, Vol. 1. East London*, p. 591.

14. T. S. and M. B. Simey, *Charles Booth, Social Scientist* (Oxford: Oxford University Pess, 1960), p. 157.

15. Norman and Jeanne MacKenzie (eds), *The Diary of Beatrice Webb*, Vol. 1 (London: Virago, 1986), p. 238.

16. Ann Oakley, *Forgotten Wives. How Women Get Written Out of History* (University of Bristol: Policy Press, 2021), pp. 25–64.

17. Booth, *East London*, pp. 37–50, 146.

18. Ibid., pp. 37–9.

19. Ibid., p. 133.

20. Pat Thane, *Old Age in English History. Past Experiences, Present Issues* (Oxford: Oxford University Press, 2000), pp. 194–212.

21. Ibid., pp. 173–7.

22. Booth, *East London*, p. 33.

23. J. H. Veit-Wilson, 'Paradigms of Poverty: A Rehabilitation of B. S. Rowntree', in David Englander and Rosemary O 'Day (eds), *Retrieved Riches. Social investigation in Britain, 1840–1914* (Aldershot: Scolar Press/Buckingham the Open University, 1995), pp. 201–40.

24. B. Seebohm Rowntree, *Poverty. A Study of Town Life* (London: Nelson & Sons, 1901), p. 17.

25. Ibid., p. 18.

26. Letter from Booth, July 1901, Rowntree, *Poverty*, pp. 355–6.

27. Rowntree, *Poverty*, p. xix.

28. Ibid., p. 117ff.

29. Ibid., pp. 40–1.

30. Ibid., pp. 85–6.

31. Ibid., p. 71.

32. Ibid.

33. Ibid., pp. 87, 188–226.

34. Ibid., p. 73.

35. Ibid., p. 74.

36. Ibid., p. 83.

37. Ibid., pp. 82–4.

38. pp. 167–8.

39. pp. 436–43.

40. pp. 150–1.

41. I. Gazeley and A. Newell, 'Rowntree Revisited: Poverty in Britain, 1900', *Explorations in Economic History* 37, no. 2 (2000): pp. 174–88.

42. Veit-Wilson, 'Paradigms', pp. 213–17.

43. Rowntree, *Poverty*, p. 355.

44. Ibid., p. 261.

45. Ibid., p. 281.

46. Ibid., p. 360.

47. Ibid., p. 36.

48. Mark Freeman *Social Investigation and Rural England, 1870–1914* (Martlesham: Boydell Press, 2000).

49. A. L. Bowley and A. R. Burnett-Hurst, *Livelihood and Poverty: A Study in the Economic Conditions of Working-Class Households in Northampton, Warrington, Stanley and Reading* (London: G. Bell, 1915).

50. Maud Pember Reeves, *Round about a Pound a Week* (London: Virago, 1979, reprinted), pp. 146–58.

51. Ibid., p. 146.

52. Thomas Piketty, *Capital in the Twenty-First Century* (Cambridge, MA: Harvard University Press, 2017), p. 326.

53. Dwork, *War is Good*, p. 93ff.

54. Martin Daunton, *Trusting Leviathan. The Politics of Taxation in Britain, 1799–1914* (Cambridge: Cambridge University Press, 2001), pp. 330–74. Picketty, *Capital*, p. 630ff.

55. Thane, *Old Age*, pp. 216–35.

56. George K. Behlmer, *Child Abuse and Moral Reform in England, 1870–1908* (Stanford: Stanford University Press, 1982).

57. Ibid., pp. 78–118.

58. Daunton, *Trusting Leviathan*, pp. 361–5.

59. Ibid., p. 35.

60. William Beveridge, *Unemployment: A Problem of Industry* (London: Longmans, 1909); Jose Harris, *William Beveridge. A Biography*, revised edition (Oxford: Oxford University Press, 1997), pp. 138–97.

61. William Ashworth, *The Genesis of Modern British Town Planning* (London: Routledge, 1954, reprinted 1968).

Chapter 3

1. Picketty, *Capital*, p. 597.

2. Ibid., p. 641.

3. Richard Roberts, *Saving the City. The Great Financial Crisis of 1914* (Oxford: Oxford University Press, 2013).

4. Sylvia Pankhurst, *The Home Front* (London: Cresset, 1987, reprinted 1932), p. 19.

5. Susan Pedersen, *Family, Dependence and the Origins of the Welfare State. Britain and France 1914–1945* (Cambridge: Cambridge University Press,1993), pp. 108–15.

6. Pat Thane and Tanya Evans, *Sinners? Scroungers? Saints? Unmarried Motherhood in England in the Twentieth Century* (Oxford: Oxford University Press, 2012), pp. 11–13.

7. Thane, *Old Age*, pp. 302–4.

8. J. M. Winter, *The Great War and the British People* (London: Macmillan, 1985), p. 236.

9. Pedersen, *Family Dependence*, p. 112.

10. Susan Pedersen, *Eleanor Rathbone and the Politics of Conscience* (New Haven: Yale University Press, 2004).

11. B. R. Mitchell and P. Deane, *Abstract of British Historical Statistics* (Cambridge: Cambridge University Press, 1962), p. 65.

12. A. L. Bowley, *Prices and Wages in the UK, 1914–20* (Oxford: Oxford University Press, 1921).

13. Joseph Melling, *Rent Strikes. Peoples' Struggle for Housing in West Scotland,1890–1916* (Edinburgh: Polygon, 1983).

14. Sean Damer, 'State, Class and Housing: Glasgow 1875–1919', in *Housing, Social Policy and the State*, ed. Joseph Melling (London: Croom Helm, 1980), p. 93.

15. Joseph Melling, 'Clydeside Housing and the Evolution of State Rent Control', in Melling, *Housing*; Melling, *Rent Strikes*; David Englander, *Landlord and Tenant* (Oxford: Oxford University Press, 1983), Ch 10–12.

16. Arthur Marwick, *The Deluge. British Society and the First World War* (London: Pelican, 1967), p. 133.

Notes

17. Winter, *Great War*, pp. 108–15.

18. Bernard Waites, *A Class Society at War: England, 1914–1918* (Oxford: Berg, 1987).

19. Carol Dyhouse, 'Women Students and the London Medical Schools, 1914–1939: The Anatomy of a Masculine Culture', in Dyhouse, *Students*, pp. 137–55.

20. Avner Offer, *The First World War: An Agrarian Interpretation* (Oxford: Oxford University Press, 1991).

21. Martin Daunton, *Just Taxes. The Politics of Taxation in Britain, 1914–1979* (Cambridge: Cambridge University Press, 2002), pp. 47–9.

22. Mitchell and Deane, *Historical Statistics*, pp. 394, 398.

23. Daunton, *Just Taxes*, p. 36.

24. Thane, *Old Age*, pp. 309–11; Winter, *Great War*, pp. 189–203.

25. Winter, *Great War*, pp. 48–64.

26. Thane and Evans, *Sinners?*, pp. 13–18.

27. Margaret Llewelyn Davies (ed.), *Maternity. Letters from Working Women* (London: G. Bell, 1915, reprinted Virago, 1978), pp. 23–4.

28. Ibid., pp. 141, 148.

29. P. Grant, 'Voluntarism and the Impact of the First World War', in *The Ages of Voluntarism. How We Got to the Big Society*, ed. Matthew Hilton and James McKay (London: British Academy/Oxford University Press, 2011), pp. 27–46.

30. Sandra Stanley Holton, *Feminism and Democracy. Women's Suffrage and Reform Politics in Britain, 1900–1918* (Cambridge: Cambridge University Press, 1986), p. 130.

31. Speech in Wolverhampton, 24 November 1918.

32. Caitriona Beaumont, *Housewives and Citizens. Domesticity and the Women's Movement in England, 1928–64* (Manchester: Manchester University Press, 2013).

33. Pat Thane, *The Foundations of the Welfare State*, 2nd edn (London: Longman, 1996), pp. 130–2.

34. Thane, *Old Age*, pp. 311–18.

35. Mark Swenarton, *Homes Fit for Heroes* (London: Heinemann, 1981).

36. Harris, *Beveridge*, pp. 246–56.

37. Thane, *Foundations*, pp. 141–3.

38. Winter, *Great War*, pp. 273–8.

39. Board of Trade, *Report on the State of Employment in the United Kingdom in July 1918*, p. 1.

Chapter 4

1. Justin Davis Smith, *100 Years of NCVO and Voluntary Action. Idealists and Realists* (London: Palgrave Macmillan, 2019).

2. Thane and Evans, *Sinners?*, pp. 29–53.

3. Kate Bradley, *Poverty, Philanthropy and the State. Charities and the Working Classes in London, 1918–1979* (Manchester: Manchester University Press, 2009), and *Lawyers for the Poor. Legal Advice, Voluntary Action and Citizenship in England, 1890–1990* (Manchester: Manchester University Press, 2019).

4. R. Mortimore and A. Blick (eds), *Butler's British Political Facts* (London: Palgrave Macmillan, 2018), p. 666.

5. Alastair J. Reid, *United We Stand. A History of Britain's Trade Unions* (London: Allen Lane, 2004), pp. 182–5.

6. P. A. Ryan, '"Poplarism" 1894–1930', in *The Origins of British Social Policy*, ed. Pat Thane (London: Croom Helm, 1978), pp. 56–83.

7. W. R. Garside, *British Unemployment 1919–1939. A Study in Public Policy* (Cambridge: Cambridge University Press, 1990).

8. Adrian Bingham, *Family Newspapers. Sex, Private Life and the Popular Press, 1918–1978* (Oxford: Oxford University Press, 2009).

9. Hollis, *Ladies Elect*, p. 486.

10. Pat Thane, 'What Difference Did the Vote Make?', in *Women, Privilege and Power. British Politics, 1750 to the Present*, ed. Amanda Vickery (Stanford: Stanford University Press, 2001), pp. 253–88; Helen Glew, *Gender, Rhetoric and Regulation. Women's Work in the Civil Service and the London County Council, 1900–1955* (Manchester: Manchester University Press, 2016).

11. A. H. Halsey and J. Webb (eds), *Twentieth Century British Social Trends* (London: Macmillan, 1999), p. 488.

12. Ibid., p. 487.

13. Melling, *Housing, Social Policy and the State*, p. 116.

14. Ryan, 'Poplarism', pp. 75–6.

15. Laurence Goldman, *The Life of RH Tawney. Socialism and History* (London: Bloomsbury Academic, 2014).

16. *Report of the Consultative Committee to the Board of Education on the Education of the Adolescent* (London: HMSO, 1927).

17. Paul Johnson, 'The Employment and Retirement of Older Men in England and Wales, 1881–1981', *Economic History Review* 47, no. 1 (1994): pp. 106–28.

18. Thane, *Old Age*, pp. 318–23.

19. Ibid., pp. 323–7.

20. Stuart Ball, 'Baldwin, Stanley, (1867–1947)', *Oxford Dictionary of National Biography*, online edition, January 2011. www.oxforddnb.com.

21. J. Skelley (ed.), *1926. The General Strike* (London: Lawrence and Wishart, 1976).

22. Thane, *Foundations*, p. 174.

23. M. A. Crowther, *The Workhouse System 1834–1929* (London: Batsford, 1981), pp. 88–112.

24. Ibid.

25. Anne Crowther, *British Social Policy 1914–1939* (London: Macmillan, 1988), pp. 40–6.

26. Thane and Evans, *Sinners?*, pp. 29–53.

27. Crowther, *Social Policy*, pp. 52–6.

28. Ibid., p. 15.

29. A. B. Atkinson and S. Morelli, www.chartbookofeconomicinequality, 2014 (accessed 23 November 2023).

30. Ross McKibbin, *Classes and Cultures, England, 1918–1951* (Oxford: Oxford University Press, 1998), pp. 37–40.

31. Guy Routh, *Occupation and Pay in Great Britain, 1906–1979* (London: Macmillan, 1980), pp. 120–1.

32. Noreen Branson, *Britain in the Nineteen Twenties* (London: Weidenfeld and Nicolson, 1975), p. 92.

33. D. Caradog Jones (ed.), *The Social Survey of Merseyside* (Liverpool: Liverpool University Press and Hodder and Stoughton, 1934).

34. Ian Gazeley, *Poverty in Britain, 1900–1965* (London: Palgrave Macmillan, 2003), p. 82.

Chapter 5

1. John Davis, *A History of Britain, 1885–1939* (London: Macmillan, 1999), p. 187.

2. Mitchell and Deane, *British Historical Statistics*, p. 66.

3. Dulcie M. Groves, 'Women and Occupational Pensions,1870–1983' (PhD thesis, King's College, London, 1986).

4. *Report of the Committee on Pensions for Unmarried Women* (HMSO, 1939), Cmd 5991.

5. Claire Debenham, *Birth Control and the Rights of Women. Post-suffrage Feminism in the Early Twentieth Century* (London: IB Tauris, 2014).

6. K. O. Morgan, 'Addison, Christopher First Viscount Addison, 1869–1951)', *ODNB*, 2004, online edition, January 2011, https://www.oxforddnb.com.

7. David Marquand, *Ramsey MacDonald* (London: Jonathan Cape, 1977), p. 610.

8. Dudley Baines, 'Recovery from Depression', in *Twentieth Century Britain. Economic, Social and Cultural Change*, ed. Paul Johnson (London: Longman, 1994), p. 195; F. Capie, *Depression and Protectionism in Britain Between the Wars* (London: Routledge, 1983, reprinted 2013).

9. N. Branson and M. Heinemann, *Britain in the Nineteen Thirties* (London: Weidenfeld and Nicolson, 1971), pp. 187–9.

10. Davis, *History of Britain*, p. 213.

11. Ibid., p. 214.

12. Ibid., p. 215; Garside, *British Unemployment*, pp. 66–87.

13. John Bew, *Citizen Clem. A Biography of Attlee* (Portsmouth: Riverrun, 2016).

14. Thane, *Foundations*, p. 171.

15. Ian Gazeley and Pat Thane, 'Patterns of Visibility: Unemployment in Britain during the 19th and 20th centuries', in *Forming Nation, Framing Welfare*, ed. Gail Lewis (London: Routledge, 1998), pp. 181–226.

16. Ann Oakley, *A Critical Woman. Barbara Wootton, Social Science and Public Policy in the Twentieth Century* (London: Bloomsbury, 2011).

17. Davis, *History of Britain*, p. 219.

18. Thane, *Old Age*, p. 331.

19. J. Stevenson, *Social Conditions in Britain between the Wars* (London: Penguin, 1977), Ch. 3.

20. Melling, *Housing*, pp. 127–33.

21. Gazeley, *Poverty*, p. 74.

22. Ibid., pp. 74–5.

23. Thane, *Old Age*, pp. 436–8.

24. Margery Spring Rice, *Working Class Wives. Their Health and Conditions* (London: Penguin 1939, reprinted London: Virago, 1981).

25. Ibid., p. 86.

26. Debenham, *Birth Control*.

27. Ibid.; Beaumont, *Housewives and Citizens*, pp. 81–7.

28. S. Szreter and K. Fisher, *Sex Before the Sexual Revolution: Intimate Life in England, 1918–1963* (Cambridge: Cambridge University Press, 2010).

29. I. Loudon, *Death in Childbirth. An International Study of Maternal Care and Maternal Mortality, 1800–1950* (Oxford: Oxford University Press, 1994), pp. 240–6.

30. Barbara Brookes, *Abortion in England, 1900–1967* (London: Routledge, 1988), p. 27.

31. Ibid., p. 43.

32. Ibid., p. 51.

33. C. L. Mowat, *Britain Between the Wars* (London: Methuen, 1972), pp. 512–13.

34. Pat Thane, 'The Debate on the Declining Birth-Rate in Britain: The "Menace" of an Ageing Population, 1920s–1950s', *Continuity and Change* 5, no. 20 (1990): pp. 283–305.

35. Ina Zweiniger-Bargielowska, *Managing the Body. Beauty, Health and Fitness in Britain, 1880–1939* (Oxford: Oxford University Press, 2011).

36. Thane, *Foundations*, p. 177ff.

37. B. S. Rowntree, *Poverty and Progress* (London: Longmans, Green and Co, 1941), pp. 29–30.

38. Gazeley, *Poverty*, p. 67.

39. Rowntree, *Poverty*, p. 126.

40. Ibid., pp. 108–9.

41. Gazeley, *Poverty*, pp. 86–7.

42. John Boyd Orr *Food, Health and Income* (London: Macmillan, revised 1937), p. 7.

43. Mowat, *Britain*, p. 461.

44. Gazeley, *Poverty*, p. 67.

45. J. Kuczynski, *Hunger and Work* (London: Lawrence and Wishart, 1938), p. 26.

46. Thane, *Foundations*, p. 204.

47. A. B. Atkinson, *The Economics of Inequality* (Oxford: Clarendon Press, 1975), p. 134.

48. A. L. Bowley (ed.), *Studies in the National Income 1924–1938* (Cambridge: Cambridge University Press, 1944).

Chapter 6

1. R. M. Titmuss, *Problems of Social Policy. History of the Second World War, UK Civil Series* (London: HMSO and Longmans, Green Co, 1950); Maggie Andrews, *Women and Evacuation in the Second World War. Femininity, Domesticity and Motherhood* (London: Bloomsbury, 2019); John Welshman, *Churchill's Children: The Evacuation Experience in Wartime Britain* (Oxford: Oxford University Press, 2010).

2. Titmuss, *Problems*, pp. 142–82.

3. James Hinton, *Women, Social Leadership and the Second World War. Continuities of Class* (Oxford: Oxford University Press, 2002), pp. 20–2.

4. Penny Summerfield, 'The "levelling of class"', in *War and Social Change. British Society in the Second World War*, ed. Harold. L. Smith (Manchester: Manchester University Press, 1986), pp. 196–8.

5. Anne Hardy, *Health and Social Medicine in Britain since 1860* (London: Palgrave, 2001), p. 124.

6. Daunton, *Just Taxes*, pp. 179–80.

7. Mortimore and Blick, *Facts*, p. 647.

8. Paul Addison, *The Road to 1945* (London: Jonathan Cape, 1975).

9. Ibid., p. 167.

10. Glew, *Gender, Rhetoric and Regulation*, p. 137.

11. Hardy, *Health and Medicine*, pp. 110–38.

12. Brian Abel-Smith, *The Hospitals, 1800–1948* (London: Heinemann, 1964), pp. 424–71.

13. J. M. Winter, 'The Demographic Consequences of the War', in Smith, *War and Social Change*, pp. 154–6.

14. Ibid., pp. 168–7.

15. Addison, *Road to 1945*, pp. 174–8; Ashworth, *Genesis of Modern British Town Planning*, pp. 191–237.

16. Beaumont, *Housewives and Citizens*, p. 171.

17. Ibid., pp. 173–4.

18. Harris, *Beveridge*, p. 363.

19. W. Beveridge, *Insurance for All and Everything* (London: Daily News, 1924); Thane, *Old Age*, pp. 318–23.

20. Thane, *Old Age*, pp. 356–63.

21. Ibid.

22. *Social Insurance and Allied Services*. Report by Sir William Beveridge. Cmd. 6404 (HMSO, 1942). Para 8.

23. Ibid., para 107.

24. Pat Thane, 'The Women of the British Labour Party and feminism, 1906–1945', in *British Feminism in the Twentieth Century*, ed. Harold L. Smith (Cheltenham: Edward Elgar, 1990), pp. 128–31; Pedersen, *Eleanor Rathbone and the Politics of Conscience*; Oakley, *Forgotten Wives*, pp. 135–74.

25. Kathleen Kiernan, Hilary Land, and Jane Lewis, *Lone Motherhood in Twentieth Century Britain* (Oxford: Oxford University Press, 1999), pp. 179–80.

26. Cmd 6404, para 8.

27. Angus Calder, *The Peoples' War. Britain 1939–1945*, 2nd edn (London: Panther, 1971), p. 609.

28. Harris, *Beveridge*, pp. 365–432.

29. Ibid., pp. 432–43.

30. Lucy Noakes, 'War and Peace', in *Women in Twentieth Century Britain*, ed. Ina Zweiniger-Bargielowska (London: Pearson Education, 2001), p. 310.

31. Ibid., p. 307.

32. Lucy Noakes, *War and the British: Gender and National Identity, 1939–1990* (London: IB Tauris, 1997).

33. Harold L. Smith, 'The Effect of the War on the Status of Women', in Smith, *War and Social Change*, pp. 210–11.

34. Beaumont, *Housewives and Citizens*, p. 145.

35. Sheila Ferguson and Hilde Fitzgerald, *Studies in the Social Services.* History of the Second World War (London: HMSO and Longman Green, 1954), p. 178, n. 1.

36. Ibid., pp. 190–1.

37. Beaumont, *Housewives and Citizens*, pp. 138–41.

38. Ibid., pp. 146–53.

39. Mitchell and Deane, *Historical Statistics*, Table 16, p. 46; B. R. Mitchell and H. G. Jones, *Second Abstract of British Historical Statistics* (Cambridge: Cambridge University Press, 1971), Table 14, p. 30.

40. Mitchell and Deane, *Historical Statistics*, Table 10, pp. 30–3, Table 8, pp. 21–2.

41. Thane, 'The Debate on the Declining Birth-Rate'; Eva M. Hubback, *The Population of Britain* (London: Penguin, 1957).

42. Virginia Wimperis, *The Unmarried Mother and her Child* (London: George Allen and Unwin, 1960), Appendix Table 2a.

43. Ferguson and Fitzgerald, *Social Services*, p. 103.

44. Ibid., pp. 93–4.

45. *Registrar General's Statistical Review of England and Wales for the Six Years 1940–1945, Text, Vol. 11, Civil*, p. 144.

46. Ibid., p. 95.

47. Thane and Evans, *Sinners?*, pp. 54–81.

48. Lucy Bland, *Britain's Brown Babies. The Stories of Children Born to Black GIs and White Women in the Second World War* (Manchester: Manchester University Press, 2019); Thane and Evans, *Sinners?*, pp. 76–8; Ferguson and Fitzgerald, *Social Services*, pp. 131–2.

49. Ferguson and Fitzgerald, *Social Services*, p. 104.

50. Thane and Evans, *Sinners?*, pp. 79–81.

51. Bernard Crick, *George Orwell: A Life* (London: Secker and Warburg, 1980), pp. 463–4.

52. Ferguson and Fitzgerald, *Social Services*, pp. 126–7.

53. Helen Jones (ed.), *Duty and Citizenship: The Correspondence and Papers of Violet Markham ,1896–1953* (Cheltenham: The Historians' Press, 1994).

54. Helen Jones, 'Markham, Violet Rosa (1872–1959)', *ODNB*, 2004, www.oxforddnb.com.

55. *Report of the Committee on Amenities and Welfare, Conditions in the Three Women's Services*, 1942, Cmd 6384, 31, 50.

56. Jose Harris, 'Political Ideas and the Debate on State Welfare', in Smith, *War and Social Change*, pp. 233–43.

Chapter 7

1. David Butler and Gareth Butler, *Twentieth Century British Political Facts, 1900–2000* (London: Macmillan, 2000), p. 158.

2. Harriet Jones and Michael Kandiah (eds), *The Myth of Consensus. New Views on British History, 1945–64* (London: Macmillan, 1990); Rodney Lowe, 'The Second World War, Consensus and the Foundation of the Welfare State', *Twentieth Century British History* 2 (1990): pp. 152–82.

3. *Times*, 5 June 1945.

4. Asa Briggs, *Michael Young: Social Entrepreneur* (London: Palgrave, 2001); Matthew Hilton (ed.), 'Michael Young in Retrospect', *Contemporary British History* 19, no. 3 (September 2005): pp. 277–320.

5. Quoted by John Maynard Keynes, *Economic Consequences of the Peace* (London: Macmillan, 1919), p. 133.

6. Pat Thane, 'Labour and Welfare', in *Labour's First Century*, ed. Duncan Tanner, Nick Tiratsoo, and Pat Thane (Cambridge: Cambridge University Press, 2000), pp. 81–3.

7. Harris, *Beveridge*, p. 452.

8. Michael Young, *For Richer for Poorer*. Report to Labour Party Research Department (1951), quoted in Briggs, *Michael Young*, p. 201; Pat Thane, 'Michael Young and Welfare', in Hilton, 'Michael Young in Retrospect', p. 293.

9. Used frequently in C. R. Attlee, *The Social Worker* (London: G. Bell and Sons, 1920).

10. Harris, *Beveridge*, p. 452.

11. David Kynaston, *Austerity Britain, 1945–1951* (London: Bloomsbury, 2007), p. 173.

12. Daunton, *Just Taxes*, p. 180.

13. Ibid., pp. 194–228.

14. Atkinson, *Economics of Inequality*, p. 134.

15. Butler and Butler, *Facts*, p. 400.

16. *Daily Mail*, 3 July 1946.

17. Ina Zweiniger-Bargielowska, *Austerity Britain. Rationing, Controls and Consumption, 1939–1955* (Oxford: Oxford University Press, 2000), pp. 83–4, 215–18.

18. Ibid., pp. 214–26.

19. Kynaston, *Austerity Britain*, p. 257.

20. Correlli Barnett, *The Audit of War. The Illusion and Reality of Britain as a Great Nation*, 2nd edn (London: PaperMac, 1987); Jose Harris, 'Enterprise and the Welfare State', in *Britain since 1945*, ed. T. Gouvish and A O. Day (London: Macmillan, 1991), pp. 39–58.

21. Jim Tomlinson, 'Welfare and the Economy: The Economic Impact of the Welfare State, 1945–1951', *Twentieth Century British History* 6, no. 2 (1995): pp. 219–20.

22. Halsey and Webb, *British Social Trends*, p. 224.

23. Nick Tiratsoo, *Reconstuction, Affluence and Labour Politics: Coventry, 1945–1960* (London: Routledge, 1960); Junichi Hasigawa, *Replanning the Blitzed City Centre* (Buckingham: Open University Press, 1992).

24. Constance Rollett, 'Housing', in *Trends in British Society since 1900*, ed. A. H. Halsey (London: Macmillan, 1972), pp. 302–5.

25. John Campbell, *Nye Bevan. A Biography* (London: Hodder and Stoughton, 1987); Charles Webster, *The National Health Service: A Political History*, 2nd revised edn (Oxford: Oxford University Press, 2002).

26. Thane, *Old Age*, p. 446.

27. Hugh Pemberton, 'Politics and Pensions in Post-War Britain', in *Britain's Pensions Crisis. History and Policy*, ed. Hugh Pemberton, Pat Thane, and Noel Whiteside (London: Oxford University Press/The British Academy, 2006), pp. 43–6.

28. Rodney Lowe, *The Welfare State in Britain since 1945* (London: Palgrave, 2005), p. 157.

29. Thane and Evans, *Sinners?*, pp. 106–9.

30. Harris, *Beveridge*, pp. 451–3.

31. Jenny Keating, *A Child for Keeps. A History of Adoption in England, 1918–1945* (London: Palgrave, 2009), pp. 190–4.

32. Thane and Evans, *Sinners?*, p. 107.

33. Davis Smith, *100 Years of NCVO*, p. 102.

34. Nicholas Deakin and Justin Davis Smith, 'Labour, Charity and Voluntary Action: The Myth of Hostility', in Hilton and McKay, *The Ages of Voluntarism*, pp. 69–93.

35. Davis Smith, *100 Years*, pp. 102–4.

36. Hinton, *Women, Social Leadership and the Second World War*, pp. 198ff.

37. Ibid., p. 202ff.

38. Oliver Blaiklock, 'Advising the Citizens: Citizens' Advice Bureaux, Volunteers and the Welfare State in England, 1938–1961' (PhD thesis, King's College, London, 2012).

39. Tanya Evans, 'Stopping the Poor Getting Poorer: The Establishment and Professionalization of Poverty NGOs, 1945–1995', in *NGOs in Contemporary Britain. Non-State Actors in Society and Politics since 1945*, ed. Nick Crowson, Matthew Hilton, and James Mackay (London: Palgrave, 2009), pp. 147–63; Pat Thane, 'Voluntary Action in Britain since Beveridge', in *Beveridge and Voluntary Action in Britain and the Wider British World*, ed. Melanie Oppenheimer and Nicholas Deakin (Manchester: Manchester University Press, 2011), pp. 121–34.

40. Cretney, *Family Law*, p. 316; Hansard (House of Commons Debates), 15 December 1948, vol. 459, col. 1221.

41. Cretney, *Family Law*, pp. 314–18; R. I. Morgan, 'The Introduction of Civil Legal Aid in England and Wales, 1914–1949', *Twentieth Century British History* 5, no. 1 (1994): pp. 38–76. Bradley, *Lawyers for the Poor*.

42. Helen Bolderson, 'The Origins of the Disabled Persons Employment Quota and its Symbolic Significance', *Journal of Social Policy* 9, no. 2 (1980): pp. 160–86; Jameel Hampton, *Disability and the Welfare State in Britain. Changes in Perceptions and Policy, 1948–1979* (University of Bristol: Policy Press, 2016), p. 148ff.

43. Butler and Butler, *Facts*, p. 400.

44. William Beveridge, *Full Employment in a Free Society* (London: Allen and Unwin, 1944), p. 21.

45. Noel Whiteside, 'Towards a Modern Labour Market? State Policy and the Transformation of Employment', in *Moments of Modernity. Reconstructing Britain, 1945–1964*, ed. Becky Conekin, Frank Mort, and Chris Waters (Lewes: Rivers Oram, 1999), pp. 76–95; Gordon Phillips and Noel Whiteside, *Casual Labour and the Unemployment Question in the Port Transport Industry, 1880–1970* (Oxford: Oxford University Press, 1985).

Notes

46. Zweiniger-Bargielowska, *Austerity*, p. 25.

47. Richard Vinen, *National Service: Conscription in Britain, 1945–1963* (London: Allen Lane, 2014).

48. A. J. Hammerton and A. Thomson, *Ten Pound Poms. Australia's Invisible Migrants* (Manchester: Manchester University Press, reprinted 2012).

49. Thane, 'The Debate on the Declining Birth-Rate', p. 301.

50. Pat Thane, 'Towards Equal Opportunities? Women in Britain since 1945', in *Britain since 1945*, ed. Terry Gourvish and Alan O' Day (London: Macmillan, 1991), pp. 191–5.

51. Ibid.

52. Veronica Beechey and Tessa Perkins, *A Matter of Hours* (Minneapolis: University of Minnesota Press, 1987), p. 16.

53. Linda McDowell, *Working Lives. Gender, Migration and Employment in Britain, 1945–2007* (Oxford: Wiley-Blackwell, 2013), p. 79.

54. Ibid., pp. 83–94.

55. Ibid., pp. 71–94. Linda McDowell, *Migrant Women's Voices. Talking About Life and Work in the UK since 1945* (London: Bloomsbury, 2016).

56. McDowell, *Working Lives*, p. 78.

57. Colin Holmes, 'Immigration', in Gourvish and O'Day, *Britain since 1945*, pp. 209–18; M. Phillips and T. Phillips, *Windrush: The Irresistible Rise of Multi-Cultural Britain* (London: Harper Collins, 1998).

58. Jane Lewis, *The End of Marriage? Individualism and Intimate Relations* (Cheltenham: Edward Elgar, 2001), p. 30.

59. Kiernan et al., *Lone Motherhood*, p. 60ff.

60. Ibid., p. 35.

61. Wimperis, *The Unmarried Mother and Her Child*, Table 4.

62. Ibid., p. 4.

63. Ibid., pp. 124–6.

64. Butler and Butler, *Facts*, p. 236.

65. James Hinton, 'Women and the Labour Vote, 1945–1950', *Labour History Review* 57 (1992): pp. 59–66.

66. Peter Clarke, *Hope and Glory. Britain 1900–2000*, 2nd edn (London: Pelican, 2004), pp. 227–31.

67. Andrew Thorpe, *A History of the Labour Party*, 4th edn (London: Palgrave Macmillan, 1997, 2014), pp. 132–4.

68. Alec Cairncross, *Years of Recovery. British Economic Policy 1945–1951* (London: Methuen, 1985).

69. Stehen Fielding, Peter Thompson, and Nick Tiratsoo, *England Arise! The Labour Party and Popular Politics in 1940s Britain* (Manchester: University Press, 1995), p. 200.

70. Jim Tomlinson in Tanner et al., *Labour's First Century*, 'Labour and the Economy', pp. 57–60.

71. Cairncross, *Years of Recovery*, pp. 507–9.

72. Peter Townsend, *Poverty in the United Kingdom* (London: Pelican, 1979), p. 123.

Chapter 8

1. Nicolas Crafts, 'Economic Growth During the Long Twentieth Century', in *The Cambridge Economic History of Modern Britain, Vol II, !870 to the Present*, ed. Roderick Floud, Jane Humphries, and Paul Johnson (Cambridge: Cambridge University Press, 2014), pp. 45–9.

2. Tomlinson, 'Labour and the Economy', in Tanner et al., *Labour's First Century*, pp. 57–60.

3. Howard Glennerster, *British Social Policy since 1945* (Oxford: Blackwell, 1995), p. 86; Helen Jones, *Health and Society in Twentieth Century Britain* (London: Longman, 1994), pp. 117–47.

4. B. Seebohm Rowntree and G. S. Lavers, *Poverty and the Welfare State. A Third Social Survey of York Dealing only with Economic Questions* (Longman: Green and Co, 1951).

5. Gazeley, *Poverty*, pp. 168–73; A. B. Atkinson et al., 'Poverty in York: A Re-analysis of Rowntree's 1950 Survey', *Bulletin of Economic Research* 3 (1981), pp. 59–71.

6. (London: Conservative Political Centre, 1952), p. 5.

7. Roy Parker, 'The Struggle for Clean Air', in *Change, Choice and Conflict in Social Policy*, ed. P. Hall, H. Land, R. Parker, and A. Webb (London: Heinemann, 1975), pp. 371–409.

8. Butler and Butler, *Facts*, pp. 356–7.

9. Ibid., p. 357.

10. R. A. Butler, *Art of the Possible* (London: Hamish Hamilton, 1971), p. 173.

11. Butler and Butler, *Facts*, p. 427.

12. J. K. Galbraith, *The Affluent Society* (London: Pelican 1962, reprinted 1962, 1963).

13. Glew, *Gender, Rhetoric and Regulation*, pp. 157–67.

14. Elizabeth M. Meehan, *Women's Rights at Work. Campaigns and Policy in Britain and the United States* (London: Macmillan, 1985), pp. 35–55.

15. Thorpe, *Labour Party*, p. 141.

16. Sally Sheard, *The Passionate Economist. How Brian Abel-Smith shaped Global Health and Social Welfare* (University of Bristol: Policy Press, 2014), pp. 84–8.

17. Glennerster, *Social Policy*, pp. 92–3.

18. *Encounter Magazine*, July 1960.

19. *The Times*, 22 July 1957, quoted Kevin Jefferys, *Retreat from New Jerusalem. British Politics, 1951–1964* (London: Macmillan, 1997), p. 65.

20. Glennerster, *Social Policy*, pp. 82–5.

21. Ibid., p. 84.

22. C. A. R. Crosland, *The Future of Socialism* (London: Jonathan Cape, 1956), p. 355.

23. Ibid.

24. D. Butler and A. King, *The British General Election of 1964* (London: Macmillan, reprinted 2008), p. 40.

25. Louise A. Jackson with Angela Bartie, *Policing Youth. Britain 1945–1970* (Manchester: Manchester University Press, 2014).

26. J. Bowlby, *Child Care and the Growth of Love* (London: Pelican, 1953).

27. Butler and King, *British General Election*, p. 39.

28. Richard Hoggart, *The Uses of Literacy* (London: Penguin, 1969), pp. 318–46.

Notes

29. Thane, 'Michael Young', pp. 293–9.

30. Thane and Evans, *Sinners?*, pp. 92–4.

31. V. Klein, *Britain's Married Women Workers* (London: Routledge, 1957).

32. N. Seear, V. Roberts, and J. Brick, *A Career for Women in Industry* (London and Edinburgh: Oliver and Boyd, 1964); Thane, 'Towards Equal Opportunities?', pp. 200–2.

33. Hannah Gavron, *The Captive Wife: Conflict of Housebound Mothers* (London: Routledge, 1966, Pelican, 1970).

34. Clarke, *Hope and Glory*, pp. 284–6.

35. Halsey and Webb, *British Social Trends*, pp. 225–6.

36. Stephen Brooke, 'Slumming in Swinging London: Class, Gender and the Post-War City in Nell Dunn's *Up the Junction*', *Cultural and Social History* 9 (2012): pp. 429–44; Stephen Brooke, *Sexual Politics. Sexuality, Family Planning and the British Left from the 1880s to the Present Day* (Oxford: Oxford University Press, 2011), pp. 156–8.

37. Arthur Koestler (ed.), *Suicide of a Nation? An Enquiry into the State of Britain Today* (London: Hutchinson, 1963).

38. David Butler and Richard Rose, *The British General Election of 1959* (London: Macmillan, 1960), pp. 20, 27.

39. Thane, *Old Age*, pp. 373–6.

40. Mark Jarvis, *Conservative Governments, Morality and Social Change in Affluent Britain* (Manchester: Manchester University Press, 2005), p. 65.

41. Mark Abrams and Richard Rose, *Must Labour Lose?* (London: Penguin, 1960); Thorpe, *Labour Party*, pp. 145–51.

42. Glennerster, *Social Policy*, p. 88.

43. Ibid.; Nicolas Timmins, *The Five Giants. A Biography of the Welfare State* (London: Fontana, 1996), pp. 209–11.

44. Clarke, *Hope and Glory*, pp. 277–82.

45. Thorpe, *Labour Party*, pp. 150–4.

46. Bingham, *Family Newspapers*, pp. 148–51, 254–7.

47. David Edgerton, *Warfare State. Britain 1920-1980* (Cambridge: Cambridge University Press, 2006).

48. Thorpe, *Labour Party*, pp. 153–6; Ben Pimlott, *Harold Wilson* (London: Harper Collins, 1993).

49. Clarke, *Hope and Glory*, pp. 293–5.

50. Glennerster, *Social Policy*, p. 94.

51. A. B. Atkinson, *Incomes and the Welfare State. Essays on Britain and Europe* (Cambridge: Cambridge University Press, 1995), p. 17.

52. Butler and Rose, *British General Election of 1959*, p. 14.

Chapter 9

1. Alec Cairncross, *The British Economy since 1945. Economic Policy and Performance, 1945-1995*, 2nd edn (Oxford: Blackwell, 1995), p. 152.

2. Roy Hattersley, 'Harold Wilson's Moral Crusade can Still be a Rallying Cry', *Guardian*, 15 October 2014.

3. Cairncross, *British Economy*, pp. 154–5.

4. Jo Workman, 'Paying for Pedigree? British Business Schools and the MBA Degree' (Unpublished D. Phil., University of Sussex, 2005).

5. Harold Wilson, *Purpose in Politics* (Littlehampton Book Services, 1964), p. 3.

6. Richard Coopey, 'Industrial Policy in the White Heat of the Scientific Revolution', in *The Wilson Governments, 1964–1970*, ed. Richard Coopey, Stephen Fielding, and Nick Tiratsoo (London: Pinter, 1993), pp. 102–22; Edgerton, *Warfare State*, pp. 244–51.

7. Halsey and Webb, *British Social Trends*, pp. 224–32.

8. Phoebe Hall, 'Creating the Open University', in Hall et al., *Change, Choice and Conflict in Social Policy*, pp. 155–276.

9. R. H. S. Crossman, *Diary of a Cabinet Minister, Vol. 1: Minister of Housing 1964–1966* (London: Hamish Hamiton, Jonathan Cape, 1975).

10. Glennerster, *Social Policy*, pp. 103–11.

11. Brian Abel-Smith and Peter Townsend, *The Poor and the Poorest* (London: Bell and Co, 1965).

12. Michael Harrington, *The Other America: Poverty in the United States* (London: Macmillan, 1962; Penguin 1966).

13. Sheard, *The Passionate Economist*, p. 1.

14. Pat Thane and Ruth Davidson, *The Child Poverty Action Group 1965–2015* (London: CPAG, 2016), www.cpag.org.uk.

15. Hampton, *Disability and the Welfare State*, pp. 88–96.

16. Mathew Hilton, Nick Crowson, Jean-Francois Mouhot, and J. MacKay, *A Historical Guide to NGOs in Britain. Charity, Civil Society and the Voluntary Sector since 1945* (London: Palgrave, 2012), pp. 45–6.

17. A. Holden, *Makers and Manners. Politics and Morality in Post-War Britain* (London: Politico's, 2004), pp. 122, 171–2.

18. Thorpe, *Labour Party*, pp. 174–5.

19. Bingham, *Family Newspapers?*, p. 87.

20. Holden, *Makers and Manners*, p. 131.

21. Ina Zweiniger-Bargielowska, 'Explaining the Gender Gap', in *Conservatives and British Society, 1880–1990*, ed. Martin Francis and Ina Zweiniger-Bargielowska (Cardiff: University of Wales Press, 1996), pp. 192–224.

22. Coopey, 'Industrial Policy'.

23. Ibid., p. 111.

24. Edgerton, *Warfare State*, pp. 251–60.

25. Coopey, 'Industrial Policy', p, 112.

26. Edgerton, *Warfare State*, pp. 266–9.

27. N. Woodward, 'Labour's Economic Performance 1964–1970', in Coopey, Fielding, and Tiratsoo, *Wilson Governments*, pp. 88–9.

28. *The Report of the Committee on the Civil Service.* Cmnd 3638 1968.

Notes

29. Thane and Davidson, *CPAG*, pp. 14–15; Evans, 'Stopping the Poor Getting Poorer'; Thane and Evans, *Sinners?*, pp. 136–8.

30. Hampton, *Disability and the Welfare State*, pp. 83–130; Gareth Millward, 'Social Security Policy and the Early Disability Movement-Expertise, Disability and the Government, 1965–1977', *Twentieth Century British History* 26, no. (2015): pp. 274–97.

31. Alan Holmans, 'Housing', in Halsey and Webb, *British Social Trends*, p. 479.

32. Glennerster, *Social Policy*, pp. 141–5.

33. K. O. Morgan, *Callaghan. A Life* (Oxford: Oxford University Press, 1998), p. 292.

34. Thane and Davidson, *CPAG*, pp. 16–17; Frank Field, *Poverty and Politics. The Inside Story of the Child Poverty Action Group's Campaigns in the 1970s* (London: Heinemann, 1982), pp. 29–37.

35. Kiernan et al., *Lone Motherhood*, p. 22.

36. Glennerster, *Social Policy*, pp. 126–9.

37. Claire Hilton, *Improving Psychiatric Care for Older People: Barbara Robb's Campaign, 1965–1975* (London: Palgrave, 2017).

38. Halsey and Webb, *British Social Trends*, p. 195.

39. Alan Walker (ed.), *Public Expenditure and Social Policy* (London: Heinemann, 1982).

40. Jonathan Gershuny and Kimberly Fisher, 'Leisure', in Halsey and Webb, *British Social Trends*, pp. 720–49.

41. Butler and Butler, *Facts*, p. 372.

42. Amanda Root, 'Transport and Communications', in Halsey and Webb, *British Social Trends*, p. 460.

43. Morgan, *Callaghan*, pp. 303–6.

44. Crossman, *Diaries of a Cabinet Minister, 1966–1968*, Vol. 2, p. 407, 3 July 1967.

45. David Butler, 'Electors and Elected', in Halsey, *Trends in British Society since 1900*, p. 318.

46. Holden, *Makers and Manners*, p. 128.

47. Ibid., p. 129.

48. Peter Tatchell, 'Fifty Years of Gay Liberation? In Britain it's Barely Four', *The Guardian*, 23 May 2017, p. 31.

49. Holden, *Makers and Manners*, p. 126.

50. Ibid., pp. 133–4.

51. Witness seminar, 'The Making of the Abortion Act, 1967', King's College London Archive Centre, 2001.

52. David Coleman, 'Population and Family', in Halsey and Webb, *British Social Trends*, p. 50.

53. Lesley A. Hall, *Sex, Gender and Social Change in Britain since 1880* (London: Macmillan, 2000), pp. 176–7; Hera Cook, *The Long Sexual Revolution. English Women, Sex and Contraception, 1800–1975* (Oxford: Oxford University Press, 2004), pp. 296–317.

54. Holden, *Makers and Manners*, pp. 185–90.

55. Kiernan et al., *Lone Motherhood*, p. 35.

56. Butler and Butler, *Facts*, p. 350.

57. Kiernan et al., *Lone Motherhood*, p. 42.

58. Claire Langhamer, *The English in Love: The Intimate Story of an Emotional Revolution* (Oxford: Oxford University Press, 2013).

59. Cretney, *Family Law*, pp. 318–91.

60. Ibid., pp. 134–6, 420–1.

61. Ibid., p. 379, n. 392.

62. Ibid., pp. 145–57.

63. Butler and Butler, *Facts,* pp. 347, 353.

64. Clarke, *Hope and Glory*, p. 321; Butler and Butler, *Facts*, p. 351.

65. W. W. Daniel, *Racial Discrimination in England: Based on the PEP Report* (Harmondsworth: Penguin, 1968); Nicolas Deakin, *Colour Citizenship and British Society* (London: Panther, 1970).

66. Robert J. Whybrow, *Britain Speaks Out, 1937–1987. A Social History as Seen Through the Gallup Data* (London: Macmillan, 1989), p. 87.

67. Ibid., pp. 87–8.

68. Mel Porter and Becky Taylor, 'Gypsies and Travellers', in *Unequal Britain. Equalities in Britain since 1945*, ed. Pat Thane (London: Continuum, 2010), pp. 71–104.

69. Meehan, *Women's Rights at Work*, pp. 43–56.

70. Barbara Castle, *Fighting All the Way* (London: Pan 1993), pp. 408–9.

71. Ibid., p. 412.

72. Ibid., p. 427.

73. A. B. Atkinson, 'Distribution of Income and Wealth', in Halsey and Webb, *British Social Trends*, p. 354.

74. Whybrow, *Gallup Data*, pp. 93–4.

75. Gazeley, 'Income and Living Standards', in Floud et al., *Cambridge Economic History of Modern Britain*, p. 160.

76. Atkinson, *Incomes and the Welfare State*, p. 17.

77. Townsend, *Poverty in the United Kingdom*, p. 272ff.

Chapter 10

1. Tim Bale, *The Conservatives since 1945. The Drivers of Party Change* (Oxford: Oxford University Press, 2012), p. 154.

2. Thane and Davidson, *CPAG*, pp. 18–19.

3. Butler and Butler, *Facts*, p. 357.

4. Ibid.

5. Michael Hill, *The Welfare State in Britain. A Political History since 1945* (Cheltenham: Edward Elgar, 1993), p. 100.

6. A. H. Halsey, 'Further and Higher Education', in Halsey and Webb, *British Social Trends,* p. 226.

7. Butler and Butler, *Facts*, p. 386.

8. Reid, *United We Stand*, pp. 327–8.

9. Cairncross, *The British Economy since 1945*, pp. 182–3.

10. David Reynolds, *Britannia Overruled. British Policy and World Power in the Twentieth Century*, 2nd edn (London: Routledge, 2000), pp. 241–9.

Notes

11. Cairncross, *The British Economy*, pp. 182–93.

12. Reid, *United We Stand*, pp. 328–9.

13. Clarke, *Hope and Glory*, pp. 338–9.

14. Reid, *United We Stand*, p. 385.

15. D. Healey, *The Time of My Life* (London: Michael Joseph 1989), p. 292.

16. Richard Roberts, *When Britain Went Bust. The 1976 IMF Crisis* (London: OMFIF, 2016), p. 33.

17. Mortimore and Blick, *Facts*, p. 447.

18. Clarke, *Hope and Glory*, p. 352.

19. Kitson and Michie, 'The de-industrial revolution', in Floud et al., *Cambridge Economic History*, pp. 310–25.

20. Roberts, *When Britain Went Bust*, p. 34.

21. Reid, *United We Stand*, p. 387.

22. James Callaghan, *Time and Chance* (London: Collins, 1987), p. 426.

23. Roberts, *When Britain Went Bust*, p. 7.

24. Ibid., pp. 54–94.

25. Healey, *Time of My Life*, p. 432.

26. Kathleen Burk and Alec Cairncross, *'Goodbye Great Britain': The 1976 IMF Crisis* (New Haven: Yale University Press, 1992), pp. 225–6.

27. Roberts, *When Britain Went Bust*, pp. 105–19.

28. Castle, *Fighting*, p. 461; Sheard, *The Passionate Economist*, pp. 318–21.

29. Glennerster, *Social Policy*, pp. 113–14.

30. Castle, *Fighting*, pp. 469–70.

31. Thane and Davidson, *CPAG*, pp. 21–2; Sheard, *Passionate Economist*, pp. 325–7; Field, *Poverty and Politics*, pp. 43–9.

32. Thane and Evans, *Sinners?*, pp. 161–7.

33. Ibid., pp. 166, 171–4.

34. Glennerster, *Social Policy*, pp. 132–3; Hampton, *Disability and the Welfare State*, pp. 181–230.

35. Hill, *Welfare State*, pp. 116–18.

36. Nicolas Timmins, 'Maria Colwell's Death Led to Legislation over Two Decades', *Independent*, 24 March 1994.

37. George Smith, 'Schools', in Halsey and Webb, *British Social Trends*, p. 199.

38. Ibid., pp. 208–16.

39. Holmans, 'Housing', in Halsey and Webb, *British Social Trends*, p. 479.

40. Eve Setch, 'The Women's Liberation Movement in Britain, 1969–1979: Organization, Creativity and Debate' (PhD thesis, Royal Holloway College, London, 2000).

41. Brixton Black Women's Group, 'Black Women Organizing', *Feminist Review* 17 (Autumn 1984): pp. 84–8; Natalie Thomlinson, *Race, Ethnicity and the Women's Movement in England, 1968–1993* (London: Palgrave Macmillan, 2016).

42. Women and Equality Unit, *Key Indicators of Women's Position in Britain* (UK Government: Department of Trade and Industry, 2001), p. 83.

43. Meehan, *Women's Rights at Work*, pp. 72–96; A. Zabalza and Z. Tzannatos, *Women and Equal Pay: The Effects of Legislation on Women's Employment and Wages in Britain* (Cambridge: Cambridge University Press, 1985).

44. Ina Zweiniger-Bargielowska, 'Housewifery', in Zweiniger-Bargielowska, *Women in Twentieth Century Britain*, p. 158.

45. Ibid., p. 160.

46. Wybrow, *Gallup*, p. 102.

47. Dyhouse, *Students*, p. 99.

48. Butler and Butler, *Facts*, p. 366.

49. Lori Williamson, *Power and Protest. Frances Power Cobbe and Victorian Society* (Lewes: Rivers Oram, 2005) pp. 80–4.

50. Erin Pizzey, *This Way to the Revolution –A Memoir* (London: Peter Owen, 2013).

51. Cretney, *Family Law*, pp. 753–5.

52. www.amnesty.org.uk/violence-against-women#.VMTOG1. Accessed 25 January 2015.

53. Louise Jackson, *Women Police. Gender, Welfare and Surveillance in the Twentieth Century* (Manchester: Manchester University Press, 2006), pp. 185–93.

54. Bingham, *Family Newspapers?*, pp. 155–6.

55. Coleman, 'Population and Family', in Halsey and Webb, *British Social Trends*, p. 62.

56. Jane Lewis, *The End of Marriage?*; Langhamer, *The English in Love*.

57. Coleman in Halsey and Webb, *British Social Trends*, p. 34.

58. Lewis, *The End*, p. 35.

59. Bill Osgerby, *Youth in Britain since 1945* (Oxford: Blackwell, 1998), pp. 123–33.

60. Nick Kimber, 'Race and Equality', in Thane, *Unequal Britain*, pp. 37–9.

61. Porter and Taylor, 'Gypsies and Travellers', in Thane, *Unequal Britain*, pp. 84–7.

62. Thorpe, *Labour Party*, pp. 195–6; Christopher Harvie, 'The Politics of Devolution', in *A Companion to Contemporary Britain,1939–2000*, ed. Paul Addison and Harriet Jones (Oxford: Blackwell, 2005), pp. 434–5; Christopher Harvie and Peter Jones, *The Road to Home Rule* (Edinburgh: Edinburgh University Press, 2000); T. M. Devine, *The Scottish Nation 1799–2007. A Modern History* (London: Penguin, 2012); K. O. Morgan, *Wales. Rebirth of a Nation, 1880–1980* (Oxford: Oxford University Press, 1987), pp. 376–408; Morgan, *Callaghan*, pp. 677–9.

63. Lawrence Black and Hugh Pemberton, 'The Winter of Discontent in British Politics', *Political Quarterly* 80, no. 4 (2009): pp. 553–61.

64. Mortimore and Blick, *Facts*, p. 646.

65. Gazeley, 'Income and Living Standards', in Floud et al., *Cambridge Economic History*, p. 160.

66. Atkinson, *Incomes and the Welfare State*, p. 17.

67. Anthony F. Heath, *Social Progress in Britain* (Oxford: Oxford University Press, 2018), p. 27.

68. J. Cribb et al., *Living Standards, Poverty and Inequality in the UK* (London: Institute for Fiscal Studies, 2012), p. 84.

69. Andy Beckett, *When the Lights Went Out* (London: Faber and Faber, 2009), p. 420.

70. Mortimore and Blick, *Facts*, p. 645.

71. Ibid., p. 641.

Chapter 11

1. Thames TV 13 Dec 1982. Available on the Thatcher Foundation Website: https://www.margaretthatcher.org.

2. Tim Bale, *Conservatives since 1945*, p. 246.

3. Butler and Butler, *Facts*, p. 309.

4. Andrew Blick, *People Who Live in the Dark: The History of the Special Adviser in British Politics* (London: Politico's, 2004).

5. P. Dorey, 'The Stepping Stones Programme: The Conservative Party's Struggle to Develop a Trade Union Policy 1975–1979', *Historical Studies in Industrial Relations* 35 (2014): pp. 89–116.

6. Reid, *United We Stand*, pp. 396–400.

7. Mortimore and Blick, *Facts*, p. 647.

8. Nicholas Crafts, 'Economic Growth', in *The British Economy since 1945*, ed. N. Crafts and N. Woodward (Oxford: Oxford University Press, 1991), p. 285.

9. Wybrow, *Gallup*, p. 121.

10. Ibid.

11. Crafts, 'Economic Growth during the Long Twentieth Century', in Floud et al., *Cambridge Economic History*, p. 46.

12. Richard Vinen, *Thatcher's Britain. The Politics and Social Upheaval of the 1980s*, 2nd edn (London: Simon and Schuster, 2010), pp. 106–7.

13. Ibid., pp. 195–200.

14. John Hills and Beverley Mullings, 'Housing: A Decent Home for All at a Price within their Means?', in *The State of Welfare. The Welfare State in Britain since 1974*, ed. John Hills (Oxford: Oxford University Press, 1990) pp. 135–201.

15. John Hills, 'Housing: A Decent Home within the Reach of Every Family', in *The State of Welfare. The Economics of Social Spending*, 2nd edn, ed. H. Glennerster and John Hills (Oxford: Oxford University Press, 1998), p. 127.

16. Ibid., p. 132.

17. Glennerster, *Social Policy*, pp. 187–8.

18. Vinen, *Thatcher's Britain*, p. 204.

19. Ibid., p. 205.

20. Thatcher, *The Downing St Years* (London: Harper Collins, 1993), p. 8.

21. Glennerster, *Social Policy*, pp. 171–3.

22. P. Dorey, 'A Farewell to Alms: Thatcherism's Legacy of Inequality', *British Politics* 10 (2015): p. 87.

23. H. Glennerster, 'Education', in Glennerster and Hills, *The State of Welfare*, p. 33.

24. Ibid., pp. 27–74.

25. Thorpe, *Labour Party*, pp. 210–13.

26. Vinen, *Thatcher's Britain*, p. 128.

27. Thorpe, *Labour Party*, p. 213.

28. R. Gildea, *Backbone of the Nation. Mining Communities and the Great Strike of 1984–1985* (New Haven: Yale University Press, 2023); Reid, *United We Stand*, pp. 402–6; Vinen, *Thatcher*, pp. 38–9; Vinen, *Thatcher's Britain*, pp. 154–77.

29. Thorpe, *Labour Party*, p. 215.

30. Evans, *Thatcher*, p. 30.

31. Butler and Butler, *Facts*, p. 401.

32. Evans, *Thatcher*, pp. 58–62; Vinen, *Thatcher's Britain*, p. 125.

33. Martin Evans, 'Social Security: Dismantling the Pyramids?', in Glennerster and Hills, *The State of Welfare*, p. 299.

34. Ibid., p. 270.

35. Glennerster, *Social Policy*, pp. 183–5.

36. Peter Riddell, *The Thatcher Government* (Oxford: Blackwell, 1985), p. 137.

37. Peter Townsend and Nick Davidson (eds), *The Black Report* (London: Pelican, 1982).

38. Ibid., p. 2.

39. Ibid., p. 51.

40. Ibid., pp. 3–4.

41. Julian Le Grand and Polly Vizard, 'The National Health Service: Crisis, Change or Continuity?', in Glennerster and Hills, *The State of Welfare*, pp. 78–9.

42. Eliza Filby, *God and Mrs Thatcher. The Battle for Britain's Soul* (London: Biteback, 2015), pp. 171–3.

43. Ibid., pp. 174–6.

44. Vinen, *Thatcher's Britain*, p. 197.

45. Ibid., p. 199; Evans, *Thatcher*, pp. 34–7.

46. Kynaston, *The City of London*. Vol. 4 *A Club No More, 1845–2000* (London: Chatto and Windus, 2001), p. 713.

47. Vinen, *Thatcher's Britain*, p. 183.

48. Kynaston, *The City*, p. 713.

49. Filby, *God*, p. 340.

50. Butler and Butler, *Facts*, p. 427.

51. Filby, *God*, p. 342.

52. Kynaston, *The City*, p. 718.

53. Atkinson, *Inequality*, pp. 156–7.

54. David Butler, *British General Elections since 1945* (Wiley: Blackwell, 1989), p. 64.

55. *Woman's Own*, 31 October 1987.

56. Glennerster, 'Education: Reaping the Harvest?', in Glennerster and Hills, *The State of Welfare*, p. 33.

57. Ibid., pp. 27–74; Evans, *Thatcher*, pp. 70–4.

58. George Smith, 'Schools', in Halsey and Webb, *British Social Trends*, p. 194ff.

59. J. W. B. Douglas, J. M. Ross, and H. R. Simpson, *All Our Future. A Longitudinal Study of Secondary Education* (London: Panther, 1971), pp. 42–7; Michele Cohen, 'Knowledge and the Gendered Curriculum: The Problematisation of Girls Achievement' (2004), www.historyandpolicy.org/policy-papers/category/michele-cohen.

60. B. Parekh, *The Future of Multi-ethnic Britain* (London: Runnymede Trust, 2000).

61. Glennerster, 'Education', pp. 57–63.

62. Ibid., pp. 36–7. John Charmley, *A History of Conservative Politics since 1830*, 2nd edn (London: Palgrave, 2008), p. 225.

63. Halsey, 'Further and Higher Education', in Halsey and Webb, *British Social Trends*, p. 239.

64. Glennerster, *Social Policy*, pp. 47–8.

65. Hill, *The Welfare State*, p. 153.

66. Hills, 'Housing', p. 134.

67. Ibid., pp. 153–5.

68. Ibid., p. 149.

69. Ibid., p. 151.

70. Matthew Hilton, James McKay, Nicholas Crowson, and Jean-François Mouhot, *The Politics of Expertise: How NGOs Shaped Modern Britain* (Oxford: Oxford University Press, 2013), p. 199.

71. M. Drake, M. O'Brien, and T. Biebuyck, *Single and Homeless* (HMSO, 1981), Department of the Environment; Hilton et al., *Politics of Expertise*, pp. 237–8.

72. Hills, 'Housing', p. 134.

73. Ibid., p. 142.

74. Ibid., pp. 147–9; Holmans, 'Housing', in Halsey and Webb, *British Social Trends*, p. 479.

75. Maria Evandrou and Jane Falkingham, 'The Personal Social Services', in Glennerster and Hills, *The State of Welfare*, pp. 189–256.

76. Ibid., pp. 200, 242–5; Thane, *Old Age*, pp. 428–35.

77. Evandrou and Falkingham, 'The Personal Social Services', in Glennerster and Hills, *The State of Welfare*, p. 208.

78. Glennerster, *Social Policy*, p. 209.

79. Evandrou and Falkingham, 'The Personal Social Services', in Glennerster and Hills, *The State of Welfare*, pp. 203–4.

80. Thatcher, *Downing Street Years*, p. 608.

81. Le Grand and Vizard, 'The National Health Service', in Glennerster and Hills, *The State of Welfare*, p. 80.

82. Glennerster, *Social Policy*, pp. 203–8.

83. Evans, *Thatcher*, pp. 68–9.

84. Le Grand and Vizier, 'The National Health Service', in Glennerster and Hills, *The State of Welfare*, p. 91.

85. Ibid., p. 91.

86. Social and Community Planning Research, *British Social Attitudes. Cumulative Sourcebook: The First Six Surveys* (London: Gower, 1992), F11.

87. ONS, *Statistical Bulletin. Older People's Day*, 30 September 2010, p. 3.

88. J. Gill and D. Taylor, *Active Ageing: Live Longer and Prosper* (London: UCL School of Pharmacy, 2012).

89. Women's Royal Voluntary Service, 'Gold Age Pensioners: Contribution Outweighs Cost by £40 Billion' (2011), www.goldagepensioners.com.

90. Holden, *Makers and Manners*, p. 227.

91. Ibid.

92. Thatcher, *Downing St Years*, pp. 630–1.

93. Ibid., p. 628.

94. Wybrow, *Gallup*, pp. 135–8.

95. *British Social Attitudes. Cumulative Sourcebook: The First Six Surveys,* Tables N1–16–25, N2–2.

96. Jeffrey Weeks, Brian Heaphy, and Catherine Donovan, 'Families of Choice: Autonomy and Mutuality in Non-Heterosexual Relationships', in *Changing Britain. Families and Households in the 1990s,* ed. S. McRae (Oxford: Oxford University Press, 1999), pp. 297–316.

97. Quoted Hilary Macaskill, *From the Workhouse to the Workplace: 75 Years of One-Parent Family Life, 1918–1939* (London: NCOPF, 1993), p. 45.

98. Thatcher, *Downing St Years*, p. 630.

99. Mavis MacLean with Jacek Kurzewski, *Making Family Law: A Socio-legal Account of Legislative Process in England and Wales* (Oxford: Hart, 2011).

100. V. Berridge, 'Crisis? What Crisis?', *Health Service Journal*, 8 August 1996, pp. 20–1.

101. Holden, *Makers and Manners*, p. 252.

102. Mel Porter, 'Gender Identity and Sexual Orientation', in Thane, *Unequal Britain*, pp. 153–4.

103. Nehring, 'Social Movements', in Addison and Jones, *Companion*, p. 394.

104. Holden, *Makers and Manners*, p. 256.

105. *British Social Attitudes*, Tables M-1, 3–7.

106. E. Breitenbach and F. Mackay, 'Feminist Politics in Scotland from the 1970s-2000s: Engaging with the Changing State', in Breitenbach and Thane, *Women and Citizenship in Britain*, pp. 157–9.

107. P. Chaney, 'Devolution, Citizenship and Women's Political Representation in Wales', in Breitenbach and Thane, *Women and Citizenship in Britain*, pp. 189–208.

108. Kimber, 'Race and Equality', in Thane, *Unequal Britain*, pp. 38–40.

109. Porter and Taylor, 'Gypsies and Travellers', in Thane, *Unequal Britain*, pp. 85–8.

110. Evans, *Thatcher*, pp. 62–4; Vinen, *Thatcher's Britain*, pp. 261–3.

111. Charmley, *Conservative Politics*, p. 237.

112. Evans, *Thatcher*, p. 119.

113. House of Commons *Debates, Hansard*, 6th series, Vol. 170, col. 525, 3 April 1990.

114. Cribb et al., *Living Standards, Poverty and Inequality in the UK.*

115. Evans, *Thatcher*, p. 118.

Chapter 12

1. Glennerster, *Social Policy*, p. 213.

2. N. Panchamia and P. Thomas, *The Next Steps Initiatives* (Institute for Government), www.InstituteforGovernment.org.uk.

3. Kevin Theakston, 'A Permanent Revolution: The Major Governments and the Civil Service', in *The Major Premiership. Politics and Policy under John Major 1990–1997*, ed. Peter Dorey (London: Palgrave, 1999), p. 28.

Notes

4. Blick, *People Who Live in the Dark.*

5. Charmley, *Conservative Politics*, pp. 242–4.

6. Clarke, *Hope and Glory*, p. 408.

7. Ibid., p. 409.

8. Ibid., pp. 278–9.

9. Clarke, *Hope and Glory*, pp. 413–16.

10. Glennerster, 'Education', in Glennerster and Hills, *The State of Welfare*, pp. 27–74.

11. Hills, 'Housing', in Halsey and Webb, *British Social Trends*, p. 142.

12. Ibid., pp. 122–88.

13. Le Grand and Vizard, 'The National Health Service', in Glennerster and Hills, *The State of Welfare*, pp. 104–5.

14. Evandrou and Falkingham, 'The Personal Social Services', in Glennerster and Hills, *The State of Welfare*, pp. 196–9.

15. Thane and Evans, *Sinners?*, pp. 184–6.

16. *Community Care*, 5 August 1993, p. 3.

17. *Guardian*, 6 July 1993.

18. *Community Care,* 5 August 1993, p. 3; Thane and Evans, *Sinners?*, pp. 187–8.

19. *Daily Mail*, 5 July 1993,

20. National Council for One Parent Families (NCOPF), *Annual Report*, 1994/5, p. 3.

21. *Independent*, 6 July 1993; *Guardian*, 7 July 1993.

22. *Independent*, 6 July 1993.

23. Single Parent Action Network, *Positive Images, Negative Stereotypes* (Bristol, 1993), pp. 31–4.

24. NCOPF, *Annual Report, 1993/4*, p. 2.

25. Cribb et al., *Living Standards, Poverty and Inequality in the UK* (London: IFS, 2012), p. 84.

26. Thane and Evans, *Sinners?*, pp. 193–4.

27. Cretney, *Family Law*, pp. 761–3.

28. Hill in Dorey, *The Major Premiership*, p. 171.

29. Simon Millar, 'Disability', in Thane, *Unequal Britain*, p. 170.

30. HC, *Debates Hansard*, Vol. 244, cols 759–60, 16 June 1994.

31. Millar, 'Disability', pp. 171–2.

32. Ibid., p. 178.

33. Pat Thane, 'Demographic Futures: Addressing Inequality and Diversity Among Older People', in *New Paradigms in Public Policy*, ed. P. Taylor-Gooby (London: Oxford University Press/British Academy, 2013), pp. 150–1.

34. Gazeley, 'Income and Living Standards', in Floud et al., *Cambridge Economic History*, p. 170.

35. Thane, 'The Debate on the Declining Birth-rate in Britain'.

36. Pat Thane, 'Older People and Equality', in Thane, *Unequal Britain*, pp. 16–19.

37. Thane, 'Older People', pp. 17–18.

38. Gazeley, 'Income and Living Standards', in Floud et al., *Cambridge Economic History*, p. 160ff.

39. Ibid., p. 163.

40. Ibid., pp. 169–72.

41. Peter Scott, 'The Household Economy since 1870', in Floud et al., *Cambridge Economic History*, p. 382.

42. Kimber, 'Race and Equality', in Thane, *Unequal Britain*, pp. 41–2.

43. Butler and Butler, *Facts*, p. 564.

44. See p. 206.

45. Kimber, 'Race and Equality', in Thane, *Unequal Britain*, p. 41.

46. Peter Brierley, 'Religion', in Halsey and Webb, *British Social Trends*, p. 662.

47. Filby, 'Religion and Belief', in Thane, *Unequal Britain*, p. 62.

48. Porter and Taylor, 'Gypsies and Travellers', in Thane, *Unequal Britain*, pp. 88–92.

49. Timothy J. Hatton, 'Population, Migration and Labour Supply: Great Britain, 1871–2011', in Floud et al., *Cambridge Economic History*, p. 108.

50. Sara Connolly and Mary Gregory, 'Women and Work since 1970', in *Work and Pay in Twentieth Century Britain*, ed. Nicholas Crafts, Ian Gazeley, and Andrew Newell (Oxford: Oxford University Press, 2007), pp. 160–3.

51. Evandrou and Falkingham, 'Personal Social Services', in Glennerster and Hills, *The State of Welfare*, p. 217.

52. Ruth Lister, 'The Family and Women', in *The Major Effect*, ed. Anthony Seldon and Dennis Kavanagh (London: Macmillan, 1994), pp. 357–9.

53. Clarke, *Hope and Glory*, pp. 409–12.

Chapter 13

1. Philip Cowley, 'Parliament', in *Blair's Britain 1997–2007*, ed. Anthony Seldon (Cambridge: Cambridge University Press, 2007), p. 16.

2. Paul Fawcett and R.A.W. Rhodes 'Central Government' in Ibid., p. 93.

3. David Butler and Dennis Kavanagh (eds), *The British General Election of 2001* (London: Palgrave 2002), pp. 235–7, 256–8, 299, 304ff; Geoffrey Evans and James Tilley, *The New Politics of Class. The Political Exclusion of the British Working Class* (Oxford: Oxford University Press, 2017), pp. 170–7.

4. Butler and Kavanagh, *General Election, 2001*, p. 2.

5. Thane, 'Labour and Welfare', in Tanner, Tiratsoo, and Thane, *Labour's First Century*, pp. 80–2.

6. Abigail McKnight, 'Employment: Tackling Poverty Through "Work for Those Who Can"', in *A More Equal Society? New Labour, Poverty, Inequality and Exclusion*, ed. John Hills and Kitty Stewart (University of Bristol: Policy Press, 2004), pp. 23–46.

7. Robert Taylor, 'New Labour, New Capitalism', in Seldon, *Blair's Britain*, pp. 232–3.

8. Breitenbach and Thane, *Women and Citizenship*, pp. 171–3, 190–2.

9. Lowe, *The Welfare State*, pp. 429–30.

10. Helen McCarthy, 'Gender Equality', in Thane, *Unequal Britain*, pp. 120–2.

11. Taylor, 'New Labour, New Capitalism', p. 220.

12. McKnight, 'Employment', pp. 23–46.

13. Taylor, 'New Labour, New Capitalism', pp. 235–7.

14. Thane and Davidson, *CPAG*, pp. 6–10.

15. Tony Blair, 'Beveridge Revisited: A Welfare State for the 21st Century', in *Ending Child Poverty: Popular Welfare for the 21st Century*', ed. Robert Walker (University of Bristol: Policy Press, 1999), p. 7; Stewart, 'Equality and Social Justice', in Seldon, *Blair's Britain*, p. 441.

16. Thane and Evans, *Sinners?*, p. 196.

17. Stewart, 'Equality and Social Justice', in Seldon, *Blair's Britain*, pp. 425–6.

18. Ibid., pp. 419–21.

19. Ibid., pp. 421–4.

20. Ibid., pp. 426–8.

21. Alan Smithers, 'Schools', in Seldon, *Blair's Britain*, p. 372, n. 28.

22. Ibid., p. 381.

23. Smithers, 'Schools', in Seldon, *Blair's Britain*, pp. 378–9.

24. John O'Leary, 'Higher Education', Seldon, *Blair's Britain*, p. 468.

25. Halsey, 'Higher and Further Education', in Halsey and Webb, *British Social Trends*, p. 229.

26. O'Leary, 'Higher Education', Seldon, *Blair's Britain*, p. 475.

27. Dennis Kavanagh, 'The Blair Premiership', in Seldon, *Blair's Britain*, p. 11.

28. N. Bosanquet, 'The Health and Welfare Legacy', in Seldon, *Blair's Britain*, pp. 393–4.

29. M. Marmot, *Fair Society, Healthy Lives. Strategic Review of Health Inequalities in England* (2010), www.marmotreview.org.

30. Ibid.

31. Holden, *Makers and Manners*, pp. 368–9.

32. Ibid., p. 372.

33. Ibid., p. 373.

34. David Willetts, *The Pinch. How the Baby Boomers Took Their Children's Future-and Why They Should Give it Back* (London: Atlantic Books, 2010); E. Howker and S. Malik, *Jilted Generation: How Britain has Bankrupted its Youth* (London: Icon Books, 2010).

35. Thane, 'Demographic Futures', pp. 151–4.

36. Picketty, *Capital*, p. 29.

37. Home Office Citizenship Surveys 2002–2011, https://www.ukdataservice.ac.uk.

38. Thane, 'Demographic Futures', pp. 152–4.

39. Pensions Commission, First Report, *Pensions: Challenges and Choices* (The Stationery Office, 2004); Second Report, *A New Pension Settlement for the Twenty-first Century* (2005); Final Report: *Implementing an Integrated Package of Pension Reforms* (2006).

40. Marmot, *Fair Society, Healthy Lives*.

41. Thane, 'Older people and Equality', pp. 17–21.

42. Ibid.

43. Ibid., p. 19.

44. Ian Bache and Neill Nugent, 'Europe', in Seldon, *Blair's Britain*, p. 541.

45. Sarah Spencer, 'Immigration', in Seldon, *Blair's Britain*, p. 352.

46. Ibid., p. 343, n. 6.

47. Ibid., p. 344.

48. Tania Burchardt, 'Selective Inclusion: Asylum Seekers and Other Marginalized Groups', in Hills and Stewart, *A More Equal Society?* pp. 219–27.

49. Spencer, 'Immigration', pp. 354–5.

50. Kimber, 'Race and Equality', in Thane, *Unequal Britain*, p. 41.

51. Kimber, 'Race and Equality', in Thane, *Unequal Britain*, p. 42; Y. Li, F. Devine, and A. Heath, *Equality Group. Inequalities in Education, Employment and Earnings: Research Review and Analysis of Trends over Time.* Research Report No.10. Equality and Human Rights Commission, www.equalityhumanrightscommission.com

52. Kimber, 'Race and Equality', pp. 43–5.

53. Porter and Taylor, 'Gypsies and Travellers', pp. 92–102.

54. McCarthy, 'Gender and Equality', p. 116.

55. Ibid., pp. 117–18; Halsey and Webb, *British Social Trends*, pp. 210–12, 226, 234.

56. Equality and Human Rights Commission, *Sex and Power: Who Runs Britain, 2008?* (London: EHRC, 2008), pp. 5–7.

57. *Stop Gap*, the Fawcett Society Magazine (Autumn 2008), pp. 10–11.

58. Holden, *Makers and Manners*, pp. 336, 343–5.

59. Porter, 'Gender Identity and Sexual Orientation', in Thane, *Unequal Britain*, pp. 156–9; Holden, *Makers and Manners*, pp. 336–43.

60. Holden, *Makers and Manners*, pp. 346–8.

61. Ibid., p. 128.

62. Ibid., pp. 356–7.

63. Porter, 'Gender Identity', p. 158.

64. Ibid., pp. 159–61.

65. Tony Blair, Fabian Society pamphlet, 2002.

66. Stewart, 'Equality and Social Justice', p. 430.

67. John Hills, *Good Times, Bad Times. The Welfare Myth of Them and Us* (University of Bristol: Policy Press, 2015), p. 132; Stewart, 'Equality and Social Justice', pp. 434–5.

68. Stewart, 'Equality and Social Justice', p. 433.

69. Hills, *Good Times*, pp. 28–31.

70. Ben Page, 'Culture and Attitudes', in Seldon, *Blair's Britain*, pp. 436–67.

71. Dennis Kavanagh and Philip Cowley, *The British General Election of 2010* (London: Palgrave, 2010), p. 3.

72. The Equality Trust, *How Has Inequality Changed* (London: Equality Trust, 2016), www.equalitytrust.org.uk (accessed 22 November 2023); Tom Sefton and Holly Sutherland, 'Inequality and Poverty under New Labour', in Hills and Stewart, *A More Equal Society?*, pp. 231–50.

73. Polly Toynbee and David Walker, *The Verdict. Did Labour Change Britain?* (London: Granta, 2010).

Notes

74. Equality Trust, *How has Inequality Changed.*

75. Evans and Tilley, *The New Politics of Class*, p. 170ff.

Chapter 14

1. M. Marmot et al., *Build Back Fairer. The Covid-19 Marmot Review. The Pandemic, Socioeconomic and Health Inequalities in England* (London: The Health Foundation, 2020).

2. Pat Thane, 'The "Big Society" and the "Big State": Creative Tension or Crowding Out?', *Twentieth Century British History* 23, no. (2012): pp. 408–29.

3. Nicholas Timmins, *The Five Giants. A Biography of the Welfare State*, 3rd edn (London: Harper Collins, 2017), p. 662.

4. John Harris, 'I'm Caught in This Cycle of Debt. It's Never-ending', *Guardian*, 1 June 2022.

5. Age UK, *The Real Impact of Raising the State Pension Age.* January 2023, www.ageuk.org.uk (accessed 23 November 2023).

6. Department of Health and Social Care, 'Closed Consultation. Aligning the Upper Age for NHS Prescription Charge Exemption with the State Pension Age', 2 September 2021.

7. *Guardian,* 30 May 2023.

8. *Universal Credit. Welfare that Works*, Department of Work and Pensions, 11 November 2010, Foreword by Iain Duncan Smith, p. 5.

9. Ruth Patrick, Kate Andersen, Mary Reeder, Aaron Reeves, and Kitty Stewart, *Needs and Entitlements. Welfare Reform in Larger Families* (London, 17 July 2023), https://www.largerfamiliesstudy (accessed 24 November 2023).

10. United Nations General Assembly. Human Rights Council, *Visit to the United Kingdom of Great Britain and Northern Ireland*. Report of the Special Rapporteur on Extreme Poverty and Human Rights (New York, 23 April 2019).

11. Mark Creagh, *Work Intensification* (London: TUC, July 2023).

12. B. Campbell et al., *Interim Report, The Commission on the Future of Employment Support* (London: Institute for Employment Studies and Financial Fairness Trust, July 2023).

13. https://www.cpag.org.uk (accessed 24 November 2023).

14. J. Cribb, A. N. Keiller, and T. Waters, *Living Standards, Poverty and Inequality in the UK, 2018* (Joseph Rowntree Foundation, 2018), www.jrf.org.uk/uk-poverty-causes-costs-and-solutions. www.resolutionfoundation.org/publications/the-living-standards-audit-2018/.

15. Joseph Rowntree Foundation, *UK Poverty 2023. The Essential Guide to Understanding Poverty in the UK* (York, 2023), p. 91. https://www.jrf.org.uk.

16. The Trussell Trust, *1.5m Food Parcels Distributed as Need Continues to Rise*, 8 November 2023,

17. *The Guardian, 3* November 2022.

18. *Guardian*, 'Britain Violating International Law over Poverty Rates, Warns UN Envoy', 6 November 2023.

19. Ibid.

20. D. Hirsch and J. Stone, 'Local Indicators of Child Poverty After Housing Costs 2019/20', May 2021. Centre for Research in Social Policy at Loughborough University for the End Child Poverty Campaign.

21. Joseph Rowntree Foundation, *UK Poverty 2023*, p. 39.

22. Marmot et al., *Build Back Fairer*, pp. 15–16.

23. Centre for Ageing Better, *State of Ageing 2023* (London, 2023), https://ageing-better.org.uk (accessed 26 November 2023).

24. MBRRACE-UK, *Saving Lives, Improving Mothers' Care*, November 2022. MBRRACE-UK was established by the Healthcare Quality Improvement Fellowship to investigate annual deaths in pregnancy, childbirth and the year after birth of mothers in UK.

25. Amelia Gentleman, *The Windrush Betrayal. Exposing the Hostile Environment* (London: Guardian, Faber, 2019).

26. Luke Sibieta, 'The Crisis in Lost Learning Calls for a Massive National Policy Response', *Institute for Fiscal Studies*, 1 February 2021, www.ifs.org.uk/publications/152891.

27. 'Coronavirus (COVID-19) Infection Survey UK' (London: Office of Public Statistics, 29 January 2021).

28. Marmot et al., *Build Back Fairer*, pp. 15–16.

29. UK Government, *Coronavirus (COVID-19) in the UK. Daily Update*, 2 February 2021, https://coronavirus.data.gov.uk.

30. S. Ray-Chaudhuri, T. Waters, and X. Xu, *Recent Changes to Universal Credit Have Much Smaller Effect on Poverty than £20 Uplift* (London: Institute for Fiscal Studies, 9 July 2023).

31. Joseph Rowntree Foundation, *UK Poverty 2023*.

32. Office of National Statistics, *Annual Survey of Hours and Earnings*, 2020.

33. Fawcett Society, *Building Back Fairer for Women and Girls* (London, 2021).

34. Joseph Rowntree Foundation, *UK Poverty 2020/21. The Leading Independent Report* (York, 14 December 2021), p. 26.

35. N. Finney, J. Nazroo, L. Bécares, D. Kapadia, and N. Schlomo (eds), *Racism and Ethnic Inequality in a Time of Crisis. Findings from the Evidence for Equality National Survey* (University of Bristol: Policy Press, 2023).

36. *BBC News*, 11 October 2022.

37. 'Councils Spend £500m on Beds in Worst Care Homes', *Guardian*, 24 March 2023.

38. Ibid.

39. *Key Facts and Figures about Caring* (Carers UK, 2023), https://www,carersuk.org.

40. Joseph Rowntree Foundation, *UK Poverty 2023*, https://www.jrf.org.uk.

41. Denise Wilkins, 'Unpaid Carers Like Me Prop Up a Failing System', *Guardian*, 3 June 2023.

42. 'Army of Volunteers to Be Recruited to Help with Social Care Crisis', *Guardian*, 7 June 2023.

43. *Guardian*, Leader, 5 June 2023 'For-profit businesses make worse carers. It's time to admit privatisation failed'.

44. Royal College of Surgeons of England, *Age Still a Barrier to Surgery, RCS and Age UK Warn* (London, 3 July 2014).

45. 'Sharp Increase in Child Poverty in Midlands and North of England', *Guardian*,14 October 2020.

46. Joseph Rowntree Foundation, *UK Poverty 2023*, pp. 27–8, 31–3.

47. Credit Suisse, *Global Wealth Report 2022*, https://www,credit.suisse.com.

48. Bea Boileau and David Sturrock, *Bank of Mum and Dad Drives Increasing Inequalities in Early Adulthood* (London: Institute for Fiscal Studies, 13 February 2023).

49. 'Income Inequality' (London: Office of National Statistics, 7 January 2022).

50. Teachers Pensions, 'Female Retirees Receive 28% Less a Year than Men', *Guardian*, 16 October 2021.

51. 'Women Would Need to Work 37 Years More than Men to Make up Huge Pension Deficit', *Guardian*, 6 March 2021.

52. 'Cost of Living Crisis Forces More Over-70s to Carry on Working', *Guardian*, 1 May 2023.

53. 'North-East of England Passes London as Area with Highest Child Poverty', *Guardian*, 12 July 2022.

54. The Trussell Trust, *State of Hunger*. Year 2, main report. May 2021, https://www.trusselltrusr.org.

55. 'Bank of Food Banks. Gordon Brown: "I Never Thought we'd Go Back to This"', *Guardian*, 12 November 2022.

56. https://www.trusselltrust.org (accessed 26 April 2023).

57. 'Soaring Costs Force Highest Ever Numbers to Seek Food Bank Aid', *Guardian*, 26 April 2023.

58. 'Living Standards, Poverty and Inequality in the UK 2020' (London: Institute for Fiscal Studies, 2020).

59. 'Half of 3.1m Children of UK Lone Parents Living in Poverty, Research Reveals', reporting research by IFS and JRF yet to be published, *Guardian*, 4 July 2023.

60. CPAG Briefing, 'Six Years in: The Two-Child Limit', 6 April 2023, https://www.cpag.org.uk/topic/two-child-limit.

61. New Economics Foundation, *A Fair Start for All* (London, 20 November 2023), https://neweconomics.org/a-fair-start-for-all (accessed 26 November 2023).

62. MBRRACE-UK, 'Saving Lives, Improving Mothers' Care', November 2022.

63. 'UK's Cost of Living Crisis May Increase Death Rate During and after Pregnancy, Warns WHO', *Guardian*, 16 January 2023.

64. David Odd et al., 'Child Mortality in England during the First Two Years of the Covid-19 Pandemic', *Journal of the American Association*, 2023, https://jamanetwork.com. https://www.ncmd.info/publications.

65. 'Black Babies "Three Times as Likely to Die as White Babies"', 10 November 2023.

66. National Housing Federation, *310,000 Children in Overcrowded Homes Forced to Share a Bed with Parent or Siblings*, 19 April 2023.

67. '"Shocking" Increase in No-Fault Evictions as Ban Stalls', *Guardian*, 10 November 2023.

68. Department of Levelling Up, Housing and Communities, *Statutory Homelessness in England*, January to March 2023, https://www.gov.uk/government/statistics/statutory-homelessness-in-england-january-to-march-2023.

69. *Guardian*, 6 November 2023.

70. L. Bannister et al., *An Essentials Guarantee: Reforming Universal Credit to Ensure We Can Afford the Essentials in Hard Times* (Joseph Rowntree Foundation and Trussell Trust, 27 July 2020), https://www.jrf.org.uk/report/guarantee-our-essentials.

71. A. Clegg, D. Ghalani, Z. Charlesworth, and T.-M. Johnson, *Missing Out: £19billion of Support is Unclaimed Each Year* (London: Policy in Practice, April 2023), https://policyinpractice.co.uk

72. https://www.ncvo.org.uk/news-and-insights/news-index/time-well-spent-2023/#/.

73. *Time Well Spent, 2023* (London: NCVO, 2023); *UK Giving 2023, A Study of Charitable Giving in the UK* (London: Charities Aid Foundation, 2023).

74. https://www.cafonline.org/docs/default-source/about-us-research/uk-giving-2022.pdf

75. *Performance Tracker 2023. Cross-Service Analysis* (London: Institute for Government October 2023), https://www.instituteforgovernment.org.uk

76. 'Excess Deaths Caused by Cold Homes "Rose by Almost 50% Last Winter"', *Guardian*, 7 September 2023.

77. *Stagnation Nation* (London: The Resolution Foundation, July 2022).

78. National Institute for Economic and Social Research, 9 August 2023, https://www.niesr.ac .uk/publications/uk-heading-towards-five-years-of-lost-economic-growth.

Chapter 15

1. Picketty, *Capital*, p. 597.

2. Ibid., p. 746.

3. Ibid., p. 753.

4. Ibid., p. 423.

5. L. Calafafi, J. Froud, C. Haslam, S. Johal, and K. Williams, *When Nothing Works. From Cost of Living to Foundational Liveability* (Manchester: Manchester University Press, 2023), Ch. 1, Section 3.1.

6. Picketty, *Capital*, p. 660.

7. Malcolm Torry, *Basic Income. A History* (Cheltenham: Edward Elgar, 2021).

8. Daniel Button and Anna Coote, *A Social Guarantee. The Case for Universal Services* (London: New Economics Foundation, September 2021).

9. 'Benefits are Too Low and the Idea of an Essentials Guarantee is a Good One', *Guardian*, 1 September 2023.

10. Matthew Oakley, *A New Framework for Tackling Poverty* (London: Poverty Strategy Commission, September 2023), https://povertyandstrategycommission.org.uk/ tacklingpoverty/.

11. 'Surviving Not Living': Warning Over Worsening Levels of Poverty in UK', *Guardian*, 5 September 2023.

BIBLIOGRAPHY

Abel-Smith, Brian (1964), *The Hospitals, 1800–1948*, London: Heinemann.
Abel-Smith, Brian and Peter Townsend (1965), *The Poor and the Poorest*, London: George Bell and Co.
Abrams, Mark and Richard Rose (1960), *Must Labour Lose?* London: Penguin.
Addison, Paul (1975), *The Road to 1945*, London: Jonathan Cape.
Age UK (2023, January), *The Real Impact of Raising the State Pension Age*. Available online: www.ageuk.org.uk (accessed 22 November 2023).
Andrews, Maggie (2019), *Women and Evacuation in the Second World War: Femininity, Domesticity and Motherhood*, London: Bloomsbury.
Ashworth, William (1954, repr. 1968), *The Genesis of Modern British Town Planning*, London: Routledge.
Atkinson, A.B. (1975), *The Economics of Inequality*, Oxford: Clarendon Press.
Atkinson, A.B. (1995), *Incomes and the Welfare State: Essays on Britain and Europe*, Cambridge: Cambridge University Press.
Atkinson, A.B. (1999), 'Distribution of Income and Wealth', in A.H. Halsey and J. Webb (eds), *Twentieth Century British Social Trends*, 348–84, London: Macmillan.
Ball, Stuart (2011, January), 'Baldwin, Stanley, (1867–1947)', in *Oxford Dictionary of National Biography*, online edition. Available online: www.oxforddnb.com.
Bale, Tim (2012), *The Conservatives Since 1945: The Drivers of Party Change*, Oxford: Oxford University Press.
Baines, Dudley (1994), 'Recovery from Depression', in P. Johnson (ed), *Twentieth Century Britain: Economic, Social and Cultural Change*, 188–202, London: Longman.
Barnett, Corelli (1987), *The Audit of War: The Illusion and Reality of Britain as a Great Nation*, 2nd edn, London: PaperMac.
Beaumont, Caitriona (2013), *Housewives and Citizens: Domesticity and the Women's Movement in England, 1928–64*. Manchester: Manchester University Press.
Beckett, Andy (2009), *When the Lights Went Out: What Really Happened to Britain in the Seventies*, London: Faber and Faber.
Beechey, Veronica and Tessa Perkins (1987), *A Matter of Hours*. Minneapolis: University of Minnesota Press.
Behlmer, George K. (1982), *Child Abuse and Moral Reform in England, 1870–1908*, Stanford: Stanford University Press.
Berridge, Virginia (1996), *AIDS in the UK: The Making of Policy 1981–1994*. Oxford: Oxford University Press.
Beveridge, William (1909), *Unemployment: A Problem of Industry*, London: Longmans.
Beveridge, William (1924), *Insurance for All and Everything*, London: Daily News.
Beveridge, William (1942), *Social Insurance and Allied Services*, Report. Cmd. 6404, London: HMSO.
Beveridge, William (1944), *Full Employment in a Free Society*, London: Allen and Unwin.
Bew, John (2016), *Citizen Clem: A Biography of Attlee*, Portsmouth: Riverrun.
Bingham, Adrian (2009), *Family Newspapers: Sex, Private Life and the Popular Press, 1918–1978*. Oxford: Oxford University Press.

Black, Lawrence and Hugh Pemberton (2009), 'The Winter of Discontent in British Politics', *Political Quarterly*, 80 (4): 553–61.

Blaiklock, Oliver (2012), 'Advising the Citizens: Citizens' Advice Bureaux, Volunteers and the Welfare State in England, 1938–61', PhD thesis. King's College, London.

Blair, Tony (1999), 'Beveridge Revisited: A Welfare State for the 21st Century', in Robert Walker (ed), *Ending Child Poverty: Popular Welfare for the 21st Century*, 7–20. Bristol: University of Bristol, Policy Press.

Bland, Lucy (2019), *Britain's Brown Babies: The Stories of Children Born to Black GIs and White Women in the Second World War*. Manchester: Manchester University Press.

Blick, Andrew (2004), *People Who Live in the Dark: The History of the Special Adviser in British Politics*, London: Politico's.

Board of Education (1927), *Report of the Consultative Committee on the Education of the Adolescent*, London: HMSO.

Booth, Charles, ed. (1889), *Labour and Life of the People*, 3 vols, London and Edinburgh: Williams and Norgate.

Booth, Charles (1901–3), *Life and Labour in London*, 17 vols, London: Macmillan and Co.

Booth, Charles (1894), *The Aged Poor in England and Wales*, London: Macmillan and Co.

Bolderson, Helen (1980), 'The Origins of the Disabled Persons Employment Quota and Its Symbolic Significance', *Journal of Social Policy*, 9 (2): 169–86.

Bowlby, John (1953), *Child Care and the Growth of Love*, London: Pelican.

Bowley, A.L. (1921), *Prices and Wages in the UK, 1914–20*. Oxford: Oxford University Press.

Bowley, A.L., ed. (1944), *Studies in the National Income 1924–1938*. Cambridge: Cambridge University Press.

Bowley, A.L. and A.R. Burnett-Hurst (1915), *Livelihood and Poverty: A Study in the Economic Conditions of Working-Class Households in Northampton, Warrington, Stanley and Reading*, London: G. Bell and Sons.

Bradley, Kate (2009), *Poverty, Philanthropy and the State: Charities and the Working Classes in London, 1918–79*. Manchester: Manchester University Press.

Bradley, Kate (2019), *Lawyers for the Poor: Legal Advice, Voluntary Action and Citizenship in England, 1890–1990*. Manchester: Manchester University Press.

Branson, Noreen (1975), *Britain in the Nineteen Twenties*, London: Weidenfeld and Nicolson.

Branson, Noreen and Margot Heinemann (1971), *Britain in the Nineteen Thirties*, London: Weidenfeld and Nicolson.

Breitenbach, Esther and Fiona Mackay (2010), 'Feminist Politics in Scotland from the 1970s–2000s: Engaging with the Changing State', in E. Breitenbach and P. Thane (eds), *Women and Citizenship in Britain and Ireland in the Twentieth Century: What Difference Did the Vote Make?* 153–70, London: Continuum.

Brierley, Peter (2000), 'Religion', in A.H. Halsey and J. Webb (eds), *Twentieth Century British Social Trends*, 650–74, London: Macmillan.

Briggs, Asa (2001), *Michael Young: Social Entrepreneur*, London: Palgrave.

Brooke, Stephen (2011), *Sexual Politics: Sexuality, Family Planning and the British Left from the 1880s to the Present Day*. Oxford: Oxford University Press.

Brooke, Stephen (2012), 'Slumming in Swinging London: Class, Gender and the Post-war City in Nell Dunn's *Up the Junction*', *Cultural and Social History*, 9 (3): 429–49.

Brookes, Barbara (1988), *Abortion in England, 1900–1967*, London: Routledge.

Burchardt, Tania (2004), 'Selective Inclusion: Asylum Seekers and Other Marginalized Groups', in J. Hills and K. Stewart (eds), *A More Equal Society? New Labour, Poverty, Inequality and Exclusion*, 209–30. Bristol: University of Bristol, Policy Press.

Burk, Kathleen and Alec Cairncross (1992) *'Goodbye Great Britain': The 1976 IMF Crisis*, New Haven: Yale University Press.

Bibliography

Burnett, John (1978), *Plenty and Want*, Aldershot: Scolar.
Butler, David (1972), 'Electors and Elected', in A.H. Halsey (ed), *Trends in British Society Since 1900*, 227–47. London: Macmillan.
Butler, David (1989), *British General Elections Since 1945*, Oxford: Wiley Blackwell.
Butler, David and Butler Gareth (2000), *Twentieth Century British Political Facts, 1900–2000*, London: Macmillan.
Butler, David and Dennis Kavanagh, eds. (2002), *The British General Election of 2001*, London: Palgrave.
Butler, David and Anthony King (2008, reprinted), *The British General Election of 1964*, London: Macmillan.
Butler, David and Richard Rose (1960), *The British General Election of 1959*, London: Macmillan.
Butler, R.A. (1971), *Art of the Possible*, London: Hamish Hamilton.
Button, Daniel and Anna Coote (2021, September), *A Social Guarantee: The Case for Universal Services*, London: New Economics Foundation.
Cairncross, Alec (1985), *Years of Recovery: British Economic Policy 1945–51*, London: Methuen.
Cairncross, Alec (1995), *The British Economy Since 1945: Economic Policy and Performance, 1945–95*, 2nd edn, Oxford: Blackwell.
Calafafi, L., J. Froud, C. Haslam, S. Johal, and K. Williams (2023), *When Nothing Works: From Cost of Living to Foundational Liveability*. Manchester: Manchester University Press.
Calder, Angus (1971), *The Peoples' War: Britain 1939–1945*, 2nd edn, Beaconsfield: Panther.
Callaghan, James (1987), *Time and Chance*, London: Collins.
Campbell, John (1987), *Nye Bevan: A Biography*, London: Hodder and Stoughton.
Capie, F. (1983, repr 2013), *Depression and Protectionism in Britain Between the Wars*, London: Routledge.
Castle, Barbara (1993), *Fighting All the Way*, London: Pan.
Chaney, Paul, (2010), 'Devolution, Citizenship and Women's Political Representation in Wales', in E. Breitenbach and P. Thane (eds), *Women and Citizenship in Britain and Ireland in the Twentieth Century: What Difference Did the Vote Make?* 189–208. London: Continuum.
Charmley, John (2008), *A History of Conservative Politics Since 1830*, 2nd edn, London: Palgrave.
Clarke, Peter (2004), *Hope and Glory: Britain 1900–2000*, 2nd edn, London: Penguin.
Cohen, Michele (2004), 'Knowledge and the Gendered Curriculum: The Problematisation of Girls' Achievement'. Available online: www.historyandpolicy.org/policy-papers/category/michele-cohen (accessed 25 November 2023).
Coleman, David (2000), '"Population and Family" in Halsey and Webb', in A. H. Halsey and J. Webb (eds.), *Twentieth Century Social Trends*, 27–93. London: Macmillan.
Connolly, Sara and Mary Gregory (2007), 'Women and Work Since 1970', in N. Crafts, I. Gazeley, and A. Newell (eds), *Work and Pay in Twentieth Century Britain*, 142–77. Oxford: Oxford University Press.
Coopey, Richard (1993), 'Industrial Policy in the White Heat of the Scientific Revolution', in R. Coopey, S. Fielding, and N. Tiratsoo (eds), *The Wilson Governments, 1964–1970*, 102–22, London: Pinter.
Cook, Hera (2004), *The Long Sexual Revolution: English Women, Sex and Contraception, 1800–1975*. Oxford: Oxford University Press.
Crafts, Nicholas (2014), 'Economic Growth during the Long Twentieth Century', in Roderick Floud, Jane Humphries, and Paul Johnson (eds), *Cambridge Economic History of Modern Britain*, Vol. 2, *1870 to the Present*, 26–59. Cambridge: Cambridge University Press.
Creagh, Mark (2023, July), *Work Intensification*, London: Trades Union Congress.
Cretney, Stephen (2003), *Family Law in the Twentieth Century, A History*. Oxford: Oxford University Press.

Cribb, Jonathan, et al. (2012), *Living Standards, Poverty and Inequality in the UK*, London: Institute for Fiscal Studies.

Cribb, Jonathan, et al. (2018), *Living Standards, Poverty and Inequality in the UK, 2018*. Joseph Rowntree Foundation. Available online: www.jrf.org.uk/uk-poverty-causes-costs-and -solutions. (accessed 22 November 2023).

Crick, Bernard (1980), *George Orwell: A Life*, London: Secker and Warburg.

Crosland, C.A.R. (1956), *The Future of Socialism*, London: Jonathan Cape.

Crossman, R.H.S. (1975), *Diary of a Cabinet Minister, Vol.1: Minister of Housing 1964–66, Vol. 2: 1966–68*, London: Hamish Hamilton and Jonathan Cape.

Crowther, M.A. (1981), *The Workhouse System 1834–1929*, London: Batsford.

Crowther, M.A. (1988), *British Social Policy 1914–1939*, London: Macmillan.

Damer, Sean (1980), 'State, Class and Housing: Glasgow 1875–1919', in Joseph Melling (ed), *Housing, Social Policy and the State*, 73–112, London: Croom Helm.

Daniel, W.W. (1968), *Racial Discrimination in England: Based on the PEP Report*, London: Penguin.

Daunton, Martin (2001), *Trusting Leviathan: The Politics of Taxation in Britain, 1799–1914*. Cambridge: Cambridge University Press.

Daunton, Martin (2002), *Just Taxes: The Politics of Taxation in Britain, 1914–1979*. Cambridge: Cambridge University Press.

Davies, Margaret Llewelyn, ed. (1915), *Maternity. Letters from Working Women*. London: G. Bell, repr London, Virago, 1978.

Davis, John (1999), *A History of Britain, 1885–1939*, London: Macmillan.

Deakin, Nicholas (1970), *Colour, Citizenship and British Society*, Beaconsfield: Panther.

Deakin, Nicholas and Justin Davis Smith (2011), 'Labour, Charity and Voluntary Action: The Myth of Hostility', in M. Hilton and J. McKay (eds), *The Ages of Voluntarism. How We Got to the Big Society*, 69–93, London: Oxford University Press, British Academy.

Debenham, Claire (2014), *Birth Control and the Rights of Women: Post-suffrage feminism in the Early Twentieth Century*, London: IB Tauris.

Devine, T.M. (2012), *The Scottish Nation 1799–2007: A Modern History*, London: Penguin.

Dorey, Peter (2014), 'The Stepping Stones Programme: The Conservative Party's Struggle to Develop a Trade Union Policy 1975–9', *Historical Studies in Industrial Relations*, 35 (35): 89–116.

Dorey, Peter (2015), 'A Farewell to Alms: Thatcherism's Legacy of Inequality', *British Politics*, 10 (1): 79–98.

Douglas, J.W.B., J.W. Ross, and H.R. Simpson (1971), *All Our Future: A Longitudinal Study of Secondary Education*, London: Panther.

Dwork, Deborah (1987), *War Is Good for Babies and Other Young Children: A History of the Infant and Child Welfare Movement in England, 1898–1918*, London: Routledge.

Dyhouse, Carol (2006), *Students: A Gendered History*, London: Routledge.

Edgerton, David (2006), *Warfare State: Britain 1920–1980*. Cambridge: Cambridge University Press.

Englander, David (1983), *Landlord and Tenant*. Oxford: Oxford University Press.

Evandrou, Maria and Jane Falkingham (1998), 'The Personal Social Services', in H. Glennerster and J. Hills (eds), *The State of Welfare: The Economics of Social Spending*, 2nd edn, 189–256. Oxford: Oxford University Press.

Evans, Geoffrey and James Tilley (2017), *The New Politics of Class: The Political Exclusion of the British Working Class*. Oxford: Oxford University Press.

Evans, Martin (1998), 'Social Security: Dismantling the Pyramids?', in H. Glennerster and J. Hills (eds), *The State of Welfare: The Economics of Social Spending*, 2nd edn, 257–307. Oxford: Oxford University Press.

Bibliography

Evans, Tanya (2009), 'Stopping the Poor Getting Poorer: The Establishment and Professionalization of Poverty NGOs, 1945–95', in N. Crowson, M. Hilton, and J. MacKay (eds), *NGOs in Contemporary Britain: Non-State Actors in Society and Politics Since 1945*, 147–16, London: Palgrave.

Ferguson, Sheila and Hilde Fitzgerald (1954), *Studies in the Social Services: History of the Second World War*, London: HMSO and Longman Green.

Field, Frank (1982), *Poverty and Politics: The Inside Story of the Child Poverty Action Group's Campaigns in the 1970s*, London: Heinemann.

Fielding, Stephen, Peter Thompson, and Nick Tiratsoo (1995), *'England Arise!' The Labour Party and Popular Politics in 1940s Britain*. Manchester: Manchester University Press.

Filby, Eliza (2015), *God and Mrs Thatcher: The Battle for Britain's Soul*, London: Biteback.

Finney, N., J. Nazroo, L. Bécares, and S.L.N. Kapadia, eds. (2023), *Racism and Ethnic Inequality in a Time of Crisis: Findings from the Evidence for Equality National Survey*. Bristol: University of Bristol, Policy Press.

Freeman, Mark (2000), *Social Investigation and Rural England, 1870–1914*, Martlesham: Boydell Press.

Galbraith, J.K. (1962), *The Affluent Society*, London: Pelican.

Gavron, Hannah (1966), *The Captive Wife: Conflict of Housebound Mothers, 1970*, London: Routledge and Pelican.

Garside, W.R. (1990), *British Unemployment 1919–1939: A Study in Public Policy*. Cambridge: Cambridge University Press.

Gazeley, Ian (2003), *Poverty in Britain, 1900–1965*, London: Palgrave Macmillan.

Gazeley, Ian (2014), 'Income and Living Standards', in Roderick Floud, Jane Humphries, and Paul Johnson (eds), *Cambridge Economic History of Modern Britain*, Vol. 2, *1870 to the Present*, 151–80. Cambridge: Cambridge University Press.

Gazeley, Ian and Andrew Newell (2000), 'Rowntree Revisited: Poverty in Britain, 1900', *Explorations in Economic History*, 37 (2): 174–88.

Gazeley, Ian and Pat Thane (1998), 'Patterns of Visibility: Unemployment in Britain During the 19th and 20th Centuries', in G. Lewis (ed), *Forming Nation, Framing Welfare*, 181–226, London: Routledge.

Gentleman, Amelia (2019), *The Windrush Betrayal: Exposing the Hostile Environment*, London: Guardian, Faber.

Gershuny, Jonathan and Kimberly Fisher (2000), 'Leisure', in A. H. Halsey and J. Webb (eds), *Twentieth Century Social Trends*, 620–49. London: Macmillan.

Gildea, Robert (2023), *Backbone of the Nation: Mining Communities and the Great Strike of 1984–85*, New Haven: Yale University Press.

Gill, J. and D. Taylor (2012), *Active Ageing: Live Longer and Prosper*, London: UCL School of Pharmacy.

Glennerster, Howard (1995), *British Social Policy Since 1945*, Oxford: Blackwell.

Glennerster, Howard (1998), 'Education: Reaping the Harvest?', in H. Glennerster and J. Hills (eds), *The State of Welfare: The Economics of Social Spending*, 2nd edn, 27–74. Oxford: Oxford University Press.

Glew, Helen (2016), *Gender, Rhetoric and Regulation: Women's Work in the Civil Service and the London County Council, 1900–55*. Manchester: Manchester University Press.

Goldman, Lawrence (2014), *The Life of R.H. Tawney: Socialism and History*, London: Bloomsbury Academic.

Grant, Peter, 'Voluntarism and the Impact of the First World War', in M. Hilton and J. McKay (eds), *The Ages of Voluntarism. How We Got to the Big Society*, 27–46. London: Oxford University Press/British Academy.

Groves, Dulcie M. (1986), 'Women and Occupational Pensions,1870–1983', PhD thesis. King's College, London.

Hall, Lesley A. (2000), *Sex, Gender and Social Change in Britain Since 1880*, London: Macmillan.

Hall, Phoebe (1975), 'Creating the Open University', in Phoebe Hall, Hilary Land, Roy Alfred Parker, and Adrian Leonard Webb (eds), *Change, Choice and Conflict in Social Policy*, 155–276. London: Heinemann.

Halsey, A.H., '"Further and Higher Education"', in A. H. Halsey and J. Webb (eds), *Twentieth Century Social Trends*, 221–53. London: Macmillan.

Hammerton, A.J. and A. Thomson (2012), *Ten Pound Poms. Australia's Invisible Migrants*. Manchester: Manchester University Press.

Hampton, Jameel (2016), *Disability and the Welfare State in Britain. Changes in Perceptions and Policy, 1948–1979*. Bristol: University of Bristol, Policy Press.

Hardy, Anne (2001), *Health and Social Medicine in Britain Since 1860*, London: Palgrave.

Harrington, Michael (1962), *The Other America: Poverty in the United States*, London: Macmillan.

Harris, Jose (1986), 'Political Ideas and the Debate on State Welfare', in H.L. Smith (ed), *War and Social Change: British Society in the Second World War*, 233–63. Manchester: Manchester University Press.

Harris, Jose (1991), 'Enterprise and the Welfare State', in Terry Gouvish and Alan O' Day (eds), *Britain Since 1945*, 39–58. London: Macmillan.

Harris, Jose (1994), *Private Lives, Public Spirit: Britain 1870–1914*, London: Penguin.

Harris, Jose (1997), *William Beveridge: A Biography*, 2nd edn, Oxford: Oxford University Press.

Harvie, Christopher (2005), 'The Politics of Devolution', in P. Addison and H. Jones (eds), *A Companion to Contemporary Britain,1939–2000*, 427–43. Oxford: Blackwell.

Harvie, Christopher and Peter Jones (2000), *The Road to Home Rule*. Edinburgh: Edinburgh University Press.

Hasigawa, Junichi (1992), *Replanning the Blitzed City Centre*, Buckingham: Open University Press.

Hattersley, Roy (2014), 'Harold Wilson's Moral Crusade Can Still Be a Rallying Cry', *Guardian*, 15 October.

Hatton, Tmothy J. (2014), 'Population, Migration and Labour Supply: Great Britain, 1871–2011', in Roderick Floud, Jane Humphries, and Paul Johnson (eds), *Cambridge Economic History of Modern Britain*, Vol. 2, *1870 to the Present*, 95–121. Cambridge: Cambridge University Press.

Healey, Denis (1989), *The Time of My Life*, London: Michael Joseph.

Heath, Anthony F. (2018), *Social Progress in Britain*. Oxford: Oxford University Press.

Hennock, E.P. (2007), *The Origin of the Welfare State in England and Germany 1850–1914*. Cambridge: Cambridge University Press.

Hill, Michael (1993), *The Welfare State in Britain: A Political History Since 1945*, Cheltenham: Edward Elgar.

Hills, John (1998), 'Housing: A Decent Home within the Reach of Every Family', in H. Glennerster and J. Hills (eds), *The State of Welfare: The Economics of Social Spending*, 2nd edn, 122–88. Oxford: Oxford University Press.

Hills, John (2015), *Good Times, Bad Times: The Welfare Myth of Them and Us*. Bristol: University of Bristol, Policy Press.

Hills, John and Beverley Mullings (1990), 'Housing: A Decent Home for All at a Price within Their Means?', in J. Hills (ed), *The State of Welfare: The Welfare State in Britain Since 1974*, 135–201. Oxford: Oxford University Press.

Hilton, Claire (2017), *Improving Psychiatric Care for Older People: Barbara Robb's Campaign, 1965–75*, London: Palgrave.

Hilton, Matthew, ed. (2005, September), 'Michael Young in Retrospect', *Contemporary British History*, 19 (3): 277–9.

Bibliography

Hilton, Matthew, Nick Crowson, Jean-Francois Mouhot, and James MacKay (2012), *A Historical Guide to NGOs in Britain. Charity, Civil Society and the Voluntary Sector Since 1945*, London: Palgrave.

Hinton, James (2002), *Women, Social Leadership and the Second World War: Continuities of Class*. Oxford: Oxford University Press.

Hinton, James (1992), 'Women and the Labour Vote, 1945–50', *Labour History Review*, 57 (3): 59–66.

Hirsch, D. and J. Stone (2021, May), 'Local Indicators of Child Poverty after Housing Costs 2019/20', Centre for Research in Social Policy at Loughborough University for the End Child Poverty Campaign.

Hoggart, Richard (1969), *The Uses of Literacy*, London: Penguin.

Holden, Andrew (2004), *Makers and Manners: Politics and Morality in Post-war Britain*, London: Politico's.

Hollis, Patricia (1987), *Ladies Elect: Women in English Local Government, 1865–1914*. Oxford: Oxford University Press.

Holmans, Alan (1999), '"Housing"', in A.H. Halsey and J. Webb (eds), *Twentieth Century British Social Trends*, 469–510, London: Macmillan.

Holmes, Colin, 'Immigration', in T. Gourvish and A. O' Day (eds), *Britain Since 1945*, 209–32. London: Macmillan.

Holton, Sandra Stanley (1986), *Feminism and Democracy: Women's Suffrage and Reform Politics in Britain, 1900–1918*. Cambridge: Cambridge University Press.

Home Office, *Citizenship Surveys 2002–11*. Available online: https://www.ukdataservice.ac.uk (accessed 22 November 2023).

Howker, E. and S. Malik (2010), *Jilted Generation: How Britain Has Bankrupted Its Youth*, London: Icon Books.

Hubback, Eva M. (1957), *The Population of Britain*, London: Penguin.

Humphreys, Robert (1995), *Sin, Organized Charity and the Poor Law in Victorian England*, London: Macmillan.

Jackson, Louise A. (2006), *Women Police: Gender, Welfare and Surveillance in the Twentieth Century*. Manchester: Manchester University Press.

Jackson, Louise A. and Angela Bartie (2014), *Policing Youth: Britain 1945–70*. Manchester: Manchester University Press.

Jarvis, Mark (2005), *Conservative Governments, Morality and Social Change in Affluent Britain*. Manchester: Manchester University Press.

Johnson, Paul (1994), 'The Employment and Retirement of Older Men in England and Wales, 1881–1981', *Economic History Review*, 47 (1): 106–28.

Jones, D. Caradog, ed. (1934), *The Social Survey of Merseyside*. Liverpool University Press and London, Hodder and Stoughton.

Jones, Harriet and Michael Kandiah, eds. (1990), *The Myth of Consensus: New Views on British History, 1945–64*, London: Macmillan.

Jones, Helen, ed. (1994a), *Duty and Citizenship: The Correspondence and Papers of Violet Markham, 1896–1953*, Cheltenham: The Historians' Press.

Jones, Helen (1994b), *Health and Society in Twentieth Century Britain*, London: Longman.

Jones, Helen (2004), 'Markham, Violet Rosa (1872–1959)', *ODNB*. Available online: www.oxforddnb.com.

Joseph Rowntree Foundation (2023), *UK Poverty 2023: The Essential Guide to Understanding Poverty in the UK*. Available online: www.jrf.org.uk/work/uk-poverty-2023-the-essential -guide-to-understanding-poverty-in-the-uk (accessed 31 January 2014).

Kavanagh, Dennis and Philip Cowley (2010), *The British General Election of 2010*, London: Palgrave.

Keating, Jenny (2009), *A Child for Keeps. A History of Adoption in England, 1918–45*, London: Palgrave.

Keynes, John Maynard (1919), *The Economic Consequences of the Peace*, London: Macmillan.

Kiernan, Kathleen, Hilary Land, and Jane Lewis (1999), *Lone Motherhood in Twentieth Century Britain*. Oxford: Oxford University Press.

Kimber, Nick (2010), 'Race and Equality', in P. Thane (ed), *Unequal Britain: Equalities in Britain Since 1945*, 29–52, London: Bloomsbury.

Kitson, Michael and Jonathan Michie (2014), 'The De-industrial Revolution: The Rise and Fall of UK Manufacturing, 1870–2010', in Roderick Floud, Jane Humphries, and Paul Johnson (eds), *Cambridge Economic History of Modern Britain*, Vol. 2, *1870 to the Present*, 302–29. Cambridge: Cambridge University Press.

Klein, Viola (1957), *Britain's Married Women Workers*, London: Routledge.

Koestler, Arthur, ed. (1963), *Suicide of a Nation? An Enquiry into the State of Britain Today*, London: Hutchinson.

Kynaston, David (2001), *The City of London. Vol.4 A Club No More, 1845–2000*, London: Chatto and Windus.

Kynaston, David (2007), *Austerity Britain, 1945–51*, London: Bloomsbury.

Langhamer, Claire (2013), *The English in Love: The Intimate Story of an Emotional Revolution*. Oxford: Oxford University Press.

Le Grand, Julian and Polly Vizard (1998), 'The National Health Service: Crisis, Change or Continuity?', in H. Glennerster and J. Hills (eds), *The State of Welfare: The Economics of Social Spending*, 2nd edn, 7–121. Oxford: Oxford University Press.

Lewis, Jane (2001), *The End of Marriage? Individualism and Intimate Relations*, Cheltenham: Edward Elgar.

Loudon, I. (1994), *Death in Childbirth: An International Study of Maternal Care and Maternal Mortality, 1800–1950*. Oxford: Oxford University Press.

Lowe, Rodney (1990), 'The Second World War, Consensus and the Foundation of the Welfare State', *Twentieth Century British History*, 1 (2): 152–82.

Lowe, Rodney (2005), *The Welfare State in Britain Since 1945*, London: Palgrave.

Macaskill, Hilary (1993), *From the Workhouse to the Workplace: 75 Years of One-Parent Family Life, 1918–1939*, London: National Council for One Parent Families.

MacKenzie, Norman and Jeanne, eds. (1982–5), *The Diary of Beatrice Webb*, 4 Vols, London: Virago.

MacLean, Mavis with Jacek Kurzewski (2011), *Making Family Law: A Socio-Legal Account of Legislative Process in England and Wales*, Oxford: Hart.

Marmot, Michael (2010), *Fair Society, Healthy Lives. Strategic Review of Health Inequalities in England*. Available online: https://www.gov.uk/research-for-development-outputs/fair-society -healthy-lives-the-marmot-review-strategic-review-of-health-inequalities-inEngland-post -2010 (accessed 22 November 2023).

Marmot, Michael, et al. (2020), *Build Back Fairer. The Covid-19 Marmot Review. The Pandemic, Socioeconomic and Health Inequalities in England*, London: The Health Foundation.

Marquand, David (1977), *Ramsay MacDonald*, London: Jonathan Cape.

Marwick, Arthur (1967), *The Deluge: British Society and the First World War*, London: Pelican.

McCarthy, Helen (2010), 'Gender Equality', in P. Thane (ed), *Unequal Britain: Equalities in Britain Since 1945*, 105–24, London: Bloomsbury.

McDowell, Linda (2013), *Working Lives: Gender, Migration and Employment in Britain, 1945–2007*, Chichester: Wiley-Blackwell.

McDowell, Linda (2016), *Migrant Women's Voices: Talking About Life and Work in the UK Since 1945*, London: Bloomsbury.

McKibbin, Ross (1998), *Classes and Cultures, England, 1918–51*. Oxford: Oxford University Press.

Bibliography

McKnight, Abigail (2004), 'Employment: Tackling Poverty through "Work for Those Who Can"', in J. Hills and K. Stewart (eds), *A More Equal Society? New Labour, Poverty, Inequality and Exclusion*, 23–46. Bristol: University of Bristol, Policy Press.

Meehan, Elizabeth M. (1985), *Women's Rights at Work: Campaigns and Policy in Britain and the United States*, London: Macmillan.

Melling, Joseph, ed. (1980), *Housing, Social Policy and the State*, London: Croom Helm.

Melling, Joseph (1983), *Rent Strikes. Peoples' Struggle for Housing in West Scotland, 1890–1916*, Edinburgh: Polygon.

Millar, Simon (2010), 'Disability', in P. Thane (ed), *Unequal Britain: Equalities in Britain Since 1945*, 163–88, London: Bloomsbury.

Millward, Gareth (2015), 'Social Security Policy and the Early Disability Movement-Expertise, Disability and the Government, 1965–77', *Twentieth Century British History*, 26 (2): 274–97.

Mitchell, B.R. and P. Deane (1962), *Abstract of British Historical Statistics*. Cambridge: Cambridge University Press.

Mitchell, B.R. and H.G. Jones (1971), *Second Abstract of British Historical Statistics*. Cambridge: Cambridge University Press.

Morgan, K.O. (1987), *Wales: Rebirth of a Nation, 1880–1980*. Oxford: Oxford University Press.

Morgan, K.O. (1998), *Callaghan: A Life*. Oxford: Oxford University Press.

Morgan, K.O. (2004), '"Addison, Christopher First Viscount Addison, 1869–1951"', *ODNB, Online Edn.* (accessed January 2011). Available online: https://www.oxforddnb.com (accessed 24 November 2023).

Morgan, R.I. (1994), 'The Introduction of Civil Legal Aid in England and Wales, 1914–1949', *Twentieth Century British History*, 5 (1): 38–76.

Mortimore, Roger and Andrew Blick, eds. (2018), *Butler's British Political Facts*, London: Palgrave Macmillan.

Mowat, C.L. (1972), *Britain Between the Wars*, London: Methuen.

Murphy, Kate (2016), *Behind the Wireless: A History of Early Women at the BBC*, London: Palgrave Macmillan.

National Council of Voluntary Organizations (2023), *Time Well Spent*, London: NCVO.

Nehring, Holger, 'The Growth of Social Movements', in P. Addison and H. Jones (eds), *A Companion to Contemporary Britain,1939–2000*, 389–406. Oxford: Blackwell.

Noakes, Lucy (1997), *War and the British: Gender and National Identity, 1939–1990*, London: IB Tauris.

Noakes, Lucy (2001), 'War and Peace', in Zweiniger-Bargielowska, Ina (ed), *Women in Twentieth Century Britain*, 307–20, Harlow: Pearson Education.

Oakley, Ann (2011), *A Critical Woman: Barbara Wootton, Social Science and Public Policy in the Twentieth Century*, London: Bloomsbury.

Oakley, Ann (2021), *Forgotten Wives: How Women Get Written Out of History*. Bristol: University of Bristol, Policy Press.

Offer, Avner (1991), *The First World War: An Agrarian Interpretation*. Oxford: Oxford University Press.

Osgerby, Bill (1998), *Youth in Britain Since 1945*, Oxford: Blackwell.

Pankhurst, Sylvia (1987), *The Home Front*, London: Hutchinson, 932, reprinted London, Cresset.

Parekh, Bhikhu (2000), *The Future of Multi-ethnic Britain*, London: Runnymede Trust.

Parker, Roy (1975), 'The Struggle for Clean Air', in P. Hall, H. Land, R.A. Parker, and A.L. Webb (eds), *Change, Choice and Conflict in Social Policy*, 371–409. London: Heinemann

Pedersen, Susan (1993), *Family, Dependence and the Origins of the Welfare State. Britain and France 1914–1945*. Cambridge: Cambridge University Press.

Pedersen, Susan (2004), *Eleanor Rathbone and the Politics of Conscience*, New Haven: Yale University Press.

Pemberton, Hugh (2006), 'Politics and Pensions in Post-war Britain', in H. Pemberton, P. Thane, and N. Whiteside (eds), *Britain's Pensions Crisis: History and Policy*, 39–63, London: Oxford University Press. The British Academy.

Pensions Commission (2004), *First Report, Pensions: Challenges and Choices*, London: The Stationery Office; Second Report, *A New Pension Settlement for the Twenty-first Century* (2005); *Final Report: Implementing an Integrated Package of Pension Reforms* (2006).

Phillips, Gordon and Noel Whiteside (1985), *Casual Labour and the Unemployment Question in the Port Transport Industry, 1880–1970*. Oxford: Oxford University Press.

Phillips, M. and T. Phillips (1998), *Windrush: The Irresistible Rise of Multi-cultural Britain*, London: Harper Collins.

Piketty, Thomas (2017), *Capital in the Twenty-First Century*, Cambridge: Harvard University Press.

Pimlott, Ben (1993), *Harold Wilson*, London: Harper Collins.

Pizzey, Erin (2013), *This Way to the Revolution –a Memoir*, London: Peter Owen.

Porter, Mel (2010), 'Gender Identity and Sexual Orientation', in P. Thane (ed), *Unequal Britain: Equalities in Britain Since 1945*, 125–62, London: Bloomsbury.

Porter, Mel and Becky Taylor (2010), 'Gypsies and Travellers', in P. Thane (ed), *Unequal Britain: Equalities in Britain Since 1945*, 71–104, London: Bloomsbury.

Reeves, Maud Pember, (1913), *Round about a Pound a Week*, London: G.Bell and Sons, reprinted. London: Virago 1979.

Registrar General, *Statistical Review of England and Wales for the Six Years 1940–1945, Text, Vol. 11, Civil*.

Reid, Alastair J. (2004), *United We Stand: A History of Britain's Trade Unions*, London: Allen Lane.

Reynolds, David (2000), *Britannia Overruled: British Policy and World Power in the Twentieth Century*, 2nd edn, London: Routledge.

Riddell, Peter (1985), *The Thatcher Government*, Oxford: Blackwell.

Rice, Margery Spring (1939), *Working Class Wives: Their Health and Conditions*, London: Penguin, repr. London, Virago, 1981.

Roberts, Richard (2013), *Saving the City: The Great Financial Crisis of 1914*. Oxford: Oxford University Press.

Roberts, Richard (2016), *When Britain Went Bust: The 1976 IMF Crisis*, London: OMFIF.

Rollett, Constance (1972), 'Housing', in A.H. Halsey (ed), *Trends in British Society Since 1900*, 284–320. London: Macmillan.

Root, Amanda (1999), 'Transport and Communications', in A.H. Halsey and J. Webb (eds), *Twentieth Century British Social Trends*, 437–68, London: Macmillan.

Routh, Guy (1980), *Occupation and Pay in Great Britain, 1906–79*, London: Macmillan.

Rowntree, Benjamin Seebohm (1901), *Poverty. A Study of Town Life*, London: Nelson.

Rowntree, Benjamin Seebohm (1941), *Poverty and Progress*, London: Longmans, Green and Co.

Rowntree, Benjamin Seebohm and G.S. Lavers (1951), *Poverty and the Welfare State: A Third Social Survey of York Dealing Only with Economic Questions*, London: Longman, Green and Co.

Ryan, P.A. (1978), 'Poplarism 1894–1930', in Pat Thane (ed), *The Origins of British Social Policy*, 56–83, London: Croom Helm.

Scott, Peter (2014), 'The Household Economy Since 1870', in Roderick Floud, Jane Humphries, and Paul Johnson (eds), *Cambridge Economic History of Modern Britain*, Vol. 2, *1870 to the Present*, 362–86. Cambridge: Cambridge University Press.

Seear, N., V. Roberts, and J. Brick (1964), *A Career for Women in Industry*, Edinburgh: Oliver and Boyd.

Bibliography

Sefton, Tom and Holly Sutherland (2004), 'Inequality and Poverty Under New Labour', in J. Hills and K. Stewart (eds), *A More Equal Society? New Labour, Poverty, Inequality and Exclusion*, 231–50. Bristol: University of Bristol, Policy Press.

Seldon, Anthony, ed. (2007), *Blair's Britain 1997–2007*. Cambridge: Cambridge University Press.

Seldon, Anthony and Denis Kavanagh, eds. (1994), *The Major Effect*, London: Macmillan.

Setch, Eve (2000), 'The Women's Liberation Movement in Britain, 1969–1979: Organization, Creativity and Debate', PhD thesis. London: Royal Holloway College.

Sheard, Sally (2014), *The Passionate Economist: How Brian Abel-Smith Shaped Global Health and Social Welfare*. Bristol: University of Bristol, Policy Press.

Simey, T.S. and M.B. Simey (1960), *Charles Booth, Social Scientist*. Oxford: Oxford University Press.

Single Parent Action Network (1993), *Positive Images, Negative Stereotypes*, Bristol: Single Parent Action Network.

Skelley, J., ed. (1926), *The General Strike*, London: Lawrence and Wishart.

Smith, George (1999), 'Schools', in A.H. Halsey and J. Webb (eds), *Twentieth Century British Social Trends*, 179–220, London: Macmillan.

Smith, Harold L. (1986), 'The Effect of the War on the Status of Women', in H.L. Smith (ed), *War and Social Change: British Society in the Second World War*, 208–29. Manchester: Manchester University Press.

Smith, Justin Davis (2019), *100 Years of NCVO and Voluntary Action: Idealists and Realists*, London: Palgrave Macmillan.

Social and Community Planning Research, (1992), *British Social Attitudes: Cumulative Sourcebook: The First Six Surveys*, London: Gower.

Stevenson, J. (1977), *Social Conditions in Britain Between the Wars*, London: Penguin.

Summerfield, Penny (1986), 'The "Levelling of Class"', in H.L. Smith (ed), *War and Social Change: British Society in the Second World War*, 196–8. Manchester: Manchester University Press.

Swenarton, Mark (1981), *Homes Fit for Heroes*, London: Heinemann.

Szreter, S. and K. Fisher (2010), *Sex Before the Sexual Revolution: Intimate Life in England, 1918–1963*. Cambridge: Cambridge University Press.

Tatchell, Peter (2017, 23 May), 'Fifty Years of Gay Liberation? In Britain It's Barely Four', *The Guardian*.

Thane, Pat, ed. (1978), *The Origins of British Social Policy*, London: Croom Helm.

Thane, Pat (1990a), 'Government and Society in England and Wales, 1750–1914', in F.M.L. Thompson (ed), *The Cambridge Social History of Britain 1750–1950*, Vol. 3, 1–62. Cambridge: Cambridge University Press.

Thane, Pat (1990b), '"The Debate on the Declining Birth-Rate in Britain: The 'Menace'" of an Ageing Population, 1920s–1950s"', *Continuity and Change*, 5 (2): 283–305.

Thane, Pat (1990c), 'The Women of the British Labour Party and Feminism, 1906–1945', in H.L. Smith (ed), *British Feminism in the Twentieth Century*, 128–31, Aldershot: Edward Elgar.

Thane, Pat (1991), 'Towards Equal Opportunities? Women in Britain Since 1945', in T. Gourvish and A. O' Day (eds), *Britain Since 1945*, 183–208. London: Macmillan.

Thane, Pat (1996), *Foundations of the Welfare State*, 2nd edn, London: Longman.

Thane, Pat (2000a), 'Labour and Welfare', in D. Tanner, N. Tiratsoo, and P. Thane (eds), *Labour's First Century*, 80–119. Cambridge: Cambridge University Press.

Thane, Pat (2000b), *Old Age in English History: Past Experiences, Present Issues*. Oxford: Oxford University Press.

Thane, Pat (2001), 'What Difference Did the Vote Make?', in A. Vickery (ed), *Women, Privilege and Power. British Politics, 1750 to the Present*, 253–88, Stanford: Stanford University Press.

Thane, Pat (2005), 'Michael Young and "Welfare"', *Contemporary British History*, 19 (3): 293–300.

Thane, Pat (2010), 'Older People and Equality', in P. Thane (ed), *Unequal Britain*, 7–28. London: Bloomsbury.

Thane, Pat (2011), 'Voluntary Action in Britain since Beveridge', in M. Oppenheimer and N. Deakin (eds), *Beveridge and Voluntary Action in Britain and the Wider British World*, 121–34. Manchester: Manchester University Press.

Thane, Pat (2012), 'The "Big Society" and the "Big State": Creative Tension or Crowding Out?', *Twentieth Century British History*, 23 (3): 408–29.

Thane, Pat (2013), 'Demographic Futures: Addressing Inequality and Diversity among Older People', in P. Taylor-Gooby (ed), *New Paradigms in Public Policy*, 139–66. London: Oxford University Press. British Academy.

Thane, Pat and Ruth Davidson (2016), *The Child Poverty Action Group (1965–2015)*, London: CPAG. Available online: https://cpag.org.uk/about-cpag/our-history. (accessed 22 November 2023).

Thane, Pat and Tanya Evans (2012), *'Sinners?' Scroungers? Saints? Unmarried Motherhood in England in the Twentieth Century*. Oxford: Oxford University Press.

Thatcher, Margaret (1993), *The Downing St Years*, London: Harper Collins.

Theakston, Kevin (1999), 'A Permanent Revolution: The Major Governments and the Civil Service', in P. Dorey (ed), *The Major Premiership: Politics and Policy under John Major 1990–97*, 28, London: Palgrave.

Thomlinson, Natalie (2016), *Race, Ethnicity and the Women's Movement in England, 1968–93*, London: Palgrave Macmillan.

Thorpe, Andrew (2014), *A History of the Labour Party*, 4th edn, London: Palgrave Macmillan.

Timmins, Nicolas (1995), *The Five Giants: A Biography of the Welfare State*, 3rd edn, 2917, London: Harper Collins.

Tiratsoo, Nick (1960), *Reconstruction, Affluence and Labour Politics: Coventry, 1945–1960*, London: Routledge.

Titmuss, Richard M. (1950), *Problems of Social Policy: History of the Second World War, UK Civil Series*, London: HMSO and Longmans, Green Co.

Tomlinson, Jim (1995), 'Welfare and the Economy: The Economic Impact of the Welfare State, 1945–1951', *Twentieth Century British History*, 6 (2): 194–219.

Tomlinson, Jim (2000), 'Labour and the Economy', in D. Tanner, N. Tiratsoo, and P. Thane (eds), *Labour's First Century*, 466–79. Cambridge: Cambridge University Press.

Torry, Malcolm (2021), *Basic Income: A History*, Cheltenham: Edward Elgar.

Townsend, Peter (1979), *Poverty in the United Kingdom*, London: Pelican.

Townsend, Peter and Nick Davidson, eds. (1982), *The Black Report*, London: Pelican.

Toynbee, Polly and David Walker (2010), *The Verdict. Did Labour Change Britain?* London: Granta.

United Nations General Assembly. (2019, 23 April), *Visit to the United Kingdom of Great Britain and Northern Ireland. Report of the Special Rapporteur on Extreme Poverty and Human Rights*, New York: Human Rights Council.

Veit-Wilson, J.H. (1995), 'Paradigms of Poverty: A Rehabilitation of B.S. Rowntree', in David Englander and Rosemary O' Day (eds), *Retrieved Riches. Social investigation in Britain, 1840–1914*, Aldershot/Buckingham: Scolar Press/the Open University.

Vinen, Richard (2010), *Thatcher's Britain. The Politics and Social Upheaval of the 1980s*, 2nd edn, London: Simon and Schuster.

Vinen, Richard (2014), *National Service Conscription in Britain, 1945–63*, London: Allen Lane.

Waites, Bernard (1987), *A Class Society at War: England, 1914–1918*, Oxford: Berg.

Walker, Alan, ed. (1982), *Public Expenditure and Social Policy*, London: Heinemann.

Webster, Charles (2002), *The National Health Service: A Political History*, 2nd revised edn, Oxford: Oxford University Press.

Bibliography

Weeks, Jeffrey, Brian Heaphy, and Catherine Donovan (1999), 'Families of Choice: Autonomy and Mutuality in Non-heterosexual Relationships', in S. McRae (ed), *Changing Britain. Families and Households in the 1990s*, 297–316. Oxford: Oxford University Press.

Welshman, John (2010) *Churchill's Children: The Evacuation Experience in Wartime Britain.* Oxford: Oxford University Press.

Whiteside, Noel (1999), 'Towards a Modern Labour Market? State Policy and the Transformation of Employment', in B. Conekin, F. Mort, and C. Waters (eds), *Moments of Modernity: Reconstructing Britain, 1945–1964*, 76–9, Lewes: Rivers Oram.

Whybrow, Robert J. (1989), *Britain Speaks Out, 1937–87: A Social History as Seen Through the Gallup Data*, London: Macmillan.

Williamson, Lori (2005), *Power and Protest: Frances Power Cobbe and Victorian Society*, Lewes: Rivers Oram.

Willetts, David (2010), *The Pinch: How the Baby Boomers Took Their Children's Future- and Why They Should Give It Back*, London: Atlantic Books.

Wilson, Harold (1964), *Purpose in Politics*, London: Weidenfeld and Nicolson.

Wimperis, Virginia (1960), *The Unmarried Mother and Her Child*, London: George Allen and Unwin.

Winter, J.M. (1985), *The Great War and the British People*, London: Macmillan.

Winter, J.M. (1986), 'The Demographic Consequences of the War', in H.L. Smith (ed), *War and Social Change: British Society in the Second World War*, 154–6. Manchester: Manchester University Press.

Women and Equality Unit (2001), *Key Indicators of Women's Position in Britain*. London: UK Government, Department of Trade and Industry.

Workman, Jo (2005), 'Paying for Pedigree? British Business Schools and the MBA Degree', Unpublished DPhil. University of Sussex.

Young, Michael (1951), *For Richer for Poorer*. London: Labour Party Research Department.

Zabalza, A. and Z. Tzannatos (1985), *Women and Equal Pay: The Effects of Legislation on Women's Employment and Wages in Britain*. Cambridge: Cambridge University Press.

Zweiniger-Bargielowska, Ina (1996), 'Explaining the Gender Gap', in M. Francis and I. Zweiniger-Bargielowska (eds), *Conservatives and British Society, 1880–1990*, 192–224. Cardiff: University of Wales Press.

Zweiniger-Bargielowska, Ina (2000), *Austerity Britain: Rationing, Controls and Consumption, 1939–55*. Oxford: Oxford University Press.

Zweiniger-Bargielowska, Ina (2001), 'Housewifery', in I. Zweiniger-Bargielowska (ed), *Women in Twentieth Century Britain*, 149–64, Harlow: Pearson Education.

Zweiniger-Bargielowska, Ina (2011), *Managing the Body: Beauty, Health and Fitness in Britain, 1880–1939*. Oxford: Oxford University Press.

INDEX

Index